Management Accounting and Control Systems

Management Accounting and Control Systems

An Organizational and Sociological Approach

Second Edition

Norman Macintosh and Paolo Quattrone

A John Wiley and Sons, Ltd, Publication

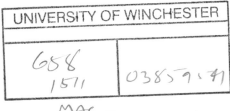
This edition first published 2010
Copyright © 2010 John Wiley & Sons Ltd

First edition published in 1994 by John Wiley & Sons Ltd. Copyright © John Wiley & Sons Ltd

Registered office
John Wiley & Sons Ltd, The Atrium, Southern Gate, Chichester, West Sussex, PO19 8SQ, United Kingdom

For details of our global editorial offices, for customer services and for information about how to apply for permission to reuse the copyright material in this book please see our website at www.wiley.com.

The right of Norman Macintosh and Paolo Quattrone to be identified as the authors of this work has been asserted in accordance with the Copyright, Designs and Patents Act 1988.

Library of Congress Cataloging-in-Publication Data

Macintosh, Norman B.
  Management accounting and control systems : an organizational and sociological approach / Norman Macintosh and Paolo Quattrone. – 2nd ed.
    p. cm.
  Includes bibliographical references and index.
  ISBN 978-0-470-71447-8 (pbk.)
  1. Managerial accounting. 2. Management information systems. 3. Organizational behavior.
I. Quattrone, Paolo, 1968- II. Title.
  HF5657.4.M27 2010
  658.15'11—dc22   2010008442

A catalogue record for this book is available from the British Library.

Typeset in 9/13 Kuenstler 480 BT Roman by Thomson Digital, New Delhi, India
Printed in Great Britain by Antony Rowe, Chippenham, Wiltshire

Contents

Preface

The idea for a second edition of this book dates back some years. Norman and I were attending the annual congress of the European Accounting Association in Göteborg and, while we were sitting on the comfortable chairs in the lecture theater, Norman told me: "I was thinking of you as coauthor for new edition of the *Management Accounting and Control Systems* book. What do you think?" I was thrilled and honored. I knew that this was going to be a tremendous experience for me and so it has been.

Those who have had the opportunity to work with Norman know that it is a pleasure and also a learning journey—a journey that may bring you to the most interesting and remote places, although at that time I had not discovered how remote these could be. To my great pleasure, Norman organized a visit to the lakes up in Ontario where we spent five days. The new structure of the book took shape there at Dorothy's Fishing Lodge in the complete isolation typical of the end of the fishing season. Well, not *complete* isolation. There was our landlord, who managed the lodge and was at the same time a great cook, the head of the local fire brigade (of which he was the only member) and the carpenter for the entire area; three dogs; and, finally, an unspecified number of fleas Foucauldianly disciplined not to leave the dogs and the carpet in front of the beautiful, warm, wood-burning stove. We had a great time and also ventured into an exploration of the lake on a small boat piloted by Norman. On that trip we soon realized how important the idea of checks and balances are—that small boat would not have passed any of the former and lacked all of the latter!

I am grateful to Norman for his hospitality and for the great opportunity. The photo you see below is a small tribute to him. I hope I was up to his expectations.

He is not the only person who accompanied me in this journey and who deserves my thanks. I will thank those who have contributed to the development of this book in the order in which they did so. The first is Salvador Carmona. I turned to him to ask advice on the whole project. He warned me how much I would regret taking on such a big task during the revision work and how a much greater joy would make me happy at the end of it. He was right.

I also have to thank those who have provided us with advice on how to revise the book. Other than the anonymous referees, to whom we are grateful, we have to name

Angelo Ditillo and Sten Jönsson who provided us with extremely useful advice, and we apologize if they will not recognize all of their suggestions in the new edition.

I want to thank warmly my undergraduate students at Christ Church, Oxford, who have all gone through most of the esoteric material of this new edition: from the Ignatian Spiritual Exercises to the Balanced Scorecard. They have been very patient and, with their comments and questions, have helped me enormously in making abstract and theoretical material accessible. I will remember many of the tutorials spent with them in my rooms in College with joy as the few last remnants of a truly academic life. I also have to thank my MBA students at the Saïd Business School, Oxford, and now at IE Business School in Madrid, for having provided me with great practical insights on the use of accounting when I taught them, or having talked about the Parmalat scandal and the issues of governance, ethics and financial reporting associated with it. They shared their experiences with me and I am grateful for this.

Christopher Lewis, the Very Revd Dean of Christ Church, made me reflect on the similarities between business, religious practices and liturgies, something I then developed in a few works of mine and tried to incorporate in some of the chapters of this new edition.

Danielle Logue's help was fundamental at a time when it was difficult to progress with the work and her assistance made me regain the right pace, at least for a little while! Some colleagues have passed me their papers and unpublished work for me to look at and get inspirations. Carlos Ramirez and Marc Ventresca are amongst these and I am grateful for this. More than anyone else, Cristiano Busco has provided me with a lot of material that we are using in joint works and that is reproduced in this new edition. I want to thank him for not having doubted even for a second that I could use that material here.

Some young economists have given us the courage to write that the training in mainstream economics and finance courses is similar to religious indoctrination and inculcates in students a doubtful ethical attitude towards the world. Of course responsibility for what is written is only ours but Charles Brendon, Emanuele Ferragina, and Ferdinando Giugliano have spent time reading some of the material now reproduced here and for this we are very grateful.

Julia Ortega at IE Business School helped in editing pictures and references and deserves a lot of thanks for the time she helped me to save.

The last part of this book was written during my visit to Stanford University School of Education as Fulbright New Century Scholar to study business education. Some of the reflections prompted by this project have been incorporated in the book (and made me think of at least another one!) and I have to thank the generosity of the Fulbright Commission for having made these reflections possible. At Stanford, the hospitality and intellectual stimulation of Francisco (Chiqui) Ramirez has been crucial in setting the tone of some of the latest material I worked on. Chats with Gili Drori, John Meyer, Woody Powell, Mitchell Stevens, Marc Ventresca and the colleagues at the various workshops held at the Stanford Humanities Center have been extremely useful in helping me to understand how important a move back to the humanities and education is in business training.

Last but not least, this book would not have been completed without the patience, help and stubborn will to see it finished of Nicole Burnett and Steve Hardman at John Wiley & Sons, Ltd. Thanks to them for having been so nicely polite when I delayed the date of delivery of the manuscript for the nth time, and for being supportive for the entire duration of the project.

This is not the first time-consuming project that I have carried out. Sabrina, my wife, knows this far too well. She has all of my gratitude for her incredible patience, fantastic support, and undeserved love. However, this is certainly the first project that has taken away my time with our little ones, Vittoria and Carolina. Therefore this book is dedicated to them, in the hope that when they hear the word "Papà" they do not turn to a PC or pick up the phone believing that their father strangely preferred to live in them rather than at home. Kids are the best for looking at things from new perspectives and make us all aware of a need for a change in our point of observation. This book is written in response to that need.

Paolo Quattrone,
Madrid

About the Authors

Paolo Quattrone is Professor of Accounting and Management Control at IE Business School, Madrid. Before joining IE, he was Reader in Accounting at the Saïd Business School and Official Student (i.e. Fellow) of Christ Church at the University of Oxford. A truly international scholar, he has conducted research and taught at the Universities of Catania, Kyoto, Madrid *Carlos III*, Manchester, Oxford, Palermo, Siena, Stanford and Luigi Bocconi of Milan. Paolo Quattrone has published widely on the interface between management control and information technologies, the history of accounting and management practices and thinking, and the managerialization of higher education institutions. He has been recently awarded a Fulbright New Century Scholar award to conduct research on the changes in business education. Professor Quattrone is also a member of the Standing Scientific Committee of the European Accounting Association, and he serves as book editor for the *European Accounting Review*. He also sits on the editorial boards of major academic journals such as *Accounting; Auditing and Accountability Journal*; *Accounting Organizations and Society*; the *British Accounting Review*; *Critical Perspectives of Accounting*; the *Accounting Historians Journal*; *Journal of Management and Governance*; *Organization*; and *Qualitative Research in Accounting and Management*.

Norman B. Macintosh, Professor Emeritus at Queen's University, Canada, has published widely in refereed accounting and organizational behavioural journals, and has been on the editorial board of eight accounting journals. His research into accounting and control systems has drawn on a number of disciplines including: human relations, psychological behaviour, organizational theory, sociology, philosophy, history, philosophy, and post-structuralism. He has served as visiting professor and invited seminar presenter at universities around the world and has been active in presenting conference papers including keynote and plenary sessions. He has served on the executive of the American Accounting Association and as Chair of its Accounting, Behavior and Organizations Section and he received the Canadian Distinguished Contribution to Accounting Thought and the Outstanding Contribution to Accounting Education awards. He has developed executive education seminars on accounting, control, and information systems and has served as consultant to large multinational firms and small businesses.

PART 1

AN INTRODUCTION TO MACS: ISSUES, CASES, AND PERSPECTIVES

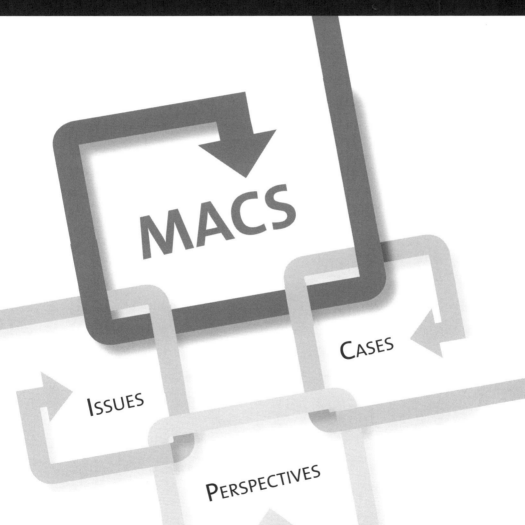

MACS

ISSUES

CASES

PERSPECTIVES

Issues: Why Management Accounting and Control Systems (MACS)?

In this chapter:

1.1 Why are MACS so Important?

1.2 What are MACS?

1.3 The Structure of the Book

1.1 Why are MACS so Important?

Control might be the most contentious word of our time. Half of the world thinks of control as coercion and oppression and protests that we should have less of it; the rest believes that society is pretty much out of control and that we need more of it. Either way, and regardless of one's political stance, control is a phenomenon that requires careful study if we are to make sense of our world. This book is about one very important and specific sort of control: *management accounting and control systems* (MACS).

It is not too great an exaggeration to say that MACS are so important and ubiquitous today that, if accountants and information people wrapped up their systems and took them home, the whole process of producing society's material goods and services, along with the governance of the social order, would grind to a standstill. Banks would close, factories would produce goods at random, supermarkets would be out of many products and over-stocked on others, police would arrest and release the wrong people, and the military would not have a clue which way to point their missiles. These controls are the central nervous system of the immense organism that we call "society," although sometimes people believe that they are only an unimportant technical matter.

Even in the early part of the twentieth century, MACS were recognized as essential to the affairs of large corporations. Firms such as BP, Deutsche Bank, FIAT, and Shell in Europe and DuPont, General Motors, Sears, Standard Oil of New Jersey, and Bethlehem Steel in the US all developed early forms of management accounting and control. It should be no surprise that issues of control have always existed and date from much earlier than the rise of corporations as we know them nowadays. Think of the Kingdom of Egypt,[1] the Roman Empire, the administrative features of medieval and modern religious societies:[2] MACS have always been there, in various forms and degrees, functioning in different ways and following various aims but all geared towards ensuring some kind of order. They are an integral part of the systems attempting to govern organizations, corporations and whole societies[3] and trying to guarantee their survival and endurance.

As Alfred Sloan, former chief executive officer (CEO) of General Motors, explained in his memoirs:

> Financial method is so refined today that it may seem routine; yet this method—the financial model as some call it—by organizing and presenting the significant facts about what is going on in and around a business, is one of the chief bases for strategic business decisions. At all times, and particularly in times of crisis, or of contraction or expansion from whatever cause, it is of the essence in the running of a business. (Sloan, 1963, p. 118)

The globalization of these same corporations, along with newcomers and their counterparts in other capitalist countries, the spread of managerial thinking, and the role played by large transnational consulting firms have made financial controls even more vital today. When controlling a highly complex and multifaceted operation in over 150 countries around the globe, a common language is essential. That language, even more universal today than English, is accounting and finance.

Management accounting and control systems are the principal means by which a few meganational enterprises virtually rule our contemporary world. Journalist Janet Lowe, in her carefully researched and disturbing book, *The Secret Empire*, convincingly documents how 25 multinational corporations, which developed out of the reach of public control, have become the new center of power of the world. Similarly, Michael Hardt and Antonio Negri have illustrated that this empire has now spread across national boundaries at the expense of large numbers of citizens. Its combined financial resources—sales and assets—exceed that of all but half-a-dozen or so nation states. The men at the desks at the top of these meganationals (there are virtually no women at the top) run their vast empires with highly sophisticated financial control systems.[4] These allow them to govern vast conglomerates of human and financial resources at leisure from their soft chairs, without having to move from their beautiful offices at their headquarters. Management accounting and control systems are an integral part of this staggering development.[5] These goliaths could not exist without them.

1.2 What are MACS?

This book is about MACS. Sometimes they are referred to as *planning and control systems*, sometimes *management control systems*, and sometimes simply *control* systems. We call them *management accounting and control systems* to signal our primary concern with management accounting systems such as the annual operating budget for a division of a multinational conglomerate, or a standard costing system for a factory, or a case-mix costing system for a hospital. This is control in the tactical sense.

If understood in this narrow sense, management accounting may seem fairly easy to define. It is

> the process of identification, measurement, accumulation, analysis, preparation, interpretation, and communication of information that assists executives in fulfilling organizational objectives . . . a formal mechanism for gathering and communicating data for the ends of *aiding* and *coordinating* collective decisions in light of the overall goals or objectives of an organization. (Horngren and Sundem, 1990, p. 4)

However, management accounting is also about control in its broad sense. Strategic planning systems, standard operating rules and procedures and informal controls such as charismatic leadership and the fostering of a clanlike atmosphere are examples of how complicated it is to make someone do something. This is control in the large. So we use the term "control" to signal that the book also deals with other related administrative devices that organizations use to control their managers and employees. "Control" has an interesting etymology dating back to the Latin *contra*, "opposite," and *rotulus*, "a script," and draws upon an opposition between two poles: a "rôle" a (role-player) who acts to a script, and a "contre-rôle" (counter-role), which monitors the role player's compliance. This etymology says a lot about the purpose of control: it is about making sure (or having the impression) that someone and/or something that plays a "role" (for instance an employee or a machine on the shopfloor) follows the script. Yet, there needs to be a wise balance between an excess of control, which would lead to resistance and organizational turmoil, and a lack of it, which would cause organizational chaos and disintegration. How and why such a balance exists is a matter of effective control. This book is about understanding it.

Our premise is that management accounting systems are only a part, albeit usually a very important part, of the entire spectrum of control mechanisms used to motivate, monitor, measure, and sanction the actions of managers and employees in organizations and to coordinate these with the other components that make organizations what they are: machines, information and communication technologies and the like. So, to understand the workings of management accounting systems fully it is necessary to see them in relation to the entire array of control mechanisms used by organizations. Our aim is for the reader to develop a strategic perspective of MACS in this larger context.

1.3 The Structure of the Book

The book has four parts as illustrated in Figure 1.1.

Part One introduces the issues that the book intends to address. It defines the contours of MACS. These are then exemplified in Chapter 2, which provides the empirical base of the book. In that chapter we will introduce four cases that contribute to a clear understanding of the features, problems and practical considerations involved when dealing with MACS. Part One also outlines various perspectives from which MACS can be considered. These have been arranged into two groups for simplicity.

The first main group of perspectives is characterized by a strong and positive belief in "reality" and is made of three further subgroups. The first subgroup posits individuals and individual agencies as the cornerstone of theorization on MACS. The second subgroup takes the organization as the pillar for theorization. In the third subgroup, certain contextual factors, such as the social environment in which individuals and organizations operate, shape the contours, purposes, uses and functioning of MACS.

The second main group of perspectives is characterized by a strong belief in the constructed nature of MACS—that is, they do not have given features and purposes but, rather, their features are defined in networks of relationships. Three further subgroups seek to explore this relationist view. The first focuses on the interaction between structures and

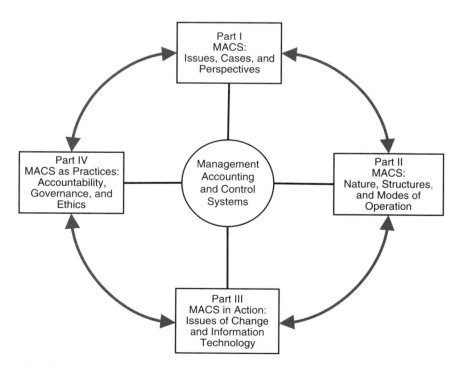

Figure 1.1   The structure of the book

agencies; the second takes the notion of practice as the key element to study MACS; and the third views actors as networks and thus espouses a view of MACS as key nodes in a nest of business and organizational relationships.

Part Two deals with the *nature, structures* and *modes of operation* of MACS. Chapter 4 views these systems as dealing with issues of information and power, and how this creates forms of organizational control. The focus on information and how it creates power within organizations helps us to link economic views of MACS with other more sociologically informed views. Chapter 10 will address this relationship between information, knowledge and power as part of one of the specific aspects of the way in which MACS work in practice. Chapters 5 and 6 deal with the structure of MACS—that is, the mechanisms that are put in place within organizations to make control operate at various levels. We will deal with the dilemma of markets versus hierarchies to address the problem of resource allocation and how, within hierarchies, various mechanisms of control (mechanical, organic, cybernetic and strategic) are operationalized to make sure that some kind of organizational order is achieved. This description is then integrated, in Chapter 7, with the various modes of operation that control systems can present in different organizational forms and environmental situations.

Part Three presents a shift from the analysis of these systems as abstract formulations, and as generalizations from practice, to a discussion of the ways in which these systems work in daily organizational action. Chapter 8 will describe various models of change to explain how MACS participate in, and are shaped by, processes of organizational change. Amongst the changes that have characterized the recent evolution of these systems is the now-ubiquitous presence of information technology (IT) as an integral part of organizational control, not only in the form of microtechnology but also at a level where it affects notions of control and its functioning. These issues are discussed in Chapter 9.

Part Four looks at MACS *in* and *as* practices. In particular, Chapter 10 views these systems as an integral part of the mechanism of social order directed to the exercise of power and the creation of specific kinds of citizens and people. This happens through particular mechanisms of control in various organizations, which make some behaviors more appropriate than others; through the combination of organizational and macroinstitutional pressure to make societies ordered and citizens governable; and, finally, through the existence of specific training regimes that inform and shape the ways in which MACS are enacted in practice, and lead to the creation and pursuit of specific visions and notions of rationality. Chapter 11 deals with these issues at an ethical and societal level and views issues of control, governance and accountability not simply as organizational problems but as specific forms of arranging and governing societies. Management accounting and control systems are seen as possessing the ability to cement or disrupt organizations and societies.

The book intends to cover some conventional themes of accounting and control but from a different perspective. In doing so, it seeks to provide a perspective rather than offering a complete view on these issues. We are aware that some themes are not treated in the book (for example the growing phenomenon of interorganizational relationships) but we hope we can provide the tools to equip the reader with a different approach to view them. And we may still deal with them in a future edition of the book!

Endnotes

1. See Ezzamel and Hoskin (2002).
2. Quattrone (2004, 2009).
3. See, for instance, Miller and O'Leary (1987).
4. For an inside look at how these meganationals are run with financial controls, see Sampson's exposé (1974) of the rise and fall of International Telephone and Telegraph Company (ITT).
5. See Latour (1987) and Quattrone and Hopper (2001, 2005). The ethics of this kind of concentration is addressed in some detail in Part Three of this book.

Further Readings

Those who are interested in knowing more about current issues in MACS can look at:

- Bhimani, A. (ed.) (2006) *Contemporary Issues in Management Accounting*, Oxford University Press, Oxford.
- Chapman, C., Hopwood, A. and Shields, M. (2007) *Handbook of Management Accounting Research* (2 vols), Elsevier, Oxford.
- Drever, M., Stanton, P., McGowan, S. (2007) *Contemporary Issues in Accounting*, John Wiley & Sons, Inc., New York.
- Hopper, T., Scapens, R., Northcott, D. (2007) *Issues in Management Accounting* (3rd edn), Prentice Hall, Financial Times, London.
- Macintosh, N., Hopper, T. (eds) (2005) *Accounting: The Social and the Political*, Elsevier, Oxford.

2

Cases: Building the Empirical Basis of the Book

In this chapter:

2.1 Introduction

Management accounting and control systems are intrinsically practical. This does not necessarily mean that they originate from the realm of practice (they may—but not always and not exclusively) but these systems are created, in most cases, to be operationalized, to be implemented, in other words to be "practiced," even though sometimes they are not.[1] In fact, sometimes accounting calculations are not used for decision making but only to legitimate decisions already taken.[2] However, the intent is to have them appear as if they can deliver something useful and, indeed, often they do. Thus there is no real schism between theory and practice—for a system to be practiced requires a great deal of theoretical understanding of how people think, how machines work and how organizations behave.

What follows is a series of four case studies of MACS. They illustrate the subject matter of this book in some detail and provide it with empirical support. The case studies are: the Society of Jesus, Wedgwood Potteries, Empire Glass, and Johnson & Johnson. Each case represents an instance of a control system that is well thought out and effective in its design, its structure, and how it works—its process. Each study is inextricably linked to a very well-defined historical era (the Early Modern period, the beginning of the Industrial Revolution, the post-Second World War period, and the late twentieth century capitalism, respectively). We will refer to these studies throughout the book.

These cases reveal the technical evolution that has taken place in accounting and control systems over the past four and a half centuries. However, rather than treating them simply as demonstrating the state of the art in management accounting and control in four different eras, we want to use them to illustrate different degrees of complexity in accounting and control matters, which are not necessarily related to a linear evolution of these notions and practices. In this respect, the cases are examples of how management accounting and control issues can be interpreted from different perspectives. Technical evolution is important but how we see management accounting and control in trying to understand how they work is also important, if not more so.

The Jesuit case illustrates the surprisingly complex machinery of controls that the Society of Jesus developed after its foundation in 1540. The Wedgwood Potteries case describes a 1770s management accounting system—one of the first at the dawning of the Industrial Revolution. Empire Glass documents the almost textbook design and use of financial controls in the early 1960s in the bottle-making division of a packaging industry giant. The Johnson & Johnson case shows how a very successful multinational healthcare conglomerate uses its sophisticated MACS to manage its sundry subsidiaries spread around the globe. We begin with the remarkable story of the Society of Jesus and its fascinating "accounting for sins."

2.2 The Society of Jesus[3]

The Society was founded by Saint Ignatius of Loyola (1491–1556) in 1539, and received the formal approval of Pope Paul III through the Papal Bull *Regimini militantis Ecclesiae* on 27 September 1540, taking the Italian name of *Compagnia di Gesù*. Originally, the project of Ignatius and his companions was to go to Venice, from where they were to embark on a "pilgrimage to Jerusalem in order to engage the ministry there." They went to Rome and offered their services to the Pope, but only because they did not find a passage to the Holy Land.[4] This says much about how chance and serendipity affect people and organizations.

The principles for structuring the Order were outlined in the *General Constitutions* of the Society. They made it a very hierarchical organization. It was organized in Assistances (e.g. Italy) and Provinces (e.g. Sicily), to which the Jesuit Colleges and Houses belonged. Assistants, Provincials, and Rectors were appointed directly by the General of the Society, who was elected by a General Congregation and placed at the top of this hierarchy. The General, the Provincial, and the Rector were assisted by a Procurator, who was in charge of administrative and accounting issues. The Rector was also supported by a Prefect, who dealt with pedagogical issues. It should not be surprising to see hierarchical forms of organization so early in the history of modern times for, in fact, hierarchy comes from *hiereus* (priest) and *hieros* (what is holy), and *arkhe* (rule): hence sacred or priestly rule[5]—an etymology that is illuminating but always forgotten.

The Order's activities mainly concerned its missions around the world, the education of members and young lay pupils, and various businesses that provided resources for this (education was, in fact, provided free of charge). Despite the supposed rigidity implied by the hierarchical structure, the Order was characterized by great flexibility and a capacity for adaptation to the most disparate lands and situations in which it operated (for instance, the Jesuits successfully reached India and Japan before the end of the sixteenth century). This approach was facilitated by a system of self-discipline, outlined in the *Spiritual Exercises* and inserted in the grand design of the *Constitutions*. Central to these *Exercises* was the individual and his self-control.[6] In order to achieve this combination of control and flexibility, the Order developed three forms of accounting and accountability in the various activities they carried out, which presented remarkable similarities. These systems are described below.

Accounting for the College

The College (see Figure 2.1) represented the primary unit of the Jesuit organization and it was here that the main peripheral activities of the Order were conducted. Generally, each College had several sources of income: legacies and annuity payments (for the foundation

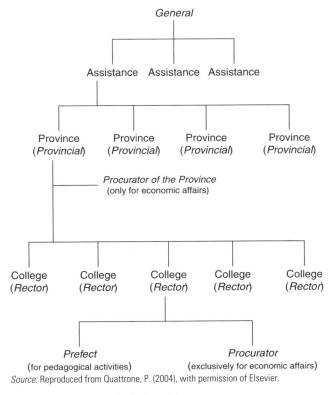

Source: Reproduced from Quattrone, P. (2004), with permission of Elsevier.

Figure 2.1   The hierarchical organization of the Society of Jesus

of the College and for donations received), farms, and rents (from letting houses and from leasing land and small farms).

Figure 2.2 illustrates the typical *Entrata e Spesa Generale* of a Sicilian College (AD 1665), in this case the *Casa del Noviziato* of Palermo. Examples of the accounts include: *Viatici* (travel expenses), *Elemosine*, (donations given and received), *Porto di lettere* (expenses for correspondence), *Infermeria* (infirmary), *Contribuzioni diverse* (contributions to the Province), *Salari diversi* (wages for people employed in the house), *Loheri di case* (rents and relative maintenance expenses), *Magazzini* (warehouse for such foodstuffs as wine, grain, and oil), *Spesa ordinaria* (food purchases for the house), *Forno* (bakery expenses), and *Masserie* (expenses and revenues related to the management of farms). Each of these accounts represented a revenue and/or cost center for which a Jesuit member was responsible.

The College's economic activities were formally regulated through the directives that emanated from the *Instructio pro admistratione rerum temporalium collegiorum ac domorum probationis Societatis Jesu*, written by Valentino Mangioni S.J. in 1649. The *Instructio* ruled the relationships among the Provincial, the Rectors of the various colleges and the Procurators of the colleges. These rules, in brief, concerned what today would be described as management control and auditing. The Provincial's main concern was to ensure that the directives received from Rome were implemented in the various Colleges of the Province. He made periodical visits to the Colleges or sent an assistant (the *Padre visitatore*) to perform this task and to check the accounting books of each College under his jurisdiction.

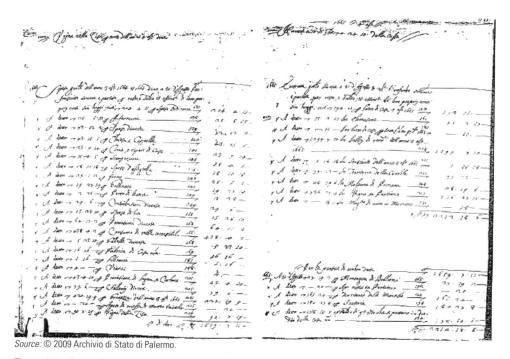

Source: © 2009 Archivio di Stato di Palermo.

Figure 2.2   The profit and loss account (*Entrata e Spesa Generale*) of the *Casa del Noviziato* of Palermo 1665)

The Rector and the Procurator of the College had to be prepared to provide the Provincial on demand with an account of the state of College affairs.

The success of the Sicilian Province may be partly attributed to the fact that the Procurator of the Province was Ludovico Flori, the well-known author of *Trattato del modo di tenere il libro doppio domestico col suo essemplare* (1636), an accounting treatise expressly written for the Sicilian Colleges.

The double-entry accounting system described by Flori in the *Trattato* was an effective combination of analysis and synthesis. It contained a detailed chart of accounts (*Lista* or *Rubrica*), and the profit or loss shown in the income statement (the *Entrata e Spesa Generale*) was the result of a progressive aggregation of the revenues and expenses generated by each "business area" of the College.

The features of the Society's accounting system are interesting and surprising. They show that sophisticated accounting techniques were in place for management control as early as the sixteenth century. However, as we stated in the previous pages, we do not want to use these cases to show the development over time of MACS. With the Jesuit case, instead, we want to show how these are rarely only an economic matter.

In order to do so, we now explore the other forms of controls that the Society deployed since its foundation. This will also explain why the more conventional bookkeeping of the College was so sophisticated: it originated not only from a need for economic control but from a need for the control of each Jesuit and his soul.

Accounting for Sins

The basis of the control system of the Society was the Ignatian Spiritual Exercises and the accounting for sins described therewith. In the first week of the Exercises, the exercitant was asked to make "a moral inventory" of his life[7] through an examination of conscience intended to prepare the soul for confession. He was asked to interrogate himself on his daily sins. For each sin committed from the moment of rising until the first examination, the exercitant was required to enter a dot on the upper line of the first "g" (which probably referred to the Italian word *giorno*, day), as shown in Figure 2.3. This step was followed by "one's resolution to do better during the time until the second examination" (SE, 25), which was made that night after supper. At that time other dots were placed on the lower line of the "g," and the letter was examined to see if the situation had improved or worsened over the course of the day. This examination was to be repeated each day of the week (from Sunday, the biggest "g," to Saturday, the smallest one).

Through this examination, a distinction was established between the controller and the controlled. This distinction constitutes the cornerstone of every system of accounting, accountability and management control. Interestingly, the distinction existed even without a physical distinction between these two figures: the distinction only occured here thanks to the inscription of the sins on a piece of paper, which made the Jesuit member reflect on his "self."

Thus the Exercises constituted a building block of the Jesuit Order's accountability and management control system: a continuous process of definition, which allowed both control (through examination) and flexibility. The Exercises pay obsessive attention to categories.

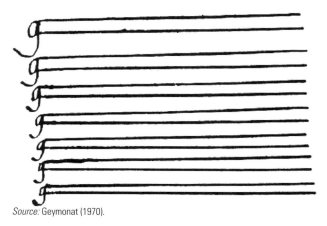

Source: Geymonat (1970).

Figure 2.3 Accounting for sins in the Ignatian Spiritual Exercises

The Exercises were organized as a hierarchical tree in which each exercise was divided into prayers, preludes, points, and colloquy, and these, in turn, were subdivided into other more analytical categories.[8] It is not surprising, then, that the accounting treatise by Flori, the dispositions of the *Instructio*, the organization of the various forms of controls within the College and elsewhere in the Order reflected this way of viewing and organizing the world. In other words, the Exercises created and transmitted to the Jesuit member a sort of "accounting" passion, which would have shaped his entire life and his range of activities. The same passion for accounting also characterized the *Accounting for the Soul*.

Accounting for the Soul

The Society of Jesus grew very rapidly and by 1615 the Order attained a worldwide presence, with 372 Colleges and 123 Residences (*Domus Professae*) for its c.13 000 members. These numbers show that the Society was an organization of considerable size.

Keeping the periphery close to the Jesuit headquarters in Rome required a constant flow of information from the periphery to the center and vice versa. The form and timing of all correspondence was thus strictly prescribed in the *Formula Scribendi* in order to facilitate storage and access in the general archive of the Society in Rome (the Archivum Romanum Socistatis Iesu). This archive constituted more than a collection of letters. Given the amount of information it stored, it was an instrument of governance and management control.

The *Catalogi* were most important items in this correspondence, and in particular those sent every three years—the *Catalogi triennales*—which comprised three parts. The first, the *Catalogus primus* gave personal details about the members (i.e. name, surname, age or date of birth, place of birth, role within the Order) (see Figure 2.4, where the record No. 22 refers to Lodovico Flori, author of the famous *Trattato* (1636)).

The second, the *Catalogus secundus*, gave personal details about the character and attitudes of each member.

Source: © 2010 Society of Jesus.

Figure 2.4 *Cataiogus primus*

The *Catalogus secundus* was also called *secretus*, for it did not report the names of the Jesuit members on whom the information was collected. In order to know the identity of the member, one was required to match the ordinal number on the page of the *Catalogus secundus* with the number and name of the Jesuit member as it appeared in the *Catalogus primus*.[9] Only the recipient of the two *Catalogi*—i.e. the controller—could therefore identify to which Jesuit member the evaluations referred. The *Catalogus tertius* gave details about economic activities, reproducing the balance sheet of each College—information that was then "consolidated" in the *Stato temporale dei Collegi d'Italia*, a book that summarized all the balance sheets of the Italian Colleges.

The *Catalogus secundus* (see Figure 2.5) represented what could be called *accountability for the soul*. The dimensions chosen in the heading of each column (ingeniousness, intellect, prudence, experience, ability to profit from studies, character, and talents) made visible those aspects of the soul that were important in making the good "soldier," the good teacher, the good "manager": in short, the good Jesuit. Through a methodical assessment of each Jesuit by grading and ranking the qualities mentioned above in a four-point scale

Figure 2.5 *Catalogus secundus*

from *malus* to *optimum*, this set of practices highlighted some aspects of Jesuit life while obscuring others.

The upper left corner of the form, which is a matrix with the people on the vertical axis and the qualities requested/monitored on the horizontal axis, represented an imaginary eye overlooking each individual member of the society. "Accounting for the soul" and "accounting for sins" of the Spiritual Exercises allowed the General to supervise (*episcopio*) his Order. Paraphrasing Latour (1987, p. 220), through the accurate and recursive process of accumulation of information on the Jesuit members, Colleges, and Provinces, the General could now *see* them, at leisure, in his own office in Rome, without any pressing need to visit them. He was able to act at a distance through the accounting devices (Robson, 1991, 1992) which were developed in the various geographical and virtual spaces that the Order created and occupied. The General was thereby empowered, an attribute reflected in his nickname, the "Black Pope," after the color of his garments.

The Accounting and Accountability System of the Society

The description above may make the reader think that this disciplinary gaze dominated the whole Order and forced members to obey central directives. However, if this were the case, the control system would have generated resistance and, above all, rigidity. This would have made the successful expansion of the Society impossible. In fact, the Jesuit hierarchical systems of control did not work in this way.

The Jesuit members did not perform the directives of the General because they were requested to do so. Rather they did so because the system allowed them to make these directives theirs. For example, in the Spiritual Exercises, the search for God was a search for their self. What God, good and evil were was always left to a process of definition. Following the Standard of God or Lucifer (as requested by the Exercises) was the enactment of members' ideals, guided but not constrained by the directives of the center. Through the various accounting and accountability practices devised by the Order, control was achieved by a fusion of self and common interest. Accountability and accounting devices thus played a crucial role in making the combination of control and flexibility possible.

In this sense, the hierarchy as well as the ordered accounting records shown in Figures 2.1–5, are only incomplete attempts to reduce the irreducible complexity of human beings and relations to a common rationale. Such attempts, whether they are underpinned by economics, pedagogy, politics or faith, are always destined to remain incomplete. The development of accounting and accountability practices in the Society of Jesus in the sixteenth and seventeenth centuries, cannot be reduced to an economic argument, as suggested by mainstream interpretations, which view these practices merely as tools for measuring and allocating the economic resources that facilitate the formation of hierarchies. A strictly economic analysis of the nature and role of accounting as an instrument for allocating, monitoring, and administering resources within the hierarchical structure of the Society of Jesus would leave undiscovered important aspects of the accounting practices deployed by the Order to control its multifaceted activities. "Accounting for sins" and "accounting for the soul" would be left at the margin of the control history of the Jesuits. This history would therefore be limited to the technical aspects of the accounting systems devised to manage the Jesuit Colleges. Instead, management control goes beyond the technical and the Jesuit case is an enlightening example of how this was the case in historical terms, as it is in contemporary organizations.

Summary

The Society of Jesus expanded very rapidly since its foundation in 1540. This expansion was facilitated by the development of a series of controls, which spanned from the individual self to the whole Order, passing via the organizational unit of the College. The Jesuit case illustrates how the understanding of MACS cannot be reduced to an economic argument or any other form of reductionist explanation. Instead it emphasizes the manner in which controls operate (through the practice of the Spiritual Exercises) and how this allows the presence of both order and flexibility within organizations. These are themes that will surface throughout the entire book.

2.3 Wedgwood Potteries[10]

Josiah Wedgwood sat in his small, sparsely furnished office, staring at the spreadsheets he had been working on over for nearly a month. It was a rainy day in August 1772, the year when a major recession swept through Europe, causing sales of fine pottery to plummet. Wedgwood believed that if he could calculate the costs for his various pottery products it would help his firm survive the depression without laying off any of his carefully trained workforce.

But something was amiss. Wedgwood had worked out in great detail the costs of labor, clay, and other materials for each product line. He had also figured in the costs of overseers, clerks, incidentals, and other indirect expenses and estimated their loading on specific products. He then meticulously developed the cost for each product down to a halfpenny. Next, he calculated the profit margins for each piece and every batch of pottery using selling prices. In the aggregate, they did not agree with the overall costs and profits included in the financial accounting reports prepared by his head clerk. He went over his calculations again and again until he convinced himself they were roughly accurate.

For some time Wedgwood had harbored an uneasy feeling about the head clerk's propriety. He was suspicious, for instance, about the cash accounting. It always arrived a couple of months late, yet came up spot on whenever the head clerk produced a bank reconciliation and cash report. He decided to launch an inquiry into the affairs of the counting house. His hunch proved accurate. The difference in Wedgwood's figures was not due to any miscalculations on his part. The head clerk, in cahoots with his underlings, had been stealing cash and fixing the books for some time. But that was not all.

A detailed investigation revealed a distressing state of affairs. Wedgwood described the situation in a letter to his London marketing partner, Bentley: "The Plan of our House in Newport Street is rather unfavourable to virtue and good order in young men," the housekeeper was "frolicking with the cashier," the head clerk was "ill with the foul disease" and had "long been in a course of extravagance and dissipation far beyond anything he has from us (in a lawful way) would be able to support." Embezzlement, blackmail, extravagance, and dissipation were the order of the day.

Wedgwood acted without hesitation. He dismissed the head clerk, replacing him with a trusted employee from his own office. He sacked the cashier and most of the other employees. He set up a new system of weekly cash reporting and bank reconciliations. He put into effect a policy that customers' accounts must be settled weekly and that all receipts be taken to Bentley for depositing. He soon "put things to right in the counting house."

Wedgwood's cost accounting system had rescued the company from internal destruction. It also helped to overcome the potential ravages of a severe economic depression. Wedgwood used his costing system in a systematic and detailed way, to analyze the effect of possible product price cuts, calculate the cost savings accruing from scheduling longer production runs of specific products, determine optimum wage scales, set sound hiring policies, and calculate the most efficient assignment of workers to the production process. While many of his competitors went bankrupt, Wedgwood weathered the storm. Once again his costing system came to the rescue.

As the depression eased and sales recovered, Wedgwood continued to use his new management accounting system to maximum advantage as a powerful tool in managing his business. Cost accounting and control proved an essential ingredient in Wedgwood's success in the subsequent period of high demand, rising prices, and spectacular profits. The man who single-handedly invented his own detailed cost accounting became a legend in his time for this and other innovations in the techniques of management control.

Strategic Planning

Wedgwood started his pottery operation near Burslem, Staffordshire, England in 1759 with only a couple of leased sheds, two kilns, a small amount of family financial backing, and one employee—a cousin. The operation grew rapidly. Within two years it was a typical potbank operating under the traditional guild system with a dozen men and boys, a rudimentary division of duties, a relaxed master-apprentice hierarchy, no formal rules, and a small output of undistinguished pottery sold to the local gentry. Burslem alone could count 150 such potbanks.

For Wedgwood, however, this was only a beginning. A small, lame, God-fearing man, he harbored much greater ambitions. He foresaw a golden opportunity in the spectacular rise in demand for fine pottery precipitated by the general increase in the English economy, the spectacular rise in the standard of living, the rapid growth in tea and coffee drinking habits, and the penchant in the colonies for imported fineries from England. Wedgwood reckoned he could monopolize this burgeoning market by manufacturing large quantities of very high quality earthenware *and* selling it at a price lower than his competitors.

With this strategy clearly in mind, Wedgwood carried out literally thousands of experiments with various clays and kiln techniques. Eventually his remarkable persistence paid off handsomely. He developed the formulae for what was to become a renowned label, the *Queen's Ware* line, so named because it graced the table of the Queen of England. Armed with a product of superior quality, suitable for the upper class, he sensed that if he could mass produce it he could cash in handsomely on the rapidly growing middle-class market. Wedgwood never forgot that he was in business to make money.

Yet one big obstacle stood in his path. Transportation in England, particularly around Staffordshire, remained primitive. This made it extremely difficult to get cheap raw materials in and, even more distressing, to get the finished product out to markets in London, the rest of England, and overseas. Getting finished pottery to Bentley's London marketing arm was a treacherous undertaking. Typically, a potter lost one-third of every shipment by packhorse over the muddy ruts that passed for roads between Staffordshire and London. Breakage and theft were common. In consequence, Wedgwood organized the potters in his region to petition Parliament for a turnpike and a canal system linking with existing rivers.

The petition proved successful. When the canal was completed Wedgwood built his dream factory, Etruria, alongside the canal. Modeling it after his friend Boulton's metal manufactory, he constructed five separate buildings in an arc alongside the canal. He situated the raw material house at one end on the water and built the packing and shipping house on the other end, also on the water. With the wheels, pottery-making equipment and kilns in the middle, production flowed smoothly along the arc. Clay and materials arrived at one end and fine pottery emerged from the other.

Control and Discipline: The Missing Link

Affairs were definitely on the upswing. Wedgwood had his dream factory, a reliable transportation system, a unique product, a brilliant competitive strategy, and a solid marketing operation run by his partner in London. But one more stumbling block proved to be his biggest obstacle—turning an obstinate, slovenly, intemperate band of employees into a disciplined productive workforce.

The English working class at the time consisted of peasants and serfs who had been driven off the farms and pressed into unfamiliar nonagricultural work. On the whole they tended to be illiterate, ignorant, and lazy. Drinking and carousing on the job was the norm. Work habits were slipshod and wasteful. As was their custom, they would work for a few days and then take off with their earnings for long bouts of debauchery and gambling. They also participated in the frequent fetes, fairs, and holy days, which featured cockfighting, bullbaiting, and visits to brothels. Every Monday was a holiday for merrymaking, gambling, drunkenness, gluttony, and carousing. All of this was a source of great distress for the ambitious and religious Wedgwood. Something was urgently needed to tame and discipline his recalcitrant workforce.

Happily, Wedgwood's run of good fortune continued. John Wesley, the founder of the Methodist movement (a brand of Protestantism) had just moved to Staffordshire. He and Wedgwood became friends. Wesley's inspired preaching soon attracted larger and larger congregations. He specifically railed at the working class, chastising them that their savage, drunken, licentious, and gambling ways were sinful in the eyes of God, exhorting them to give up their evil ways in favor of a pious life, and warning them that, unless they changed, they would never reach the kingdom of heaven where they could be with Christ for eternity. Over time, Wesley's influence proved remarkable. Little by little Wedgwood's workers began to give up their egregious vices to live sober and respectable lives.

At the same time, Wedgwood instituted a series of controls at the factory. To begin with he published a book of potter's instructions. It described in fine detail the specific rules that were to be followed for each task in the production process. Such meticulous spelling out of duties and procedures was essential to making quality pottery. A little dirt, a marred piece of clay, some small error at any stage of production spoiled the entire batch of pottery. The instructions also contained detailed descriptions of proper decorum while at work. There was to be no drinking, gambling, swearing, or debauchery at Etruria.

In order that there be no mistake about the instructions and rules, Wedgwood spelled out a system of stiff fines for specific misdemeanors and disobedience. For example, a worker could lose 10% of his weekly wages for bringing ale into the factory, for writing obscenities on the wall, or for gambling on the premises. Habitual violators and anyone abusing an overlooker were sacked on the spot. Wedgwood also kept an eye out for any "natural" leaders in the workforce and the moment they challenged him or his potter's instructions, he got rid of them.

However, the pottery soon grew too large for Wedgwood to keep a personal watch over the workforce. He solved this problem by installing a layer of overseers, clerks, and supervisors to make sure that his instructions and rules were carried out to the word. Wedgwood also designed a career structure whereby the more obedient and better workers could advance to more highly skilled jobs and subsequently join the ranks of supervisors. Some historians credit Wedgwood with inventing hierarchical supervision and establishing the traditions of the overseer class. In any event, the idea of a cadre of supervision proved so successful it was soon copied in other potteries and industries.

Wedgwood's next control was a primitive clocking-in system. Employees were given tickets with their name on them. They put these in a box when reporting for work in the morning and when returning after lunch. The potter, instead of doing the rounds, merely recorded times of arrival on a board, checked the box, and investigated any absences. This was an early instance of management by exception.

Wedgwood followed up his instructions in person. He could be found almost any day stumping through his five sheds, telling, showing, and scolding his workers. He was well known for raging over a speck of dirt, smashing substandard batches of pottery, and writing on the workbenches in chalk, "This won't do for Josiah Wedgwood." He also constantly harassed his clerks and overseers to be diligent in the extreme when watching the workers, making sure that no dirt got into the clay and that the potters followed his instructions to the letter.

Unlike most owners at the time, Wedgwood also paid close attention to his employees' quality of life at home as well as on the job. He made sure that his shopfloor conditions were clean, dust-free, and well ventilated and better than other Staffordshire manufacturing workplaces. He also offered a wage scale that was the highest in the area. He went out of his way to encourage and praise individuals for hard work and good effort, in addition to chastizing them for shoddy output, thus maintaining a judicious balance between sticks and carrots. And he took a keen personal interest in the spirituality and health of his employees and their families.

Wedgwood's human resources plan, as it might be called today, was a success. Although he demanded more from his employees, worked them for longer hours, and supervised them more closely than was usual in other potbanks, the workers believed him to be a kind and good employer. Wedgwood asked and got much more from his employees, who worked a great deal more diligently and productively than did workers in competitive firms. These measures were not purely altruistic. Competitors frequently tried unsuccessfully to hire away his best employees, not least because they hoped to steal Wedgwood's secret formulae for fine pottery.

Summary

Wedgwood's superior management methods enabled him not only to survive a severe economic depression when numbers of other potters went bankrupt but also to outstrip his competition during the boom years. Much of this success can be attributed to his innovative experiment in cost accounting. While others were making crude guesses as to their costs and ignoring relevant details in their account and waste books, Wedgwood made substantial use of his cost accounting system. It taught him about economies of scale, informed him about profit margins of his various pattern lines, guided him in wage decisions and pricing policies, and exposed dishonest employees. He considered it, along with his well-guarded formulae for fine pottery, as one of his most valuable competitive weapons.

What is remarkable about the Wedgwood saga is that he put in place a sophisticated, effective, and smoothly functioning control system. In addition to his cost accounting system, this included his detailed potter's instructions; personal observation, criticism, and directives; hierarchical surveillance by a cadre of overseers and supervisors; a system of positive and negative sanctions; cooptation of the best workers into the supervisory cadres; concern for employees' quality of working life; social control in the form of Wesley's Christian preaching; and a clear strategic plan. It would not be wrong to say that Wedgwood had literally and single-handedly invented what we call today management planning and control systems.

The results proved spectacular. By 1775, Wedgwood employed over 150 workers in five specialized shops, whose work was supervised by a fully trained cadre of overseers and clerks. And by 1790, what was once a modest potbank now boasted a diligent and dedicated workforce of more than 200 men, women, and children performing highly specialized tasks under vigilant and systematic supervision. Not surprisingly, he outstripped his competition in quality of pottery, efficiency of operations, and discipline of workforce. His beloved Etruria factory became a showcase for the nation. When he died in 1795, Wedgwood's estate exceeded £500 000, a staggering fortune in those days.

2.4 Empire Glass

We move on nearly 200 years to the early 1960s for a look at the financial control system at the Empire Glass Company (EG). Empire Glass is a diversified container company manufacturing and marketing glass, metal, plastic, and paper containers of all sorts.[11] The company is organized into product divisions, with operating responsibility delegated to the divisions, each of which is run by a divisional vice-president, supported by functional line managers and several staff officers, who report to the executive vice-president at headquarters.

Headquarters (HQ) consists of a small group of executives, a handful of clerks and three financial officers: the controller, the chief accountant, and the treasurer. The controller's office employs only the controller and one assistant. These HQ executives rely almost exclusively on EG's MACS to run the company. We now look in on the glass division and one of its seven glass plants where James Hunt is the plant manager.

It is early in November 1963 and Mr. Hunt sits in his office poring over the October batch of profit planning and control reports (PPCRs). These contain highly detailed financial information about almost every aspect of the plant's operations as well as comparative data for the previous month, the previous month a year ago, and the year to date. Importantly, the annual bonus for the management team at each plant is tied to attaining 90 % of budgeted profit for the year. Sales from Hunt's plant for the year are running 3 % below target, so it is going to be necessary to reduce costs substantially for the next six or seven weeks in order to reach or exceed the profit target for the year. Hunt is confident this can be accomplished.

The management accounting reports consist of five PPCRs, which cover every aspect of a plant's operations. PPCR #1 contains 39 line items summarizing the plant's financial performance, including gross and net sales, fixed, discretionary, and variable costs, as well as a host of statistics such as profit/volume ratio, manufacturing efficiency indexes, return on capital, and capital turnover. Five other PPCRs provide the details behind the data in PPCR #1. The reporting system also includes PPCRs that contain the same information consolidated at the divisional level and financial information on almost every nook and cranny of each plant as well as for the division as a whole.

Under EG's incentive scheme plant management team members can earn a bonus of between 25 % and 30 % of their annual salaries for achieving 90 % of the plant's budgeted profit for the year. Once this is accomplished, it is also possible to earn another bonus of up to 25 % of salary for meeting cost reduction and efficiency targets. Further, managers can earn up to 20 % more by exceeding the plant profit target. The bonus scheme has been in effect for several years.

When asked by the case reporter if there might be slack in some accounts that could be used to reduce budgeted expenses when results fall below target levels, Hunt responds:

> No, we never put anything in the budget that is unknown or guessed at. We have to be able to back up every single figure in the budget. We have to budget our costs at standard assuming that we can operate at standard. We know we won't all the time. There will be errors and failures, but we are never allowed to budget for them. (Dalton and Lawrence, 1971, p. 143)

After carefully scrutinizing the October financial reports, Hunt schedules a special meeting of all line and staff management people and supervisors. The purpose of the meeting, he tells the case reporter, is to get things straightened out.

> The thing we have to do now is kick those accounts in the pants that are not making the savings they planned to make . . . The thing to do now is to get everyone together and excited about the possibility of doing it. We know how it can be done. Those decisions have already been made.
>
> It's not unattainable even though I realize we are asking an awful lot from these men [the workforce].
>
> You see we are in a position now where just a few thousand dollars one way or the other can make a big difference in the amount of bonus the men get. There is some real money on the line. It can come either from a sales increase or an expense decrease, but the big chunk has to come out of an expense decrease.
>
> We never fight about the budget. It is simply a tool. All we want to know is what is going on. Then we can get to work and fix it. There are never any disagreements about the budget itself. Our purpose this afternoon is to pinpoint those areas where savings can be made, where there is a little bit of slack, and then get to work and pick up the slack. (Dalton and Lawrence, 1971, p. 153 Source: R.D Irwin, Homewood IL.)

Hunt opens the meeting by expressing his disappointment with the October financial results and pinpointing those areas with good results and those with poor numbers. The plant accountant then calls on each individual with poor numbers to explain why. Hunt exhorts each in turn to do better with statements like "that's not good enough," or "get things straightened out now," or "do better for the rest of the year." He also makes it perfectly clear that he wants everyone to communicate to him as soon as problems come up with meeting their part of the profit budget.

The plant accountant then reviews in detail the budgeted targets for November, discussing for each account what specific savings in November and December can be expected. Hunt closes the meeting with a no-holds-barred pep talk:

> There are just a couple of things I want to say before we break up. First, we have got to stop making stupid errors in shipping. Joe, (foreman of shipping) you have absolutely got to get after those people to straighten them out. Second, I think it should be clear, fellows, that we can't break any more promises. Sales is our bread and butter. If we don't get those orders out in time we'll have no one but ourselves to blame for missing our budget. So I just hope it is clear that production control is running the show for the rest of the year.
>
> Third, the big push is on now! We sit around here expecting these problems to solve themselves, but they don't. It ought to be clear to all of you that no problem gets solved until t's spotted. Damn it, I just don't want any more dewy-eyed estimates about performance for the rest of the year. If something is going sour we want to hear about it. And there's no reason for not hearing about it. (Pounds the table, then his voice falls and a smile begins to form.) It can mean a nice penny in your pocket if you can keep up the good work. That's all I have got to say. Thank you very much.

These efforts pay off. The plant exceeds its profit budget in the year and beat its operating efficiency and cost reduction targets by a comfortable margin. The managers and supervisors, as in previous years, receive a sizable bonus.

Background

Empire Glass competes in an industry that is monopolized by a few companies. Quality across the industry is very high and price competition is virtually nonexistent (on occasion some companies have been accused by the government of price collusion). However, large customers, such as brewing companies, soft drink corporations, and large packing plants, play off the various glass companies if quality, delivery, or service standards are not met. Consequently, while glass firms compete on the basis of service and delivery, efficient low-cost production is essential to make profits.

Empire Glass's glass products division produces glass products in thousands of different sizes, shapes, colors and with many different decorations. They include food, soda, and beer bottles. Nearly all sales are made to order with a typical lead time of two to three weeks between delivery and order. Empire Glass's production process, originally a craft enterprise, is now almost fully automated due to its recent heavy capital investments in the most up-to-date production machinery. Quality is critical and a mistake anywhere in the production cycle (melting, filling the moulds, blowing, annealing, cooling, or coating) results in high rejection rates. Glassmaking, once the purview of highly skilled artisans, now comes under the discipline of the machine.

Most jobs in the plant require little skill. Output is machine driven and the workers, little more than machine tenders, have virtually no control over either the pace of work or the production methods. The higher skilled jobs include mold making, machine repairing, and machine changeover and setup. Employees are unionized with bargaining conducted at the national level. Wages are relatively high. All employees below the supervisory level are paid on an hourly basis and do not participate in bonus schemes.

Planning and control at EG is elaborate, systematic, and formal. In May each year, the planning and control process starts when the glass products division vice-president estimates sales, profits, and capital expenditure needs for the next year. The vice-president also outlines planned capital spending requirements for the next five years. These data, along with estimates of long-term market and sales trends, are then submitted to HQ.

Meanwhile, the HQ market research department is busy preparing detailed market predictions for the glass industry for the next year and two or three more years. These estimates are based on thorough reviews and consideration of all relevant economic factors for each product line. They submit these forecasts to the divisions for review, criticism, and adjustment.

At the same time each district sales manager prepares a forecast of sales for his or her district by estimating sales on a customer-by-customer basis. The divisional office amalgamates these estimates and then compares the total with the HQ market research department's top-down forecast. The district forecasts are then consolidated and reviewed by the divisional marketing manager but no changes are made in district sales managers' targets without their consent.

Headquarters also provides guidance at this stage if requested. But once the sales budget is approved by divisional marketing managers no one is relieved of responsibility for meeting the sales budget without the approval of division top management. At the same time, the divisional marketing managers cannot make changes to the sales budget without the explicit agreement of all parties responsible for meeting the budget.

This process is repeated at HQ and divisional levels until everyone agrees the sales budgets are sound. Only then are they approved by the divisional vice-president and the HQ executive vice-president and president. At this stage each level of management becomes fully responsible for its own share of budgeted sales. The sales budget, now fixed in stone, cannot be changed without the approval of HQ top management.

After the sales budget receives final approval, the divisional sales budgets are broken down and allocated to the various plants for manufacture and shipment. The plant sales budget is further broken down by month, price, volume, and end use. This information is then used by each plant to prepare its profit budgets. Standard variable cost information for each product and estimated fixed costs and overheads are used to estimate gross and net profit. Plant executives prepare budgets for each operation, cost center, and department in their plants.

Participation in preparing the plant budget is widespread. Each production section in the plant estimates the physical requirements of the sales plan (for instance, tons of raw material, labor hours, and machinery hours) necessary to produce budgeted sales. Costs are budgeted based on standards developed by industrial engineers at the plant and at the divisional headquarters. Estimated cost reductions (such as expected variances from standards due to improved methods and fixed cost improvement programs) are incorporated into the budget figures by the plant industrial engineer in conjunction with the plant manager, the assistant plant manager, and the plant supervisors. It is felt that such widespread involvement results in general commitment to meet targets.

Before submitting the plant budget to headquarters each plant receives an on-the-site visit during the summer by a group of HQ and divisional executives. Typically, this group includes the HQ controller and his assistant as well as members of the divisional manufacturing staff. During these visits, which last from half a day to a day, the budget is discussed in detail with the plant manager and his management team. The group also tours the plant, paying particular attention to the details of the maintenance and capital replacement budgets. The purpose of these visits is to acquaint the executives with the proposed plant budget and to guide the plant manager regarding corporate expectations concerning projected profit levels.

The divisional vice-president also reviews each plant's budgets "keeping in mind the corporate headquarter's expectations." At this stage plant managers are sometimes asked to cut their budgeted expenses. Then, in September, each plant submits its budget to headquarters for consolidation with those of other plants. When the executive vice-president at headquarters and the divisional vice-president are satisfied, they submit the consolidated budget to the president who accepts it or sends it back for modification. In December, the budget is presented to the Empire Glass board of directors for final approval.

During the year, HQ and divisional offices use the PPCRs to monitor closely each plant's performance. On the sixth working day of each month the plants wire key operating variances to headquarters. These are summarized on a variance analysis sheet and sent the next day to all key HQ executives. This sheet highlights variances in critical areas and helps headquarters to take timely action. Along with the PPCR reports, plant managers also submit their most current estimates of key operating variances for the coming month and the next quarter. This exercise is believed to force plant managers to look at where their programs are going rather than run the plants using a day-by-day fire-fighting mentality.

The actual results come in on the eighth working day of each month. Executives at HQ then review each PPCR on a management-by-exception basis, looking only at numbers in excess of budget targets. Plant managers include written commentaries for variances, explaining where they went off base. Net sales, gross margins, price and mix changes, and manufacturing costs receive particularly close attention. Executives at HQ and divisional executives also watch fixed-cost and capital expenditure items closely to keep a careful eye on whether or not the plants carry out their planned capital expenditure and maintenance programs. Plant managers must submit written explanations if these programs are not carried out or if they exceed budget allowances.

The financial controls allow the company to identify trouble spots in advance. Depending on the magnitude of the problem, headquarters might ask for daily reports from the plants. In some cases they dispatch HQ or divisional staff experts into a particular plant to help resolve the problem. Although plant managers are not required to take the experts' advice, they are expected to accept their help gratefully.

While the operating budgets are fixed in stone in December, changes can be made if, early in the year, sales decline and if plant managers can convince headquarters that the change is permanent. No changes are permitted, however, if sales decline unexpectedly towards the end of the year as in Hunt's situation described above. In this case, the HQ controller asks the plant managers to review their profit budgets with the plant staff, looking for places where cost reduction and expense cuts will do the least harm including expenditures that can be eliminated or delayed until the subsequent year. When sales exceed budget, the plants are not allowed to keep the extra profits that accrue.

Sales and plant relations, while typical in terms of cooperation and conflict, also have a unique side to them. In theory, sales has the final say but in practice it is the other way around because the plants control production, quality, scheduling, and delivery. Nevertheless, if an important customer wants a rush order, the plant tries to accommodate the customer even if it upsets production schedules by disrupting runs already in process, thus increasing costs.

Importantly, both the plants and the sales organization have a common interest through the budgeting and bonus systems in seeking sales. The plants have a material interest in the customer's welfare because plant profit depends on sales as well as cost efficiency. Sales managers also earn a substantial bonus at year end if budgeted sales levels are met. Thus, the incentive to meet the budget is substantial throughout the organization. And it is very unusual for either plant or sales management personnel not to meet the annual targets and not get their bonuses.

Several other controls operate alongside the planning and budgeting system. Detailed formal job descriptions exist for all employees above the level of assistant supervisor. Industrial engineering personnel measure and set standards for all jobs up to supervisor level. Standards are also developed by divisional engineers for each machine when the equipment is first used. These standards are subsequently used to compare performance across plants and in the preparation of costing data in the budgets.

Industrial engineers perform job studies throughout the year to reduce costs. Each month, headquarters prepares and distributes bar charts comparing and ranking divisions and plants across the company on manufacturing efficiency. As quality is critical, all output is inspected both electronically and visually by inspectors. These controls complement the PPCR system.

Managers throughout the company seem highly satisfied with the management planning and control system. Executives at HQ believe that the system's focus on planning is very valuable, especially when so many people up the line and down in the field units are involved. The field people, in turn, value the management prerogatives that the control system offers them. They do not see it as a straitjacket. Rather, they feel that it gives them almost total freedom to carry out the planned programs. Moreover, managers and supervisors at the plant level are well informed about the plans, budgets, standards, and targets, and respond in a positive fashion to them. In recent years, the glass division increased its share of market slightly and was one of the industry leaders in profit performance.

Summary

The Empire Glass case illustrates how planning and budgeting systems act as an integral part of management control systems through a series of incentives. This is typical of divisionalized firms such as EG where this system goes into even minute aspects of the plant's operation through the preparation of detailed PPCRs, which are then used to manage the daily operations of the firm and achieve budgeted profits. The PPCRs are an illuminating example of how abstract objectives are translated into powerful control metrics, which act as a disciplinary gaze to make sure that, from the plant to the HQ, there is a constant flow of communication and controls.

2.5 Johnson & Johnson[12]

Background

We move on again but this time only a couple of decades to look at the MACS at Johnson & Johnson (J&J), a global conglomerate that develops, manufactures and markets a wide variety of healthcare products. Products ranged from Band-Aids and disposable diapers to highly sophisticated lab equipment and surgical devices, as well as hospital management systems. Sales in the late 1980s approached $10 billion and the firm employed over 75 000 people in 75 countries. In recent years surveys have consistently rated J&J as one of the best managed companies on the Fortune 500 list. The reason for this lies in large part with the company's commitment to, and sophisticated use of, its unique MACS.

The headquarters executive group play a key role in this system. The group consists of 12 members including the chief executive officer (CEO), the president, the chief financial officer, the vice-president of administration and eight executive committee members (ECMs). Each of J&J's 155 subsidiaries reports to headquarters through one of these ECMs. Remarkably, this small group of executives at headquarters in New Jersey is able to run a complex, giant empire spread around the globe.

Johnson & Johnson's decentralized organizational philosophy is a key feature of the management control system. Each subsidiary is treated as an autonomous, independent, integral business in its own right. The subsidiary president, in most instances a citizen of the country involved, takes full responsibility for the subsidiary's strategy and operations. Unlike most large, complex organizations, J&J does not have a strategic planning staff at headquarters nor does it have any explicit global corporate strategy outside the strategic business plans for its subsidiaries. Against this background we look in on the action at the Codman & Shurtleff (C&S) subsidiary as its executives work on the June update of the operating budget.

The June Update at C&S

It is a warm Boston spring day in May. Codman & Shurtleff's executive team is sitting around a solid oak table in the executive boardroom poring over the sheaf of financial reports and plans. President Roy Black called the meeting to review the preliminary figures assembled by the vice-president of information and control for the annual June update of the annual operating budget.

The June update involves re-estimating and revising all budget estimates, right down to the lowest-level expense center, for the rest of the year. These estimates and the actual results to date are used to update the forecast for the remainder of the year. The numbers indicate that C&S will be $2 million short of its profit target for the year. The June update is due at J&J's headquarters in New Jersey in a week.

The profit shortfall is due to a mixture of events that were unforeseen the previous September when the profit budget was put together. Actual sales and estimates for the rest of the year are running nicely ahead of budget due in part to the earlier-than-expected introduction of a new product. Actual expense and estimates for the rest of the year, however, are running over budgeted targets largely because of three unanticipated events: higher than predicted start-up costs of a recently combined manufacturing facility, an unfavorable product mix variance, and a larger than anticipated drop in US currency that pushed costs up on specialty instruments purchased from a J&J European subsidiary.

Roy Black begins the meeting by asking his vice-president of marketing if he could "give something" (Anthony, Dearden, and Govindarajan, 1992, pp. 485–86). The latter shakes his head and replies:

> I've been working with my people looking at price and mix. At the moment, we can't realistically get more price. Most of the mix variance for the balance of the year will be due to increased sales of products that we are handling under the new distribution agreement. The mix for the remainder of the year may change, but with 2700 active products in the catalogue, I don't want to move too far from our original projections. My expenses are cut right to the bone. Further cuts will mean letting staff go.

Roy Black nods and turns to his vice-president of business development:

> You and I should meet to review our research and development priorities. I know that Herb Stolzer [J&J's headquarters executive committee liaison member for C&S] will want to spend time reviewing the status of our programs. I think we should be sure that we have cut back to reflect our spending to date. I wouldn't be surprised if we could find another $400 000 without jeopardizing our long-term programs.

He then closes the meeting:

> Well, it seems our work is cut out for us. The rest of you keep working on this. Excluding R&D, we need at least another $500 000 before we start drawing down our contingency fund. Let's meet here tomorrow at two o'clock and see where we stand.

Mr Black, the vice-president of new development, the vice-president of marketing, and the vice-president of information and control meet again that evening to review all R&D projects included in the current year's budget. They review the priority and progress of all major projects searching for projects that can be deferred or terminated because of changing market conditions. Roy Black then asks the vice-president of business development to meet with his staff the next morning to scrutinize the 40 or so active R&D projects for potential savings to the tune of $400 000.

The next afternoon he chairs another meeting of his executive team. The vice-president of product development reports that his group has come up with $300 000 of savings and is working on the other $100 000. The vice-president of marketing, after some queries from Black regarding inventory levels, allows that there might be savings by providing faster turnaround on the core of critical products and by putting high-specialty items on a 90-day made-to-order delivery basis. The vice-president of human resources reports that an early retirement initiative will eliminate 14 jobs in the personnel department. Roy Black then asks his executives to go back to their departments and chip 2% off their operating expenses.

In total, the projected savings, including the remaining $100 000 from R&D, will reduce the projected profit shortfall to $200 000. This is sufficient, Roy Black believes, to allow C&S to draw down on its contingency fund for the rest. Each subsidiary has a contingency expense account built into its annual operating budget. The amount depends on negotiations with the corporate office and is based on the perceived uncertainty in achieving the budget profit target. The June update is complete and will be sent to C&S's executive committee member for approval. The above decisions and actions are motivated in large part by J&J's MACS, which is described next.

The Business Plan

The business plan is the overall strategic framework for the subsidiary's competitive stance. It consists of three parts: a mission statement, a detailed competitive marketing plan, and a simple financial forecast. The mission statement defines, in general terms, the focus for the subsidiary's products and markets. Codman & Shurtleff's mission statement, for example, states its mandate as a primary focus on neurospinal surgery worldwide. All new R&D products as well as any business acquisitions are screened carefully to see if they fit under this umbrella.

The heart of the business plan is the marketing plan. It describes in detail how the subsidiary intends to compete in each major segment of its business. It also includes a concise summary of all major competitors' strategies along with an estimate of their sales and profits. The marketing plan then becomes the basis for each department head in the subsidiary to develop a plan for his or her area of responsibility.

The financial part of the business plan consists of only four numbers: sales volume, net revenue, net income, and a return-on-investment index. It also includes a qualitative description of how these figures are to be achieved. A unique feature of the business plan is that once the four numbers are approved they remain fixed for the next five-year period. For example, if 1989 was the first year of the five-year period, the financial forecast for the four numbers is made for the years 1996 and for 2001. These numbers then remain fixed until 1994 when a new forecast will be made for the years 2001 and 2006. The mission statement, the marketing plan, the departmental plans, and the financial plan are combined into the business plan and bound in a formal document.

The logic behind fixing the financial forecasts for a five-year period is to make sure managers do not become totally caught up in the daily routines and tactical problems of running a complex business. The business plan exercise forces them not to lose sight of long-run and strategic opportunities and helps them to maintain a dialog between qualitative and quantitative plans. When formulating the business plan, managers are constantly made aware of previous and current financial forecasts. Likewise, when making financial forecasts, they are constantly aware of strategic and marketing plans. In order to further reinforce this back-and-forth process, a subsidiary cannot get capital expenditure funds for future opportunities unless they are identified in the business plan.

Company executives believe that locking-in the financial forecasts in the business plan for each five-year period is the cornerstone of J&J's MACS. Since the same two planning years are analyzed repeatedly over the five-year period by managers, many different perspectives throughout the subsidiary are brought to bear on business possibilities, problems, and issues. And managers are forced to repeatedly reconsider how the competitive environment has changed since the initial forecasts were made and what action is needed to compete effectively according to the plan. This process continuously forces managers to articulate strategic qualitative plans with financial results and targets in the annual profit budget.

The timetable for preparing the business plan is as follows. During the first half of the year, the business plan is discussed, debated, and adjusted by the subsidiary's top management group over a five-month period. Then in June, they meet with the subsidiary's executive committee member for an on-the-site, no-holds-barred, let-the-hair-down meeting. During this grueling two- or three-day session, the executive committee member challenges all aspects of the plan, exposes its basic assumptions, airs concerns about the particulars of the marketing strategy, questions the validity of the financial forecasts, and presses the subsidiary managers to spell out specifically how they expect to meet the numbers. The meeting ends when the executive committee member declares the plan to be sound and workable.

The subsidiary president then summarizes the business plan in a two-page report and submits it to headquarters. In September, the HQ executive committee meets to debate and approve each subsidiary's business plan, formally presented by the subsidiary president. These meetings feature frank, hard-hitting discussions and debate and adjustments to the business plan are common at this stage. Finally, when the HQ executive committee is satisfied, the business plan is approved.

Profit Budget

The approved business plan becomes the guiding framework for the preparation of the annual profit budget for the coming year. Throughout each subsidiary, managers, down to department level, prepare detailed financial estimates for their particular responsibility center. They also prepare a second-year forecast, but in less detail. In putting together the profit budget, managers keep a close eye on the financial numbers in the business plan and on the second-year forecast in the previous year's profit budget. Thus, the current year's profit budget is integrated with the thinking expressed in the business plan and in the prior year's profit budget.

Subsidiaries compile the first draft of the profit budget late in the summer. The various managers in each subsidiary are brought into the process as early as possible to complete their part. Each department prepares its own forecast, where applicable, of sales revenues, operating expenses, and capital expenditures for the coming year. Revenues and expenses as well as key balance sheet accounts are also broken out on a month-by-month basis. Production cost estimates are based on standard costs. Research and development expenses pose a special problem because a subsidiary's project list is usually too long to support it in its entirety. Research and development expense targets have to be determined by ranking projects in terms of the expected sales, expenses, and production capacity requirements.

All this information is consolidated and compared with the second-year forecast in the previous year's profit budget. If the first consolidation indicates a shortfall relative to that forecast, special budget presentations are held where each department manager is asked to remove any budget slack and meet the earlier targets. The second-year forecast is also useful in hindsight as an indicator of how well the managers plan and perform. This widespread participation, company officials believe, helps to gain commitment on the part of managers throughout the subsidiary to meet the targets in the profit budget.

When the subsidiary's top management group is satisfied, they meet in October to discuss the profit budget with their executive committee member. The latter reviews it in detail looking for any differences in the new profit budget from the second-year forecast in the previous year's profit budget or from the financial figures in the current strategic business plan.

During this meeting, the amount of the subsidiary's contingency expense allowance to be included in the profit budget is negotiated and finalized. This allowance acts as a cushion against unpredictable events such as currency devaluations, inflation fluctuations, and supply price changes. Subsidiaries are allowed to draw down on their contingency fund when actual profits fall below budget targets and a reasonable explanation of the shortfall is forthcoming. The idea behind the contingency fund account is to mitigate any propensity by subsidiary managers to deliberately build slack into their budgets. When all agree on the profit plan in November, the executive committee member presents the subsidiary's profit budget to the HQ executive committee for final approval.

Each month starting in January, actual performance relative to the targets in the profit budget is monitored closely both at headquarters and in the subsidiary. Each week the subsidiaries submit a report to headquarters on sales performance, which the designated executive committee member reviews. The subsidiary president submits a monthly management report to headquarters highlighting key financial accounts and comparisons with the previous month and with budget targets. This report includes a written explanation of any significant variances. Clearly, all parties keep a close eye on progress towards the profit target throughout the entire year.

The profit budget is revised three times during the year. The March revision consists of an update by the subsidiary's executive committee member who presents its most recent estimate of the sales and profit for the current year to the HQ executive committee. This information is based on estimates provided by the subsidiary president. The more extensive June update was described earlier. Finally, the November revision, presented to the HQ executive committee at the same time as the profit budget for the coming year, features a close look at results for the first ten months and a revised profit budget for the last two months. The November revision also requires updates from all departments in the subsidiary, but not in the same detail as for the June revision.

Reward System

Johnson & Johnson's unique salary and bonus system is an integral part of the control system and merits special mention. The HQ executive committee decides the salary and bonus for each subsidiary president and its other top executives but the subsidiary president has complete discretion in salary and bonus matters for all other employees in the subsidiary. These decisions, importantly, are not tied to any predetermined formula such as achievement of financial targets in the profit budget or the business plan. The logic is that these are bound to be inaccurate given the diversity and unpredictability of changes in the healthcare industry. Rather, initiatives taken to increase market share, efforts to introduce new products, and steps taken to develop long-term competitive advantages, along with energy put into increasing the current year's sales and profits, count heavily. These subjective assessments far outweigh objective criteria.

Reflections on the Control System

The case reporter asked several J&J executives for their opinion of the company's MACS. They unanimously expressed great pride in it and saw it as one of the corporation's distinctive competences. They believed it to be a big factor in gaining a competitive edge over rival firms. Roy Black, who had been with J&J for 25 years in various line and staff positions at headquarters and in subsidiaries, responded that the control system's big plus is that it kept him and his managers aware throughout the entire year of the long-term strategic plan as well as the importance of achieving the annual profit. He put it this way:

> We should always be thinking about such issues, but it is tough when you are constantly fighting fires. The Johnson & Johnson system forces us to stop and really look at where we have been and where we are going. We know where the problems are. We face them every day. But these meetings force us to think about how we should respond and to look at both the upside and downside of changes in the business. They really get our creative juices flowing.
>
> Some of our managers complain. They say that we are planning and budgeting all the time and that every little change means that they have to go back and rebudget the year and the second-year forecasts. There is also some concern that the financial focus may make us less innovative.

But we try to manage this business for the long term. We avoid at all costs actions that will hurt us long term. I believe that Herb Stolzer is in complete agreement on that issue. (Anthony, Dearden and Govindarajan, 1992, p. 495)

It is important to understand what decentralized management is all about. It is unequivocal accountability for what you do. And the Johnson & Johnson system provides that very well.

Summary

The J&J case clearly illustrates how contemporary multidivisional organizations are run by numbers. Targets such as return on investment, profit and the like are all forms of controlling without detailing what the divisional managers should be doing. These managers are left with autonomy, within reason and within the planning and budgeting process constraints. Of course, while this can allow for flexibility, it can also lead to rigidities. The key task of the controller is to decide where to strike the balance.

2.6 Summary and Conclusions

This book deals with MACS from an organizational sociology perspective. Today these systems play a huge role in the management of society's major institutions and both private and public sector corporations. We began our journey into their organizational aspects by describing the MACS in four organizations. The cases also illustrate the evolution of these systems over the past five centuries.

Well before the Industrial Revolution, the Society of Jesus developed very sophisticated systems of managerial control and human accountability. This shows how issues of management control are rarely a purely economic matter. They are instead intertwined with other matters, which, in the case of the Jesuit Order, concerned religion, education, politics, and their missions. Without its specific management control systems the Order would have not spread across the world as quickly as it did. Indeed this example teaches us that very little is new in management control while quite a lot is to be learned if we adopt a new perspective and look at MACS in nonconventional ways.

At the dawn of the Industrial Revolution, Josiah Wedgwood single-handedly invented his own cost-accounting system along with a host of other valuable controls. He used it to sharpen his intuition when making strategic pricing, production, and hiring decisions and to supplement his many other control devices. Here, as much as in the previous case, we witness the combination of economic concerns with religious, social and cultural beliefs and habits. Would Wedgwood have developed the sophisticated incentive system without his religious inspiration?

Two hundred years later, at Empire Glass, we saw a sophisticated and highly detailed management accounting system that covered every nook and cranny of the organization. In this management accountant's paradise a handful of executives at headquarters and in the divisional offices simply ran the company by the numbers.

A couple of decades later, at J&J, we witnessed another metamorphosis in management accounting and control. An elaborate strategic planning system was grafted onto the traditional profit budget system. Managers at all levels in the subsidiaries were constantly interacting with and adjusting strategic business plans as well as profit budgets, while a dozen or so executives at headquarters kept up a vigilant surveillance of the subsidiaries' plans and results.

The job of top management at J&J differed markedly from the work of Josiah Wedgwood. Wedgwood formulated the business strategy, researched and developed the product, designed and organized the factory, and kept a close personal watch over the workers. At J&J, in stark contrast, the top executive's job is almost purely control. Johnson & Johnson's elegant and sophisticated MACS allow them to rule a vast healthcare conglomerate operating around the globe with hundreds of thousands of products and employees. For top executives, control at a distance has replaced actually doing business.

Enterprises like J&J have emerged today as the dominant form of organization. These goliaths command resources in excess of those of all but a dozen nation states. Such an eventuality would have been unthinkable in Josiah Wedgwood's day. There are, of course, many ways to account for the miracle of the meganational conglomerate form of economic power. Some would point to their vast storehouses of proprietary scientific and technical knowledge. Others might attribute a good deal of weight to their marketing skills. Still others would point to random events and lucky breaks. Be that as it may, it does not seem too great an exaggeration to say that, without concomitant advances in control systems, such enterprises could not exist.

Each of these four case histories represents an instance of what we would consider to be sound management control systems, but there are important differences in their design, implementation and in how managers can understand their nature and functioning. In the next chapter we look at theoretical frameworks that go some way towards explaining such variations.

Endnotes

1. See Quattrone (2009).
2. See also Burchell *et al.*'s (1980) rationalization machine.
3. This case draws on Quattrone (2004).
4. See O'Malley (1994, p. 142).
5. See Höpfl (2000).
6. The character of the Society, as defined by Saint Ignatius in the *Spiritual Exercises* and in the *Constitutions*, was quite different from that of the medieval religious Orders. First and foremost, the Jesuits were animated by an activism previously unknown in the Catholic Church, where monastic organizations were devoted to contemplation and isolation. The Jesuits' aim was to take them outside the cloister for "the salvation of souls," requiring them to engage in numerous activities—notably, missionary, educational, and economic enterprises but also theater and dance. Unlike members of other Catholic Orders, the Jesuits could take a fourth vow (unconditional and prompt obedience to the Pope, *sine ulla tergiversione aut excusatione*), in addition to the three vows of chastity, poverty, and obedience normally assumed by members of other religious orders.

This fourth vow, along with the words of Saint Ignatius, who described the Order as the Militia of Christ, the harsh discipline imposed on its members, and its hierarchical structure, resulted in a Society that was often compared to an army in service to God.

7. See O'Malley (1994).

8. See Barthes (1976, pp. 57ff).

9. In Figures 2.4 and 2.5, for example, one can find the report on Lodovico Flori, the accountant of the Sicilian Province, No. 22, page 6—the number on the top right of the *Catalogi primus* and *secundus*. On this structure also see Lamalle (1981–2, p. 101).

10. The source material for this synopsis is reported in McKendrick (1961, 1970) and Langton (1984). The Wedgwood case has been the focus of more than 50 000 articles and papers.

11. The case study is reported in Dalton and Lawrence (1971) and Anthony, Dearden and Govndarajan (1992).

12. The source material for this case history is reported in Anthony, Dearden and Bedford (1989) and in Anthony, Dearden and Govindarajan (1992).

Further Readings

For other cases in MACS see:

- Groot, T. and Lukka, K. (eds) (2000) *Cases in Management Accounting: Current Practices in European Companies*, Pearson Education, Harlow.

For further works on case study and qualitative methodologies in accounting and beyond see:

- Cooper, D. and Morgan, W. (2006) Case study research in accounting. *Accounting Horizons*, **22** (2), 159–78.
- Humphrey, C. and Lee, B. (eds) (2004) *The Real Life Guide to Accounting Research. A Behind-the-Scenes View of Using Qualitative Research Methods*, Elsevier, Oxford.
- Quattrone, P. (2006) The possibility of the testimony. A case for case study research. *Organization*, **13** (1), 143–57.
- Ryan, B., Scapens, R. and Theobold, M. (2002) *Research Method and Methodology in Finance and Accounting* (2nd edn), Thomson, London.

Perspectives: A Toolbox to Understand MACS

In this chapter:

3.1 Introduction

3.2 Believing in Reality: Positive Faith in Individuals, Needs, and Structures

3.3 Believing in Relations: Relativist Faith in Interactions, Actions, and Networks

3.4 Summary and Conclusions

3.1 Introduction

This book does not deal with the finer procedural and technical aspects of accounting. It does not discuss the principles and rules for calculating management accounting entries and preparing reports, nor does it cover the application of quantitative techniques and spreadsheets to the work of management accountants.[1] It does not focus on the influence of social psychological factors such as participation, leadership, group dynamics, and personality. There are already many excellent books covering these aspects of management accounting.[2]

Rather, this book takes an organizational sociology approach to the study of MACS and intends to show how this approach can complement other perspectives that are also treated in the book. What do we mean by an "organizational sociology approach"? With our approach we would like to escape two temptations. On the one hand, it would be seductive to explain the nature, functioning and change of MACS by relying on grand and overarching forces. Thus it would be easy to say that these are somehow dependent on ideas such as "context," "environment," "market," "the economy" and the like. This is typical of much straightforward sociology, but it leaves out key organizational elements of these systems. On the other hand, it would be easy to assume the existence of an omniscient rational human agent as the creator of MACS: the unbiased user of neutral and effective management tools.

Instead we would like to focus our attention on problems faced by everyone who encounters MACS. These problems relate to the nature, design and implementation of such systems and to the difficulties in using these tools effectively in daily practice. This is why we discuss the nature, structure, and change of MACS in the chapters that follow. These are issues that can be viewed from different perspectives and ours is one amongst many.

There are two reasons for taking a different approach.[3] First, there are management accounting books that already focus mainly on management accounting from a technical point of view.[4] Second, there are far fewer books that look at MACS from a sociological perspective and even fewer that grant organizations and organizing activities a primary role in the way in which these systems emerge, spread and are used. Organizations are the most prominent social institutions of our time; we are born, raised, educated and employed in them and we even retire and die in them. Management accounting and control systems are pervasive in organizations; however they do not exist in a vacuum but in a network of relationships, which, in various degrees, have an impact on what is controlled, how and why.

Organizational sociologists study organizations, including their MACS, from a sociological perspective. However, sociology too is made of many paradigms, research traditions and ways of looking at how societies and institutions work. So which one should we choose?

"Society" is a word that comes from the Latin *socius*, "ally," which stresses the importance of the ties that make a society a collectivity.[5] Thus, for us, MACS are a way of making, managing and maintaining such relationships and they are thus important not only for the functioning of organizations but also for our understanding of how collectivities work. More specifically, sociology, and the sociology that inspires some of the arguments of this book, involves the systematic study of the development, structure, interaction, and *collective* behavior of organized groups of human beings. So while the sociologist aims to comprehend individuals, such as managers, as *social* beings who can be understood from their relations with other human beings, artifacts, social context and the society of which they are part, we aim to understand the social nature of MACS.

Our aim, in this book, is not to undermine the microanalytical approach of many managerial attempts to understand accounting, but rather to complement it with developments in organizational sociology and possibly overcome this dichotomy by relying on a relational view of actors and institutions. Control is never, as the Jesuit case illustrated, something that can be isolated or reduced either to micro actors (such as the *homo oeconomicus*) or macro construction (such as an abstract idea of culture or society). These need to be studied for their relational nature. As control—coercion, compliance, and cooperation—is at the heart of organizational sociology, studying management accounting from this vantage point could be of considerable help to accountants and financial executives in developing a strategic and global perspective of the way MACS work.

This book also advocates the use of models and theories to help analyze MACS, problems, and issues. Models and theories are ways of interpreting and understanding these complex systems. A model is a simplified (or cleaned-up) representation, which identifies a few important dimensions or variables of the real thing and packages it into a comprehensive conceptual net. A theory is a way of seeing a problem, a description that provides insights on how the dimensions and variables are related or intertwined. Models and theories help us to see and understand things that we might otherwise overlook. However, by making some of these relationships visible and intelligible, they also obscure and exclude other possible vistas on management control problems. This is why we need to be acquainted with various forms of explaining and interpreting organizations and controls. Knowing one perspective only is too reductionist given the complexity of the phenomenon.

Instead of learning by trial and error or making do with personal experience in several organizations, the knowledge of a constellation of models and theories can help accountants diagnose and explain the workings of a system in a more systematic and sophisticated way. The result should be greater effectiveness. Thus, in a very real sense, an organizational sociology approach can make management accountants and financial executives more competent and more influential. After all, accounting and financial discourse is one of the most pervasive and important voices in today's world; a strategic and global perspective, in addition to technical and micro perspectives, seems crucial.

Accounting theories tend to line up into distinctive paradigms about organizations and the social world. There are many to choose from and this book includes several.[6] But models and theories come in different forms and this always makes their classification difficult, never objective, and attempts at classification are often subject to harsh criticism. We thus decided to keep things simple in choosing ordering principles. Hence we first grouped together those perspectives on the study of MACS that assume that an organization's social system consists of concrete, empirical phenomena that exist independently of the managers and employees who work there. We then divided these approaches into three large categories, which move from the individual to the context as the explanatory variable in understanding organizational phenomena and the nature and functioning of MACS. At the other end of the spectrum there are approaches that assume the relational nature of organizational phenomena: these do not exist in a vacuum but are interlinked and their nature and functioning is the ongoing result of a continuous process of interaction. We then classified these into three further categories, which view relations as interactions between agents and structures as being shaped in and by practices and, finally, as being agents themselves.

This book outlines a number of frameworks for investigating and understanding MACS. The frameworks have been carefully selected in order to offer a cross section of the perspectives described above. Each was selected because it offered a unique and valuable way to look at these systems. Such a wide sweep brings with it the advantage of broadening horizons well beyond the traditional approach of information for decision and control. It possesses the obvious advantage of opening up fresh vistas and providing new insights, but it may bring with it the feeling that such an expansion has been won at the cost of importing into our knowledge base a certain measure of confusion and disagreement about the best approach.

One way to handle this feeling is to adopt the view that no one paradigm is best. This means realizing that there are different possible self-contained traditions and ways of making sense of the organizational ramifications of MACS and that we can judge each according to its own standards and purpose. Such a relativistic stance may not sit well with those who believe there must be one best perspective, or with those who believe that accounting knowledge rests on some ideal foundational scheme that we can discover. While such idealism is to be admired, the reality is that accounting, like most bodies of knowledge, has yet to achieve such a state, and will possibly never reach this plateau. Even physics, the crown prince of the sciences, lacks a general theory to unify the quantum theory of particles with concepts of relativity that Einstein formulated. Relativism does not necessarily mean that "anything goes" but it seeks to acknowledge the multiple nature, purposes and uses of MACS. So it should not be a surprise that accounting has competing and conflicting theories. If anything, what surprises is that there are still some who believe that a best way exists!

Instead of looking for the ultimate paradigm, we aim more modestly to bring to the attention of management accounting practitioners a number of paradigms that look at different dimensions and aspects of these systems and to illustrate how to use them in a practical way. We do this with a variety of case histories, which breathe life into what might otherwise seem dry and inert. We show how to put frameworks into action for analyzing, diagnosing, and prescribing for real MACS problems and issues.

Thus, our *modus operandi* differs from both the traditional case method and the conventional theoretical approach. The case method treats each situation as unique with issues and problems that can be identified and sorted out diagnostically by drawing on intuition and insight derived from an in-depth analysis of the situation at hand. In contrast, the theoretical approach focuses heavily on the knowledge content of the subject in order to get across the theoretical concepts and the elegance of their interrelationship within the theory. Often oversimplified examples, such as a children's lemonade stand, are provided to illustrate the theory but little concern is shown for practical application. The aim is to acquire a deep understanding of theories for appropriate application in the future. If the traditional case method is like a rich and fascinating story about a problem looking for a solution, the conventional theoretical approach is like an elegant and powerful solution looking for a problem.

This book veers away from any such theoretical–practical duality. Instead, it aims to show that both are important, that theory and practice are inextricably intertwined Theory is always there in practice, regardless of how implicit or commonsensical it may appear. Likewise, practice is always present in the theory, no matter how thinly disguised. In this book, the theories are used to sensitize understanding of practical situations to vital but easily overlooked aspects of the situation at hand. And the case histories are used to bring to life what otherwise might come across as inert abstractions.

But it is also a slippery slope. The frameworks tend to focus on a few variables at the expense of excluding others that may also be vital. Moreover, there is no guarantee that different individuals, even though they rely on the same framework, will reach an identical understanding. The frameworks do not inevitably generate correct answers. There is still a great deal of individual skill and judgment that goes into the analysis. The richly painted case analyses presented here are idiosyncratic and are not deemed to be definitive solutions. Rather, they are offered as illustrations of one way to interpret the case situation using the syntax, concepts, and relationships included in the particular framework at hand. Nevertheless they are considerate and serious attempts to use the frameworks in a valuable way.

What follows is an introduction to the main perspectives that we will refer to in this book. We clearly do not intend to provide a complete and exhaustive illustration of them (and we could not, even if we wished to do so).

Being conscious that our classification is subject to criticism, we wanted to provide readers with basic instruments to create their own. Those philosophers who wish to make a further exploration in this perilous territory can begin their journey by looking at the list of references provided at the end of this chapter.

3.2 Believing in Reality: Positive Faith in Individuals, Needs, and Structures

Do you believe in reality? Your answer will very likely be a resounding "yes," and it would be difficult to not agree with you. In fact, most of modern science is based on the assumption that reality exists independently of how we study it and of which perspectives and technologies we employ in this study. Some economists and students of MACS share the same view and often apply methodologies used in the natural sciences to analyze the way organizational control systems work. They describe variables, set forth testable hypotheses, collect quantitative data, and undertake statistical analysis. Like the particle physicist, they assume themselves to be neutral, objective, and value-free observers of the MACS under investigation. Scientific positivism is *de rigueur*.

This belief can be operationalized through various methodologies. Various management accounting and control theories are underpinned by realist assumptions as we have defined them here. We have organized the following sections in a range from a faith in individuals and individualism as the key explanatory variable of organizational phenomena, to a belief in societal context as the cause of changes in contemporary capitalist societies, accounting systems and the like. These sections will give you a flavor of such perspectives.

3.2.1 Individualism: Positive, Rational, and Market Beliefs

Assume that you were asked to understand how societies, organizations, MACS work, of what they are made and what for. What would you do? You would very likely begin to "analyze" your object of study. But what does it mean to analyze a problem or an organizational phenomenon?

Analysis is an interesting word which needs to be well understood in order to comprehend the tenets of methodological individualism.[7] We often assume that we know its meaning as we are asked to analyze problems since primary school. But do we really know what it means "to analyze things"? And, have we reflected on how we are building an explanation of organizational phenomena when we do so through analysis?

Let us look at a very practical management accounting and control tool: ratio analysis. Why do we call this technique to assess firms' performance "ratio *analysis*"? Why don't we call it "ratio *synthesis*"? And what do we do when we do "ratio analysis"? How do we build an explanation of organizational performance through ratios?

We often ask our students these questions when we teach our courses. The most common answer we receive is that we call it "analysis" because it provides an "interpretation" of how the firm is doing. Well . . . if this were the answer, we would call it "ratio hermeneutics" as hermeneutics is the art of interpreting signs. But we all keep calling it "ratio analysis." Why?

The etymology of the word "analysis" may help. "Analysis" comes from ancient Greek, *analyein,* which means "to break things up"—that is, to separate a whole into its components parts. Thus to do ratio analysis, to understand a firm's performance, means to understand this performance by breaking it up into those components that improve or worsen it. The Du Pont method and the pyramid of ratios that it creates are the classical example of methodological individualism in management accounting: the whole performance of the firm is explained through the behavior of a series of ratios that relate to specific areas of such a firm in a progressive journey towards the minutest parts.

Methodological individualism therefore does not grant any explanatory power to the whole or to "collective" terms such as "organization," "society," "state" and the like. It assumes an ideal continuity and causal relationship between microphenomena and macrophenomena, explaining the latter in terms of the former's behavior.

This methodology in constructing explanations is underpinned by some ontological assumptions and has consequences.[8] The assumption is that organizational phenomena are stable and independent of our observations. Hence the term "positivism"—that is, a positive description of reality rather than a normative prescription of what should happen.[9] A financial analyst would break organizational performance down to the smallest part, as a Newtonian physicist would do, both being inspired by the same positivist beliefs.

This faith in a positive knowledge of reality has consequences. If organizational phenomena are independent of our observations, then it is just a matter of correctly linking information with actions: greater knowledge should lead to better actions and the extent to which this happens makes agents more or less rational. In a sense this positive belief in reality makes it difficult to escape from a normative prescription of behavior. The space where these beliefs take shape is the market, nowadays increasingly seen as a metaphor for the solution of all human problems.

Economists, and thus also those accountants who view accounting as being all about economics, rely heavily upon methodological individualism to construct their theories. For them, macro-aspects such as market fluctuations in demand are explained in terms of microbehaviors such as changes in consumers' aptitudes. Such ideas lie at the core of neoclassical economics, where individual behavior is used to explain how entire economic systems work: this is the product of a sum of individual behaviors. Aggregates such as organizations can thus be viewed as coalitions of individuals in equilibrium or a sum of individual contracts formulated in a market. Management accounting and control systems are crucial in this milieu as they provide supposedly neutral information to rational decision makers whose actions will make organizations and (internal or external) markets work.

We will see that this is a very powerful framework given its simplicity and seductive logic. We will also see, though, that, like any other explanation, this partial and reductionist view cannot be used as the only way of understanding MACS.

3.2.2 Functionalism: On Being "Fit"

It seems that everyone is in favor of effectiveness and efficiency. Everybody likes to achieve objectives that have been set and to do so with the least possible consumption of resources. It is difficult to go against the rhetoric of these powerful constructs.[10]

Of course a belief in these two principles follows the same assumption as the previous methodology—that we can easily identify what these objectives are, as well as the related means to achieve them. Notions such as the "utility function," or more simplistically the idea of an identifiable "need," open the way to value judgments about whether an action is more or less functional to their satisfaction. Based on the notion of "organism," as a body made of organs that play specific functions to guarantee its survival, functionalism has been developed in sociology and other cognate areas such as organization studies.

Scholars of MACS are not exempt from this seductive idea. Their concern is to make MACS function more effectively. So they search for workable solutions to practical problems, which will help accountants and managers achieve a better alignment of these systems with other organizational elements and forces. Their aim is pragmatic—to achieve better regulation and control of the status quo.

Possibly the most successful example of a very functionalist approach to management accounting is the development of activity-based costing (ABC) and its variations such as activity-based management (ABM). The proponents of ABC claim that conventional management accounting systems, which allocate overheads to cost objects according to a volume-related cost allocation base, fail to recognize how external environments have changed with respect to customer requirements, technologies, methods of production and so forth. Old accounting systems fail to recognize these changes and thus do not provide useful and functional information. Activity-based costing takes these changes into account and uses cost drivers that tend to reflect the increased complexity of the market, production and technology environment. For those seduced by the functionalist ABC message, conventional cost accounting systems introduce and produce some dysfunctionalities, which need to be corrected in order for the organization to be able to satisfy customer needs and to be more in tune with external market, production and technological changes taken as independent variables.

The corollary of this functionalist perspective is a firm belief in a notion of "fitness"—some behaviors, systems, and organizational forms are more "fit" to survive in a given environment and others are not. The idea of "fitness" is powerful when management scholars and consultants have to explain why the implementation of accounting and information systems fails: they fail because of a dysfunctionality in these systems; a lack of fit between design and action, training and use, information needed and information produced, to name only some of various possibilities.

The functionalist approach, for better or worse, remains a dominant paradigm for most MACS thinking, especially in its contingency-driven explanations. For the most part, functionalists take power and political arrangements as given and so treat the existing power structure as unproblematic, while contextualism regards this power as the quintessential feature of its explanation.[11]

3.2.3 Contextualism: Culture, Society, and Resistance

Think of crime. Then ask a psychologist and a sociologist to give an explanation for its worrying growth. The psychologist would try to explain it by digging into the history of the individuals involved in it. The sociologist would blame society for the bad influence on the individuals committing it. The former blames individuals and agency, the latter society and the contexts in which these crimes take place. Of course this is a crude dichotomy and it is clear that neither the first nor the second explanation is entirely right: they both contain elements of truth.

However, this example helps us to introduce the last of the realist methodologies that we will be addressing in this chapter. It also leads us directly to the core assumption of this explanation—that human beings are political and social animals and society has an enormous, and sometimes unavoidable, effect on them.

Accounting researchers have attempted to reintroduce these political and sociological issues into our understanding of MACS by abandoning individual agency and market exchange as the basis of their analysis of the nature and role of these systems.[12] The focus has instead been on another sphere of relationships at the level of social structures and contexts. In this socio-structural sphere attention is paid to nontransactional relationships rather than transactional and economic ones.[13] Accounting, like other management practice, is seen as a means through which standards of appropriateness are transmitted across different social contexts.[14] If we stay with the example of the success of the ABC system—from this viewpoint this success would be explained as a form of imitation rather than as a rational and functional response to an existing need for better financial management information. Firms adopt ABC because other firms do so and because society requires its use as a legitimating action in the battle to attract resources in a given market or field of expertise.

Contextualism interprets single actions and human behavior within the unique context that "determines" them.[15] Such a methodological position translated into the accounting domain explains the role of accounting within organizations via a strategy that privileges the structures (for example, language, cultural settings) in which individuals and organizations find themselves embedded. The passive conditioning of individuals by institutions represents the cornerstone on which such theories can be built, and constitutes a way of constructing theories that is quite contrary to that adopted by methodological individualism. However, like methodological individualism and functionalism, contextualism assumes that social systems have a concrete and real ontological existence—that is, they are independent of the actions of the individuals who suffer from this influence.

For some of the theorists in these studies, the existence of such overarching structures generates a state of dynamic tension for social organizations: two basic opposing forces or principles are locked in a dialectic contradiction whereby they operate in terms of, but also run counter to, each other. Secondary contradictions are also present, but they arise as a consequence of the primary contradiction. The contradiction between the two forces is seen as an intrinsic aspect of any organization and basic to the integration of its systems.

Radical structuralists, for example, try to uncover the role that MACS play in supporting and maintaining a mode of organization whereby a small minority of executives and managers rule and exploit the rest of the employees scattered across the organizational landscape.[16] Importantly, these dynamics are more readily discerned in crisis situations than during periods of surface stability when underlying structural contradictions and tensions are camouflaged. The labor process framework and the historical–dialectical model in Chapter 4 are of this type.

All social systems are seen to be inherently changeful. At any time, one of the two fundamental forces in the system has the upper hand, but only temporarily, and it can be overturned by the other. Radical structuralists pay particular attention to the way those with power (usually a small elite) hold the rest in check by means of their control over and use of power resources including MACS. The radical structuralist aims to develop possibilities for effecting a radical overhaul of any such coercive status quo.

The radical humanist approach is a variation of the radical structuralist explanation, which draws on this dialectical relationship to call for activism and change. Radical humanists assume a subjective social world but, in contrast to some extreme relativist and interpretivist positions, which will be discussed in the next section, they adopt a radical change position.[17] Radical humanists aim for a people-oriented vision of MACS practices whereby humanistic ideals and values come before organizational purpose. Like radical structuralists, they see MACS as vehicles for elites to take advantage of other managers and employees. They see this suppression stemming not from concrete, real, and independent forces and institutions such as the state, capitalism or bureaucracy, but from the traps that organizational participants construct themselves.

Radical humanists contend that managers and employees socially construct organizational control structures and processes, but later, through a process of reification, come to experience them as outside forces rather than as extensions of themselves. They argue that relations of power in organizations acquire their force just as much from subordinates' enactment of the prevailing structures of control and domination as they do from superordinates' initiatives. In consequence, managers and employees are prone to take on a false consciousness about the coercive nature of their working life. Individuals socially construct realities of which they then remain victims. They become happy slaves or misinterpreters of the basic source of their suppression themselves.

Radical humanists have both enlightenment and emancipatory aims. The enlightenment goal is for agents to see through their self-induced fettered existence whereas the emancipatory aim calls for them to regain power and responsibility for their self-constructed social world. It is possible, radical humanists believe, for managers and employees to realize that the social structures that discipline and control them are merely language games (albeit extremely serious ones) whereby socially constructed narratives and metaphors dictate the terms of social actions and interactions. Thus, the possibility opens up for the actors to understand these dynamics and restore power to themselves. People are not for organizations; organizations are for people.

The notion of strategy as ideology (see Chapter 6), for instance, draws on radical humanist ideas. The dialectic control model outlined in Chapter 4 is developed along radical humanist lines. It argues for empowering employees by letting them take control of the design and running of MACS in order to rehierarchize organizational goals in such a way as to put their needs for employment, stability, and interpersonal relationships at the top, instead of a hierarchy where the market price of the company's stock and cost cutting come ahead of employee imperatives. Humanistic ideals, not materialistic goals, would reign.

Most of the structuralist and radical movements have sought to profess change to subvert the status quo. However, the assumption that powerful dominating structures are present has been criticized for attributing excessive passivity to individual behaviors. Paradoxically theories predicating change have been constructed assuming the inherent stability and dominance of these structures. The approaches which will be examined in the following section, although not always driven by this radical attention to change, have subverted the starting point of the theorization and assumed the relativity of these structures to explain how they change, even though they are not always primarily concerned with issues of change.

3.3 Believing in Relations: Relativist Faith in Interactions, Actions, and Networks

Management accounting and control systems can be viewed from a less objectivist and realist point of view, which abandons the abstractions of economic approaches and enters into the realm of interactions, actions, and networks. Economic models, biological metaphors and structuralist understandings of management accounting are useful but they leave little room for interpretation, subjectivity and relativism in constructing an understanding of the information that these system produce, how this information is used, and with what consequences.

Alternative approaches have thus developed in accounting research. Concepts such as postmodernism and its variations, once almost unknown in accounting circles, have become, at least among certain academics, quite common. Recent studies in law, philosophy, architecture, history, communications and information studies, geography, visual arts, and women's studies have profoundly influenced the methods and theories of a variety of disciplines in the human sciences, including accounting, as a fresh and vital development.[18] They have highlighted how the project of modernity, with its belief in the power of science and technology, has failed. Thus some have argued that "we have never been modern"[19] although we have always aspired to become so.

Highly sophisticated technologies, mass media, and a homogenized global marketplace dominate the contemporary world, making it appear as quintessentially modern. However with this faith in modernity comes also a quasimystical belief in the power of numbers, science and technology. In this respect, there is not a great difference between the mysticism of the Middle Ages and the modern faith in science. Once both have been demystified, there is a need for new concepts, theories, and methodologies to understand the contemporary world in which we live.

Accounting, as the quintessential administration practice, has been central to this attempt to make our lives more scientific through effective MACS. However, the idea that these systems provide full control is fading out. That control remains a chimera is now increasingly becoming a commonplace although the desire for some kind of social order is still pressing.

Most recent approaches to MACS have thus abandoned the dominant methods and theories of so-called modernity (such as structural and radical functionalist ideas) in favor of poststructuralist tools. These include genealogical historical analyses of the human sciences and their related practices; deconstructivist interrogation of ruling ideas and canonical texts; dedoxification of scientific methods; and strategies for defining and constructing one's own individuality. Poststructural tools are used to create legitimate spaces for discourses and groups previously marginalized by modernist perspectives with their hegemonic tendencies.

But perhaps the distinguishing feature of the poststructuralist approach is its negation of structuralist and objectivist claims that more or less permanent, subsurface structures, such as the invisible hand of the market or the forces of capitalism, running deep and strong, give the true meaning of the surface world, which merely copies them. For poststructuralists, such an idea is simply a politically loaded language game. Instead they see the sociocultural landscape as a collage of unanchored, free-floating, and competing discourses.

These alternative approaches, which have taken various names throughout the recent history of accounting theories,[20] differ from the realist methodologies in two major respects. First, the focus is not only on getting the organization to run more smoothly, but also to produce rich and deep understandings of how managers and employees in organizations understand, think about, interact with, and use MACS. These studies result in thick narratives about the way accountants and managers make sense of these systems through studying how various kinds of interactions happen: hence the term "interactionists."

The other major difference is that interactionists do not believe in the existence of any one single, objective, concrete organizational reality. Instead, they contend that each organizational participant interprets the situation in his or her own way and, more importantly, that their understandings become very real to them because they react to events and situations on the basis of these personal meanings.[21] Moreover, in doing so, they interact both with other managers and employees, who bring with them their private meanings, and with other technologies, which mediate the construction of these meanings. Relying on personal reflections and interactions, managers and employees construct and transform the meaning of accounting and control systems as they go along, always paying close attention to how others see them and the situation at hand.

For the interactionists the meaning of an accounting system does not stem predominantly from social structures that exist independently from accountants and managers. Nor are they seen to be the result of the manager's psychological makeup. Although the manager must use language to construct meanings, the words used do not have fixed, stable meanings. Instead, they take on meaning only within a context, at the moment when they are used and in the nest of relationships in which they are used. The organizational world is thus seen to be constructed as a result of ongoing relationships between changing agencies and structures, or via the training that informs organizational practices, or in networks of relationships that can sometimes take a dialogic form (as in the case of structuration). Relativism, from these perspectives, does not necessarily mean that all being equal and relative nothing can be done to change society. Quite the contrary—the assumption that everything can be thought to be equal and the acknowledgment that power relationships and domination is simply the result of certain historical and material configurations makes change a possibility rather than an utopian ideal. Relativism, from these perspectives, should perhaps be renamed "relationism," to indicate that these approaches have a relational view of the world and of societies.

3.3.1 Structuration: Structure, Actions, and Systems

The methodologies described in the previous sections begin with a focus on individuals and single components of a system and end with the power that structures have in dictating people's behavior.[22] Paradoxically, these explanations finish by presenting similar characteristics and, for example, the power of the market can be seen as an overarching force that dominates individuals!

In order to escape from the dichotomy that seems to have trapped sociological thinking, the past decades have seen a valuable development of interpretations which try to grant equal power to structure and agency. The outcome of these efforts is knows as structuration.[23]

Structuration theory is concerned with the interplay of structures and agency in the production, reproduction, regulation, and change of social orders. Structure, the codebook for social behavior, exists in virtual time and space, is drawn upon by agents as they act and interact in specific time–space settings, and is itself the outcome of those actions and interactions. This process, known as structuration, denotes the duality of structure.

Agents, however, are not merely social dupes. They are purposive and know a great deal about why they act in the way they do. They can and do provide rationales for their actions and interactions. However, although many of the consequences of agents' behavior are intended and known, other consequences may be both unintended and unknown. In their reflexive monitoring of action in social settings, agents rely on both their discursive and practical consciousness and are motivated by an unconscious need for ontological security.

Structuration takes place along the dimensions of signification, domination, and legitimation. Signification structures involve semantic rules that are drawn on to produce meaning. Domination structures involve resources that are used to produce power. And legitimation structures involve norms and values involved in the production of morality. These three dimensions of social systems are inextricably intertwined and are considered separately for analytical purposes only. In social interactions, agents always draw on these dimensions as an integrated set. In combination, the three structural dimensions influence the social actions and interactions of agents in organizations and institutions. They serve to constrain and coerce agents, but at the same time they function to gain the cooperation necessary to maintain the social order.

Management accounting systems represent modalities of structuration in each of the three dimensions. In the signification dimension, they are the interpretive schemes that managers use to interpret past results, take actions, and make plans. In the domination dimension, they are a facility that management at all levels can use to coordinate and control other participants. In the legitimation dimension, they communicate a set of values and ideals about what is approved and what is disapproved; they justify the rights of some participants to hold others accountable; they legitimate the use of certain rewards and sanctions. Through the modalities described above, management accounting provides for the binding of social interactions in organizations across time and space as well as in some situations for their radical change.

In studying management accounting and control in practice it is always important to recognize the way in which the three dimensions are intertwined. By signifying what counts, management accounting provides a discourse[24] for the domination structure through which some participants are held accountable to others, while at the same time it provides legitimacy for the social processes that are involved. Thus, signification in management accounting terms is implicated in both the legitimation and domination structures, and as such is an important resource in structuring relations of power. However, the structural properties of management accounting are neither wholly explicit, nor unchanging. They can change as they are drawn upon and reproduced in their use by organizational participants.

A major gain from structuration theory is that issues of power and morality become highly explicit. Management accounting and control systems are seen to do much more than provide information to decision makers for purposes of scorekeeping, attention directing, and problem solving. Many accounting scholars have recently sounded the alarm that to leave relations of domination and legitimacy out of the equation and to view the world only in terms of a collection of individual actors is to miss some very important and essential aspects of accounting systems.[25] In consequence, the degree to which accountants and the systems they design are deeply involved in the social relations of domination and morality is beginning to dawn on most thoughtful academics and practitioners. When this notion really hits home, we will likely see a wholesale revolution in the way we think about MACS. Structuration theory distinguishes between structure, agency, and system. Social systems have structures which are the codes for social actions, while agency is the actions of individual members of the system. Agents draw on structures during social action and, as they do so, they produce and reproduce discernibly similar social practices across space and time. So structuration theory, and this is the point to underline, in contrast with many social theories, includes *both* structures and agency. Thus it subsumes two otherwise fundamentally antagonistic positions: the structuralist position, where social life is determined by impersonal, objective social structures, and the existentialist humanist position, where social life is a product of the individual agent's subjective, existentialist choice making.

We will return to the features and functioning of structuration processes when dealing with issues of change (Chapter 8). This brief introduction provides you with a useful bridge between the realist perspectives and those that will be discussed below.

3.3.2 Practices: MACS Uses and Training Regimes

The word "practice" is possibly becoming one of the most fashionable in accounting and management studies. Indeed there is some talk of a "practice turn" in the social sciences and accounting.[26]

What does it mean to state that management accounting and control theories are practices? As the etymology suggests, the word "practice" is something that has some practical relevance. In this sense, the etymology does not add any new nuance to the common understanding of the nature of MACS. They are indeed systems that have to prove themselves to be useful, although this utility may not be relegated to the realm of economic efficiency but can expand into the usefulness that these systems display in, for example, legitimizing past decisions. Some of you may have seen the film *Brassed Off*.[27] The film is the story of a brass band at a mine in a small village in Yorkshire (in the north of England). Most see a love story in this film. An accounting scholar instead views it as a fascinating accounting drama on how management accounting calculations and figures can be used in these two different manners. On the one hand, the accountant in love with the personage interpreted by a young Ewan McGregor used her accounting expertise to show that the mine to be closed was in fact efficient and profitable. On the other hand, the managing director of that same mine used other management accounting calculations and figures to justify *ex post* the political decision that that mine should be closed irrespectively of whether it was profitable: the British government had already decided to downsize the entire mining industry in Great Britain, regardless of the sorts of individual sites, including the mine of this lovely community and its brass band—something that made the miners "brassed off!"

This is a typical example of how accounting "systems" can actually be used "in practice" for many different purposes. In this sense, the practice turn in accounting alerts us to the way in which MACS can be used in ways which are far beyond the intentions of the original designers.[28] The notion of "practice" thus reminds us that a practice is something that is done and performed. It is in performing management accounting techniques, rather than in the abstract design of some economist, that the nature, functioning, and utility of the technique itself is defined and constantly modified.

However, not everything that is practiced—not everything that is done and performed—becomes a practice in the sense we would like to convey in this section. Some activities can be done occasionally and have a practical relevance but they do not assume the importance that MACS have because of this. These systems are so pervasive across organizations and societies because they are the result of specific training regimes. These might be certified accounting qualifications or other knowing systems—i.e. principles according to which we organize the world around us. An example will clarify this latter point. Take the case of the balanced scorecard. What you have there is a "vision" placed at the center of a figure made of four perspectives. As mentioned in the introduction to this book, this constitutes a common and consolidated practice of organizing our knowledge about a given subject, be this a speech to be given by expert orator or the performance of a firm. They both refer to some rhetorical principles that are part of our training from the moment we enter our first classroom at the age of five.[29] A practice is thus the result of specific discourses, habits or methods of knowing, all constructing a view and providing an account for the world around us.

It is thus the method, not the content, which makes management accounting and control an interesting practice. To look at how management accounting is done "in practice" is not enough (and would fall back into a positivist approach). The notion of practice that we assume in this book instead refers to shared ways of doing which are assured by the existence of certain kinds of training regimes, of certain discourses, of specific methods which spread across geographical and temporal contexts, becoming dominant. And because they provide a method but not content, MACS have a tendency to become what they are not[30]—that is, they have a multiple nature, which is ready to display itself in various guises when practiced. Think of ABC: two systems will never look the same but they will always be made of what seem to be cost drivers and cost pools. They can be used for different purposes, even at the same time, while seeming apparently the same.

In the accounting literature there has been a considerable amount of work in this direction. Foucauldian approaches, in their governmentality[31] and disciplining[32] variations, for example, are good examples of this emphasis on practice as part of broader knowing and normalizing systems. This emphasis has also been placed on some historical works that link developments in humanistic knowledge to the development of accounting.[33] The notion of practice as resulting from clear training regimes has also been useful in understanding the role that professions and professionalization have in the construction of both the professional and of what counts as legitimate knowledge in a given field.[34]

The notion of practice, which we have illustrated in this section, is the trait union between the previous perspective (characterized by the interaction between structure and agency as one of its main tenets), and the following, where the nature and uses of management accounting and control systems are defined in nets of relationships formed in the use of these systems.

3.3.3 Actor-networks: Actions and Diffused Agencies

Ask yourself whether:

> you can, with a straight face, [keep] . . . hitting a nail with *and without* a hammer, boiling water with *and without* a kettle, fetching provisions with *or without* a basket, walking in the street with *and without* your clothes, zapping a TV set with *or without* a command, slowing down a car with *or without* a speed-bump, keep track of your inventory with *or without* a list, run your company with *or without* book-keeping . . . (Latour, 2005, p. 71).

If you can hit a nail without a hammer, boil water without a kettle and, above all, run a company without book-keeping then actor-network theory (ANT) is not the right perspective for you. But if you can't, then it may be.

Actor-network theory seeks to do many things. Amongst these, one is to rethink issues of agency in organizations and assess how agencies emerge from the relations existing between "actants."[35] Now, think of various management accounting techniques and information technologies. You can conceive of these as having a neutral influence in the decision-making process. If this is the case, again, ANT is not the right perspective for you. But if you think that they have a role in how decisions are made then ANT may shed some light on how these techniques and technologies play a role in governing and controlling contemporary organizations.

But why should MACS be seen as having a role in shaping human decision making? Well, the first answer to this question is that they provide information and this constitutes the basis for further decision making. The second answer is more profound and requires us to go back to the example opening this section. You would not consider zapping without a remote control. Leaving your comfortable arm chair every ten seconds would be too tiring and tedious and you would finish up liking a TV program that you would have otherwise hated. The same happens with MACS. You would not even imagine the possibility of expanding a company without their support and this already illustrates that these "nonhuman" techniques do have an impact on how humans think and act.

This does not mean, though, that these techniques have a determinist, structural and functional impact on management's behavior (as otherwise we would be back to a structuralist explanation). Quite the contrary. Actor-network theory seeks instead to understand how agencies are diffused across a network of actants. They do not reside either in the mind of the manager or exclusively in the objects and techniques that they utilize in their daily jobs. How this diffusion happens, what effects it produces on individuals and organizations, and how individuals, organizations and societies are affected by the ways in which these techniques and technologies are deployed are the issues that one can understand through ANT lenses. These lenses focus on minute variations, relationships and events that seem irrelevant and that instead count significantly. For ANT, they make a difference and thus need to be accounted for in order to understand what influences management behavior. Clearly MACS are full of these variations and ANT can assist one to get used to recognizing them. As Bruno Latour, one of the major exponents of this approach, noted, ANT is about the study of these details. To understand MACS one needs to observe them both when they are theorized and also as they are practiced, as both observations will reveal how they influence the construction of a given view of organizations and their performance.

3.4 Summary and Conclusions

This chapter has provided a framework that may be helpful in mapping various forms of understanding of MACS. The chapter has not dealt explicitly with the features of these systems but mainly with the perspectives from which one can look at them.

Our mapping began from familiar territory: the view that organizational phenomena are quite stable and independent of our observations. This assumption implies that MACS should aim at faithfully representing these phenomena to aid rational decision making and improve organizational efficiency. The method adopted for gaining this knowledge is analytical, breaking the problem to be solved down to its smallest possible part. Ratio analysis is a paradigm to pursue this approach and its methodology is based on individualism.

This emphasis on efficiency is also shared by those approaches that abandon a monolithic view of reality and assume that environments change and vary. Management accounting and control systems in this case have to adapt to an external environment, expressed in terms of some kind of variable (technology, market conditions, and the like). If they do, then these systems are "fit" and functional to the pursuit of organizations' aims. If they do not, then they are dysfunctional and this lack of fitness becomes the scapegoat for every organizational problem. Functionalism is the label chosen to describe this approach.

This move from the individual to the environment drives a further shift towards "the context" as the explicatory variable of the nature, use and functioning of management accounting systems. The systems construct realities, which then determine human and organizational behaviors. Overarching structures reign sovereign and make human existence miserable, in the worst case, or with little room for diversity and maneuver in the better ones. If the "context" rules then contextualism describes this perspective.

These realist assumptions are abandoned when one enters the realm of interactions. In order to escape an exclusive focus on either the individual or the context, structuration approaches seek to establish a more interpretive approach to the role that MACS play in organizations and societies. Their nature, uses and functionalities change with time as the result of this interaction between individual agency and technical structure. The resulting effect is structuration, as a process dependent on both context and the interpretation of the user.

This emphasis on the performance of these systems is what inspires those who believe in a practice approach. Management accounting and control systems can be used differently when practiced, and often they are. Yet, training regimes and knowing systems affect the way in which we use these systems in forms that are open to exploration. The "practice turn" in the study of MACS is already happening.

Once MACS are viewed as practices, it is easy to see how the nature and functionality of these systems depends on their configuration, and on the way in which they are implemented and interact with other systems and with their users. We thus enter the realm of actor-network approaches where the nature and functionality of MACS is diffused across a network of relationships involving, for example, technologies (such as Enterprise Resource Planning systems), regulations and standards (such as the International Financial Reporting Standards), and so forth.

In summary, we have tried to provide a map to show the various forms and uses of MACS. As with every classification, the overview that we provided in this chapter is incomplete—it is biased by our preferences and depends on our personal and academic histories and worldviews. However, once you have read the remaining chapters and expanded your knowledge of MACS through the various readings we provide at the end of each chapter (and other readings) we believe it can provide a starting point from which you can then create your own understanding of what these systems are and do. Management accounting and control systems are fluid and changing entities. Defining them once and for all would limit your ability to comprehend how they work, how they produce effects on your lives and on those who work with you. It is much better, at this stage, to provide you with different ways of seeing them and also to warn you that these views are always partial.

Endnotes

1. See Bhimani *et al.* (2008), Ezzamel (1992), Kaplan and Atkinson (1989) and Scapens (1985) for books regarding the application of calculative techniques to management accounting.
2. See Emmanuel, Otley and Merchant (1992), Macintosh (1985) and Parker, Ferris and Otley (1989) for coverage of the microbehavioral approach to behavioral accounting.
3. See Czarniawska (1997) for an overview and description of the approach that we would like to follow in interpreting organizations.
4. The exceptions are books by Puxty (1993) and Roslender (1992); both are excellent.
5. See Latour (2005).
6. See Hopper and Powell (1985) for an overview of the various paradigms and related accounting studies, and Chua (1986) for a review of their epistemological and ontological assumptions.
7. Individualism makes single actors and one-to-one transactions the cornerstone of social theory (see Donzelli, 1986; Nagel, 1963, 1968; Salmon, 1989; Sparti, 1995). They discover elements of systems and their interrelationships—be they organizations, accounting systems, or economies. They then behave as individual agents according to either full or bounded economic rationality to exploit this knowledge (see Donzelli, 1986; Friedman, 1935; Hodgson, 1988; Robbins, 1932). Behavior is presumed to be purposeful and in accordance with knowledge of an external reality possessing a firm ontology. Elements, be they individuals or transactions, and their interrelationships are building blocks for constructing knowledge as a whole—be it about an organization or an entire economic system. Contextualism, in contrast, emphasizes how situational factors and social collectivities shape individuals' construction of meanings, which form the basis for purposeful behavior. It gives explanatory power to concepts such as "society," "culture," and "institutions." Individualism looks for the smallest building blocks or atoms of the observed phenomena to build the whole upwards, whereas contextualism explains phenomena through larger social constructs, i.e. it builds theory downwards.
8. For some others, instead, this methodology is the result of a given belief in specific realist ontological assumptions. See Laudan (1977). The definition of the terms "ontology," "methodology" and "epistemology" used here is drawn from Laudan's concept of "research tradition" (Laudan, 1977, pp. 78–81), and from their etymological analysis. As it is widely known, the etymology of the term "ontology" derives from the Greek *on, ontos* (present participle of *einai*, to be) and *logos* (discourse). Analogously, the etymology of the term "methodology" derives from the Greek *meta* (after), *hodos* (a way), and *logos*; that of "epistemology" from *episteme* (knowledge) and *logos*. Traditionally, these terms have been used to describe the research of the true essence of the "being," of the best scientific method and of the "true" knowledge, respectively. But it might be argued that their etymology is not in contrast with "weak" interpretations of them (Vattimo, 1983) According to the etymological analysis, "ontology" is a *discourse on the object* of knowledge (entities and processes of a domain of study, Laudan, 1977, p. 81). Analogously, "methodology" is a *discourse*

on the subject of knowledge (ways in which theories are constructed in that domain, Laudan, 1977, p. 81). "Epistemology" is thus a *discourse on knowledge* and these terms can therefore be deprived of the metaphysical and transcendental features that have characterized their history.

9. For neoclassical economics there is virtually no difference between social and natural science. Friedman stated: "positive economics is, or can be, an objective science, in precisely the same sense as any of the physical science" (1935, p. 181). Thus, in neoclassical economics, individual behavior, far from being "subjective," ideally becomes isomorphic to whatever, *ceteris paribus*, it should be. The same distinction between positive economics and normative economics becomes subtle, with "that which is" being almost identical to "that which should be." The conditions of absolute truthfulness posited by neoclassical economics in the *explanans* of the deductive-nomological model implicitly conceive of a rational man who has absolute knowledge of his phenomenal dominion (see Simon, 1983). Assumed to know all the available alternatives, he can order his preferences. In so doing the rational economic man reduces everything to "numbers." For this reason the economic aspect of a given transaction is representative of all the other aspects involved in decision making. According to Robbins: "by itself the multiplicity of ends has no necessarily interest for the economist . . . when time and means for achieving ends are limited *and* capable of alternative application, *and* the ends are capable of being distinguished in order of importance, then behaviour necessarily assumes the form of choice . . . *It has an economic aspect*" (1932, p. 84; last emphasis added).

10. See Hansen and Mouritsen (1999).

11. Not all functionalists ignore politics and change. But those that do consider power and global goals see them as up for grabs in a pluralistic (and changeful) setting where all have a chance to become part of the "dominant coalition." Thus, the manager is considered to be either an astute or a naive politician.

12. See the classic Tinker, Merino and Neimark (1982).

13. Meyer and Rowan note that: "Quite beyond the environmental interrelations suggested in open systems theories, institutional theories in their extreme forms define organizations as dramatic enactments of the rationalized myths pervading modern societies, *rather than as units involved in exchange*—no matter how complex—with their environments" (1977, p. 47, emphasis added).

14. See Mouritsen (1994).

15. See Sparti (1995, pp. 175–80).

16. See Tinker (1980) and Tinker and Neimark (1987) for a seminal accounting study along these lines.

17. See Puxty (1993, Chapter 6) for a detailed (if partial) review of this paradigm.

18. See and Best and Kellner (1991) and Sarup (1993) for excellent introductory coverage of post-modernity and poststructural developments.

19. Latour (1991).

20. These go under the name of "critical accounting" (see, for instance, Arrington and Puxty, 1991; Broadbent, Laughlin and Read, 1991; Chua, 1986; Hopper, Storey and Willmott, 1987; Neimark, 1990; Neimark and Tinker, 1986; the special issue of *Critical Perspectives on Accounting*, No. 1, March, 1994), "interpretivist research" (see for instance Ahrens and Chapman, 2007a, b; Chua, 1986), "naturalistic research" (natural or naturalistic models—Abdel-khalik and Ajinkya, 1979, 1983; Boland and Pondy, 1983; Tomkins and Groves, 1983; Hopper, Storey and Willmott, 1987), "subjectivist research" (Boland, 1989). These various approaches depart from the monolithic, but very clear, assumption of the realist approaches and are inspired by critical, postmodern and poststructuralist philosophies. See Chua (1988) and Covaleski and Dirsmith (1990) for useful overviews of the interpretivist paradigm in accounting.

21. A striking example supporting interactionist beliefs comes from Perrow (1970) who reports the case of two juvenile delinquent institutions. In one case, the authorities saw the situation in terms of a lack of authority and discipline in each of the delinquent's lives. So they set up a highly autocratic, military-like organization and meted out large doses of discipline. In the second case, the authorities saw each delinquent as a unique case study to be treated and understood in his or her own right. This institution featured highly organic and peer-type person-to-person relationships between counsellors and detainees. The reality in each case was socially constructed but, importantly, resulted in totally different control structures and processes.

22. Oldroyd (1986).

23. See Giddens (1984) and, in management accounting, Macintosh and Scapens (1990) and Burns and Scapens (2000).

24. In this sense, a discourse can be said to be the "outcome" of signification, or, in other words, its instantiation in practice.

25. See Burchell *et al.* (1980), Cooper (1980), Tinker (1980) and Tinker, Merino and Neimark (1982) for pioneer articles making this point. See also Covaleski, Dirsmith and Jablonsky (1984) and Covaleski and Dirsmith (1988) for the importance of relating accounting to relations of power.

26. For a review of the "practice turn" in accounting see Ahrens and Chapman (2007a, b). For more in general see Schatzki, Cetina and von Savigny (2001).

27. If not, watch it: it is a good film! *Brassed Off* is a 1996 film by Mark Herman, starring Pete Postlethwaite, Tara Fitzgerald and Ewan McGregor. We will refer to it later on in the book.

28. We will come back to this point when we will, for example, discuss issues of management accounting change and how this is coupled with the development of information technologies in ways that are yet to be discovered.

29. On this point see Quattrone (2009).

30. See Hopwood (1987).

31. See, for instance, Miller and O'Leary (1987, 1994a).

32. See for example, Hoskin and Macve (1986, 2000).

33. Quattrone (2009) and Thomson (1991), both looking at accounting as a rhetorical practice.

34. See Ramirez's (2001) work inspired by Bourdieu.

35. Actor-network theory, drawing on Greimas's semiotics, uses the notion of "actant" rather than "actor" to stress the importance that "nonhumans" (such as the hammer, the nail and the remote control of the example in the text) have in shaping human actions. In this sense, these actions, and the related agencies, cannot be defined as "human" only, but they result from a hybrid combination in which the boundary of the "human" and the "nonhuman" becomes blurred.

Further Readings

You can usefully do some further readings in each of the areas below:

On the philosophy and sociology of the sciences see:

- Oldroyd, D. (1986) *The Arch of Knowledge. An Introductory Study of the History of the Philosophy of Science*, New South Wales University Press, Kensington.
- Woolgar, S. (1988) *Science: The Very Idea*, London, Routledge.

On organization theory and accounting see:

- Ahrens, T. and Chapman, C. (2007) Theorizing practice in management accounting research, in *Handbook of Management Accounting Research* (eds Chapman, C., Hopwood, A., Shields, M.), Elsevier, Oxford, vol. 1, pp. 99–112.
- Baxter, J. and Chua, W. (2003) Alternative management accounting research—whence and whither. *Accounting, Organizations and Society*, **28** (2–3), 97–126.
- Burrell, G. and Morgan, G. (1979) *Sociological Paradigms and Organizational Analysis*, Heinemann, London.
- Hopper, T. and Powell, A. (1985) Making sense of research into the organizational and social aspects of management accounting: a review of its underlying assumptions. *Journal of Management Studies*, **22** (5), 429–65.
- Quattrone, P. (2000) Constructivism and accounting research: towards a trans-disciplinary perspective. *Accounting, Auditing and Accountability Journal*, **13** (2), 130–55.
- Ryan, B., Scapens, R. and Theobold, M. (2002) *Research Method and Methodology in Finance and Accounting* (2nd edn), Thomson, London.

PART II

THE NATURE, STRUCTURES, AND MODES OF OPERATION OF MACS

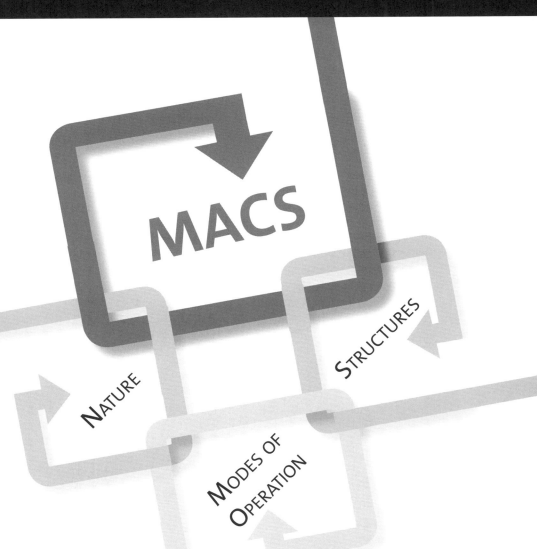

4

The Nature of MACS: Information, Power, and Control

4.1 Introduction

Chapter 2 described four cases in some detail, focusing on the MACS in these organizations. Chapter 3 also offered an overview of various perspectives that can be of some use in interpreting MACS. The reason for doing so was to identify the subject matter of this book clearly, to demonstrate the vital role these systems can play in organizations and to illustrate their richness and complexity. Yet no useful body of knowledge can rest on the assumption that each case is unique and can be understood primarily on the basis of experience and intuition. In consequence, most fields of knowledge about organizations started out with the alternative premise that there are essential and universal elements and general principles that are applicable to all complex systems. Management accounting is no exception. This chapter looks at five major universal paradigms.[1]

The first of these, *agency theory*, depicts the organization as a web of two-person contracts between owner and employees where the owner (or principal) uses accounting information to control the employee-manager who acts as the owner's agent. Agency theory, situated solidly in the structural functionalist paradigm, treats accounting systems and agents as commodities in order to bring the analytical techniques of neoclassical economics to bear on problems of control such as employee sloth and deceit. In sharp contrast, the second framework, the *informational nerve center* picture, sees the manager as immersed in collecting, storing and disseminating formal and, particularly, informal information during a frantic and relentless round of brief encounters. The nerve center framework, following the subjective interpretivist paradigm, relies on sociopsychological role theory to make sense of the manager's chaotic life. The third framework examines MACS for their symbolic nature. *Accounting symbolism*, the name for this approach, still tries to establish a relationship between information gathering and decision making. However, it seriously questions the assumption that a relationship between managerial knowledge and action in fact exists. Based on empirical observation, those who believe in the symbolic nature of MACS believe that managers collect far more information than they can process. Accounting information is thus collected but not properly used or not used at all and therefore it has more a symbolic rather than functionalist nature. The *labor process* view, the fourth paradigm addressed in this chapter, follows the radical structuralist tradition and situates the manager in a contradictory position as both the victim and user of MACS. It applies notions of deskilling and cheapening of wage labor to raise important issues about accounting and control systems. Finally, the *dialectic control* framework highlights how organizations historically evolve thanks to dialectic tensions existent in the system. It is the continuous tension amongst organizational elements that makes organizations evolve along a path but equally change over the time of this evolution. The General Electric case described in the final section provides an illustration of this form of evolution where path dependencies, tensions and finally change are all related to the nature of GE's management control and accounting systems. We will also relate these five views to the cases illustrated in Chapter 2.

While these five paradigms are somehow competing ways of thinking about the role of MACS, each has something vital to say about them.

4.1.1 Dealing with Information: Agency Theory and the "Principal versus Agent" Problem

The agency theory view of management accounting usually assumes a world of explicit or implicit two-person contracts between owner and employee in which both parties behave in a rational utilitarian fashion motivated solely by self-interest. It depicts the agency relationship as a contract under which the owner (or principal) delegates decision-making authority to the manager (agent) who then performs services on behalf of the owner. Given that agents are utility maximizers, it seems the agent will not always take actions that are in the principal's best interests. The owner, however, can limit such aberrant behavior by incurring auditing, accounting, and monitoring costs and by establishing, also at a cost, an appropriate incentive scheme (Jensen and Meckling, 1976).

Most proponents of agency theory do not really believe the organizational world consists mainly of bilateral contractual relationships. Rather, they hold that this portrayal can be used advantageously to shed light on and develop insights into the way accounting and information systems can be used by owners to control employees and managers. Importantly, by positing a contractual world, agency theorists can proceed by relying solely on neoclassical economic theory and the techniques of information economics. Agency theory is built around the key ideas of self-interest, adverse selection, moral hazard, signaling, incentives, information asymmetry, and most pervasively, the contract.

Self-Interest

Agency theory has its roots planted firmly in neoclassical economics, which has always made self-interest its basic platform. The self-interest theme stems from the influential writings of Hobbes, Smith, and Spencer, three giants of social philosophy. Thomas Hobbes (1588–1679), living in an era of tumultuous political, economic, and spiritual upheaval, pictured human beings as wholly selfish and, when living in the state of nature, leading a solitary, poor, nasty, brutish, and short life. The individual's happiness came from getting what one desires. One's desires were deemed to be goods. Moreover, Hobbes argued, people are fundamentally equal in terms of strength, ability, and hopes for attaining these goods but since everyone is motivated by and is equal in the attributes needed for satisfying self-interest, everyone's hopes and happiness are constantly threatened. The individual's life, it seemed, was permanent and constant misery.

In contemplating this miserable state of affairs, Hobbes suggested a way out. The key, he surmised, lay in enlightened self-interest. The individual must create some sovereign, central power (king, parliament, state, whatever) and agree to be governed by it. The sovereign's job is to remove the threats to the individual inherent in the state of nature. Importantly, the sovereign acquires the right of power and command from "man's" consent, not from some divine being. And from command comes law, justice, morality, and civilization. In return, the enlightened but still self-interested individual must not only consent to the rules of the sovereign but must also take on the duty of obedience. Command, consent, and duty emerged as the essential ingredients of Hobbes' social contract.

A century later, the self-interest theme received a large boost from Adam Smith (1723–90) who, in his monumental treatise, *Inquiry into the Nature and Causes of the Wealth of Nations*, worked out an intriguing and elegant theory of the political economy of self-interested effort guided by the invisible hand of the marketplace. Smith was greatly influenced by the French physiocratic school of economics, which believed that wealth was not merely possessions of land, gold, silver, livestock, castles, and so on, but also arose from labor on land. The physiocrats also held that wealth must be circulated through the nation (just as blood flows through a healthy body) and should not be hoarded in counting houses and treasuries. Smith held, against the physiocrats, that labor created wealth not just on the land, but wherever it performed, particularly in the manufactory. Moreover, he concluded, it worked in a miraculous fashion when specialized into discrete tasks. Specialized labor, not nature, which was already in abundance, was the source of a nation's wealth.

Smith held, however, that labor must be free to circulate to perform wherever the individual might detect some personal advantage in meeting the needs of others. There was no need for any central direction for this circulation because the laws of the market (not the laws of nature or a sovereign) automatically work things out. Self-interest directs labor towards those needs for which others willingly pay. For example, the factory owner, driven into action by other people's self-love, makes pins to take advantage of his specialized abilities to make a profit, not out of benevolence towards humankind. But if the owner is able to command an exorbitant price and impressive profits, capital will circulate as others will rush in, also make pins, charge less, and take away business. Similarly, if the owner pays workers too little they will circulate elsewhere to earn a better wage. In both instances, it is competition which produces the unexpected result, social harmony.

Competition for labor, moreover, not only regulates its price, but also directs it towards the quantity of goods society desires. If society wants more zippers and fewer pins than currently produced, customers will scramble for zippers while the pin business will be overstocked. As the demand for zippers rises, zipper prices will increase as will the owner's profits. Conversely, the price for pins will fall and profits disappear for the pin maker who then puts the workers out on the street. These workers, however, are snapped up by zipper makers whose business is booming. Quantities of pins on the market fall while quantities of zippers rise, just what society wants. Self-interest creates competition, which keeps self-interest in check. But best of all, Smith emphasized, these laws of the market have no need of any central regulator since they work of their own accord. The market acts as its own chaperon.

Smith also reasoned that capital as well as labor must circulate freely. The profits, which accrued to the shrewd and industrious factory owner should be pumped back into the economy and put to use in more machinery. This in turn would call for more labor, so the price of labor would rise until higher wages for the working class led to better conditions for their children. More babies and children would live and a greater proportion would enter the workforce causing wages to fall again. The owner's profits, conversely, would rise and fall with the supply of wage labor. Thus, the system would automatically regulate the supply and demand for capital. Self-interested specialization of labor and the accumulation of capital would move society inexorably towards a Valhalla of material wealth and happiness.

A century later, self-interest received another boost from Herbert Spencer (1820–1903), a much acclaimed philosopher during his lifetime but hardly read today. Spencer linked economic theory to Darwin's revelations regarding the law of survival of the fittest in the natural world. Spencer argued that the individual was uniform, discrete, and ultimate and that society existed for the benefit of its members rather than, as tradition had held, its members existing for the benefit of society. The endowment of the individual with a self-regulating mechanism ensured that when each pursued his or her self-interest and private wants, the result would be the greatest possible satisfaction of everyone's wants. Rational, self-interested utilitarianism, unfettered in any way by state or sovereign, ensured the survival of society and propelled humankind along its evolutionary path towards abundance, peace, and happiness for all. Darwin's laws of nature not only prevailed over beast, bird, fish, insect, and fauna, but also over humanity.

This self-interest theme remains today as the cornerstone of neoclassical economics. So it is not surprising people see it as the foundation of the agency theory perspective of the manager. In the first instance, the manager consents to carry out certain duties as the owner's agent. Then, the owner and the manager (explicitly or implicitly) enter into a social contract whereby the duties and obligations are worked out during a bargaining process. Such arrangements provide ample opportunity, as we shall see next, for the manager to pursue self-interest with guile given the problems of adverse selection, moral hazard signaling, incentive schemes, and asymmetric information.

Adverse Selection

The adverse selection, or hidden information, problem arises when an owner puts out a contract to the market for managers. The owner sets a specified price for designated effort and output based on a probability distribution of the payoff associated with his or her prior experience with managers. While the managers are privy to private information regarding their own abilities to perform the contract, the owners have never observed the managers in action so they cannot ascertain their quality. Thus, a situation of asymmetric information arises in the market for managers.

In these circumstances, an opportunity arises for the less able managers to pursue self-interest through lack of candor and honesty as the owner is unable, at low cost, to distinguish between the managers who respond to the bid. Moreover, managers whose ability to command a higher price on the market will not regard the offer as sufficient. Nor can the latter establish that they are indeed superior as well as honest in representing their abilities and therefore entitled to a higher price, since the inferior managers, acting opportunistically, can make the same representations by withholding private information and lying about their abilities. As a result, the superior managers withdraw from the bidding. In consequence, the owner ends up paying a premium for the wrong managers, thus incurring the adverse selection cost. At the end of the day the low-quality managers, the lemons, crowd out the high-quality managers, the plums.

In order to circumvent this situation, the owner is obliged to consider several alternatives, each of which comes with a cost. For example, the owner might incur the cost of obtaining detailed information regarding the managers who submit bids. Alternatively, the owner might offer a premium price over and above the going market price. Or, the owner might purchase insurance against the risk of contracting with inferior managers. When the problem is framed this way, agency theory calls for the owner to calculate the costs and benefits of the various alternatives and, using the logic of information economics and Bayesian statistical techniques, work out a Pareto optimal solution for both parties.

Moral Hazard

The adverse selection problem concerns situations where the owners, on one side of the market for managers, before settling on a contract, cannot observe at low cost the quality of managers on the other side of the market. Along somewhat similar lines, the moral hazard

(or hidden action) problem refers to situations where owners cannot observe the actions and efforts of the managers *after* they have been hired and are now under contract. The term "moral hazard" is borrowed from the insurance industry and describing it in that setting can be helpful.

In the insurance market for bicycle theft, for example, the probability of theft may be affected by the effort and actions bicycle-owners take. For the sake of simplicity, assume all owners live in the same neighborhood and that all owners lock their bicycles, so the insurance company is not bothered by the adverse selection problem. A bicycle is more likely to be stolen from those owners who do not lock their bicycle (or use only a flimsy lock) than from those who carefully do so. But owners who take out full insurance may change their locking behavior, which affects the probability of theft.

The insurance company, recognizing this, takes into account the incentives owners have to take proper care of their bicycles. At one extreme, if no insurance is available, owners have the maximum incentive. While at the other extreme, where full insurance is available at low cost, they have the minimum incentive to take care. In the former case, owners bear the full cost of their actions and will invest in caretaking until the marginal cost of more care just exceeds its marginal benefit. In the latter case, owners have no pecuniary incentive whatsoever to lock up their bicycles securely. So it seems that too much insurance leads to inadequate care, while too little insurance leaves owners bearing most of the risk. This lack of incentive to take care is moral hazard.

Insurance companies, however, are well aware of these risks and the owner's tradeoff decision. When the company can observe the amount of care taken by the insured, they base their rates on these observations. But when they cannot observe the relevant actions, the insurers will not offer complete coverage but instead include a deductible amount that the insured has to pay on any claim. This way the insured always has *some* incentive to take care. Moreover, even if the insurance company could verify the amount of care taken *after* the fact of theft, it still would not offer complete insurance when it cannot observe the level of care taken *before* theft for, if they did, owners would rationally choose to take less care. Overcoming the moral hazard problem leaves some of the risk in the hands of the insured, at the cost of not maximizing market opportunities, thus paradoxically tampering with the law of market equilibrium.

The moral hazard problem in the firm arises in a similar fashion. The owner and the manager enter into a contractual arrangement which calls for a certain amount of input and effort on behalf of the manager. Yet, as in the bicycle example, the owner cannot directly observe the input and effort exerted. In consequence, the owner must rely on some observable output measure (profit, cost of production, sales or billings, etc.) as a basis for administering the contract. This arrangement, however, can result in a reduction of the manager's incentive to take care and to supply maximum input and effort. In terms of agency theory, this is the incentive to shirk.

The result is a loss of welfare for both owner and manager. On the one side, the owner obviously suffers because the manager shirks on inputs and effort. On the other side, the manager suffers because the owner (as with the insurance company) will arrange the contract so the manager shares some of the risk for the output. Moral hazard involves a cost for both parties. But agency theory does not rest there; the costs of adverse selection and moral hazard can be minimized through signaling.

Signaling

We saw how asymmetric information caused problems in the market for managers and resulted in adverse selection costs. So the superior managers (assuming they must bear some of the agency costs) have an incentive to try to convey to owners the fact that they are honest and superior. They would like to take actions that signal their abilities. Two such signals could be their level of education and their work experience. Let us use education, say an MBA degree, for illustration.

Superior managers might decide to acquire an MBA "sheepskin" as a signal of their competence, but they cannot do so costlessly. Attending university involves out-of-pocket costs, plus the costs of study efforts, plus the opportunity-lost costs of temporarily withdrawing from the market. Now it may or may not be the case that the MBA education increases the manager's productivity. Either way, however, there is a sheepskin cost to the manager as well as to the owner and, importantly, to society at large, especially when university education is government subsidized.

Agency theory may be helpful at this point. By putting the various opportunity costs to all parties (inferior managers, superior managers, owners, and society) into cost–payoff equilibrium models and making assumptions regarding the various parties' utilities and risks, the agency theorist can indicate under which conditions signaling leads to efficiencies (or inefficiencies) for the various parties. While it is beyond our scope here to go into details, agency theory modeling can show when equilibrium with signaling is preferred to equilibrium without it. But each situation must be analyzed on its own merits and assumptions. Signaling can make things better but it can also make things worse.

Incentive Schemes

Incentive schemes also play an important role in agency theory. Given adverse selection, moral hazard, and signaling, how can I get the managers to work hard on my behalf? That is the central problem for owners. One obvious answer is to give the manager a lump-sum fee independent of output, but then the manager might have little incentive for hard work. A better solution might be to link the payment or some part of it in some way to the output produced. In this case the owner will try to determine exactly how sensitive the payment should be to the output produced. Economists call it the efficient incentive scheme.

An efficient incentive scheme is one which ensures that the utility the manager gets from the job is at least as great as the utility available elsewhere in the market for managers. This is called the participation constraint, where the utility the manager gets from the job must be at least as great as the utility available elsewhere. Second, the owner wants to induce the manager to choose an effort level that yields the owner the greatest surplus, given that the manager is willing to work for the owner. This is the unconstrained maximization problem and is solved by choosing the effort level to make the marginal product equal the marginal cost. Finally, the owner has to determine how much to pay the manager to achieve that effort. This is the incentive compatibility constraint, which simply states that the utility to the manager from choosing the determined effort level must be greater than the utility of any other choice of effort.

A few examples may help to clarify these incentive issues. To begin with, the owner could simply rent the business to the manager for a specified price so that the manager gets all the profit produced after paying the rent. This, however, could result in too much risk for the manager. Alternatively, the owner could pay the manager a constant salary per unit of effort (where the salary rate is equal to the marginal profit of the manager at the optimal effort level) plus an amount which makes the manager indifferent between managing elsewhere and managing for the owner. This would satisfy the participant constraint. Another arrangement could be to fix the contract so that the manager, who makes the effort decision, is the residual claimant to the profit. A scheme where both parties get a fixed percentage of the profit does not lead to an efficient incentive scheme. (Either way, the owner wants a scheme whereby the manager shares in the uncertain output in a way that he or she also shares the risk.) But the effort exerted by the manager on behalf of the owner is also conditioned by private, or asymmetric, information.

Asymmetric Information

Asymmetric information is the most fundamental concept in agency theory because it gives rise to all the other problems: adverse selection, moral hazard, signaling and incentives. Asymmetrical information refers to important information to which the manager (but not the owner) is privy. A special case of asymmetrical information is impacted information, information regarding deep knowledge about one or more of the factors of production. It is very difficult and costly for the party without impacted information to achieve a state of information parity.[2] According to agency theory, managers will opportunistically exploit asymmetrical and impacted information to its fullest before, during, and after exerting effort. Driven by self-interest, they can use their private information to shirk (shrink selfishly from) responsibility and duty; to consume excessive perquisites to which they are not entitled (steal and cheat); to manipulate signals (lie or distort); and to hide their actions, private information, and information-affected special knowledge from the owner (sneakily hoard essential knowledge). There is no place for either altruistic or naive behavior in this scheme.

Normally it is impossible for the owner to observe the effort of the manager perfectly. At best the owners may observe a signal of effort, such as output. Yet even here, output also depends, in addition to the manager's effort, on factors outside the latter's control: competitors' moves, economic upturns, changes in national monetary policies, even the weather. This kind of "noise" means that a payment from the owner to the manager based on output alone will not be equivalent to a payment based on effort alone. Effort and output are always less than perfectly correlated.

The owner again faces the information asymmetry problem. The manager can select the effort level but the owner cannot observe it perfectly or costlessly. So the owner has to guess the effort from the observable output then design the optimal incentive scheme to reflect this inference problem. This involves calculating an incentive scheme that shares the risks and provides the appropriate incentives. Framing the owner–manager relationship this way, the agency theorist can apply the techniques of Bayesian decision theory, linear and dynamic programming, and equilibrium theory to various situations and calculate an arrangement where neither party can improve his or her welfare at the expense of the other. This Pareto optimal solution becomes the basis for the contract between the owner and the manager. Management accounting and control systems provide crucial information to owners for fixing, instituting, and monitoring the contract.

The Contract

The idea of the contract as the primary unit of analysis can be traced back over the years to other similar concepts. Hobbes, as we saw above, developed his idea of the social contract—consent to let some sovereign rule and duty of the individual to obey—as the fundamental bonding agent in society. A century later, Adam Smith replaced consent and duty with market exchange as the basic unit of social interaction arguing that on-the-spot exchanges were all society needed to regulate social relations. But by the end of the nineteenth century, however, industrial societies bore little resemblance to either Hobbes' rule by a sovereign or Smith's world of atomistic exchanges.

Instead, the social landscape featured large hierarchical organizations and institutions. Giant corporations, large-scale government, denominational specific churches, powerful unions, public utilities, military establishments, educational institutions, and professional associations dominated the social landscape. These hierarchies, which operated as collective action centers of economic power, exercised considerable influence over the coordination of production and the distribution of wealth and the life of the individual. This new institution-dominated world bore little resemblance to the suppositions of prevailing neoclassical economic theory. Economists scrambled back to their drawing boards to put into place a revisionist version of market economics called transaction-cost economics.

Transactions, the revisionists argued, involve more than just on-the-spot exchanges of material wealth. They also include long (even indefinite) time commitments, general (even vague) obligations, and promises of forbearance (agreement for nonaction or nonexchange). Moreover, transactions take place within and between hierarchies as well as in the marketplace. And many transactions involve the exchange of legal, moral and power conditions such as the right of a superior to command a subordinate. The transaction, it seemed, is a more fundamental unit of social interaction than is the market exchange.

This realization proved to be a milestone. It meant that economists could explain both the internal workings of hierarchies, previously only a black box in economic theory, *and* the functioning of the market using the same conceptual apparatus—transaction-cost economics. Transactions, they surmised, incur costs, over and above the "natural" price for a commodity—costs that the parties to the transaction must bear, such as the costs of negotiating, monitoring, administering, insuring, and even litigating in the case of nonperformance. As costs are a key phenomenon in economic theory, they can be analyzed using the economist's bag of tools. There was no need to muddy the waters with theories from sociology, social philosophy, psychology, or organizational theory.

These developments later gave rise to what we know today as agency theory. For agency theorists, the contractual arrangement for a transaction in a market for the sale/purchase of a commodity is exactly the same as a contractual arrangement in a firm (hierarchy) whereby one person (the principal) engages another person (the agent) to perform the service of making decisions on the principal's behalf. Importantly, agency theorists also transform the hierarchy, where the owners (superiors) have authoritarian directive and disciplinary legal and moral power over agents (subordinates), into a peer or team relationship where all the players are on an equal footing and one team member "is the *centralized contractual agent in a team productive process*" (Alchian and Demsetz, 1972).

Limitations

Agency theory offers an elegant, even alluring, way to think about MACS and to pinpoint some worrisome issues, but it has its limitations. One concern arises from its concentration on problems encountered by the owner when the manager relies on asymmetrical information to cheat and shirk. Yet it is just as reasonable to assume that the owner would also have private access to crucial information, such as the condition of the firm's production technology and its market competition, and would use it to advantage in negotiating an enforceable contract, suboptimal for the manager. Asymmetrical information is not a one-way street. That is to say, in order for agency theory to work, the markets for both managers and owners must feature pure competition where typically there are many competitors in these markets each of whom has negligible effects on prices. In today's world of large oligopolistic organizations and high unemployment rates, this seems a heroic assumption.[3]

A related but more problematical concern with agency theory centers on its treatment of the owner–manager relations of power. Transaction-cost economists gave full recognition to power relations in the hierarchy whereby fiat and command play a crucial role in coordinating production, but agency theory assumes power relations between owners, managers, and employees that are far from asymmetrical. Since employees can order the owner to pay them money or quit, thus terminating the contract as easily as can the employer, the argument goes ". . . long term contracts are not an essential attribute of the firm. Nor are 'authoritarian', 'dictatorial' or 'fiat' attributes relevant to the conception of the firm or its efficiency" (Alchian and Demsetz, 1972, p. 783). So the owner, instead of being the boss, all of a sudden becomes merely the team captain; simply the team member who acts as its central contractual agent and is thus entitled to be the residual claimant to the team's net output. Agency theory renders opaque the asymmetric power situation in the hierarchy.

Moreover, the owner-now-captain ". . . has no power of fiat, no authority, no disciplinary action differently from ordinary contracting between two people" (Alchian and Demsetz, 1972, p. 783). One is designated captain because of one's special abilities to monitor other team members for shirking but the captain will not shirk because he or she is the residual claimant. These supplementary moves are absolutely necessary to make agency theory work and they put owner and employee on an equal power footing. Issues of domination and power are central to most social and organization theories. But agency theory, having conveniently set them aside, can explain the workings of the firm on the basis of markets for managers and information.

Nevertheless, agency theory offers insights into some of the tough issues and difficult problems involved in the design of such systems. So it is not surprising that a great amount of intellectual effort by accounting academics has been exerted in working out the details.[4] Yet, this rarefied air of economic reductionism seems a long distance from the realities of managers' working lives. Next we turn to the close up observations of real managers in real organizations.

4.1.2 The Manager as Nerve Center

Our second paradigm, the manager as nerve center, also foregrounds the role of information as a central theme. But instead of portraying a disturbing picture of sloth, deceit, and mendaciousness motivated by self-interest, the picture is almost completely opposite. In sharp contrast with the agency theory portrait, or the labor process view of relentless de-skilling and degrading at lower work levels, day after day the dedicated manager is seen to put in exceedingly long and hard hours, immersed in an unrelenting stream of unconnected rounds of activities. Managers use intuition and a sixth sense, not rational calculations, to hurriedly make on-the-spot decisions, and spend most of the time gathering, storing, moving, sharing, and processing huge quantities of informal and formal information.

This view emerged unexpectedly in the 1970s as a result of a now classical field study in which the researchers followed managers around observing, recording, and asking them what they actually did (Mintzberg, 1972, 1975). The big surprise proved to be that the picture that emerged did not conform at all to the conventional managerial literature, which portrayed the work of managers as neatly working out a blueprint for the organization, making sure it is properly staffed, then using budgets and reports as feedback on progress to clearly defined ends. Instead of methodically planning organizational objectives and systematically achieving them, the managers lived in what appeared to be chaos.

So, in stark contrast to some orderly, highly controlled world, the managers encountered about 250 separate incidents per week, which on average lasted less than ten minutes. They also kept dozens of longer term projects orbiting simultaneously, periodically checking progress, juggling them a little, then relaunching them; and, importantly, they seemed to abhor reflective tasks such as planning. The managers saw their working life as disorder, brevity, and discontinuity instead of orderly progress towards predetermined contractual goals or rational calculation of how to shirk and cheat the owner. Yet the managers reportedly thrived on this chaotic existence.

Managerial Roles

In order to make some sense out of this apparent chaos the researchers pigeonholed each incident into one of three major managerial roles: decisional, interpersonal, and informational. This proved to be an insightful step. Before long, a clearer but newer picture of managerial work emerged. Decision roles took considerably less time than either of the other two. This may come as a surprise to those who teach accounting, stressing the decision-making role. This is not to say that decisional roles (entrepreneurship, disturbance handling, resource allocation, and negotiation) are not important; they are critical. Managers have the authority and responsibility to make decisions; indeed they are required to make them. Yet, surprisingly, managers in the sample spent only a fraction of their time on them.

Interpersonal roles took more time. In fact, figurehead chores, such as greeting visitors, taking important customers to lunch, attending weddings, and presenting gold watches to retiring employees, consumed about 12% of the working day. The formal authority vested in them called for the managers to spend a great deal of time in personal contact with other people, including clients, suppliers, peers, media, government officials, union representatives, professional association contacts, and trade association officers. Managers also spent a lot of time with subordinates, hiring, coaching, encouraging, reprimanding, and even firing them. Though they do not involve decision making, these interpersonal roles are important; they can be performed only by the manager.

Informational roles, surprisingly, took more time than either decision-making or interpersonal roles. Rather than behaving like wise owls in a tree, the managers acted more like trout in a mountain stream, poking briefly here, flitting there, investigating this, nibbling that, turning suddenly and darting into a new pool to repeat the process. Information seemed to be their basic source of energy. A recent field study undertaken to learn more about managers' use of management accounting systems found pretty much the same story (Bruns and McKinnon, 1993). The managers, working in a variety of large manufacturing organizations and in a variety of jobs in the US and Canada, revealed that they hungered for better information to support their work and that informal sources dominated formal ones. As in the previous study, the managers were prone to develop their own personal information networks and systems. The study concluded that managers are hungry for information to support their work. They seek information from every source available to them. Informal sources of information—face-to-face meetings, observation, telephone calls, and informal reports—dominate other sources of information for day-to-day needs and remain important for longer term needs. Unit data is the metric in which day-to-day management takes place, and financial information increases in importance and use as the management horizon lengthens (Bruns and McKinnon, 1993, p. 94).

The realities of the manager's working life, it seems, have not changed much since then.

Managerial Information Processing

Managers apparently spend the majority of their time processing information, and the manner in which they gather, store, move, and share it should be of vital interest to accounting and information systems managers. Managers receive information from external and internal sources, and they give it out in their disseminator, spokesman, and strategy-maker roles. Three aspects of this information processing activity stand out.

For one thing, each day managers collect information from a wide variety of sources. They receive mounds of e-mails. They are flooded with reports. They get briefings from their superiors and subordinates. They go on observational tours. They scan professional journals. They talk on smartphones. They grill peers and subordinates. They even plant private sources in strategic places. In fact, they spend most of their time planting, cultivating, and harvesting information from private networks.

There are good reasons for this. To be effective, managers must be the nerve centers of their organizational units. In order to perform this role they must know, not necessarily everything, but at least more than their subordinates. This is true in formal organizations and informal organizations, such as street-corner gangs. The leader is the person at the center of the information flow, not necessarily the best technical expert or the toughest street fighter, but the one who perpetually monitors the environment for information and disseminates it within the organization. Subordinates must be informed, peers must be appraised, and bosses must be briefed. Managers also speak for the unit by passing information to outsiders as required. For leaders, then, information is their most valuable asset. It is a precious commodity; and managing their private information network is their most important skill. It must be carefully husbanded, skillfully exchanged, and judiciously passed around. Information is the manager's major lever to survival.

Another outstanding feature of the way that managers process information is their predilection for soft, verbal, detailed, and current information. They reach out eagerly for every scrap, including speculation, hearsay, rumor, and gossip. They also show a strong preference for verbal communication and seem to thrive on telephones, meetings, encounters in the hall or washroom, and coffee-break chats. In fact, the managers in the survey spent nearly 80% of their working time in verbal activities; and they like their information fresh, hot, and spicy.

But managers also find information in management accounting systems, such as the annual operating budget, valuable for enacting managerial roles including decisional and interpersonal roles in addition to informational ones. A recent study found that one group of managers seemed to use budgets strategically as an aid in monitoring the environment to keep on top of trends and events and for allocating resources to areas of opportunity and need within the organization (Macintosh and Williams, 1992). The study also found that high-performing departments are headed by managers who are more active in performing managerial roles and are more involved in, and responsive to, information in budgeting systems than are their counterparts in the low-performing units.

The final striking feature of the managerial information processing is the way they use information to make decisions. Managers are constantly gathering odds and ends of data from their network. These bits and pieces are tucked away in the brain until one new piece suddenly acts as a trigger for all of it to come together, like a bolt from the blue, and form into an important message. This is not to say that managers are unthinking bundles of nerves reacting synaptically to each piece of information. Instead, it seems as if they have plans and models tucked away inside their heads to be updated as new information appears. Nevertheless, when this "ah-hah" strikes, the managers react as if charged by an electric current. They think nothing of interrupting meetings, rescheduling workdays, cancelling long-standing engagements, in order to follow the new insights.

So managers see their work as information processing. It is not aloofly orchestrating a master plan. It is not cunningly shirking while pursuing self-interest within the constraints of a contractual arrangement with the owner. And it is not deliberately deskilling and downgrading the labor force as the subjectified pawn of capitalist interest. Rather, it is frantically monitoring, storing, and disseminating information, especially the soft and current variety, then using it to make intuitive, off-the-cuff decisions. This style, it should be underlined, suits the nature of managerial work. It also matches managers' thinking processes. Just as war is too important to leave to the generals, information processing is too important to leave to the accountants. In any event, this picture of managers, obtained by actually observing what managers do, seems quite remote from the ethereal realm of economic theory.

4.1.3 The Symbolic Nature of MACs

Our next model is based on the observation that organizations and managers gather and process far more information than they can possibly use for decision making (Feldman and March, 1981). Recall that the conventional idea depicts information processing as an integral part of the decision-making process. This position assumes that during the decision process managers will secure, analyze, and retrieve information in a timely and intelligent fashion as long as its marginal cost is less than its incremental value. Yet, when they are observed at close hand, managers do not seem to carefully weigh the reliability, precision, and relevance of information. Instead, they collect and process far more information than they could ever reasonably use for decisions. Most of the information that they collect is also totally unconnected to decisions. Organizations, even the best ones, apparently overinvest in a glut of information.[5]

Commonsense Explanations

From the objective realist perspective there are several reasons for this. One explanation is that managers gather a lot of information that turns out not to be suitable for decisions. Another reason is that accounting and information systems are a free good (paid for by accounting, computing, and MIS departments), so managers take almost any formal information they are offered. Yet another commonsense reason is that managers monitor their environment for potential surprises in order to be reassured there are none. Such explanations cling to the version of managers as rational information processors.

Defensive Use

From the subjective interpretive perspective there are quite different reasons for the redundant information processing phenomenon. The first of these is related to the widespread practice in organizations of criticizing decisions after the fact. A common version of this is known as Monday-morning quarterbacking. On Monday morning, ardent home fans second-guess the decisions made on Sunday by the quarterback in the heat of the battle.

Major blunders harmful to the home team are readily apparent. What seems so clear in retrospect was not at all obvious at the time.

Similarly, managers make decisions in the face of uncertainty, knowing only too well that individuals at all levels in the organization will be quick to make *post hoc* criticisms. The inevitable judgments come in two extremes. One asserts that events occurred that were underestimated, and that the manager should have collected more information. The other concludes that events that did not occur were overestimated; the manager probably overcollected and therefore wasted information-processing efforts. The more astute managers recognize that, either way, criticisms will be forthcoming, but the majority will point to underestimates. The wiser choice is to have more information than is needed. Management accounting and control systems are valuable here as protection systems to head off the inevitable postdecision criticisms. They become the building material for constructing a formidable defense.

Offensive Use

Accounting and control systems are also used in organizations for offensive aims. The dynamics of such use are subtle but elaborate. Managers recognize that information is an important instrument of persuasion, that it can be a source of influence and power. They are, therefore, into a process whereby contending liars, competing in the persuasion game, send and receive mostly unreliable information.

This strategic use of information is a complicated game and is played under conditions of conflicting interests. Wily players do not treat information as if it were neutral and innocent. They must make inferences and discount a great deal of the perverse information they receive, recognizing full well that strategic misrepresentation is a harsh reality of organizational life. Not surprisingly, they counter by circulating strategic information of their own. This subtle game of distorting and misrepresenting information to one's own advantage stimulates an oversupply of strategic information. It is, however, a risky game and managers who are found out are prone to lose their creditability throughout the organization.

Symbolic Use

But perhaps the most pervasive reason managers and organizations collect more information than they can possible process is deeply rooted in a central ideological norm of Western civilization, *the belief in intelligent choice*. Organizations are the central arena for displaying and honoring this paramount social value. Information gathering and the use of accounting data are ritualistic assurance that one does indeed respect this central value. It is a means of reaffirming the value of rational decision making. It is a representation to others of one's competence. And it is a symbol for all to see that one believes in intelligent choice. Managers find value in accounting and control system information that has little or no relation to decision making.

Part of this myth holds that more information leads to better decisions. So, the more information a manager processes, the better he or she must be in the eyes of others. Managers establish their legitimacy by their use of information. The visible and observable aspects of gathering and storing information are not unlike the ritualistic gray suit, white shirt, and dark blue tie of the committed IBM executive of the 1990s. Information is not merely a basis for action, it symbolizes and reaffirms a core value of society. Seeking and collecting information, and this is the striking point, has symbolic value for the manager far beyond its worth in decision making. Managers establish their legitimacy by displaying their use of information. Today, the laptop computer displayed by the busy executive in airport terminals and on commuter trains signals a true believer.

Managers, especially prudent ones, posture accordingly. They diligently ask for and carefully store MACS reports. They carry them home after work in visibly bulging briefcases. They assiduously orchestrate decisions to ensure that all believe they take action only on the basis of reasonable and intelligent choice. The command of such information, the access to its sources, and the apparent application of it to decisions all work to enhance the manager's reputation for competency and to inspire the confidence of others. It symbolizes one's broad commitment to reason and to rational decisions. Management accounting and control reports take on value as symbol far beyond their worth as a basis for action.

4.2 Dealing with Power and Control

4.2.1 Labor Process

A third view of MACS emerged as part of the labor process critique of the treatment of workers in capitalist enterprises. This perspective focuses on the "sad, horrible, heart-breaking way the vast majority of my fellow countrymen and women as well as their counterparts around the world have been obligated to spend their working lives."[6] From the labor process view, management accounting systems play a crucial role in the institutionalized subordination and control of wage labor by capitalist interests.

The overriding concern of labor process theorists centers on the historical fact that the control of work has passed from the hands of the individual worker during precapitalist times to the capitalist owner class during early capitalism and subsequently into the hands of the managerial class working on behalf of owners. Since the labor process perspective draws heavily on the works of nineteenth-century political economists such as Engels (1820–95) and Marx (1818–83) a brief review of some of their key concepts—commodification, alienation, surplus value, and class contradiction—seems essential in order to realize their pertinence today.[7]

Nineteenth-Century Capitalism

Engels and Marx were first and foremost ardent and dedicated humanists. Both had witnessed first hand in the mid-1800s how Adam Smith's wonderful world of the division of labor, the invisible hand of the market, and the newly released self-interested capacity of the factory, mine, and farm owners had transformed the social landscape.[8] But instead of a Valhalla, the result for the working class was a horrific life of overcrowding in filthy slums, abject poverty, child slave labor, sexual exploitation, dirt, and drunkenness. This savage indictment of the greed and hypocrisy of the bourgeoisie went against the humanistic aim of the Enlightenment project for the individual to attain dignity and unity with self, humankind, and nature.[9]

Commodification

Commodification, a central concept in the labor process perspective, refers to an object or thing outside the human being that satisfies some material want. Examples include a bushel of wheat, a tonne of coal, a side of beef, or a suit of clothes. These commodities obtain their value simply from what they fetch in a market transaction (the exchange value) rather than from their useful qualities (the use value) or from the amount of labor necessary to produce them (the labor value). The division of work, Engels and Marx observed, had turned working-class men, women, and children into commodities.

Commodification resulted from the specialization of labor within the production process. Specialization produced "man as a commodity, the human commodity, man in the form of a commodity . . . as a mentally and physically dehumanized being" (Marx, 1944, p. 121). Moreover, "the worker becomes an ever cheaper commodity the more goods he creates. The devaluation of the human world increases in direct relation with the increases in value of the world of things" (Marx, 1944, p. 121). Under the capitalist system of production, like a machine or raw material, the worker was just a thing to be treated for whatever price it would fetch in the market for labor. No longer a whole human being with spiritual, aesthetic, and communal needs, the worker became merely another factor of production. Commodification of the worker meant that this total person had been swept away.

Alienation

According to Engels and Marx, commodification led inexorably to alienation, the estrangement of human beings from the product of their work, from other human beings, and, importantly, from oneself. Hegel (1770–1831), the great social philosopher of his time, saw alienation as a vital aspect of the human condition; the separation of body and soul, nature and intelligence, object and subject. He believed, however, that alienation could be transcended through the reason of the mind and intuition to reach a state of unified synthesis. Thus, it was possible for the individual to become truly human, far removed from animal origins and preoccupation with the problems of basic material existence. The individual could achieve an "Absolute" state of existence.

Marx, unlike Hegel, did not believe that such an unalienated condition could be achieved simply by reflection and pure thought, *logos*. Instead, he argued, alienation stems from society's way of producing its material wealth, its mode of production. The main feature of the capitalist mode of production was a class-divided social order whereby the human beings of the underdog working class produced society's material needs by dint of their labor but in return were treated as commodities by the reigning bourgeoisie class. Furthermore, the bourgeoisie maintained workers at a mere subsistence level and were quick to appropriate the lion's share of the wealth created, especially the surplus wealth produced over and above its labor cost.

Commodification and class domination, Engels and Marx reasoned, meant that the individual's human existence had lost its unity and wholeness. With the specialization and deskilling of work, the individual became alienated from the product of his or her labor. Workers no longer produced a whole product so they never saw their work completed. Moreover, deprived of any intrinsic satisfaction with their work since the finished product belonged to the factory or mine owners, the worker was separated from the product of his or her own labor only to encounter it as an alien thing in the marketplace.

Further, the system made workers compete with each other for jobs and advancement in the market for labor. This splintered the social camaraderie of working conditions that had existed in the workshops of skilled artisans. And, since one class exploited the other, the human beings of each class became estranged from those of the other. Alienation, rooted in the material existence of the capitalist mode of production, could not be exorcized by thinking it away as Hegel had held.[10] Commodification, alienation, and class domination became the building blocks for the labor process humanistic critique of the inner workings of capitalism. At bottom, however, deskilling paved the way.

Deskilling and Control

The critical problem for the capitalist enterprise in the late eighteenth and early nineteenth century turned out to be control. The owner needed to develop an effective mechanism for keeping wage labor hard at work and so adapt it to the needs of capital. Deskilling of specialized labor proved to be a highly effective way of accomplishing this. Deskilling, it is important to recognize, is different from specialization. Specialization means being an expert in the entire process of production of a commodity, such as a carriage, a house, a shirt, or a bottle of wine. In contrast, deskilling refers to the systematic emptying of a traditional craft by carefully breaking it down into basic activities then assigning each one to a single worker along with a set of minute instructions.

Deskilling worked to make wage labor more efficient, as Adam Smith had shown, but even more importantly, it transferred control of the way work was performed from the individual worker into the hands of the owner and thus to the new managerial class. This enabled managers to treat labor like all other commodities in the production process, with the aim of extracting ever increasing productivity from the individual worker. Appropriating control of the knowledge of the production process was vital to the capital accumulation process.

From a humanistic point of view, however, deskilling meant more than just the transfer of work knowledge to the managerial class. During the early stages of the Industrial Revolution, artisans of all kinds (weavers, china makers, brewers, mechanics, carpenters, instrument makers, even cigar makers) specialized in fabricating the entire product.[11] They spent long apprenticeships learning their craft, including studying the available scientific and technical knowledge underlying its practice. Weavers, for instance, not only worked with cloth but also studied biology, botany, entomology, mathematics, geometry, and music in order to develop a deep understanding of patterns and shapes. They even formed associations and societies to advance the scientific knowledge of the marvels and workings of nature. They enjoyed a cultured and intellectual existence. A century later, their offspring, now commodified, led a life of incredible poverty and degradation. Deskilling meant the obliteration of artisanship *and* the destruction of a whole civilized way of life for the craft worker.

Control of Work Process Knowledge

The transfer of the control of work from the laboring class to the owning class meant that the conception of *how* to do the job was uncoupled from its *execution*. As small firms developed into large enterprises in the late nineteenth and early twentieth centuries, their managers could systematically study work and apply science to the increasingly complex problems of the control of labor. This undertaking became the focus of the scientific management movement, spearheaded by the ardent and relentless Frederick Taylor who insisted that it was absolutely essential for management to dictate to the worker precisely how to perform each task. Management must assume the burden of " . . . gathering together all the traditional knowledge which in the past has been possessed by the workmen and then of classifying, tabulating, and reducing this knowledge to rules, laws, and formulae" (Taylor, 1911, p. 36).

Scientific management brought to an end an era where owners derived their knowledge of the work process in a haphazard and hazy way. Taylor mandated: "All possible brain work should be removed from the shop and centered in the planning and layout department" (Braverman, 1974, p. 118). Management could now fully lay out in advance the task of every worker and provide him or her with complete, detailed, written instructions regarding the exact means to be used for its completion. For the management scientist the science of work became the prerogative of management; it must never be left to the worker.

Control of Financial Information

As knowledge of the work process passed into the hands of the owners so did financial knowledge. Efficiency did not automatically accrue from technical advances. The abandonment of subcontracting, common in the mid-nineteenth century, in favor of direct control by hiring wage labor was not, in fact, more efficient, as some historians argue (Johnson and Kaplan, 1987). Rather, it was done to transfer information about costs and profits from the workers to the factory owners. Owners soon developed costing systems and records that gave them detailed knowledge of internal costs and profits and allowed them to discipline labor in an intense drive for ever more efficiency. The ultimate aim, argues the labor process view, "was to cheapen the worker by decreasing his training and enlarging his output" (Braverman, 1974, p. 118). Once again the worker was dispossessed, this time of the financial knowledge of the production process.

The advent of scientific management and the emergence of the large-scale capitalist enterprises also precipitated the rise of a new class of employees—clerical workers. The sales office handled travel to customers' factories, sales correspondence, order processing, commissions, sales analysis, advertising and promotion; while the accounting office looked after double-entry bookkeeping, financial statements, credit, collections, cash management, and shareholder records. Moreover, they were often paid double the wages on the factory floor.

As part of this development, the factory office expanded substantially. Previously, it consisted of the timekeeper and the supervisors' clerk who kept track of pay records, materials, work in progress, stages of production completion, and finished goods. To these basic duties were added production planning and scheduling, purchasing, engineering, design, and modern cost accounting systems in order to keep track of work on the shop floor. The physical work process came to be mirrored in a stream of records and accounts, a vast paper empire that had a life of its own separate from the material world on the factory floor. The labor process was writ large in the factory office.

Sophisticated and detailed cost accounting systems, driven in large part by the scientific management movement, swept through factories and clerical offices across industrialized nations and became vital. Employers already used historical cost accounting systems as a way to contain the powers of superintendents and overseers who were hired to control the workforce. Engineers, following the principles of scientific management, using stopwatches, ergonomics, and close observation, redesigned labor processes and developed time standards for work operations rather than relying on historical experience. Such data were combined with accounting information to create full-scale standard costing systems including variance reporting. Each individual worker's output could now be compared daily with scientific norms. Cost accounting emerged as a "highly effective instrument of management control and the intensification of labor" (Hopper and Armstrong, 1991, p. 420). This was not Adam Smith's *invisible hand*; but rather the very *visible fist* of owners and their managers.

The Ambiguous Status of Managers

These developments gave rise to a new occupational group—managers. The status of the new managerial class, however, remains problematic within the labor process conception of a bipolar capitalist society. On the one hand, as with the working class, managers possess neither capital nor occupational independence but rather labor for the capitalist class. Thus, it should not surprise us that managers sometimes manipulate accounting controls, such as when divisional managers engage in activities which make them score well on profit budgets but which go against the best interests of the owners (Merchant, 1985, 1987). From the labor process perspective such "manipulation of accounting controls . . . is thus more accurately portrayed as, in part, managerial resistance and coping with contradiction, rather than any failure of systems or corporate loyalty" (Hopper, Storey and Willmott, 1987, p. 452). Goal-incongruent behavior is seen to be endemic to the manager's ambiguous position in society.[12]

On the other hand, owners hire managers to act on their behalf in directing and controlling wage labor. Furthermore, managers' remuneration runs significantly above that of the workforce. So it seems fair to say that managers share with owners the surplus value produced by wage labor. Moreover, managers enjoy the prerogatives of fiat in that they hire, command, and fire workers. This seems to indicate that their interests lean more in the direction of owners than towards wage labor. So at the end of the day, labor process proponents conclude, managers' contradictory actions with regard to accounting controls, which leave them sometimes advocating and sometimes resisting, arises from their ambiguous class position (Hopper, 1990, p. 130).

4.2.2 Dialectic Controls

The final view of organizational contexts and controls is constructed using a *historical–dialectical* analysis.[13] The historical strand draws attention to the way organizations are shaped by their past and how they evolve through distinct phases over time. The dialectical strand emphasizes the inherent changefulness within any system due to a concealed but fundamental contradiction embedded in any system such as an organization.[14] The central idea is that systems exist in a state of dialectical tension and that they evolve through distinct historical phases as the contradiction is played out.

Contradiction in the dialectical sense refers, not to some logical contradiction,[15] but rather to the existence in any system of some mutually interacting but incompatible opposition between two fundamental elements or forces. The elements, locked in a relational struggle, exist in a state of *dynamic tension*. At any moment, one element gains the upper hand and represses the oppositional one. Thus the current condition of the system is seen to be the result of its most recent resolution of this struggle. Paradoxically, the essence of reality is the unity of opposites.

This current resolution, however, is only temporary. The seeds of its downfall are already planted inside the system, the reason being that the present state (or thesis) inevitably leads to excesses on the part of the temporarily superior element. Feeding off these excesses, the subordinate element rises up, overturns the hierarchy, and establishes itself in a place of privilege but, importantly, at a level that subsumes the previous resolution. However, this new synthesis is subject to the same fate as the old resolution. A new antithesis forms in opposition to the synthesis, and the process repeats.

Thus, for the dialectician the essence of reality for any system is motion, restlessness, and mutability. Its innermost being is changefulness since it consists of the unstable co-existence and perpetual resolution of the two incompatible forces. The dialectic unfolds in a way that is integral to the system but at the same time destructive of its current state. This idea of contradiction helps us ascertain the dialectical logic to any system's historical tendencies and evolution.

An Example

The classic illustration of dialectic tension is Plato's Master–Slave contradiction. Two independent people stranded on a desert island see each other as a limit to their own freedom and power over the island's natural abundance. To settle this unstable state of affairs, a struggle takes place and one conquers and enslaves the other. Although, it may seem that the Master has the upper hand and the situation is stable, such is not the case. The situation will reverse due to the contradiction concealed in the relationship.

It is the Slave, who by dint of physical labor changes the natural (material) world, gets satisfaction from this, and so develops a true self-consciousness. The Master, not recognizing the Slave as a real person worthy of an ideal consciousness, debases himself to a lower form of existence; he has not seen his own universal self in the other. Further, the Master is now dependent on the Slave for his material existence. Spiritually and materially, the Master now occupies the lower position. Control has passed from Master to Slave who now enjoys the upper hand.

Autonomy and Direction: The Basic Contradiction

The basic contradiction in our historical–dialectical model of control in organizations is the unrelenting struggle between the forces for autonomy and freedom on one side and the forces for authority and order on the other. When authority gets the upper hand, autonomy is suppressed. This resolution of the dialectic tension, however, sows the seeds for its inevitable reversal when the excesses of authority lead to its overturning by the forces for autonomy. In turn, an overdose of autonomy brings on another crisis and authority eventually comes to the fore. And so it goes on, as the organization's basic character swings back and forth, one time in favor of autonomy and the next time giving authority the nod.

The dialectic plays out as follows. When autonomy has the upper hand the outcome is innovation, creativity, and risk-taking behavior on the part of managers and employees. An overdose of autonomy, however, eventually leads to chaos, parochialism, and even anarchy. At this juncture, authority, which has been lying dormant, comes forward to gain the upper hand. The shift to authority fosters leadership, direction, and attention to global purpose. However, a surfeit of authority induces its own crisis of apathy, lethargy, and paralysis within the organization. The time has arrived for another reversal.

The model also contends that organizations tend to experience lengthy periods of evolutionary growth followed by short revolutionary periods. Each phase of evolution precipitates its own revolution and its ensuing dialectical crisis. If the firm survives the crisis, by making the correct organizational adjustment, then it moves into the next phase of prolonged evolution. During each evolutionary stage, only minor fine tuning of its overall pattern of organization and control is necessary for sustained growth. Importantly, each evolutionary phase has a characteristically distinct and dominant management style as well as its own unique management problem. And as each phase affects the subsequent phase, it too is a result of its predecessor phase.

As the dialectic process unfolds, organizations that survive each crisis develop through five distinct phases: creativity, direction, delegation, cooperation, and coordination. Each phase is shaped by historical factors including its size, the growth rate of its industry, and its previous stages of evolution and crisis. Next we sketch out these five phases, summarized in Figure 4.1.

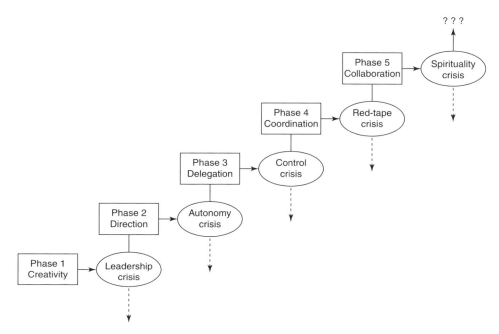

Figure 4.1   A Dialectic Model of Coordination and Control. (Solid arrows indicate successful evolution to the next phase; dashed arrows indicate failure to resolve the crisis. Adapted from Greiner (1972).)

Phase 1: Creativity

Every firm is small early on in its history. It begins its historical journey because its founder created a new product, invented a new production method, or developed a new market. The organizational climate is informal and communication is face to face. Often the founder/owner, usually highly technically or entrepreneurially skilled, relies on charismatic leadership and personal relationships for coordination and control. Employees, feeling awe and respect for the founder and his or her innovation, perform faithfully and diligently. Creativity and charisma, essential for the firm to get up and running, provide the necessary discipline and control.

Success leads to growth. Longer runs and an increasing number of changeovers characterize the production process. New capital is raised to finance increases in working capital and to purchase new production equipment. The size of the workforce expands. The founder, still relying on creativity and charisma to cope with the expansion, works harder and longer in order to keep things under control.

The founder also tends to be engrossed in selling the product and getting it through the plant as designed. Customers' demands, production mishaps, and technical breakdowns in the product consume more than the available hours in the day. Administrative practices and management systems, such as accurate cost accounting systems, inventory controls, and capital expenditure analysis, are neglected or even disdained.

Moreover, the founder no longer knows each employee on a personal basis. Nor are new employees motivated by an intense loyalty to the founder or by an enrapturement with the original innovation. Administrative systems, including formal management accounting systems, are urgently needed to bring order to the now chaotic situation. The firm faces its first perilous turning point, the *leadership crisis*.

Strong leadership and direction is needed, particularly on the administrative end. Founders now perceive themselves to be forever bogged down in mundane, petty administrative matters. Moreover, they find the new conditions much less appealing than the crusading, swashbuckling days of old. Even though they understand the need for strong leadership and direction on the administrative side of the house, and they recognize that they themselves are unsuited in temperament for the administrative life, they are reluctant to delegate these activities to a capable manager. Yet survival is contingent on sound management practices and formal systems.

Phase 2: Direction

The firms that survive the leadership crisis are those that develop sound administrative practices that provide the vitally needed direction and authority. Production scheduling and inventory controls are formalized. Written communications replace face-to-face encounters. Standards and budgets are put in place. Cost-accounting systems are introduced. Formal hierarchies and position titles are set up. The happy result is that order and routine begin to subdue chaos and uncertainty. Moreover, the new directive techniques provide a climate fostering efficient growth. The firm prospers, becomes more diverse and complex, and embarks on a sustained period of development.

The successful bureaucratization of the firm, as the dialectic predicts, precipitates its own crisis. The restriction of the prerogatives of lower level employees produces a stagnant organization. They know a great deal more about manufacturing processes, products, distribution, and customers, than do the administrators. They experience the administrative mechanisms as cumbersome, centralized, and repressive. Yet, feeling they must follow procedures, they are reluctant to take the initiative for fear of reprisal from the administrative arm. A sort of paralysis creeps in as the inevitable *autonomy crisis* hits the organization.

The solution, although drastic, is clear enough. Lower level managers need greater autonomy and freedom to act as they know best. Often this proves difficult for the administrators—after all they gained their success by being directive. Moreover, it can be troublesome for lower level managers. Used to being bossed, they are unaccustomed to making their own decisions. Yet delegation of important decisions is inescapable if the firm is to overcome the autonomy crisis and reach the next era in its historical evolution, the *delegation phase.*

Phase 3: Delegation

Rather than stubbornly adhering to a dictatorial central bureaucracy, successful firms overcome the autonomy crisis through delegation. Responsibility and authority is given to the managers of the various field units: manufacturing facilities, sales districts, marketing departments, and engineering development and research offices. These components now run their own shows. Upper managers refrain from interference in the operations of the field units by restraining themselves to management by exception on the basis of strategic plans and operating budget reports from the field. Field units are treated as autonomous profit or marketing centers. Communication from the upper echelons is infrequent as they now concentrate on acquisitions, investment, and capital market considerations and monitor the field units by means of simple reports such as a profit budget.

Delegation usually does the trick. Released from the fetters of an overzealous central bureaucracy, these managers and their subordinates experience a heightened motivation. Taking full advantage of their new-found autonomy, they now react rapidly to customers' needs, penetrate new markets, introduce advanced manufacturing technologies, and launch new products. Delegation proves to be the engine for a new and prolonged period of steady growth and progress.

As in previous phases, however, success breeds its own emergency, the *control crisis*. The autonomous managers, having developed their own fiefdoms, are reluctant to coordinate their operations with the other independent components. Opportunities to economize on purchasing, central services, technology, computing, specialized personnel, and R&D go unrealized. Moreover, arrogant parochial attitudes emerge as the various managers fiercely protect their territorial boundaries and prerogatives. The organization becomes Balkanized.

Sensing their loss of influence and direction over the diverse operating units, top management attempt to regain control for the center. Some firms opt for a return to the bureaucratic measures of the direction phase. In this case, failure is the usual outcome. The company is too diverse and complex to be run from the top. Others find and adopt a new social technology based on sophisticated integration mechanisms. The *coordination* phase is under way.

Phase 4: Coordination

The *coordination* phase features a realignment of duties throughout the organization. A new layer of management is inserted between headquarters and the field units. At the field level, the sundry operations such as various previously autonomous profit centers are merged into sector, industry, or product groups and treated as return-on-investment centers. The product group manager is given authority for nearly all phases of bringing the product to market: engineering, production, sales, marketing, and so on. Each product group is considered to be a separate autonomous business. This authority, however, is not granted without responsibility. The product group managers become responsible for achieving profit and return-on-investment targets.

At headquarters level, new staff offices are created and formal administrative systems are implemented to coordinate and control activities at product group level. Technical staff units—marketing, personnel, purchasing, engineering—are expected to provide expertise and assistance to the field. In some firms they must sell their ideas to the product groups; in others they have a direct line of authority over their counterparts in the product group. These units have the responsibility for the technical quality of their area of specialty. The result is dual lines of authority. The manager of engineering, for example, in the product group is responsible to both the HQ director of engineering and to the product group general manager.

Administrative staff offices at headquarters also become busy developing various management systems in an all-out effort to effect more control over the product groups. A host of administrative control systems are put in place including strategic planning, long-range financial plans, operating budgets, capital investment budgeting, as well as standard operating procedures, rules, and policies. While the product groups are left with as much decision-making responsibility as possible, they are required to adhere to these control and coordination systems. They must now justify their actions and decisions to the watchdogs up the line.

In order to make the new arrangements stick, stock options and company-wide profit-sharing schemes are put in place. These act as inducements for the product group managers to respond positively to the new coordination and control systems and look beyond the needs of their own component. The realignment of the field operations, the institution of coordination and control systems, and the new global outlook by field managers lead to economies throughout the firm. The result is a more effective allocation of resources and another lengthy period of profitable expansion.

After a time, however, the various technical and administrative staff offices at headquarters take on a life of their own. They become an end in their own right rather than a means to assist and guide the line operations. The result for the field managers is a feeling of being overwhelmed by a proliferation of bureaucratic paper systems. They come to resent the unsolicited advice from staff specialists who are unfamiliar with local problems and conditions. While at headquarters, staff become increasingly frustrated by the parochial attitudes and ignorance of new technical developments on the part of the field product groups. They perceive the line managers as uncooperative and stubborn. Once again success has created the conditions for a new kind of crisis and yet another transmutation. Initiative, innovation, and problem solving grind to a halt as the *red-tape crisis* strikes.

The General Appliance Corporation (GAC) provides a prime example of an organization operating in the coordination phase.[16] General Appliance Corporation, an integrated manufacturer of home appliances of all kinds, strove to be the quality-products industry leader. It operated with four product divisions, four manufacturing divisions, and six central staff offices. It treated the product and manufacturing divisions as profit centers responsible for the design, engineering, assembling, and marketing of various home appliances. The product divisions purchased 20% of their parts from outside suppliers and 80% from the manufacturing divisions; the manufacturing divisions sold 25% of their output to outside companies.

The product and manufacturing divisions dealt with each other as if they were independent companies competing in the marketplace. Headquarters held each division responsible for a budgeted amount of profit and a target return on investment. The transfer price system for internal transactions relied on market-based prices wherever possible. The various staff offices had functional authority over their counterparts, who were also responsible to their divisional general manager, in the manufacturing and product divisions but they had no line authority over the divisional general managers.

The president, deeply concerned over customer and dealer complaints about product quality and a customer survey indicating that GAC's reputation as a quality leader had deteriorated, gave the production staff vice-president of production unilateral decision power for six months to bring the quality of all products up to a satisfactory level. There was a transfer price dispute over a stove top which had been improved in quality as a result of the vice-president's mandate.

The general manager of the chrome products manufacturing division passed on the extra cost (plus a normal profit) to the electric stove division. The electric stove division rejected the revised transfer price, pointing out they had not requested the improved quality. The chrome products division argued that since they had been ordered to improve the quality by the staff vice-president, they should not have to absorb the additional cost. Negotiations led nowhere and the electric stove division appealed to the finance office to arbitrate a transfer price.

The case illustrates how firms in the coordination phase attempt to get the best of both worlds by relying on market controls, including a sophisticated transfer price system, for the manufacturing and product divisions and a parallel command organization for the technical and administrative support side of the organization. The natural tension between the two systems came to a head over the stove-top transfer price. In terms of the dialectic model, this clash can be seen as a valuable situation whereby the autonomous market-oriented product division spontaneously attempted to resist nonprofitable quality improvements, while the technically oriented staff units took on the leadership role to ensure that GAC's products were of the highest quality, regardless of cost. Rather than seeing this as a dysfunction conflict, the model suggests it may be a natural and healthy confrontation in which two sides automatically provide the necessary checks and balances on each other. Coordination phase organizations strive to manage such tensions and the inevitable conflicts arising from coordination needs without precipitating a red-tape crisis.

Phase 5: Collaboration

Efforts to manage coordination-phase tensions are frequently unsuccessful and the organization is overcome by a ponderous bureaucracy. Rule by red tape threatens to smother it. In order to surmount the new crisis, successful organizations take steps to recover interpersonal relationships and to align organizational relationships more laterally than in the coordination phase. Sometimes cross-functional teams are put together to speed up complex problem solving. Or matrix management is introduced with functional, product, and line people coming together to debate, discuss, and make decisions with no party having more formal authority than the others. Social controls, including clan-like relationships, are frequently fostered in place of formal controls. Some companies in Europe even went so far as to restructure on a democratic parliamentary basis whereby the chief executive officer (CEO) and other top executives were elected by the employees, each of whom had one vote. Either way, the emphasis is on personal interaction and positive horizontal relations.

The consequence is that power and influence of headquarters staff experts melts away. Some regroup into consulting groups who now must sell their expertise to line people.

Others are relocated into the line organization on a special assignment basis. Accounting and management information systems (MIS) departments strive to get real-time information to the right places. As these changes take place, the organizational ethos shifts from single career paths, specializing in one discipline, to a program of retraining and continuous education.

Conferences of like-minded managers and employees are held frequently. Sabbatical leave is granted so that managers can catch up on leading-edge technology, knowledge, and developments at universities, government bodies, and international institutions such as the United Nations, the World Bank, and volunteer agencies in developing countries. Experimentation is encouraged and rewards are based on personal contributions to the problem at hand, rather than to conformance with administrative systems and edicts. The result is a gradual loosening and rejuvenation of the organization.

But pressures for innovation and the psychological stress of peer-group problem solving and decision making eventually take their toll. Managers feel mentally burned out. Japanese companies are notorious in this regard, literally forcing managers to spend most weeknights entertaining customers in long bouts of drinking, eating, and carousing and to attend weekend attitude-training courses. In consequence, organizations must find ways of permitting a more balanced lifestyle for their employees. Some companies accomplish this through rest and recreation programs. Others install gymnasiums, squash and tennis courts, and arrange daily aerobics sessions and jogging groups. Some even introduce yoga classes and stress management programs.

These measures help but organizations today face a new crisis. Managers and employees still sense a lack of spirituality. The specter of the economic and the material needs of society with its discourse of markets, competition, survival of the fittest, and wealth accumulation still prevails. In all likelihood, it will be some time before spirituality pushes economics and politics off center stage. Yet there are signs. The dawning recognition of the egregious ruination of the world's life support systems—air, water, farmland, lakes, forests, the ozone layer—will eventually force us to design and give pride of place to systems of accountability that feature environment and quality of life. This *spirituality crisis* is not limited to individual corporations, it invades all aspects of the living world.

4.3 Relating Theories to Empirical Observations

4.3.1 The General Electric Case

The history of the General Electric Company (GE) vividly demonstrates aspects of the historical–dialectical model of control.[17] In 1878, a small group of electricity enthusiasts formed the Edison General Electric Company to exploit the commercial opportunity presenting itself in electricity, electric lighting, and electric motors. For the next 70 years, GE operated pretty much as a "direction phase" company with a traditional functional organizational structure featuring research, engineering, manufacturing, marketing, and financial divisions. Direction and strong leadership took GE to over \$2 billion in sales by 1950.

But in the early 1950s GE's top management sensed that the functional organizational structure was stifling innovation, flexibility, entrepreneurship, and managerial initiative throughout the company. In consequence, in a dramatic move, they reorganized GE into the delegation mode by decentralizing responsibility and authority for operations to nearly 100 product departments, treating them as profit centers. Entrepreneurship, flexibility, and aggressive marketing flourished in these new departments and GE, capitalizing on the favorable economic conditions in the next two decades, experienced an explosive growth in sales.

By 1970, GE featured 160 profit product departments reporting to headquarters through about 40 divisional general managers, who in turn reported through one of ten vice-presidents or group executives, who reported to one of three top executives at headquarters. Growth in profitability, however, lagged behind the spectacular boom in sales. Moreover, opportunities to economize by sharing R&D, technology, and administrative functions went unrealized. The company was ripe for coordination.

General Electric overlaid the department, division, and group hierarchy with a layer of strategic business units (SBUs), each of which represented, as far as possible, a stand-alone business. Headquarters also put into effect a strategic planning system that called for each SBU to prepare a strategic plan for its business. The information that emerged from the strategic planning process allowed top management to identify wasteful overlaps, initiate cross-businesses coordination, and allocate resources to areas of competitive advantage and away from areas with limited potential.

In 1977, top management added yet another layer of administration to the existing organizational structure by installing five sector vice-presidents just under the headquarter's office. Each of the five sectors—consumer products and services, power systems, technical systems and materials including aircraft and aerospace operations, industrial products and components, and international operations—represented a separate industry. The sector executive became Mr. General Electric and acted as CEO and GE's institutional leader for that particular industry. A very important part of the job for these executives was to prepare a detailed strategic plan for their sectors, reviewed by headquarters to pinpoint GE's major areas of competitive advantage, allocate resources, identify duplication and wasteful overlapping activities, and above all to exploit potential synergies across sectors and SBUs. In consequence, staff planning offices sprang up throughout GE.

Not surprisingly, as the historical–dialectical model predicts, the inevitable red-tape crisis hit GE in the early 1980s. Recognizing this threat, newly appointed CEO Jack Welch, previously SBU head of technical systems and materials and later chief executive of GE's huge consumer products and service sector, embarked on a massive restructuring and downsizing exercise. He culled the headquarters planning department to eight people from 30, reestablished responsibility for strategy to line operating managers, eliminated layers of administrative managers, pruned product lines, closed down marginal and nonproductive plants, and introduced advanced manufacturing equipment in the remaining ones. He also eliminated the five sector offices, and reorganized GE's 150 separate businesses into 15 lines of business, lumping them into three circles or groups.

When the smoke cleared towards the end of the decade, GE had divested 125 businesses and eliminated a staggering total of over 100 000 employees. For better or worse Welch had "taken out the layers," "pulled out the weeds," and "scraped off the rust" of the GE family of businesses.[18] But the inexorable, massive downsizing left GE with a dispassionate "survivor mentality" cadre of middle and lower level managers and a "running scared" workforce.[19] A *spirituality crisis* was in full swing.

In the face of this pivotal moment in GE's history, Welch embarked on a long-term "spiritual revitalization" program designed to shift managers' and workers' focus "from cost-cutting to the murky realm of human values . . . pushing soft values because he sees them as the only way to maintain the pace of GE's productivity drive . . . by inspiring the remaining workers to produce more" (Tichey and Sherman, 1993, p. 240). Welch aimed to do this by instilling throughout GE a new "spiritual credo" containing values that he hoped all employees would not only understand but, more importantly, would feel passionately about.

The new spiritual credo contained several major injunctions. For instance, all employees were warned that GE would not ensure job security—only satisfied customers could do that. They were also enjoined to develop a high level of emotional commitment to the new values. Moreover, the credo demanded that every business component achieve number one or two status globally in the design, technology, and quality of its chosen product line. In order to accomplish this, hierarchical grouping labels would be erased, cross-functional barriers would be removed, and the distinction between domestic and foreign operations would be eliminated. General Electric would become an organization without boundaries.

In order to institutionalize the new credo, Welch started at the top of the organization and set up the Corporate Executive Council (CEC) composed of GE's 30 highest ranking business unit chiefs and senior headquarters staff directors. The CEC met quarterly to discuss the most important problems facing GE at that time. In order to encourage a wide open debating style, meetings were held in a small amphitheatre along the lines of a miniature Roman coliseum. A topic would be teed up and combatants took each other on until they reached a consensus of sorts. Unlike the old days, everyone at the meeting received the details of each others' financial results.

This open atmosphere, Welch believed, induced participants to share information, generate solutions to each other's problems, and most importantly, break down parochial barriers so that good ideas mined from one part of GE were shipped to the rest of the company. By 1988, CEC executives had not only come to understand and embrace the new credo, but also they became an effective force for pushing the shared values further down in the organization. Similar councils were organized at the next level in each of the 13 major business components. Finally, in order to get employees and the workforce to "walk the new talk," Welch set Operation Work-Out in motion.

Operation Work-Out consisted of a series of meetings patterned after "good old Yankee" town meetings. Groups of 30 to 100 hourly and salaried workers within a particular business met off site for two or three days to discuss common problems. In order to promote candor, bosses were locked out during discussion times. Initially, employees spent a lot of time airing complaints and griping, but later the meetings took on a more constructive mode as participants started to identify and define work-related problems *and* to develop concrete proposals. The bosses then returned to the meeting and were required to make on-the-spot, public decisions regarding the proposals, particularly for problems which could be fixed readily. Operation Work-Out not only empowered lower-level employees but also served to expose any managers and workers who were not walking the talk.

Welch summed up the new spiritual credo this way:

> The only way I see to get more productivity is by getting people involved and excited about their jobs. You can't afford to have anyone walk through a gate of a factory, or into an office, who's not giving 120 %. I don't mean running and sweating, but working smarter. It's a matter of understanding the customer's needs instead of just making something and putting it into a box. It's a matter of seeing the importance of your role in the total process
>
> . . . The point of Work-Out is to give people better jobs. When people see that their ideas count, their dignity is raised. Instead of feeling numb, like robots, they feel important. They *are* important . . . With Work-Out and boundarylessness, we're trying to differentiate GE competitively by raising as much intellectual and creative capital from our workforce as we possibly can.
>
> Trust is enormously powerful in a corporation. People won't do their best unless they believe they'll be treated fairly—that there's no cronyism and everybody has a real shot. The only way I know to create that kind of trust is by laying out your values and then walking the talk. You've got to do what you say you'll do, consistently, over time. It doesn't mean everybody has to agree. I have a great relationship with Bill Bywater, president of the International Union of Electronic Workers. I would trust him with my wallet, but he knows I'll fight him to the death in certain areas, and vice versa. He knows where I stand. I know where he stands. We don't always agree—but we trust each other.
>
> That's what boundary-less is: An open, trusting, sharing of ideas. A willingness to listen, debate, and then take the best ideas and get on with it. If this company is to achieve its goals, we've all got to become boundary-less. Boundaries are crazy. We're not that far along with boundarylessness yet. It's a big, big idea, but I don't think it has enough on it yet. We've got to keep repeating it, letting everybody know all the time that when they're doing things right, it's boundaryless. It's going to take a couple of more years to get people to the point where the idea of boundarylessness just becomes natural. (Tichey and Sherman, 1993, pp. 248–9, NY: Harper Business.)

In order to ensure that the new values would stick, Welch revamped GE's management compensation scheme. For the top 400 executives, take-home pay would consist of 50 % bonuses while the next top 4000 managers could receive one-quarter of their compensation in the form of performance incentive bonuses. Most of these executives and managers also got stock options. Two main criteria were used for awarding bonuses and stock options: financial performance *and* demonstrated adherence to the new, shared values. The latter was measured on the basis of ratings by peers, superiors, and subordinates, as well as self-ratings. An individual's accomplishment rating thus included a pragmatic financial measurement as well as a subjective assessment of his or her emotional commitment to the new spiritual credo.

These recent developments at GE can be read as a striking example of one organization's attempt to develop a blueprint for coping with the spirituality crisis. Welch's revitalization efforts—pushing soft values, promoting a boundaryless organization, creating cross-functional situations like CEC and Operation Work-Out, assessing commitment to the new credo, encouraging a clanlike atmosphere, and diffusing the power of HQ staff experts—mirror the prescriptions of the historical–dialectical model for coping with the spirituality crisis. It remains to be seen whether or not Welch's gambit, with its injunction to "control your own destiny or someone else will," can pull GE through the current crisis. In spite of its emphasis on employee empowerment, the credo's materialistic injunction—produce or else—seems to outweigh its spiritual precepts. Either way, the GE experience provides a striking example of one organization's attempt to develop a blueprint for coping with the tensions of the collaboration phase.

4.3.2 Linking Back to the Case Studies

This chapter reviewed five prominent theories about MACS. While each may appear to have some universal validity, each provides a strikingly different version of the workings of these systems. The main tenets of these five frameworks are summarized in Table 4.1.

So we are left with five different portrayals, five different advocacy positions, five different views of the nature of MACS and how they work. The General Electric case has illustrated how the dialectic nature of control works in practice. Let us see how this and the other perspectives perform in light of the case studies in Chapter 2.

Agency Theory

Agency theory receives some support. If one could forget history, the Jesuit case could be seen through the lenses of agency theory but with some difficulties. Clearly there is a problem of managing relationships between principal (the center in Rome) and agent (the representatives of the Order in the spread periphery). The case shows signs of self interest, and adverse selection and the role of the Jesuit accountability system could be said to tackle issues of moral hazard. The same goes for signaling, incentive schemes and so forth. However, some other interesting aspects of this case would be left out by the elegant agency theory models. Amongst these, for example, the different role that accounting and accountability may have played in the Society would be overlooked. Analogously, their links with other pedagogical practices such as rhetoric, which could explain their early diffusion across the Order, would equally be shadowed. It could be said that Wedgwood's decision to pay his workers slightly more than the going rate constitutes a form of residual output sharing and thus mitigates the adverse selection problem because this practice would attract the better workers in the area. While in the Empire Glass (EG) case, since the owners cannot directly monitor the plant managers' efforts, the profit budget acts as an explicit contract for a specified output (profits and efficiency) and the bonus scheme works as a way of sharing some of the risk for output thus moderating the moral hazard problem. The Johnson & Johnson (J&J) case is less supportive of agency theory. Bonuses are deliberately uncoupled from budget performance and, since HQ executive committee members are intimately familiar with the subsidiary managers' abilities and comportment habits, the

Table 4.1 Universal perspectives.

Characteristics	Agency Theory	Nerve Center	Accounting Symbolism	Labor Process	Dialectic controls
Type of paradigm	Individualism	Functionalism	Contextualism	Contextualism: radical structuralist	Contextualism: radical humanist
Intellectual forerunners	Hobbes, Smith, Spencer	Parsons, Mead, Merton	March, Mayer & Rowan	Engels, Marx, Braverman	Plato, Hegel, Adorno
Major thesis	Agents will use asymmetrical information to pursue self-interest with guile	Managers act as informational nerve centers whose main role is the collection, storing, and dissemination of information	Managers use accounting information for defensive and offensive actions or ritualistically or symbolically to formally comply to environmental demands and institutional pressures	Capitalistic interests appropriate the technical and financial information of the labor process to weaken and exploit wage labor	Managers at the centre of opposed processes (autonomy and delegation vs. power and control)
Central focus	Asymmetrical informational relations	Manager's information processing behavior and relations	Manager's impossibility to process information, external pressures	Asymmetrical power relations	Asymmetrical power relations, dialectical tension
Main concepts	Moral hazard, signaling, asymmetric information, residual claim sharing	Decisional, interpersonal and informational roles, nerve center management	Accounting as ritual, ceremonies, legitimacy, symbolism, isomorphism, decoupling	Commodification, alienation, deskilling, class contradiction, expropriation of surplus value	Historical path dependency and evolution, change
Advocacy position	Owners	Managers	Accountants and accounting itself	Wage labor workers	Managers, wage labor workers

adverse selection problem is minimized. Furthermore, there is no indication of cheating and shirking on the part of the managers. On the contrary, they apparently put in long, difficult, and arduous hours on behalf of the company.

Nerve Center

Turning to the nerve center framework, the case studies provide a good deal of support for its main propositions. The Jesuit Order illustrates how, even in early modern times, people in charge of managing organizations (the College, the Province or the entire Order) could rely upon a huge amount of information ranging from accounting data to reports on sins committed! Yet most of this information was collected informally when visits to the Colleges and the Missions were paid by superiors. Josiah Wedgwood seems an archetype of the nerve center manager: immersed in a relentless round of seemingly unrelated events he incessantly collected, processed, and disseminated information, including financial information. Empire Glass also confirms the picture of manager as nerve center. Plant manager Hunt seemed to be constantly collecting, analyzing, and distributing information, especially data in the formal control system reports. At J&J, HQ and subsidiary executives are literally awash with information, much of it from the formal MACS. In fact, it seems as if these systems are designed at J&J to ensure managers act as nerve centers.

Accounting Symbolism

Accounting symbolism also offers some useful insight. In most of the case studies we have described so far we do not really understand the relationship between the information collected and its use for decision making. This is not only because the cases are historical but also because observation, even of contemporary cases, is always partial, and the same piece of information can have a positive relationship with decisions made while playing another role for some others. Equally, the use of this information may play a double role This is, for example, what could be said for the case of the Society of Jesus: management accounting and controls seem to play a functional and direct role in how decisions are made. However, some have argued, the collection of accounting information could have also played a symbolic role to show that the Order kept economic and religious aspects of its management well separated. This would be an example of a defensive use. Analogously, one could argue that information is collected to show an "intelligent" use, which in the context of the Order would mean a religious one. Similar arguments can apply to Josiah Wedgwood's case and the others. It is not difficult to imagine how the immense flow of information led to some defensive, offensive or symbolic use.

Labor Process

The labor process perspective performs also well. The Jesuit case has been viewed as the first example of "proto-capitalism" where accounting data was used to discipline Jesuit members working in the missions and to use their work to accumulate wealth at the center in Rome. In order to put his brilliant strategy to work, Wedgwood needed to suppress a recalcitrant and undisciplined workforce. He did this by breaking up the traditional potting operation into separate tasks and assigning each to its own small building. This tactic served to deskill the traditional potter's craft. And by applying his own version of management science (his potter's instructions which spelled out in meticulous detail how to perform the various tasks as well as proper comportment on the job) he effectively took control of the knowledge of the production process. Empire Glass also illustrates deskilling in that the workers are no longer glassblowers but mere machine tenders. Moreover, they are programmed in accordance with the industrial engineers' scientific management work studies. Thus, the workers are deprived of both the technical and financial knowledge of the production process and are in the end treated as commodities.

The cases also demonstrate the ambiguous position of managers within the relations of capitalism. Empire Glass headquarters uses the profit planning and control reports to closely monitor the managers at the glass plants. Managers show some resistance in the form of making the numbers always come up right by the end of the year. At the same time, the glass plant managers advocate the use of the controls for disciplining the supervisors and the workers. Similarly, J&J headquarters almost continuously monitors the subsidiary managers by means of the profit budget and the strategic business plan; whereas managers use them to watch over and discipline each department in the subsidiary.

Dialectic Controls

The historical–dialectical analysis also offers some insights into the cases. The Society of Jesus made the dialectic relationship between autonomy and control the key engine for its development, revolutionary phases having an apparently minor role in this evolution. Wedgwood wisely used management accounting to direct the workforce and reduce its autonomy, although it did not show the shift in power relationships that the model would predict. The EG and J&J cases are also examples of at least some of the phases through which dialectics evolves, with signs of direction, delegation, coordination and collaboration. The fact that corporations are nowadays run by numbers exemplifies the spirituality crisis that a dialectic view of MACS illustrates.

4.4 Summary and Conclusions

This chapter has reviewed five universal paradigms that try to interpret the nature of MACS. They are "universal" as each of them cannot necessarily (coherently) be combined with the others. In other words, while the empirical cases can be seen as examples of one or more of these theoretical constructions, the theories admit only with difficulty the possibility of a different view of the world. Agency theory, for instance, is driven by an owner perspective that cannot be combined with the labor process view. Analogously the manager as a nerve center posits too much trust in the manager's capability to process information while accounting symbolism views this processing as ritualistic.

In summation, *agency theory* conceives of organizations as a sum of contracts between owner and employees. It relies on the distinction between the owner (or principal) and the employee-manager (who is supposed to be the owner's agent). Agency theory, taking the owner's side, depicts employees (agents) as using their asymmetrical information advantage to opportunistically cheat and shirk on the owner. It views the contract as the central unit of analysis to understand organizations and management accounting information and controls seen as a way to mitigate such behavior.

In contrast, the *labor process* perspective is almost the antithesis of agency theory. Taking the underdog side of the exploited wage laborer, it depicts management accounting, buttressed with the techniques of management sciences, as a way for owners to deprive workers of the technical and financial knowledge of the production process, treat them as commodities, and pressure them for even more productivity. Owners also use accounting systems as a way to legitimate grabbing the lion's share of any surplus value accruing from the enterprise. The labor process perspective sees the role and historical development of MACS not as an objective, neutral enterprise, feeding information to decision makers, nor as a way for owners to counteract managers' shirking and cheating tendencies, but rather in terms of a set of broader structural power inequalities endemic to capitalist societies. These systems developed during early capitalism to secure control over recalcitrant labor and later developed into "sophisticated control mechanisms designed to ensure the institutionalized subordination of labor to the needs of capital" (Puxty, 1993, p. 78). Together with management science techniques they effected the usurpation of technical and financial knowledge of the labor process of production by owners and their manager agents from wage labor. According to labor process scholars, management accounting continues to play a crucial role in subordinating workers to contemporary capitalistic needs.

The *nerve center* portrayal is neutral in this important debate. Taking the manager's position, it portrays them as involved in a hectic nonstop round of seemingly unrelated events, all the while gathering, storing, and disseminating information including that contained in formal accounting reports.

However, it often appears, particularly from the rationalistic, objective realist perspective, that managers gather and process a great deal of redundant information. This is why MACS can be seen as having a symbolic nature.

Accounting symbolism views managers as to be using MACS to construct a reality that is personally enabling. Sometimes they use them to construct a defensible image of having followed the most competent path by gathering all the information available before making the risky decision. Sometimes they deliberately construct a false reality for other managers and assume that others do likewise. And sometimes they use them ritualistically to create a self-serving image of themselves as believers and active followers of rational choice and decision making. In each case—defensive, offensive, and symbolic—the accounting and control system is used by the manager to subjectively construct meaning.

The *dialectic control* framework depicts organizations as systems showing an intrinsic tension, which makes them evolve through distinctive phases: creativity, direction, delegation, coordination, collaboration, and eventually crisis. This model brings into the picture the need for radical changes in the status quo of autonomy–direction relations in order to overcome or avert crisis situations.

While each of the five universal theories receives some support from the evidence in the case studies, not one is fully supported or seems to perform better than the others. The reason for this may be that each puts the spotlight on different facets of MACS while ignoring or putting aside factors stressed in the others. For example, agency theory stresses the potential of agents to exploit owners due to their asymmetrical information advantage but ignores the latter's legal power of command, which accrues from ownership. The labor process framework, in stark contrast, foregrounds the power of owners to exploit workers (agents) due to their control of the technical and financial information about the production process, as well as their powerful ownership position. On the other hand, it ignores the worker's possibilities of using private information for indolence and deceptive maneuvering. The nerve center picture ignores power positions altogether. So it is hard to prefer one over the others purely on its descriptive richness or its predictive ability; it seems to depend on one's advocacy position—owner, worker, or manager. Accounting symbolism tends to view accounting either too instrumentally or too ritualistically. In the former view, it assumes that managers have full control of accounting information and can thus defend themselves or pursue offensive aims. In the latter, managers are instead seen as having too little control of accounting numbers, with these becoming simply ritual and ceremony. The dialectic approach, while acknowledging organizational tensions, views them as happening in dual relationships, ignoring the fact that these may involve more complex networks of organizational actors.

These theories take us beyond the assumption that every case is unique, and they uncover elements essential to all management accounting systems. However they do not provide much, if any, leverage on how the universal elements are capable of variation. Nor do they identify patterns to such variations. For example, the asymmetrical information problem is likely to loom larger at J&J than at EG. At EG the technology is well understood and uncertainty is low, whereas at J&J the technology is complex and uncertainty runs high. Similarly, the importance of the nerve center role looms much larger at J&J, where uncertainty runs high, than it does at EG, where certainty is the order of the day.

Moreover, there are many important factors in the cases which are not included within the scope of these frameworks. Think of religious and political issues affecting managerial decisions in the Jesuit case. Wedgwood, for example, relied more heavily for control on nonaccounting controls, such as the reforming influence of Wesley's Christian preaching, the clocking-in system, his supervisors and overseers, his potter's instructions, his daily inspection tours of the five work sheds, and his personal concern for the spiritual and physical well-being of his workers and their families. While at EG, group solidarity and the positive attitudes of the plant management group towards the company as well as for the formal accounting reports played an important part in the highly effective control we witnessed. And at J&J, the clear mandate of decentralized responsibility for business plans and their execution, along with a seasoned group of executives and managers weaned on the company's unique formal controls, played a vital role in the success of its control systems. These and other crucial factors are not addressed well by any of the three universal frameworks.

This suggests that the importance and nature of any universal elements of MACS may be contingent on impersonal forces and factors surrounding the organization, such as environment, corporate history, strategy, technology, and interdependencies. If this is so, then organizations operating in similar environments and with similar strategies, technologies, and interdependencies should exhibit similar patterns in the way they design and make use of their management accounting systems. As it turns out, a lot of work has been done investigating this idea and, as a result, there are several valuable frameworks along these lines. The next couple of chapters present several frameworks, which show how systematic differences in such impersonal forces result in patterned variations in important characteristics of MACS. This does not mean, however, that the universal frameworks are unhelpful; merely that by themselves they are not sufficient to capture all the important aspects of these systems.

Endnotes

1. We use the notion of a "paradigm" (cf. Kuhn, 1970) to describe theories that aim to construct universal explanations that can be reconciled with other such other explanations only with difficulty and thus do not admit a comparison: they are therefore incommensurable in a Kuhnian sense. A theory (even when it seeks to acheive a certain degree of generalization and abstraction) does not necessarily have these features.
2. See Williamson (1973). A university is a case in point. Faculties in the various parts of the university—nuclear physics, genetic engineering, literary theory, law, electrical engineering, and so on—are privy to information that is well beyond the ability of the president to comprehend, unless the president comes from that discipline.
3. See Perrow (1986) and Armstrong (1991) for detailed and trenchant critiques of agency theory as well as Scapens (1985) for basic exegesis of the mathematics involved in agency theory and an even-handed synopsis of its limitations and possibilities.
4. See Baiman (1982, 1990) for detailed review articles of agency theory in management accounting.
5. See Schick, Gordon and Haka (1990) for an excellent if conventional overview and discussion of the information overload phenomenon.
6. Paul Sweezy, p. xii in the foreword to Braverman (1974).
7. See Armstrong (1987, 1991), Hopper, Storey and Willmott (1987), Hopper and Armstrong (1991), Puxty (1993), and Roslender (1992) for expositions of the labor process accounting paradigm.
8. Sir John Byng, touring the North Country in 1792 is reported to have exclaimed on seeing Manchester first hand, "Oh! What a dog's hole is Manchester." (Reported in Heilbroner, 1930, p. 58.)
9. Children often proved better workers than grown-ups because they could be easily trained and controlled. It was common for half-starved, ragged, untaught children as young as seven to be working 15 hours a day, six days a week. A government commissioner described life after work this way: "I have seen wretchedness in some of its worse phases both here and upon the Continent, but until I visited the wynds of Glasgow I did not believe that so much crime, misery, and disease could exist in any civilized country. In the lower lodging-houses ten, twelve, sometimes twenty persons of both sexes, all ages and various degrees of nakedness, sleep indiscriminately huddled together upon the floor. These dwellings are usually so damp, filthy and ruinous, that no

one could wish to keep his horse in one of them" (reported in Engels, 1987, p. 79). One need only go today to Cairo, Calcutta, or Karachi to see how these slums have been exported to developing countries.

10. Similarly today, the university professor never (or only rarely) sees the product of his or her work—the completion of the student's education—and so is deprived of any intrinsic satisfaction from the work of educating students. The examination system also creates a "them and us" situation, thus estranging professor and student.

11. Braverman (1974); see particularly Chapter 5, "The primary effects of scientific management."

12. See Macintosh (1994) for a detailed discussion of this issue within the widely diversified multinational firm.

13. This framework is adapted from Greiner's (1972) model of organizational evolution and revolution.

14. "*Dialectics* come from the Greek term for dialogue, whereby a residue of give-and-take and of relentless questioning continues to inform the context. At the core of all dialectics, we find a continuation of incessant querying and an active engagement with the resistant stuff of knowledge. Dialectical inquiry is epitomized by Plato in the person and style of Socrates" (Heilbroner, 1980, p. 31).

15. A logical contradiction refers to the situation where two statements contradict each other as is the case if one statement holds "A is true" but another statement says "not A is true."

16. See Anthony, Dearden and Govindarajan (1992, p. 255) for a description of GAC.

17. This brief history relies on the case studies General Electric Company (A) and (B) in Anthony, Dearden and Bedford (1989); "Background note on management systems: 1981," *Harvard Business School*; "GE's new billion-dollar small businesses," *Business Week*, 19 December 1977; and "Why Jack Welch is Changing GE," T. Lueck, *New York Times*, 1985.

18. Tichey and Sherman (1993, p. 8). The details of this "spiritual" revival are described in some detail by Tichey and Sherman (1993), who provide an inside look at GE from the point of view of a long-time GE consultant and business professor and a senior writer for *Fortune* magazine.

19. See "An American workplace, after the deluge," Peter T. Kilborn, *The New York Times*, 5 September 1993.

Further Readings

You can usefully do some further readings in each of the areas below:

Agency theory:

- Lambert, R. (2007) Agency theory and management accounting, in *Handbook of Management Accounting Research* (eds C. Chapman, A. Hopwood and M. Shields), Elsevier, Oxford, pp. 247–68.

Nerve center:

- Bruns, W., Jr. and McKinnon, S. (1993) Information and managers: a field study. *Journal of Management Accounting Research*, Fall, 84–108.

Accounting symbolism:

- Ansari, S. and Bell, J. (1991) Symbolism, collectivism and rationality in organisational control. *Accounting, Auditing and Accountability Journal*, **4** (2), 4–27.
- Meyer, J. (1986) Social environments and organizational accounting. *Accounting, Organizations and Society*, **11** (4/5), 345–56.

Labor process:

- Hopper, T. and Armstrong, P. (1991) Cost accounting, controlling labour and the rise of the conglomerates. *Accounting, Organizations and Society*, **16** (5/6), 405–38.

Dialectic controls:

- Cooper, C., Taylor, P., Smith, N. and Catchpowle, L. (2005) A discussion of the political potential of Social Accounting. *Critical Perspectives on Accounting*, **16** (7), 951–74.
- Covaleski, M. and Dirsmith, M. (1990) Dialectic tension, double reflexivity and the everyday accounting researcher: on using qualitative methods. *Accounting, Organizations and Society*, 15, 543–73.

5

The Structures of MACS: Market, Hierarchies, and Systemic Controls

5.1 Introduction

Management accounting and control systems are pervasive in today's world. When viewed from close up, however, they seem to come in different forms and they seem to be used in different ways by different organizations. In consequence, suspecting that these variations might be related to the specific circumstances facing each organization, some researchers began to identify how variations in these circumstances lead to systematic differences in key characteristics of MACS. So they put aside the search for universal truths, such as "participative budgeting is better than imposed budgets" and "budget targets should be difficult but achievable." Instead, taking a functionalist contingency approach, they argued that an organization's performance depends on matching its control-system characteristics with the constraints of its environment and other important contextual circumstances. These efforts bore fruit. Careful studies began to identify contextual dimensions that seemed to influence the way a particular organization would design its administrative systems. The findings were used to develop general frameworks that are useful for analyzing an organization's domain, that is to say, its environmental field of action, and for prescribing the appropriate administrative controls. This chapter outlines three frameworks of this kind.

The first distinguishes between command and market controls and relates each to the type of information available to upper management. The second describes mechanistic and organic control and identifies the circumstances under which each is suitable. The last introduces two information-processing strategies for coping with information requirements. These three frameworks all fit squarely in the structural functionalist paradigm, with the market versus command control constituting an ideal link between individualism (where the units of analyses are market transactions and individual entities) and functionalism. They provide guidelines for achieving the best alignment of the organization's MACS with the type of environment and the kind of uncertainty facing the organization. These frameworks aim to provide the basic structure of how MACS could work in various organizations or in the same organization in distinct phases of its life.

5.2 Market versus Hierarchy?

Our first model of control and organizational context is anchored in some fundamental ideas from economic theory. This is why it constitutes an ideal bridge between individualism and functionalism. For the economist, the key to modern life for both the individual and the organization is *rational choice,* which, fired by the vigorous pursuit of *self-interest,* leads to *utility-maximizing* behavior. While many, if not most, economists recognize that rational utility maximizing is seldom achieved, they maintain that we can, nevertheless, be *intentionally rational* and so achieve *utility-satisfying* behavior (Cyert and March, 1963). Either way, the key to optimal behavior for the economist lies with the kind and quality of information available to the decision maker.

Kenneth Arrow, a Nobel Prize winner in economics, used the economist's toolkit of ideas in his classic article to address the issue of control in large organizations (Arrow, 1964). An organization ". . . is a group of individuals seeking to achieve some common goal, or, in different language, to maximize an objective function."[1] At the same time, however, each member also has a personal objective function, which may or may not coincide with the common goal. Thus the crucial problem for organizations is to solve the problem of ". . . how it can best keep its members in step with each other to maximize the organization's objective function" (Arrow, 1964, p. 3). This, of course, is the *goal congruence problem* so familiar to management accounting and control practitioners, academics, and students.

Further, the decision parameters for any individual are constrained by the external environment and by the decisions made by the other members. Some, but not all, of the observations about the world both internal and external to the organization are communicated to its members. So communication and information processing becomes a prime consideration in organizational design.

Managers' work is seen to consist of processing information. Managers spend most of their time sending and receiving signals from other managers and from the environment to make decisions based on their revised, current assessment of the various factors in play. In the jargon of the economist, they acquire information at a cost and use it to gain a benefit, such as better decision making, as long as the incremental gain accruing from additional processing exceeds its marginal cost.

Moreover, the process is dynamic. As decisions are made, they generate further information, which is transmitted in one form or another to the environment and to other managers. This in turn generates new decisions and more signals. At the same time, new signals are coming in, so managers are constantly revising their conditional probability distributions about the *state of nature* and calculating the effect of these new distributions on their *utility functions.* They behave in very *rational* ways.

As managers go about this process, they do so within the framework of *operating* and *enforcement* rules laid down by the organization. Operating rules instruct organizational members about how to act; they *tell* managers what to do. Enforcement rules compel them to act in accordance with the operating rules, they *persuade* them to do it. Operating and enforcement rules, the nervous system of any organization, come in two bureaucratic forms: the command organization, which implies strict hierarchical relationships, and the market organization, which tries to replicate market mechanisms to manage organizations. Each of these is outlined in Figure 5.1.

Command Controls through Hierarchies

When the upper echelons have low-cost access to the sundry conditions prevalent throughout the organization, a centralized command organization can be employed to advantage. The key factor here is the availability of omniscient information to top management. The vital coordination of individuals' efforts and interests is achieved via a structured, vertical

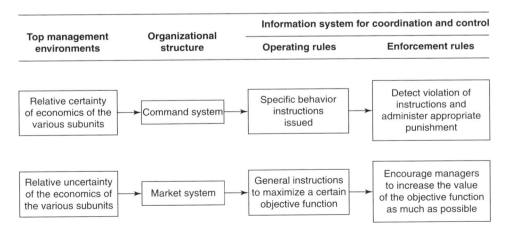

Figure 5.1   Command versus Market Control

hierarchy and general acceptance throughout the organization of the master plan made at the highest level. Control is exercised through specific detailed operating rules followed up with punitive enforcement rules. The latter are designed to detect and report violations of operating rules to upper management who then have only to reward compliance or sanction deviations. Omniscient information lends itself to a command organization.

Management accounting and control systems are an integral aspect of both the operating and enforcement rules. Top management's plans (the operating rules) are expressed in great detail in the master budget for the entire organization and in the operating budget for each component. The controller's department, closely monitoring variances from the budget, detects any deviations from the master plan. Budget performance is then used as the basis for rewarding and sanctioning managers throughout the organization. The master budget masters the organization and its individual members.

But perfect transmission and assimilation of knowledge by top management is not always possible, especially in complex, widely diversified, multinational companies. The reason for this is that managers are information channels of decidedly limited capacity. Information, especially that circulating lower down in the organization, is not necessarily transmitted to the next step up the hierarchy. Further, the absorption of every piece of information would lead rapidly to information overload on the part of sundry managers in the hierarchy.[2] After a certain level of information coming in, managers simply stop processing information.

But perhaps more importantly, in today's huge, worldwide organizations with their complex flow of products and services, lower level managers will always know much more about their spheres of activities than will higher officials. The net effect is that the centralized command management system, so well suited to the context of omniscient upper management, becomes more and more cumbersome and eventually becomes a major impediment to organizational effort.

Market Control

A widespread response is for organizations to adopt a decentralized, market-based approach to managerial arrangements. This is accomplished by rearranging the enterprise into many small, separate, widespread but related organizational subunits. These units then trade among themselves and with their external markets as if they were independent, autonomous entities. The organization is transformed into a sort of a quasi-independent, miniature free-market economy featuring free-wheeling economic subunits.

The information requirements for operating in this mode are quite different than those of the command organization. The major operating aim for each subunit is to maximize the profits of its own activity center. The enforcement rules here are designed to encourage each manager to increase profits as much as possible in his or her sphere of responsibility. Economic performance, not obedience to orders, is paramount.

This creates new demands on the management accounting system for information about the economic performance of each autonomous subunit. Management accounting and control systems shift from budgets full of highly detailed information to reports that focus on general profitability indicators such as return on investment and residual income. Reports provide a kind of market performance information in that profits are seen to measure success in the marketplace.

With each subunit vigorously pursuing its own profit, however, the various parts of the organization may work against the common organization purpose. Goal-incongruent behavior might prevail. Goal incongruence exists when the actions taken by individual managers that are in their own best interests, as far as subunit profit maximization is concerned, are not in the best interests of the overall firm. As a result, the organization might even fly apart. Some mechanism is needed to hold the separate pieces together.

The answer, according to the economist, lies in market mechanisms. External market prices and internal transfer prices provide the necessary information with which to calculate profitability, that is to say, economic performance. And need for external and internal prices places new demands on the management accounting and control departments.

Regardless of the actual external price paid, the information used for internal reporting must be based on solid, longer term market prices, not on distress prices. Where available, internal transfer prices should be based on external prices for the same goods and services. Even when these are not available, or seem inappropriate, they can be simulated. One way is to rely on engineering estimates of the cost structure of a hypothetical producer of the same product. Another way is to approximate them with the aid of mathematical programming techniques.

Such market-based information is of great value. It reveals to upper managers those component managers who are capable of prospering under competitive market conditions. By the same process the less fit managers are exposed. The invisible hand of the marketplace reaches in and disciplines the managers throughout the organization in a marvelously efficient manner.

It is important to recognize that the economist's belief in the efficacy of the market to coordinate and control individuals in society stems from Herbert Spencer's (1820–1903) evolutionary, utilitarian, and individualistic social philosophy (long since out of favor with social theorists) built on positivist scientific assumptions. For Spencer, each individual was "blessed with an automatic, self-regulating mechanism which operated so that the pursuit of self-interest and private wants would result in the greatest satisfaction of the wants of all" (Parsons, 1937, p. 4). Society would evolve until it reached the final state where each individual (free from ignorance, superstition, and fear) would stand unfettered by state or church and act "rationally." All nonrational or nonutilitarian aspects of existence were pared away in Spencer's scheme. Utilitarian economic action explained all.

In sum, for the economist, the nature of the information available to top management determines the choice of either a command or a market organization. When omniscient information is available a command structure is appropriate. When this is not the case, a market system is required where real or quasi-market prices replace perfect information. Management accounting and control systems vary depending on which of these arrangements is adopted. Importantly, neither form is perfect. Each presents unique problems for management and for management accounting. In reality, many if not most of our large, complex firms employ both types, adopting command control for some parts and market control for others.

5.3 The Metaphor of the System

The metaphor of the system has always been attractive for those who deal with issues of management control. The notion of the system, by definition, suggests an idea of order, of coordination, of efficiency. These are all concepts which are difficult to resist.[3] This is why, at least since Taylor, organizations have been seen as "machines," "organisms" or "cybernetic systems." These views all show an inner belief in order. Management accounting and controls are thus there to ensure that an organization and its members all work towards a certain stable order. Stability rather than change is the core objective of these theories.

In this chapter we will explore various models of controls which seek to serve a given notion of "organization as system." This can take the form of a machine, and therefore we will have mechanistic controls; it could be seen as an organism and then we will be talking of organic controls; or it could be seen as a thermostatic system, which tends to self-regulate and thus leads to stability, and we will then have cybernetic forms of control.

5.3.1 Mechanistic and Organic Controls

This framework stems from a milestone study by two Scottish organizational sociologists whose work caused so much excitement that senior civil servants had them put on a series of seminars around Britain for upper-echelon executives of industrial organizations (Burns and Stalker, 1961). The hopes were that the insights from their research would help British industry regain its competitive edge, boost exports, and ameliorate the critical balance of payments conundrum faced by the UK.

The researchers built their framework using a biological metaphor. As they saw it, there were two *species* of firms. One type, living in a stable environment, reproduced its social technology in a mechanical way, just as a machine faithfully repeats its motions and functions. The other species, facing shifting conditions in its environment, constantly adjusted its administrative mechanisms just as some species change their shape, color, and physiology to suit their changing habitat. Adaptation, evolution, and survival are key concerns.

The insect hive or nest provides the root metaphor for the mechanistic firm. In an ant nest, for example, each ant is born with a distinct role, which it carries out automatically during its lifetime. Some are programmed to gather food and haul it back to the anthill. Some farm fungi and raise aphids as livestock. Some act as guards and attack any potential enemies. Some do the construction and housekeeping. And some look after the breeding and the babies. These roles are programmed into the ant's genes and are mechanically reproduced generation after generation. There is no question that each ant will faithfully carry out its instructions. The ant is a social creature in the extreme and a solitary ant on its own, lost and far from the nest, cannot survive. The social order of the nest is identical today to that of its ancestors millions of years ago.

The herd provides the root metaphor for the organic firm. The great caribou herds of North America exist by migrating with the seasons in search of food. Predators and weather patterns are its greatest enemies. Some fall prey to wolves, others drown while crossing swift-running rivers, and still others die of starvation or insect bites. Males compete with each other, literally head to head, for mating rights, with the losers deferring until the next rutting season. The herd is an organic unity and social roles—leader, sentinel, protector, and breeder—are passed around and exchanged as the need arises. It is survival of the fittest all the way.

The researchers paid particular attention to the relationship between a firm's external circumstances and its *social technology*, as they aptly labeled its management systems. External circumstances refer to markets served, production techniques developed, and scientific knowledge available. Social technology pertains to the flow of formal authority, lines of communication, division of tasks, arrangements for coordination of effort across the organization, and the required planning and control systems. Social technology, they concluded, is determined largely by external circumstances.

Mechanistic Control

As evidence for this conclusion the researchers observed that some of the firms they studied operated in relatively stable environments. These had a well-defined social technology. They divided tasks and problems into distinct slots. They defined precise duties for each function. They allocated power unambiguously amongst managers. They relied heavily on vertical hierarchical arrangements. They coordinated the entire operation from the top, the only place where overall knowledge of the firm resided. Their management systems worked like a machine, constantly repeating the same motions and producing the same effects. The researchers labeled these kinds of management systems *mechanistic*.

The archetype of the mechanistic organization was a firm that produced and marketed viscose rayon filament yarn. The efficient production of rayon called for a highly predictable, precise and explicit production program. The requirements and tolerances for each stage of the production program were set down in a book called the factory bible. Each department had a copy of the bible and used it each day to control part of the program.

The management system was also devised to keep production conditions stable. Each position in the hierarchy was specialized in terms of clearly defined parameters for authority, technique, and information requirements. No one could act outside the defined limits of their position. Reports, including expected and actual performance, were produced for every position and elaborately recorded in logbooks. All departures from stable conditions were immediately reported upward. Managers throughout the hierarchy made decisions within a tightly controlled framework of familiar program expectations.

The researchers also reported that the firm had a distinctly *authoritarian* character. Superiors issued firm commands, which subordinates obediently followed and took for granted as appropriate to the work situation. Authoritarianism at work, however, did not interfere with the relations off the job; the same people interacted within friendly social activities during which all were treated as equals and peers. The stable program conditions needed to manufacture rayon called for a mechanistic, authoritarian social order which all accepted as necessary and appropriate in the plant, but not away from work.

Organic Control

Other firms, in contrast, existing in relatively more fluid environments had a quite different social technology, which the researchers labeled *organic*. Scientific knowledge moved ahead relentlessly. Manufacturing equipment and techniques constantly improved. Tolerance levels for products became ever more demanding. New products perpetually emerged in their market sectors. These environments seemed in a state of perpetual motion.

This turbulence meant that problems and actions could not be defined precisely or assigned to distinct specialist departments. Individual tasks could not be performed without knowledge of the goals and tasks of the entire organization. So a manager's methods, duties, and power arrangements had to be continually negotiated and redefined. They accomplished this through frequent and intensive interaction with other managers throughout the organization. Lateral, rather than vertical, relationships dominated. Formal definitions of hierarchy melted. Complete knowledge of the organization was no longer ascribed to top management. Environment and social technology never settled down.

An electrical engineering firm, one of the research sites, typified the organic firm. Upper management deliberately avoided assigning specific functions to particular people and they were loath to define lines of responsibility. And the makeup of the top management group fluctuated with prevailing circumstances. Managers met regularly and interacted frequently on an informal basis whenever they needed to find out what was going on or to decide what to do about a problem. All employees regardless of official rank could consult with top management or anyone else in the firm about issues and problems. All managers had an equal voice in making decisions. This organic social technology, the researchers concluded, matched the firm's unstable program conditions.

The researchers had identified two distinct types of bureaucratization, mechanistic and organic. An essential part of upper management's job, they concluded, is to interpret correctly both the degree and kind of instability in the market circumstances, manufacturing technology, and scientific knowledge facing their firms. Only then are they in a position to match the appropriate social technology with the environment. They found many firms in the sample had failed to make this analysis; consequently their form of bureaucracy proved inappropriate and ineffective.

In some instances, firms had successfully utilized the mechanistic form but had not noticed that their external circumstances had shifted from stable to unstable program conditions. They struggled on with a mismatch of unstable program conditions and a mechanistic social technology. In other instances, upper management tried to utilize an organic social technology when their external circumstances were stable. One reason was that managers had come from firms where organic arrangements worked well, so they blindly assumed they would work in their new firm. The organic type of bureaucracy including *matrix management* was trendy at the time, so consulting firms urged nearly all their clients to adopt the new fashion. And in some firms, even when the environmental–social technology mismatch had been correctly diagnosed, politics and careerism forestalled a realignment. A sinecure in a mechanistic firm can readily disappear in an organic firm.

Implications for Management Accounting and Control

This work holds special interest for our purposes because it also theorized about the appropriate type of accounting and control system for each of the mechanistic and organic types of firms. In mechanistic firms, operating in a stable environment, overall knowledge is available only at the top of the hierarchy, resulting in a simple but forceful management control system. In this, the model clearly resembles the command model of control that we saw earlier in the chapter. Superiors govern operations and work behavior by issuing strong, clear commands. Unilateral instructions flow downward and become more explicit with each successive layer of bureaucracy. Upward-flowing information, in contrast, is successively filtered out on its way to the top. As this process continues it loses its impact, accuracy, and force. This unilateral, autocratic style of control is uniquely suited to the mechanistic management system. These ideas are depicted in Figure 5.2.

In organic systems, by contrast, the management control pattern is remarkably different. All-encompassing information is no longer available at the top and often critical knowledge exists only at the tentacles of the firm. So managers seek out and interpret for themselves the information needed to perform their part of the overall task. Much back-and-forth exchange of control information ensues. Communication patterns resemble lateral consultation more than vertical command. These systems seem almost to be self-designing.

In sum, external circumstances that shape management systems also influence the shape of the appropriate accounting and control systems. The organization of the accounting department, as well as the form of the system itself, should be consistent with the overall organizational design. In centralized mechanistic firms the management accounting and control function should be centralized and unilateral. In decentralized organic firms, horizontal flows of control information should be featured. A great deal more participation and discussion with line managers is required at all levels; and decentralization of responsibility to management accounting offices down the line is a necessary aspect of successful design in organic systems. Accounting and control systems need to match both the external circumstances and the social technology.

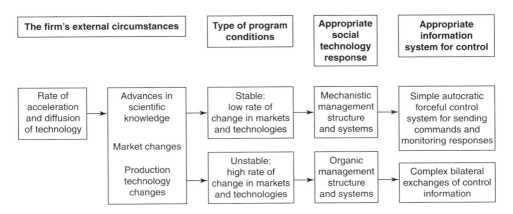

Figure 5.2 Mechanistic versus Organic Control

Before moving on to our next framework, it is important to note that most organizations include both forms of control. Other researchers, following up on the above study, noted that the type of program conditions could vary within organizations as well as between organizations.[4] Some parts of the same organization faced stable program conditions and a slow rate of acceleration in technology, while other parts faced rapidly changing program conditions and technology. Research and development departments, for example, tended to have the organic form, while production departments tended to follow the mechanistic one. In fact, purely mechanistic or organic firms are the exception rather than the rule. The important implication is that MACS should be different in form and use within the same organization, depending on the type of program conditions facing the particular component.

5.3.2 Cybernetic Controls

Our next model of context and control takes an *information processing* or *cybernetic* approach.[5] Researchers following this path focus on the decision-making and informational process aspects of organizational action, which they believe are a function of the limitations of human ability to process information. This approach aims to improve decision making by improving data collection and retrieval; building and managing useful data bases; grafting computer-based models onto human information processing and decision making; and getting online, real-time information into the decision process. The fundamental idea is to get the right amount of information into the decision-making process at the right time. But what, we might ask, determines the right amount and the right timing for information?

The answer from the information processing camp is *task uncertainty*. When task uncertainty is great, that is to say when the task is poorly understood, more information needs to be processed among decision makers to get the work done than when task uncertainty is low. Uncertainty is the difference between the amount of information already available for task execution and the amount of information required for the job. So it follows that organizational design and control is a function of the information-processing requirements necessary for task completion.

These information requirements in turn are seen as a function of three task characteristics: output diversity, input resources utilized, and the level of goal difficulty inherent in the task. The degree of diversity of output depends on the number of different products, services, and programs the organization produces and the number of markets, customers, and clients it serves. The variety of input resources utilized is measured mainly by the number of different work locations, the number of different specialists employed, and the number of different resource requirements (such as inventory and suppliers) needed to produce the outputs. The level of goal difficulty is a matter of the tolerances and quality needed in the inputs and outputs in order to meet efficiency and effectiveness expectations of customers and clients. The difference between the combined information requirements of outputs, inputs, and goal difficulty and the amount already possessed determines the level of task uncertainty.

Rules, Goals, and Hierarchies

Organizations can usually cope with task uncertainty by means of rules, goals, and hierarchies. Rules specify prescribed behavior in advance and become the organization's memory for handling routine work, thus eliminating the need for further communication between the subunits involved. New and unusual situations, however, are not covered in the rules. New information must be processed through the formal hierarchy. But hierarchies have a finite capacity to process information and after a point become overloaded. So instead of using the hierarchy, it becomes more effective to delegate decisions to the point of action and set superordinate goals (or targets) to cover interdependencies among the various subunits. Eventually rules, hierarchies, and goal setting are unable to cope with new demands for information processing. When they fail, organizations look for new strategies to cope with their information-processing needs.

Uncertainty-Reducing Strategies

When such a disparity exists between the amount of information that needs to be processed and the actual amount possessed, organizations respond by increasing the organization's capacity to process information, by decreasing the amount required, or by some combination of both. Two main strategic alternatives are available for decreasing and increasing the amount of information processing: slack resources and self-contained units.

Slack Resources

The first strategic move for reducing the quantity of information required involves creating slack resources. In place of information, slack or excess resources are used to alleviate immediate problems. Excessive inventory levels, long delivery times, extra machine capacity, overtime, and staff departments are examples of areas where slack is created rather than increasing the amount of information processed. Slack acts like a sponge to absorb information.

Self-Contained Units

The other strategy to counter insufficient information processing is to create self-contained tasks. These could take the form of a shift from an interlocking responsibility for all products to responsibility for a segment only of the organization's total products. Airplane manufacturing firms, for example, have two main choices in their organizational arrangements. The first is to allocate responsibility to product engineers, design technicians, process engineers, fabricating, assembly, and test units, and so on, with each unit having responsibility for the entire aircraft. The second choice is to organize around self-contained units by airplane section such as a wing or the tail.

The creation of self-contained units reduces the amount of information processing needed in two ways. First, it reduces output diversity. Each self-contained unit deals only with *one* body section, whereas the functional response would require each unit to deal with *all* body sections. Second, the creation of self-contained units reduces specialization. Rather than sharing process engineering across all aircraft section units, the engineers in each unit would be involved in process engineering as well as product design and quality engineering. This reduces the need for information processing *across* functional departments.

Vertical Information Processing

Two major strategies also exist for *increasing* an organization's capacity to process information. The first involves investing in vertical information systems. It is advantageous to develop new annual operating plans and budgets, rather than making incremental changes to the old ones, when, for example, uncertainty levels become intolerable. This entails collecting information and new plans at appropriate times and places instead of overloading the organizational hierarchy by forcing it to cope with a vast number of budget exceptions.

New Lateral Relations

The second strategy for increasing the capacity to process information involves the selective creation of new lateral relations. This move lowers the level of decision making to the point where the information is located, instead of transmitting it to high echelons where the decision is then made. This strategy decentralizes decision making; but it does so without calling into existence new self-contained groups.

The creation of new lateral relations can be accomplished by several means. These include: direct contact between those who share a problem; establishment of new liaison positions, such as project or product administrations, to manage interdepartmental contacts; formation of task forces, such as product or project teams; or in the extreme case employment of dual reporting relations and matrix organizational structures.

New lateral relations, however, are not a free good. They lead to an increase in the time managers must devote to the processing of horizontal information. This cost in time can be offset by moving decisions to the level where the information is located, rather than to a center high up in the organization. This has the added advantage of guaranteeing all relevant information is included in the decision processes. The result should be sounder decisions.

It is important to emphasize that these moves are not called for because of incompetent management but because the information processing and computational capacity is insufficient to deal with the complex and interdependent coordination requirements of an organization. This model of information and organizational design is summarized in Figure 5.3.

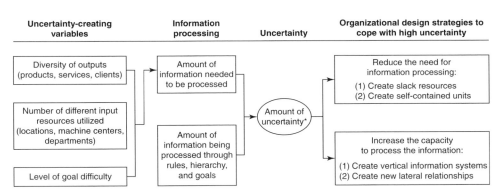

Uncertainty-creating variables	Information processing	Uncertainty	Organizational design strategies to cope with high uncertainty

*The amount of uncertainty is the difference between the amount of information needed to be processed and the amount actually processed.

Figure 5.3   An Information Processing Model

A Case History

The case history of a firm that produced different assembled mechanical devices for the aircraft industry lends vividness to this theory.

Work in this firm ranged from acquisition of raw materials to forging and stamping, to machining and the assembly of units in an orderly fashion. A conventional type of functional organizational structure was employed. Costs were under control; growth was adequate; and profits were good.

Despite these favorable conditions, management were dissatisfied with the prevailing state of affairs. Their impression was that their time was spent in dealing with short-term problems, "fighting fires," to the neglect of longer run tooling and capital investment programs. Of course, the lack of attention to longer-run problems eventually fed more fuel to the short-term "fires."

In due time a management task force was formed to study the problem. The task force produced an historical analysis of the firm's development. Members of the task force were surprised when they documented the changes that had taken place in the previous decade. The product line had doubled. The number of individual parts produced had increased by more than half, as had retooling. The number of machining and assembly stations had expanded. Quality specifications and tolerance limits had risen significantly. The production department had acquired a new expertise in dealing with exotic metals, and in order to keep up with expanding volume the number of shifts had increased from one to three. The firm had increasingly met delivery dates, while at the same time reducing inventory levels. Remarkably, until formation of the task force, the magnitude of these changes had remained almost unnoticed; but the information processed had not kept pace with production (Galbraith, 1973, pp. 67–8).

Viewed over a suitable time period, the firm had experienced substantial changes in product diversity and volume, the number of parts produced, and the requirements for retooling. Output diversity had increased significantly. Almost simultaneously, the number of input resources also increased, as witnessed by the expansion in the number of machining and assembly stations. At the same time, the goal levels required for quality, tolerance, delivery, and new metal technology had risen sharply. These changes in output diversity, input resources, and difficulty in maintaining the new goals meant that the amount of information in need of processing had grown by leaps and bounds. The result had been a large increase in uncertainty.

Once the problem had been diagnosed, management moved rapidly. They selected two of the prescribed strategic responses. First, they created more self-contained units, such as separate departments to concentrate on new products and processes. Second, they formed liaison units, including both line and staff people to handle the multifunction interdependence at low levels in the organization. In the model's terms, they brought into existence new self-contained units, and they created new lateral arrangements. These strategic alignments ameliorated the immediate problems, and management was able to concentrate on the long-run situation.

A major strength of the information processing model is its ability to frame the problem in terms of a repertoire of responses. So instead of redefining authority, responsibility, and accountability every time a storm of uncertainty passes through the environment, the problem can be resolved by judicious selection from a repertoire of strategies until the storm passes. This would avoid a series of substantial realignments from mechanistic to organic or from a command to a market structure, a phenomenon we see often—perhaps too often, many argue—in our organizations.

The case studies in Chapter 2 also illustrate some of the ideas in the cybernetic model. As Wedgwood grew, the rules, supervisory networks, and quality goals were no longer sufficient. In consequence, Wedgwood invented a vertical information system for highly detailed cost reporting, including accurate allocations of general and fixed costs. He also created self-contained units for each of the major phases of production and materials management. Interestingly the same kind of arguments could apply to the Society of Jesus, which faced similar information processing problems during its incredibly quick spread across the world, and managed them in a similar fashion.

Empire Glass headquarters relied on a highly detailed vertical information system in the form of specific plans and detailed budgets, and set up the plants as self-contained units. Given the maturity of the glass industry, the firm could ill afford slack resources. Nor did it need new lateral arrangements because both the sales organization and the plants had an important and shared stake in the form of a substantial bonus in sales, quality, and delivery targets. In the Johnson & Johnson situation, operations featured nearly 160 self-contained subsidiaries and intensive vertical information systems (the strategic business plan and the annual profit budget). All three companies judiciously selected from the model's repertoire of strategies to cope effectively with their information processing requirements.

5.4 Relating Theories to Empirical Observations

In this chapter we have introduced the idea that organizational structure and management systems might vary according to the type of environmental conditions faced, the availability or lack of information, the degree of uncertainty prevailing, and an organization's historical evolution. The contribution to control system design of this way of thinking is different from approaching management accounting and control as a problem of technical design. Rather it seeks a congruence in the characteristics of these systems with those of the organizational setting including characteristics such as environment, technology, available knowledge, type of work, uncertainty, and the state of the dominant crisis of its dialectic tension. The general thesis is that factors that shape context and organizational structure may also account for important differences in our MACS.

Conceptual apparatuses which link impersonal forces with organizational processes would seem to hold great potential for explaining some of the major variations we see in the design and use of MACS. When we see how these systems can be rearranged in various settings so that they are no longer random we may develop a clearer notion of how system designers should proceed. This proposition is demonstrated next in some detail by using the frameworks in this chapter to analyze two case studies of organizational design and control: a national consumer finance company and a high-technology computer company.

5.4.1 Transamerica Finance Company

Our first case situation is relatively straightforward. It concerns the management control system at Transamerica Finance Company (TFC), a large consumer finance company.[6]

Case Information

Transamerica Finance Company was one of the largest finance companies in the US, with hundreds of branch offices across the country. Its primary business was the acceptance of conditional sales contracts from customers who had purchased consumer goods. Usually customers could not get loans from chartered banks and so turned to commercial loan companies for finances. The company paid the retailer while the customer paid TFC in monthly instalments. It operated nationally and had several regional offices located in major cities. Branch offices were located in most cities and towns including downtown areas and suburb shopping centers. The branch offices varied in size from six to 50 personnel depending on the market served and the amount of money loaned. Branch offices received money for loans from the Central Office located in a large city in the center of the nation and at the end of each working day all branch bank accounts were closed out to a central office bank account. Branches, however, reported through one of 15 district offices to the central office.

The corporate central office functioned as the hub for strategy, policy-making and administrative systems. Central office established specific policies and procedures regarding every aspect of branch operations, including loans, collections, record-keeping, branch control and reporting methods, personnel policies, and detailed job descriptions for all branch positions and office administration procedures. These standard operating procedures, designed to ensure consistent branch operations across the nation, were contained in procedures manuals located in each branch. They emphasized that branch managers should seek new profitable accounts aggressively, make sure payments were received on time, and run a neat, tidy, and efficient office with all records and reports continually up to date.

On the third working day of the month each branch submitted to the central office, as well as to its district office, a report for the previous month. The report contained the essential statistics about branch operations, including the number and dollar value of all loans, details of collections, branch expenses by line item category, and a detailed schedule that stressed overdue accounts and delinquency rates. These reports were sent to the central office for computer analysis of branch operations including a multiple regression analysis, which analyzed office expenses and personnel levels according to the number of branch transactions for the month. The computer also compiled this information into a district report, which compared all branches in the district and ranked branch performance for each district. These reports were provided to each branch so they could compare themselves with other branches in their district. Branch managers, very sensitive about their relative performance, eagerly awaited this report each month. Interestingly, budgets and long-range plans were noticeable by their absence.

The district managers closely monitored the monthly reports, scrutinizing them for anything that appeared out of line, especially new loans and accounts that were more than 30 days overdue. If a branch seemed out of line, the district manager and a staff member paid a quick visit to get to the bottom of the problem; and, if warranted, a staff expert was assigned to the branch until performance reached a satisfactory level. In addition, each district manager conducted a thorough, onhand inspection of each branch at least once a year. During the visits, which were made on a surprise basis, the district manager and his staff performed a comprehensive audit of all loan and collection records as well as inspection of employee performance evaluation and pay rates. At the end of this visit the district manager conducted the annual performance evaluation review of the branch and assistant managers. The review included setting objectives for the next year regarding any aspect of branch operations needing attention.

More recently, TFC had installed an online computer system, which connected each branch to a large computer at the central office. Branch transactions were entered each day, and a summary of operations by branch, district, and for the entire company was submitted early the next morning to the president. Branch managers could also call for an update on their branch operations for the month to date.

Branch managers operated their branches with some autonomy, hiring and training their own staff personnel and taking full responsibility for loans, collections, and expenses. They could earn an additional 30% of their annual salary in the form of a bonus based on branch performance. In addition, company-wide contests were a regular feature, where the best-performing managers won, say, a free trip for two to Europe. Branch managers were highly satisfied with these arrangements including the controls and reports, and particularly the autonomy and responsibility that they perceived with the job.

Analysis

At first blush, the MACS at TFC seems excessively comprehensive. Standard operating procedures cover all aspects of branch operations. Every nook and cranny is monitored, reported on, and scrutinized on the spot. Surprise visits and spot checks are the order of the day and branch performance is reported daily to the president's office. It would seem to be a very oppressive and punitive control system.

Analysis of TFC's accounting information and control systems with the models earlier in this chapter, however, yields a different perspective. In terms of the mechanistic and organic control model, it is apparent that TFC has a well-defined social technology. Tasks are divided into distinct slots. Precise duties are defined for each branch position. Power and authority arrangements are unambiguously allocated to corporate, district, and branch managers. Heavy reliance is placed on vertical hierarchic arrangements, and operations are coordinated from the top, the only place where overall knowledge of the firm resides. The simple but forceful management control system reinforces this pattern. Instructions flow downward through the hierarchy, becoming more explicit at each successive layer in a unilateral and autocratic control style. Transamerica Finance Company seems almost the archetypical mechanistic firm.

This social technology, nevertheless, is well suited to the firm's circumstances. Markets are well defined. Procedures for operating a branch are well understood. Scientific knowledge is minimal. With the exception of the short-term money market, the environment is stable. Transamerica Finance Company, like most consumer financial companies, had a precarious financial structure consisting mainly of short-term money market notes, some long-term debt, and very little equity. It turns a profit on the margin between short-term borrowings and interest rates charged to customers. Consequently, it is absolutely essential that the branches are tightly controlled and responsive to calling in or expanding loans depending upon short-term fluctuations in the money market. TFC's mechanistic social technology is well matched to its operating environment.

According to the command–market model of uncertainty and control systems, TFC mirrors the centralized prototype. Top management has at its disposal, at a low cost, information about nearly everything happening anywhere in the organization. Centralized coordination is achieved through specific and detailed operating rules contained in the standard operating procedures. These are complemented by enforcement rules which detect and report violations from the procedures to upper echelons. The branches are monitored closely, and visits by district managers follow quickly if anything untoward is detected. So uncertainty is low; in fact, it cannot be tolerated because of the precarious capitalization. The centralized management system fits the top management environment perfectly.

Analysis of the TFC situation using the ideas in the information processing model of control confirms the above conclusions. Output diversity is low, goals are reasonably achievable, rules are in abundance, and reporting channels are more than adequate to handle information processing requirements. The branch offices are self-contained and highly homogeneous. Consequently, the amount of information to be processed is relatively small and most if not all is available to top management. Formal control information is simple, low in quantity, and handled readily with a straightforward but forceful vertical information system. Transamerica Finance Company has made an appropriate response to its uncertainty-creating variables.

Finally, the TFC case can also be linked to the dialectical model that we saw in Chapter 4. Sound administrative practices provide close and tight control over every activity at the branches. The formal hierarchy is clear-cut, job responsibilities are unambiguous, and direction and authority prevail. The highly directive lean and mean management control system ensures that order and routine prevail, the necessary conditions for efficient operations in a highly competitive environment. The vitally needed direction and authority are institutionalized. Moreover, TFC has taken steps to fend off any autonomy crisis. Branch managers experience a great deal of freedom to run their operations according to the standard operating procedures while healthy performance bonuses and frequent interbranch competitions with exotic prizes keep branch managers from stagnating. Transamerica Finance Company's organization functions like a well-oiled machine.

5.4.2 Apollo Computers[7]

Our second case study traces the evolution of the organizational design and control through a corporate takeover and reorganization of Apollo Computers (AC). With headquarters in Monterey, California, AC was a relatively small and successful company specializing in sophisticated computer applications. Its products included computers for advanced weaponry and space explorations; microprocessors for trains, trucks, and ships; and integrated data base management systems. Apollo Computers also conducted highly sophisticated research in sundry areas like bubble memory chips, DNA engineering and molecular rectifiers, and crystal lattice computers. At the time of the takeover, sales had grown to nearly $300 million annually from $10 million in 1978.

Case Information

Apollo Computers' organization structure before the takeover was essentially functional. Different executives were assigned responsibility for R&D, engineering, manufacturing, marketing, and finance. Interfunctional problems and issues went up the hierarchy for resolution and decisions were passed down. Top management attempted to coordinate the various functions from on high. Recently these arrangements seemed to be working less than optimally. Decisions on differences of opinions at lower levels moved very slowly up and down the vertical hierarchy. Research and development efforts were inefficiently allocated among product lines. Attractive market opportunities were lost when other companies, quicker off the mark, jumped in to steal business from under AC's nose.

The manager of organizational development had already begun to identify these problems. She concluded that the present organizational design was ill suited for exploiting new product opportunities. The different functional people simply were not working together. Many reasons were suggested for this. The managers did not know who held the responsibility and authority to develop new products. Upper management did not pay enough attention to this activity. Delays occurred as information traveled up and down the proper functional channels. R&D efforts appeared to be disproportionately allocated among product lines due to the personal influence of a few product specialists. Further, squabbles seemed continually to erupt among the functional managers over designs and production schedules. These disputes had to be sent up the line to top management and so were delayed, postponed, or even left unresolved.

These symptoms underlined the difficulties encountered by the various functional groups as they wrestled with new product development. In a few instances, however, engineers, marketing managers, and manufacturing personnel had formed informal work groups and successfully worked out common problems for specific products. As well, a partial division of executive responsibilities by product groups had been established as functional jurisdictions began to melt. Further, the controller had instituted monthly product line profit and loss statements and a few small, informal groups, composed of engineers, plant people, and marketers had sprung up to work out common problems. These people participated in company rest and recreation activities such as aerobic sessions, computer chess competitions, and "Cal-Mex" cooking seminars. During these nonwork get-togethers informal groups discussed specific product problems.

Analysis

Apollo Computers' situation can be understood using the frameworks described in this chapter. According to the mechanistic–organic model, AC operated in an unstable environment. There is ample evidence for this conclusion. Engineering technology changed rapidly. Products required a high degree of engineering competence. Apollo Computers custom-manufactured products according to the needs and whims of customers. And the market for the products had grown rapidly. Program conditions were characterized by a high rate of change in both markets and technologies.

Turning to AC's social technology, we see evidence that they were employing a mechanistic management structure. The organization was essentially functional with different executives assigned responsibility for manufacturing, marketing, engineering, and finance. Vertical hierarchical arrangements predominated for issuing orders. Conflicts went up the hierarchy for resolution and decisions were passed down. Top management attempted to coordinate the various functional units from on high. The top management structure, it would appear, was mechanistic.

According to the model, AC had a serious mismatch in that a mechanistic structure does not suit an unstable environment. In fact, signs of conflict had begun to appear as continued squabbles occurred between departments. Moreover, the informal social technology was moving towards more organic arrangements. Top management had begun to sense that the degree and kind of instability in markets and scientific technology facing the firm was not well served by its social technology.

The command–market model leads us to a similar conclusion. Top management seemed to lack information about the state of affairs, events, and problems at lower levels and at the boundaries of the organization. Enough information was not being transmitted upwards to top management. Messages travelling through the transmission channels bogged down.

As a result, operating rules issued by top management were often inappropriate, and their efforts to coordinate the complex flow of products through the functional departments to customers were ineffective. The use of the vertical channels, and attempts to follow higher level plans, meant delays which cost market opportunities. The centralized style of management arrangements was inappropriate to the amount of information available at the upper strata of the organization and top management's ability to assimilate it.

Next, the cybernetic model hinges on the difference between the amount of information required for processing relative to the amount already processed by the organization. The amount required is a composite of output diversity, input resources utilized, and the difficulty of the level of performance required. For AC's mix of activities it seems clear that the level of both output diversity and input resources utilized was high. The highly technical nature of the product lines bears witness to this conclusion. A high degree of engineering competence was required for most products.

According to the cybernetic model, the amount of information required for processing was great, if not vast. Although we have no direct documentation of the amount of information already processed by the organization, several factors indicate that it was much lower than required. Coordination of the functional departments, particularly on new product development, was not adequate. A comprehensive plan did not exist. A sense that there was a need for more communication had led to financial information being produced relating to the product line. All this suggests that a strategic organizational response was badly needed in order to close the gap between the amount of information required and the amount available.

From the perspective of the model, AC had experienced a remarkable change in its uncertainty-creating variables over the past decade. Products, services, and customers had become highly diverse. The number of departments, offices, and manufacturing centers had multiplied many times over. And the technical tolerance and quality levels for products had risen significantly. In consequence, the traditional means of handling information through rules, hierarchy, and budget targets could no longer keep up with the amount of information processing required to cope with the new uncertainty level.

Finally, this case can be easily linked to the historical–dialectical framework as it seems clear that AC was at the end of a successful and prolonged direction phase but now faced an autonomy crisis of severe proportions. The company had grown in complexity and diversity. Lower echelon employees felt restricted by a cumbersome, centralized hierarchy. They knew much more about the technology, markets, and recent scientific developments of the information technology market than did the bureaucrats at the top. The functional hierarchy, the booster engine for direction during the 1980s, was now sputtering. Within its historical dialectic, the forces of direction and leadership had severely repressed those of autonomy and creativity. A reversal seemed urgently needed if AC was to survive its autonomy crisis.

More Case Information

At this critical juncture in its history, an event occurred that may well have saved AC from stagnation and even demise. The principal owner, who had amassed a tidy fortune from AC's public offering of common shares and its stock option program, had joined an awareness cult based on the Kegon School of Buddhism, which stressed the Buddhahood of all sentient beings, the identity of nirvana and samsara, and the wisdom and compassion of the bodhisattvas. At forty-four years of age he wanted to devote the rest of his life to finding his inner spirituality and working for the green earth movement.

At the same time, three former middle-level managers of Dionysus Corporation (DC), one of the world's largest computer companies, had cashed in their stock options, taken the company's early retirement payoff, pooled their personal assets, and bought a controlling interest in AC. They believed that with proper management skills and AC's superb technical expertise, they could get the company back on track and eventually even challenge some of the world's computer giants.

The new owners moved swiftly to reorganize the company along lines similar to Dionysus. They instituted a new profit-centered organization featuring decentralized profit-responsible product groups. These groups were assisted by HQ staff departments such as R&D, engineering, software, sales, and finance. Several product departments were established within each product group. Each product group was headed by one manager in charge of marketing, engineering, and production units for his or her assigned products. Their main responsibility was to coordinate all activities of their product lines, including the HQ sales force, R&D, and engineering departments, which were not under their command. Their mandate was to assure that the products were profitable.

Within the product group, the marketing unit worked on marketing strategy, pricing, contacting customers on special requests and factory problems, promotion, and new product development. The production unit was responsible for efficient manufacturing, meeting delivery dates, and production costs. The engineering unit designed new products, devised new production processes, and worked on special customer requests. A production control manager looked after scheduling of work, supervised expediting, shipping and delivery, inventory, and purchasing. The product group managers, however, were the kingpins of the new organizational arrangements.

More Analysis

These changes correspond closely to the prescriptions of our theoretical models. They would, for example, prescribe a shift to organic management structures to suit the high rate of change in the external circumstances of their scientific knowledge, markets, and in all likelihood, their production technology. This seems to mirror the actual events. Powers and duties shifted from functional and vertical responsibility to product and lateral accountability. The product department managers became responsible for managing the lateral relationships involved in the design, marketing, production, and selling of the products assigned to them.

So they had to have considerable understanding of the various overall goals and tasks of the entire AC organization. Matters such as R&D and the sales force, however, were not under their authority. Duties and powers in these areas would be in a state of continual negotiation and flux. Top management was no longer in a position to know everything about the various product centers. The new management structure had shifted from a mechanistic to an organic social technology.

We also see that AC no longer attempted to coordinate its complex flow of products from the top of the hierarchy by issuing clear, firm commands based upon omniscient information and following up with punitive enforcement rules and sanctions. Rather, they reorganized around quasi-independent, miniature, free-market product groups—each with responsibility, if not full authority, for profitable survival in its own market sphere. A market structure replaced a command one.

In terms of our cybernetic model, the company previously seems to have experienced a gap between the amount of information required for processing and the amount available. The response followed two major strategies. First, AC created slack resources by some duplication of manufacturing resources and by investing in inside marketing personnel. Second, AC created self-contained units in the form of profit-responsible product departments. These two moves reduced the need for information processing.

At the same time, AC also increased its capacity to process information, The new product–profit responsibility required a horizontal accounting information system that provided information on financial performance for product groups. To effectively manage their new responsibilities, the product group managers needed to be involved in a significant amount of lateral communication, negotiation, and building of reliable relationships. They were required to manage the product flow from R&D through engineering, sales, manufacturing, delivery, customer service, and into the customer's plant.

The company, then, employed all four coping responses: creation of new self-contained units, employment of organizational slack, development of vertical information systems, and creation of new lateral relationships. The new organizational design seems better suited to the amount of information processing needed.

Finally, viewing the situation from the perspective of our historical–dialectical model, we see that the new owners overcame an autonomy crisis by putting into effect a decentralized organization structure anticipating an era of growth through delegation. Much greater responsibility was assigned to the product group managers. The new top executives, accustomed to the DC system of restraint from interfering in operating decisions, were more than willing to follow the path of management by exception based on periodic reports from the product groups and staff technical offices. With the dialectic tension resolved in favor of autonomy, they could concentrate on long-range planning and searching for new acquisitions that could be lined up beside the other decentralized product groups.

These moves proved to be the right formula for surmounting the autonomy crisis. Delegation of product group responsibility provided heightened motivation and creativity at lower levels. The product group managers eagerly took the bull by the horns and, taking full advantage of their greater authority and expanded mandates, responded rapidly to customers' requirements, penetrated larger markets, and developed new products. Another phase of growth and expansion was under way.

More Case History

Along with these changes came a new approach to MACS design and utilization. First, strategic planning was considered to be a live activity and was delegated to each of the product group managers. Each of these managers conducted a detailed assessment of their group's strengths and weaknesses as well as the risks and opportunities inherent in their selected product market spheres. They then prepared a qualitative report documenting the unit's competitive strategy for the next five-year period. The report included a very general balance sheet, income statement, and cashflow estimate for the next five years. This report was reviewed by a select committee of top-level executives. They reviewed it closely, especially its basic assumptions, and either approved it or asked the product group manager to take part in a face-to-face meeting where the plan would be reviewed in detail. These usually proved to be intensive and gruelling meetings and became known as hell sessions. The main focus was on opportunities that might be missed. The meeting ended when the plan was given final approval.

Each product group also prepared budgeted financial statements for the coming year. Upper management normally looked for an increase in the sales and profit targets of 40% to 60% because the computer and information technology industry was growing at this rate. Plans that came in below these levels were usually bumped up by top management to the required level. Actual performance compared to budget was reviewed monthly by upper management and each product group manager was given a formal face-to-face review every three months.

These new arrangements were received enthusiastically by the product group managers and their employees. Several managers developed their own internal operational control systems including profit–volume–cost information systems, with standards and actual outcomes to help them identify specific variances from a plan and to track down the reasons for them. Each department within the group participated in developing these data. These self-designed systems helped product group managers focus their attention and efforts on developing new products, seeking new customers, servicing old customers better, improving marketing efforts, or improving manufacturing processes. The field units were free to run their own show.

The relationship between bonuses and promotions to budget performance was deliberately left ambiguous because the industry could unexpectedly surge or go flat. The general feeling was that short-run profits were important. Furthermore, product group managers knew full well that the new owners' performance in relation to their corporate plan was being constantly monitored by stock market analysts in Los Angeles and San Diego. They also knew they were expected to take any steps necessary to meet the profit objective. During periods when they were below plan, there was considerable pressure to increase sales efforts, meet with R&D to develop new products, and to reduce asset levels.

The philosophy of control that pervaded DC's global operations had been transferred to ACs. The main feature was complete decentralization of profit responsibility but with tough built-in targets. This way profit center managers were limited in the degrees of freedom available for building in organizational slack in operating budgets. And the pressure was kept on them for growth. The philosophy held that this was an excellent way for managers to develop business acumen. Those that did were readily identified and rewarded; those that did not were quickly relegated to technical jobs or dismissed.

Further Analysis

The characteristics of the new MACS follow closely the prescriptions for firms operating in relatively unstable circumstances. Much critical environmental information about customers, technology, and markets is known only by the product group managers at the firm's lower levels. The new MACS highlights the effectiveness of the flow of product through the organization to the customer. So lateral consultation and exchange of information, especially about products and product performance, ensued. An important part of these exchanges took place during the formulation of the profit budget and later when profit performance was reported against plan.

Turning to the command–market model, since AC operated under highly uncertain circumstances it was best served by decentralized managerial arrangements which featured a free-market economy. The reason for this is that knowledge of environmental conditions, market prices, and customer idiosyncrasies were in the hands of the product group managers at the tentacles of the organization, rather than with upper management. Product group managers were closer to customers so they could respond quickly and accurately to marketplace changes. Responsibility for the profit of a cluster of products was decentralized to a product group manager who had command over most of the resources and people involved in a cluster of product–market relationships. The sundry product-based, profit centers employed by AC were an attempt to create a miniature free-market economy.

The new operating rules for the product groups were general—maximize profits and long-run growth. These operating rules were backed up by strong enforcement rules. Top management met weekly to review the performance of each product group to pinpoint trouble spots. And product group managers were given a formal performance review every three months. The mandate called for profits *and* growth.

Actual profit and sales growth performance was constantly being evaluated against planned levels. These enforcement rules were designed to encourage product group managers to increase profits and sales as much as possible within their sphere of responsibility. Managers who did so would be recognized and appreciated. The new MACS, along with the new organizational decentralization and the revised operating and enforcement rules, conform closely to the theoretical prescriptions for organizations that operate in relatively uncertain environments.

From the perspective of the cybernetic model, the new organizational design helped considerably to reduce the need for information processing in two ways. First, it reduced substantially the amount of vertical information flowing to upper management. They now relied on short, standard, and general profit budget reports from the self-contained product groups to keep track of operations. Only the self-contained units processed the specific information they needed to manage their sphere of responsibility. Lateral information flows to and from other product groups were now minimized; they were limited to exchanging sales forecast information and other strictly business transactions. These new arrangements brought the amount of information processed in line with the amount required.

Finally, these new developments fit closely with prescriptions from the historical–dialectical model. Communication between upper management and the operating product groups was now infrequent. Upper management reviewed and approved the various strategic plans, and restrained themselves to management by exception using monthly reviews of actual versus planned profits. The product groups, as witnessed by events in the AC profit center, responded very positively to their newfound autonomy. AC seems well poised to enjoy a prolonged period of steady growth and progress.

But there is no doubt that the new MACS creates a good deal of tension in the organization. The motivation to meet short-run profit and sales targets is strong, as is the motivation for long-run growth. It is up to the autonomous units to figure out the appropriate (and often difficult) trade-off between the short- and the long-run. And while participation in target setting is widespread it is clear that top management have the prerogative of having the last word in this regard. For some, the ambiguous relation between rewards and short-run budget performance might be a worrisome aspect of the new management accounting and control information systems.

Some tension was required to make the new concept of product profit centers work. The regular review of performance provided the necessary motivational force; and participation in budget setting was widespread even though top management, with their broader view of the total scheme of things, was entitled to have the final say in setting budget levels. Delegation of profit responsibility without some way of providing motivation, without a means of monitoring results, and without a recourse to adjustment of inappropriate budgets, would seem to be both impractical and imprudent. Finally, research has indicated that formula-based reward systems are more appropriate to relatively certain operating conditions than to dynamic environments. And some ambiguity in rewards keeps people on their toes.[8] This macro-perspective does provide a broader picture and the models do seem capable of giving us new insights into problems of designing effective MACS.

5.4.3 Linking Back to the Case Studies

Let's return briefly to the case studies in Chapter 2 examining each in light of some of the frameworks in this chapter. At a first glance, the Society of Jesus may appear as a classical example of command control where bureaucracy rules the organization. The problem with this view is that the Order did not operate in a stable environment and its missions were always faced with the unknown. This is why market, organic and cybernetic forms of control may be most appropriate for an understanding of the case. Indeed the Order set up a series of independent units (the Colleges) which then were coordinated through accounting and accountability systems to guarantee goal congruence. The missionary nature of the Order required the organization structure to be flexible and become fit, with the diverse and changing environments with which the organization had to interact. Analogously the flow of information from the center to the periphery and vice versa allowed a system of cybernetic adjustments that guaranteed the persistence of the Society across centuries.

Wedgwood led the potbanks in both product and production technology and his competitive strategy was light years ahead of the competition. With the exception of the period of worldwide economic recession, Wedgwood's environment was relatively stable. Not surprisingly, then, Wedgwood operated a highly mechanistic social technology. Overall knowledge of the firm was available only to him. Strong, clear commands were issued verbally during his inspection tours and were written down in the potter's instructions. His control system was simple but forceful. Thus Wedgwood seems to be a prime example of the successful employment of a mechanistic social technology that was well suited to its relatively stable environmental circumstances.

Wedgwood also seems typify the command organization. Josiah Wedgwood had low-cost and remarkably efficient access to almost complete information about the sundry conditions prevalent throughout the firm. He operated with an extremely centralized and highly structured vertical hierarchy, which he used to coordinate and control the flow of products through the organization. He wrote and disseminated specific and detailed operating rules for every aspect of the operation including comportment on the job. He followed these up with enforcement systems, which detected and punished any violations of the operating rules. Wedgwood's centralized management system, a paradigm of the command organization, was logical, internally consistent and complete.

The glass products division (GPD) of Empire Glass can also be slotted into the various frameworks. It seems to be operating under stable environmental conditions in a mature market with a commodity-type product. Once the sales forecasts are analyzed, adjusted, and agreed, the plants are given their program for the coming year. These instructions become more explicit at each successive layer of the hierarchy. They are the specific and detailed operating rules which persuade the plants to execute their programs as per the detailed plan. These are the trademarks of successful mechanistic and command organizations.

In terms of its historical evaluation, the GPD seems to fit comfortably into the direction phase of the dialectic model. Cost accounting systems had been successfully introduced, including standard costs and comprehensive budgets. A formal hierarchy with clear-cut positions had been institutionalized. Order and routine reigned and fostered a climate of efficient growth. Large-volume vertical information systems along with self-contained units, including the glass plants and the various sales districts, seem more than capable of processing the requisite information. The mechanistic social technology was well suited to a long period of evolution through direction.

Finally, turning to Johnson & Johnson, we see an outstanding example of the market-based, decentralized organization preferred by most economists. Each of their 155 subsidiaries traded with the external markets as if they were independent, autonomous units. Any trading between subsidiaries was handled on the spot by the subsidiary managers on the basis of external market prices. The operating rules dictated that each subsidiary develop a prospector strategy paying particular attention to share of market and long-run profitability. The enforcement rules encouraged each subsidiary to increase these two measures as much as possible within their own product market spheres. The use of self-contained units and a highly interactive and intense vertical information system reinforced the market-based organizational design.

5.5 Summary and Conclusions

This chapter presented three frameworks for investigating management control issues and problems. The first model, relying on a biological metaphor, saw the problem of organizational survival as one of adapting social technologies to the changes taking place in the organization's environment. The next model relied on classical economic notions to develop two caricatures of control and coordination: command-based and market-based organizations. The third model built on the cybernetic view of organizations as information-processing entities and outlined different strategies for coping with the need to reduce uncertainty when information needs exceed the organization's available processing capabilities.

Each approach contains its own biases, strengths, and limitations. Moreover, they tend to ignore agency—that is the actions and decisions of key actors who play important roles in the survival and growth of organizations. So they put aside the actions of great leaders such as Gandhi, Churchill, Gorbachev and the likes of Sloan, Iacocca, and Welch. The role of human agency will be addressed in Chapters 11, which outlines a scheme that includes *both* structures and agency. For now, it has been sufficient to concentrate on organizational context and the problems of coordination and control from an organization-in-the-round perspective.

Endnotes

1. Arrow (1964, p. 3). Arrow explains his perspective this way: "My point of view is rationalistic and derives, with appropriate changes, from the logic of choice as it has been developed in the pure economic theory of prices and the mathematics of optimization."
2. See Schick, Gordon, and Haka (1990) for an excellent review and critique of the information overload phenomenon.
3. Hansen and Mouritsen (1999).
4. See Hall (1962) for a pioneering study along these lines.
5. This model is adapted from Galbraith's (1973, 1977) pioneering work. See also Amey (1979, 1986) for a detailed and technical application of cybernetics to MACS.
6. The name of the company is disguised. The case data were collected as part of a research study reported in Daft and Macintosh (1984), Macintosh (1985), and Macintosh and Daft (1987).
7. The name of the company is disguised.
8. See Stedry (1960) and Simons (1987).

Further Readings

You can usefully do some further readings in each of the areas below:

Market and command controls:

- Williamson, O. (1991) Comparative economic organization: the analysis of discrete structural alternatives. *Administrative Science Quarterly*, **36** (2), 269–96.

Mechanistic, organic and cybernetic controls:

- Otley, D. (1983) Concepts of control: the contribution of cybernetics and system theory to management control, in *New Perspectives in Management Control* (eds T. Lowe and J. Machin), Macmillan, London.

6

The Structure and Strategy of MACS

In this chapter:

6.1 Introduction

Most authorities on organizations agree that strategy formulation is currently the single most important task of top management. In fact, the strategic planning school of management proclaims that strategy and strategic planning are the keys to the governance and control of organizations, big and small, private and public. Strategy deals with both mission and governance. Mission reflects the major aims of the organization and the tasks to be performed to attain them. Governance is the means by which the organization is controlled and regulated. While strategy and the organization's structure dictate the appropriate type of control, MACS are used to enhance and influence the strategic planning process. The basic premise is that there are important links between environment, strategy, organization structure, and management control systems and that a congruent matching of these variables is essential to performance as depicted in Figure 6.1.

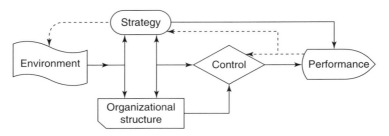

Figure 6.1   Environment, Strategy, and Control

The concept of strategy as a vital management process and its relationship with management control systems had been around in formalized form for at least a century. The interest in unraveling the vital strategy–management control system relationship has been an important topic for researchers since the late 1950s and early 1960s. Such studies included those of Burns and Stalker, Emery and Trist, and Woodward in the UK, Crozier in France, and Hofstede in The Netherlands. In the US, Chandler documented the important strategy, structure and management control systems connection in large US industrial companies in the early part of the twentieth century. These studies spawned a new organizational theory school that supplanted the classical principles of management school. While the latter had focused on key universal functions of management (plan, organize, staff, direct, and control), the former held that effective organizational control systems are contingent on key strategic variables. In the management accounting field, Anthony in his classic book, *Planning and Control Systems*, provided a framework and key concepts for understanding these relationships. Most recently, Norton and Kaplan have developed the idea of the Balanced Scorecard in order to link strategic visions to management control and performance measurement systems. From Anthony to Norton and Kaplan, it is now well established that important interrelationships exist amongst strategy, structure and control systems.

This chapter explores that relationship.[1] Its purpose is to bring together some findings and speculations about the reciprocal relationship between an organization's strategy and the design and use of its MACS.[2] To set the stage, we present a brief review of what is meant by the terms "strategy" and "strategic planning." Then we outline a framework that includes four distinct types of strategies along with the appropriate organizational structure and management control systems most appropriate to each strategy. We sketch out another conceptual scheme linking strategy and control based on the idea of product life cycle. Finally, the chapter speculates on the strategy–control relationship from the perspective of ideology in a critical social theory sense.

6.2 Strategy and Strategic Planning

Chapter 4 looked at some ways of thinking about how an organization's environment and its history affect its MACS. In Chapter 5 we illustrated how the metaphor of the organism has also been quite popular amongst management scholars. These frameworks imply that environmental and historical forces are out there beyond the organization's boundaries. This line of thought relies on a biological metaphor of survival: organisms must adapt to their environment or become extinct. We now want to revise this metaphor somewhat to argue that organizations "enact" their environment by way of strategic planning rather than simply adapting to it.

Enacting the Environment

Enactment, an important concept in the organizational behavioral literature, requires a little explaining.[3] In order to make sense out of the infinite set of variables and constantly changing events in the world in which we live, we must focus our attention on a small number of variables. So we bracket off a manageable subset for closer attention as a basis for action. Our actions, however, produce an ecological change in the environment, which appears to be in a continuous state of flux. In order to cope we again select a manageable subset, take action, produce more ecological change, and the process repeats. This ongoing process is called enactment.

An example may help. Two friends on vacation tour the same city but experience it in quite different ways. One seeks out and tours the museums, art galleries, and book stores and purchases, at a handsome price, a painting by a new artist. The other heads for the beaches, cafes, and discotheques and eventually starts a brawl that brings the police on the scene. For the arts fan, the environment appears to be civilized, calm, and lively; for the rambunctious fun lover, it seems pretentious, boisterous, and definitely action packed. Both initially faced the same circumstances but each enacted the environment—selected a subset, took action, and changed it—in a quite different way.

Organizations enact their environment in a similar way. Top executives select part of the environment for close attention and action. They describe which parts of the environment present opportunities to exploit, which parts to keep an eye on for possibilities, and which parts to avoid as dangerous. These considerations become the basis for the organization's strategic plan. Organizations choose and act on their environment and as they do so, as with our two tourists, they inevitably effect some change in it. Such choices are a result of the organization's strategy and its strategic planning process.

The enactment concept brings to the surface the fact that a strategy is very much a subjective enterprise. That is to say, a strategy is a human creation, even though in most of the management literature it is treated as an objective reality that exists outside the minds of the managers who produce it. This reification error, the process whereby human creations, such as social norms or marriage, are treated as entities created by nature or God with an existence independent of human minds, obfuscates the fact that strategy is a human creation.

The first two models in this chapter treat strategy as if it were an objective reality. Such reification permits us to analyze the strategy–control relationship from a convenient structural functionalist vantage point. The third framework, however, adopts the subjectivist position and shows how strategy works as an ideology that comes to be experienced as an objective reality by managers who feel compelled to implement its injunctions even if they go against the grain of their personal values and beliefs.

Strategy

A strategy is a master plan of the way in which an organization intends to compete in its environment, indicating the sort of structure, including coordination and control devices, that is required to implement the plan. Strategy is concerned with fundamental, large-scale problems relating to how an organization defines itself, including its relation to the environment. It is the road map for organizational effort.

The concept of strategy is not limited to business organizations. In fact, the idea was imported into business from the military where strategy means generalship and the art of war. A *stratagem* is an artifice or device for deceiving the enemy by deploying troops, ships, aircraft, and so on, in a way that imposes upon the enemy the place, the time, and the conditions for fighting that are preferred by the strategist. Business strategy still retains the spirit and jingoism of warfare, but strategy is also applied to nations, governments and government agencies, universities, and similar institutions. For individuals, strategy can be valuable as a grand plan for getting on in life.

Strategic Planning

The strategic planning process usually begins with a detailed analysis of opportunities and threats in the environment. During this process, the economic climate, availability of critical factors of production, political atmosphere, and strengths and weaknesses of competitors are carefully assessed and predictions for the future attentively considered. Will the environment be stable, or will it be turbulent? Will the environment be friendly or hostile? Will successful operations bring large rewards or will it be slim pickings? How will competitors react and compete? These are the kinds of questions that must be answered in any thorough environmental analysis.

Such analysis is followed by carefully identifying the organization's current skills, strengths, and weaknesses. Distinctive competencies, those things that it does better than most competitors, are identified and become the cornerstone of the strategic plan. This internal appraisal includes evaluation of the current product line, the state and condition of production technologies, the R&D abilities, and the capabilities of key employees. Each functional area, such as manufacturing, finance, engineering, and marketing, is carefully assessed for strengths and weaknesses. "Know thyself" is the rule.

The next phase in strategic planning involves matching distinctive competencies to opportunities uncovered during the environmental analysis stage. Success here calls for entrepreneurial skill, something we do not understand at all well. Hunch, judgment, cunning, intuition, experience, and optimism are difficult enough to define, but perhaps impossible to teach or program. Luck, chance, and random events also seem to play an important role. More an art than a rational science, entrepreneurship is nevertheless the consummate business and political skill.

The final stage in the strategic planning process consists of drafting a blueprint for an organizational structure to get the strategy into action. The blueprint outlines the appropriate way of allocating authority and responsibility, putting in place integrative and coordinative mechanisms, and most importantly for our purpose, designating appropriate control systems for measuring and rewarding performance. The control system directs resources towards accomplishment of strategic results.

Strategies and their formulators come and go. But industrial and commercial enterprises have a life of their own—one that frequently lives longer than that of the current strategy, the incumbent executives, and the present administrative systems they use to run the company. To put it differently, enterprises have a unique history that outlives individual executives, strategies, and administrative systems. The trick seems to be for the enterprise to find a viable congruence among these three elements. A crucial part of this process is to work out the appropriate match between strategy and control systems.

This point is illustrated dramatically by Alfred Chandler in his classic and seminal book, *Strategy and Structure*. Chandler documented over many years the strategic and administrative responses to their shifting environmental conditions of four US giant industrial enterprises: DuPont, General Motors, Standard Oil of New Jersey, and Sears, Roebuck & Co. Using highlights from DuPont, we illustrate this important point.[4]

6.2.1 Strategy and Control at DuPont

In 1902 the hundred-year-old DuPont company, the largest producer of black and smokeless gunpowder and dynamite in the US, nearly vanished when the president, Eugene du Pont, died suddenly and the four remaining elder partners decided to sell the company to its largest rival. The fifth partner, Alfred I. du Pont, visibly outraged, quickly arranged with his two young cousins Coleman and Pierre to buy out the other partners and run the company themselves.

The One-Man Show

Before the buyout, DuPont existed as a loose federation of small firms and plants spread around the country. Henry du Pont, president from 1850 to 1889, cunningly purchased several of the larger powder plants during the post-Civil War depression. He also ran the Gunpowder Trade Association, a cartel that set production quotas and prices for the entire industry. Henry was little interested in administrative systems. He simply told each plant what to produce and at what price to sell their quota. The absence of administrative control is evidenced by Chandler's observation that he "carried on single-handedly from a one-room office overlooking the powder mills on the Brandywine, most of the business of his company and that of the Association. He wrote nearly all the business correspondence himself by longhand" (Chandler, 1962, p. 55). It was the classical one-man show.

Centralization with Tight Controls

Upon taking over the reigns, Alfred and his cousins quickly moved to "consolidate and centralize" the company. They built a new central office in the center of Washington, where they installed a general research and development department and three new administrative line departments, one each for black powder, high explosives, and smokeless powder. Each line department was to set policy, coordinate, plan for, manufacture, form a nationwide marketing organization, and appraise the operations of its plants. The cousins also established staff offices, including treasurer, legal, real estate, purchasing, and development.

Pierre also came down hard on the du Pont's tradition of nepotism by insisting that any family and relatives be well trained and competent before assuming a position of responsibility. He also clearly defined everyone's authority and channels of communication. The new owners aimed to transform DuPont from a *laissez-faire* collection of relatively small firms to a well-managed, centralized, integrated, and tightly controlled industrial empire. A vital part of the new arrangements proved to be the treasurer's department, headed up by Pierre himself. Chandler describes the set up as follows:

> The Treasurer's Department provided the central office with even more valuable and more regular information. Beside their routine financial activities—the handling and supervision of the myriad financial transactions involved in any great industrial enterprise—the financial executives concentrated on developing uniform statistics essential to determining overall costs, income, profits, and losses. The Department, at first divided into three major units—The Treasurer's Office and the Accounting and Auditing Divisions—came to have, by the time of the First World War, additional units that administered credit and collections, salaries, and forecasts and analyses. The auditing unit gathered information on general external financial and economic conditions as well as on the company's internal performance, while the accounting office continued to develop cost data for production, sales, construction, research, and other activities. The creation of these statistical offices, like those in the sales and manufacturing departments, provided the executives administering the du Pont properties with a steady flow of accurate information. Such data were not and, indeed, could not be assembled until Pierre and Coleman had created this centralized, functionally departmentalized operating structure. (Chandler, 1962, p. 60)

These arrangements served DuPont well. They allowed the executive committee to concentrate their efforts on long-range planning and overall appraisal while the operative committee met weekly to coordinate and watch over the operations of the field units.

During this period, DuPont continued to strengthen and hone its centralized administrative systems, particularly the development of statistical reports and procedures for using financial controls. Formal financial forecasting and capital expenditure systems were developed using sophisticated return on investment estimates for the growing number of new projects and proposals including expansion of existing operations and even new ones such as chemicals. Young Donaldson Brown, working under Treasurer Raskob, devised what was to become famous and widely copied by industry in general during the rest of the century. General Motors, for example, adopted Brown's financial control chart. This was a financial control device which related rate of return on capital invested to capital turnover, sales volume, costs, and profit for overall operations as well as for almost each component throughout the enterprise. This control mechanism enabled head office executives to monitor and appraise in great detail the operations of each department by means of the common discourse of accounting.

These managerial innovations soon proved their worth many times over. The First World War led to an explosive increase in DuPont's munitions business and in its new chemical department. The centralized organization with its detailed and sophisticated financial controls "proved admirably suited to meet the needs of the resulting phenomenal growth" (Chandler, 1962, p. 66).

New Blood and Diversification

After the war the du Pont cousins, opting for a well-deserved and badly needed respite, turned the company reins over to a new set of top executives. At the time DuPont was recognized as one of the "best managed" enterprises in the world. The new top executives took stock of the situation and agreed that even more direction, coordination, and control from the center was required to cope with already large and ever-expanding operations.

At the same time, paradoxically, they decided to pursue vigorously the strategy of diversification that had been started by the previous management. Before long, many new products and markets, especially those related to its chemical operations, were added. These included, for example, artificial leather, pyroxylin, dyes, rubber, paints, varnishes, vegetable oils, and a variety of organic chemical products. The company also expanded into new geographic areas domestically as well as setting up operations in Canada and Europe.

The Great Crisis

The ensuing success of the diversification strategy, however, was to lead to a key moment in DuPont's history—one that brought the company to the brink of bankruptcy. Chandler insightfully describes the impending crisis:

> By 1919, then, the DuPont Company was rapidly changing the nature of its business. Where before the war it had still concentrated on a single line of goods, by the first year of peace it was fabricating many different products whose manufacture was closely related to the making of nitrocellulose for smokeless powder but which sold in many very different markets and in some cases used new types of supplies and materials. This strategy of product diversification was a direct response to the threat of having unused resources.
>
> Yet, in carrying out a policy of diversification to assure the long-term use of existing resources, the same executives failed to see a relationship between strategy and structure. They realized clearly that structure was essential to combine and integrate these several resources into effective production, but they did not raise the question of whether a structure created to make and sell a single line of goods would be adequate to handle several new and different products for new and different markets. (Chandler, 1962, pp. 90–1)

The problem, which went almost unnoticed at the time, proved to be that the rapid expansion into new products, industries, and geographic areas had vastly increased the demands placed on the centralized head office. Coordination requirements mushroomed. Close monitoring and performance appraisal of the operating departments greatly increased the amount of information flowing into head office. Overloaded with data and figures, top executives now had to make strategic decisions about products, equipment, and markets with which they were nearly totally unfamiliar. The centralized, functional organizational structure, with its now cumbersome and voluminous vertical information flows, was strained to bursting point.

The Solution: Found But Rebuffed

Noticing this strain and alarmed by the company's poor results during the sharp depression of 1920 and 1921, the executive committee formed an organization committee of younger key executives to study the problem. This committee called in outside experts, studied the organizational arrangements and administrative systems of eight leading industrial companies, and generally carried out their mandate in the typically methodical, rational and thorough DuPont manner. The committee's findings proved to be a watershed in DuPont's historical evolution. "Their work and the resulting report had an impact far beyond the company's immediate difficulties; for the first time a new form of management structure was proposed" (Chandler, 1962, p. 94).

They had discovered, by dint of a lot of sharp pencil pushing, that DuPont's raw and semifinished products were quite profitable, based on an ideal return on investment of 15%. Further analyses revealed, however, that DuPont's finished products for ultimate consumers were not profitable even though their chief competitors for the same products were reaping good profits. The problem, the committee concluded, must lie with the organizational structure and administrative systems. Under the current arrangements it was impossible to determine who was responsible for profits.

The committee concluded that a fundamental change in organization structure was urgently needed. DuPont should organize around product responsibility, not functional responsibility. More specifically, they proposed placing responsibility for purchasing, manufacturing, marketing, and accounting for each of the company's main product lines under one executive with the executive committee having only general supervision over these product department general managers.

Despite a very strong recommendation, the proposal was initially rejected by the executive committee. Its members argued that only closer attention to specific problems by the central office executives would solve the problem. "The answer was not reorganization but better information and knowledge" (Chandler, 1962, p. 99).

Another special committee of three older executives was formed to study the whole question of organization. Their findings not only mirrored those of the organization committee but also went further to suggest that the entire company be regrouped into product profit departments with the head office staff departments establishing and maintaining general policies and procedures to guide the line departments. Once again, however, the proposal was rejected. President Irénée du Pont, stalwart protector of the status quo and the old guard, argued against tossing out the proven organizational and administrative arrangements that had worked so well until recently. He sent the report back for more study.

In Through the Back Door

An unofficial committee without portfolio, however, brought the new ideas in through the back door. They developed a plan outlining how DuPont could make 10 % return on investment (ROI) on the paint and varnish business, presently making a loss, by regrouping it into a single unit. The executive committee, impressed by the plan, gave it the go-ahead.

Soon after, another group of executives presented a report that ostensibly recommended improvements in financial statistics but in substance calling for broadening product profit responsibility to include all the company's products. The executive committee almost immediately accepted these proposals and by 1921 DuPont "was beginning to move toward a de facto structure based on product divisions rather than functional departments" (Chandler, 1962, p. 103). The inevitable move to the delegation phase was underway.

The Reorganization Ordained

A financial crisis in the first six months of 1921 heated up the debate. Old-guard members of the executive committee, dyed-in-the-wool centralists, argued for the appointment of a strong, single, dictator-president with absolute jurisdiction and full authority to take whatever steps he felt necessary to remedy problems anywhere in the company. In opposition to this idea, the younger executives, now more than ever convinced about the need for a decentralized structure, pressed their case hard, and persevered in their struggle until finally the old guard capitulated.

The new organization featured five product (or industry) departments, eight staff departments, a treasurer's department, and an entirely distinct executive committee with no direct operating duties but with responsibility for overall planning, appraisal, and coordination. The eight staff departments were given no line authority whatsoever. Rather, they were to act as consultants to the line personnel and to provide services to the company as a whole. The treasurer's department, however, continued to have line authority for overall management accounting and control practices including the type of controls required and the time-tabling of the various reports, while the general managers of line departments looked after the details of the cost accounting methods and systems for their own components.

The new arrangements came into effect in September 1921. The results were felt almost immediately. Red-ink operations soon turned into black-ink operations. DuPont never again encountered as severe a crisis, not even during the great depression of the 1930s. While over the years new product departments have been added and a few more staff offices opened, the organization model and administrative systems have remained fundamentally the same.

The DuPont history, in sum, is a vivid example of the importance of the need for a strategy–structure–control systems match. At the turn of the century, the three cousins converted the company from a *laissez-faire* federation, run from the top as a one-man show, into a highly centralized, tightly controlled, functional organization, marketing a related group of products. A key feature of the new organization was its sophisticated, highly detailed, financial control system run by the active, energetic and professional personnel in the treasurer's office.

The company's successful diversification strategy, however, resulted in overloading the central office with information and decision making. It pushed the centralized structure, with its voluminous vertical flow of information, to the breaking point. A new decentralized structure, eventually put in place in spite of fierce resistance from old-guard executives, realigned DuPont into a set of product departments responsible for manufacturing, marketing, and purchasing. The head office top executives, with no direct operating decisions, looked after overall planning and general appraisal of the operating components. Staff offices at headquarters provided services to the line operations and to head office. The new arrangements, which brought strategy, structure, and controls into alignment, served DuPont well for the rest of the century. In 2007, DuPont was still thriving. It employed 60 000 people worldwide, operated in more than 70 countries, its revenue exceeded $29 billion and its market capitalization neared $50 billion. Its mission was to be the world's most dynamic science company and its range of products and services included agriculture, nutrition, electronics, communication, safety and protection, home and construction, transportations and apparel.

Corporate versus Business Strategy

The DuPont history provides an impressive illustration of the potential power of strategic planning as well as the importance of the strategy–control system interrelationship.[5] It is necessary, however, to distinguish between global strategy and business strategy. Large, complex, widely diversified multinational companies, which dominate the scene today, have a global or corporate strategy to define the pattern of the firm's diversified activities. Acquisitions, divestitures, joint ventures, relations with governments of nation states, and major capital market transactions are grist for the mill of global strategy.

Business unit strategy, in contrast, deals with the specifics of how particular strategic business units (SBUs) within the firm will compete, including policies for matters involving marketing, production, engineering, purchasing, R&D, and so on. It also outlines what kind of organizational structure and administrative systems are appropriate to implement the SBU strategy. In small companies, global and business strategies are usually one and the same.

6.3 Strategy and the Structure of MACS

In the recent past scholars in general management and business policy have developed typologies, following structural functionalist assumptions, which are valuable when considering the link between strategy and management control. The first typology identifies four types of organizations on the basis of their competitive strategies and outlines the best fit for each type in terms of organizational structure and management control systems.[6] The basic notion is that each type has a unique configuration of strategy, organizational structure, and management control system. The key ideas are summarized in Table 6.1.

Table 6.1 Typology of strategy, structure, and control.

Type of Organization	Strategy	Key Characteristics Structure	Control System
Defender	Aggressively maintain a prominent position in a carefully chosen, narrow product-market domain	Traditional centralized functional organization	Efficiency focus with detailed and tight controls
Prospector	Create turbulence by continually bringing new products to the market	Organic management arrangements and product group organization	Effectiveness focus accenting innovation, entrepreneurial effort and self-evaluation at lower levels
Analyzer	Highly selective in its stable sphere and rapidly copies successful innovations in its dynamic domain	Dual core organization: centralized functional for its stable domain and organic for its dynamic sphere	Tight controls and an efficiency focus for the stable sphere, and looser controls with an effectiveness focus for the dynamic domain
Reactor	A well-defined but obsolete strategy or a "running-blind" strategy	Politics and careerism dominate over any logical arrangement of authority and responsibility	Treated as merely a bookkeeping system

Before describing each of these types of organizations, a few general caveats are in order. It is important to recognize that they are presented only as archetypes; some organizations will not fit perfectly into one of the four categories. Particular firms may closely resemble one archetype at one time and another archetype at another time. A small prospector, for example, that pioneers a new technology, may metamorphose into a defender organization as other firms catch up on or copy the technology. Finally, large multinational companies around the world are made up of a portfolio of businesses including all four types. Nevertheless, the typology can be very valuable for conceptualizing the strategy–management control system relationship.

Defender Organization: Efficiency Controls

The defender organization pursues a strategy featuring a well-defined, stable, and frequently mature product market domain. It aims its products at a limited segment within the total potential market, often the healthiest and most lucrative. Within this narrow field, it tries

to offer customers a full range of products. Success for the defender depends on aggressively maintaining a prominent position in a carefully chosen market.

By carving out a narrow niche in the market, defenders can concentrate on internal processes, procedures, and problems. There is little need to scour the environment for new markets nor to diversify into unrelated products. The focus is on finding new ways to reduce production and distribution costs, cut marketing expenses, and improve product quality. Japanese auto companies in the 1970s and early 1980s typify this approach. By choosing to compete in the subcompact and compact segment of the market, aggressively reducing costs, continuing to improve their products, and pricing moderately they discouraged new competitors from attempting to enter their carefully selected market niche. Operating from this solid base in recent years, they have carefully and gradually established beachheads in the midsize and luxury segments of the auto market. "Lean and mean" is the maxim.

The traditional functional organization structure is well suited to the defender strategy. Specialists with similar skills are grouped within functional units such as manufacturing, engineering, sales, R&D, and finance. Each specialist unit becomes extremely adept at its particular task. Work flows sequentially from one unit to another. Coordination between the functional units is routine, having been initiated during the planning phase. Finally, a small group of key top managers acts as watchdogs over operations.

Defenders also have distinctive administrative features. The simple strategy allows the organization to develop formal operating procedures specifying clearly how each employee is to carry out specific duties. Production plans and coordination needs can be meticulously mapped out well in advance. Planning tends to be concentrated over a few key areas of needs. Output and cost objectives are set and translated into budgets and specific operational goals. Only then is production set in motion.

During production, control is centralized, formal, detailed, and far reaching. A small group of top management personnel, usually dominated by finance and production, keeps a close eye out for any deviations from plans. They do this by means of long-looped, vertical control systems, which reach from the top of the organization deep into the lowest levels. These controls usually focus on efficiency indices and comparisons with previous years. Formal progress reports and explanations for budget variances flow upwards from the lowest levels to the top of the hierarchy; formal standard operating procedures, job descriptions, and specific directives flow down. Formula-based bonus schemes are explicitly connected to budget performance. For defenders, with a very clear understanding of what they want to do and how to do it, tight controls fit like a glove.

In sum, defenders concentrate on narrowly defined, stable, product market domains which they aggressively defend by means of low costs, high quality, and reasonable pricing. This strategy is implemented within a functional organizational design not unlike the mechanistic organization described in Chapter 5. It features rigorous planning, long-looped vertical information flows, formalized standard procedures, and close monitoring by upper management of progress on plans. Not surprisingly, in successful defenders, business proceeds smoothly in a predictable manner. The glass products division of Empire Glass described in Chapter 2 is an archetype of the defender firm.

The Case of Glass Products Division

The glass products division (GPD) of Empire Glass is an archetypical defender. It competes with a full line of glass products ranging from small orders of fancy specialty jars, to middle-sized orders of jam and honey jars, to long-runs of standard-size beer and soft drink bottles, and it aggressively maintains a prominent position in this narrow, stable, and mature market domain.

The GPD does not invest much time in strategic planning as its strategy is clear-cut, well understood by all, and changes little from year to year. Nor does it spend much on product R&D. Instead, managers at all levels focus their energy on finding ways to reduce the costs of production, distribution, and marketing and on improving product quality. The GPD vigorously defends its market niche with continuous cost reduction and product improvement. Potential competitors think twice before taking them on and usually decide to look elsewhere for opportunities.

The GPD also typifies the defender in its organizational design. The HQ and divisional executive groups are small and financial officers play a dominant role. The glass division is organized along clear-cut functional lines. Coordination needs are taken care of in advance by means of an elaborate, careful forecasting and planning process. These plans are translated into budgets and specific operational goals which are discussed and debated at all levels until agreed upon. From then on the field units, sales districts and plants merely execute the program.

Divisional and HQ offices monitor the field units closely. Detailed profit planning and control reports, which cover nearly every aspect of operations, convey performance information from the lowest echelons to the top. Variances from the plan are analyzed in detail and explained in writing and the bonus scheme is spelled out explicitly and linked to budget performance for the year. Tight controls and close monitoring are the order of the day. The GPD is not a place that tolerates deviations from plan during execution.

For the GPD strategy, structure, and management control formed a complementary and coherent package. Not surprisingly, it not only held but also improved its market share in a highly competitive mature industry. It also recorded small but steady growth in profitability at a time when some competitors went under. The GPD is the prototype of the successful defender.

Prospector Organization: Effectiveness Controls

Organizations following a prospector strategy are almost the antithesis of defenders. While defenders focus on a narrow, well-defined product market niche, prospectors compete in a broad product market domain. Their distinctive competence lies in their ability to find and capitalize on new product opportunities before the competition. They systematically add new products, shed old ones, retrench in some markets, jump into avant-garde product lines, and buy new technology. It is almost as if they continually try to get ahead of themselves.

More accurately, prospectors deliberately create turbulence within their industries. With the environment in constant flux, prospectors bring their distinctive competencies—developing and marketing new products—into play, keeping the competition off balance.

In fact, their entire product line may undergo transformation within three or four years. The idea is to try to keep the product market domain in a state of perpetual change and so maneuver the competitive turf in its favor. While change is anathema to defenders, it is opportunity knocking for prospectors.

Prospecting calls for a unique style of management. It is not like a game of chess, where management carefully plans programs and closely monitors their faithful execution by skilled specialists down the line. It is more like a game of chance where they must roll the dice against large odds, deploying limited resources over numerous ventures and hoping for the best. So planning, such as it is, takes the form of just-in-case scenarios with only sketchy and tentative plans for contingency moves for both successful and losing ventures. And monitoring performance involves knowing when to cut the losers short and go with the winners. It is not a strategy for the cautious conservative or the weak-hearted.

Firms employing the prospector strategy also feature special organizational arrangements. Characteristically, these firms localize entrepreneurial and engineering activities by grouping them into temporary project teams and task forces where they can be most effective. Talented professionals are similarly shuttled in and out of projects as needed. The project groups are free to explore new markets and develop avant-garde products as they see fit. The necessary project coordination and integration is decentralized to coordinators at the project level rather than handled through the vertical hierarchy.

It is not surprising, then, that the product group organization fits prospectors well. All the talent necessary to research, engineer, manufacture, and market a set of related products is grouped into one organizational component. In order to give each component a free hand, formalization is kept to a minimum. Rigid planning and tight control are avoided in favor of loose, organic arrangements. Flexible, lateral relations are given priority over vertical hierarchies to give the product groups room to make important decisions.

Prospectors' MACS are designed to support these arrangements. They promote effectiveness rather than efficiency, with an emphasis on entrepreneurial effort and market results. Nevertheless, access by the product or project groups to financial performance information is essential in order to respond rapidly to market signals. In consequence, horizontal feedback loops prevail. While efficiency measures such as cost cutting are available to upper management, primary control is located within the product group, which actively assesses its own market performance. With competent, self-motivated professionals in charge, these arrangements work well.

Careful research supports these ideas. One study, for example, uncovered evidence that for high-performing prospecting firms (using return on investment as the criteria) management control systems featured output effectiveness goals, forecast data in control reports, frequent reporting, tight budget goals, and, surprisingly, an emphasis on cost control (Simons, 1987). The study also found that the use of tailor-made controls by prospectors was negatively correlated with performance. For defenders, however, performance was positively correlated with budget-formula based bonus schemes, but negatively associated with informal control information, interperiod budget performance, and output effectiveness goals. The study also confirmed that prospectors perform better in rapidly changing conditions while defenders do better in stable environments.

The prospector strategy places unique demands on the organization. Sometimes prospecting pays off handsomely and sales suddenly take off. But this puts heavy strains on employees, who must constantly deal with new and unfamiliar technology and face the frustration of never approaching optimal efficiency. At other times, market expectations may fail to materialize, causing morale to sag and, with it, the confidence and bravado essential for prospecting. Environmental turbulence induced by the prospector can cause it to spread resources and talents too thinly; then experts turn into dilettantes, merely trifling with new products and markets instead of mastering them. Volatility can mean opportunity, but also uncertainty, risk, and frustration.

Corning Glass: An Archetypical Prospector

Corning Glass (CG) seems almost the epitome of the prospector firm in terms of its strategy, organizational structure, and management control systems. It invents, develops, and produces a wide range of domestic cooking and glassware as well as specializing in related high-tech products, such as refractory materials, electronic devices, and medical instruments, which it markets around the globe. CG aims to be on the cutting edge of developments in its chosen fields and can boast of its well-earned reputation as a world leader in speciality glass and related inorganic materials products.

This strategy paid off handsomely over the years. Its reputation, growth, and profitability stemmed from its remarkable stream of inventions with superior technical qualities, including breakthroughs in heat resistance, mechanical strength, chemical stability, and light transparency. It has a 150-year history of developing life-changing innovations including the glass for Edison's light bulb, ultra-thin glass for active matrix liquid crystal displays, ceramic substrates for diesel and automative emissions control, and the first commercially viable, low-loss fiber for use in telecommunications. The market acceptance of these products resulted in an enviable record in profits growth.

Corning Glass prides itself on its technical "knowledge capital," which allowed it to bring a host of innovative leading edge products to the marketplace. These included more recently very "hi-tech" products such as active matrix liquid crystal display glass for flat panel computer screens, cellular ceramic substrates for controlling emissions from diesel engines, light-emitting diodes used for drug discovery, and low-loss optical fibre. Its expertise and values have enabled Corning to develop leading positions in their current market segments: display technologies, environmental technologies, telcommunications and life sciences. Corning Glass is a worldwide leading supplier of glass substrates for liquid crystal displays (LCDs) and cellular ceramic technologies and solutions for emissions control in mobile and stationary applications, a leading manufacturer of optical fiber and cable systems for telecomminications networks and was a leading global supplier of scientific laboratory products for more than 80 years. Corning is also a leader in providing high-performance materials for the semiconductor, lighting and ophthalmic industries.

Corning Glass could boast that it is a diversified technology company that even today concentrates its efforts on high-impact growth opportunites. It combines its expertise in specialty glass, ceramic materials, polymers and optics with strong process and manufacturing capabilities to develop, engineer and commercialize significant innovative products for the telecommunications, flat panel display, environmental, life sciences, semiconductor and other materials markets. In the 2000s, CG continued to pursue its prospector stategy. As a recent annual report stated, "We will grow the company and we will fuel that growth with global innovation. Some companies grow mainly by aqusition or mergers. But Corning grows through innovation—and that belief is deeply ingrained in our culture."

Many of CG's products are developed for original equipment manufacturers (OEMs). Upon receipt of what seems a viable OEM request, the scientists in CG's technical staffs division (TSD) get to work inventing the necessary technology. From there, projects are passed on to the manufacturing and engineering division (M&E). The M&E division, staffed by a pool of CG's best engineers, develops the applied technology working closely with the field units that will eventually produce and market the new product. Corning Glass strives to be first in the marketplace with these high growth-potential products. This lead, backed up with patents, manufacturing knowhow, and large investments in production facilities, permits CG to capitalize on its strong market position and the product's high growth potential.

This prospector strategy is accomplished by means of an organization structure featuring the functional TSD and M&E units alongside a matrix of product divisions and area managers. The product divisions are responsible for strategy formulation, resource allocation, and technological development for their assigned products. The 130 area managers are assigned responsibility for the day-to-day operations and assets in their geographic territory. The product division is broken into around seven product line divisions, 20 business groups and 60 businesses. Both the product and the geographic units share responsibility for marketing, capital investments, and acquisitions. Ambiguity and overlapping responsibilities, typical of the matrix organization, are accepted by all as going with the territory.

Corning Glass has an array of management control systems to reinforce its prospecting strategy. One important control is its strategic planning system. Each product and geographic unit prepares a business strategy plan once a year. This document features a breakdown of products on a grid including on one axis four categories of competitive strength (ranging from weak to strong) and on the other axis four categories of market life cycle (ranging from embryonic to aging). It also includes estimates of five key financial statistics (with sales as the top line and return on assets as the bottom line for the current year, the next year, and the fifth year out); a qualitative description of the unit's competitive strategy, its goals and how they would be measured; the major resources required in the next few years to implement the strategy; an analysis of the unit's competitive position, threats, risks, and opportunities; and a statement of any significant changes in the strategy since the previous year. The strategic plan is prepared annually, reviewed by the worldwide business managers and the relevant geographic area managers, and then submitted to corporate management for approval.

Large investments are controlled with a traditional capital budgetary system. Business and unit managers submit a resource request document to the corporate office outlining the resources needed for new projects and for expanding existing ones for each capital project as it arises. The request includes cashflow and rate-of-return estimates for the project and indicates how the request supports the current business strategy of the unit. In addition to money requirements the proposal also includes a request for M&E engineers. The M&E pool of talent is considered to be a much more scarce resource than is money capital.

Requests are reviewed and prioritized at the levels of worldwide business manager and geographic area manager before submission to the corporate resource allocation committee, which consists of the financial vice-president, the corporate controller, the director of strategic planning (who reports to the financial vice-president and the directors of M&E and TSD). The resource allocation committee (known as an exclusive club for accountants) recommends priorities and funding levels, including cash and M&E talent for development projects.

The business development committee, also at the corporate level, complements the resource allocation committee. Its role is to identify opportunities for new markets and products that dovetail with CG's special technological competencies and to stimulate managers to exploit new technologies and markets. Thus, it acts as a counterbalance to the natural tendency of the accountant's club to stifle creativity, initiative, and enthusiasm of the unit managers necessary for the prospecting strategy.

The business strategies and resource requests are the basis for the annual operating budget and the annual capital budget. All units down to plant level prepare the traditional operating revenue and expense budget including three measures of profit: gross margin, operating margin, and contributed margin (after assigned corporate expenses). They also prepare and submit return on assets (ROA) and other standard financial ratios, as well as a capital expenditure budget for the coming year.

Variance from budgeted operating margin, however, is considered the most important statistic. Fifty percent of a manager's salary increase is directly tied to the manager's operating margin variance. The individual performance factor (IPF), the other half weight, includes the manager's ability to meet the budgeted operating margin. Bonuses for corporate executives and divisional managers, however, are based on corporate profit only. Corning Glass's compensation system also includes the typical stock option participation plan to help soften the emphasis on operating margin.

In sum, CG has a well-defined strategy of seeking leadership in its preselected market domains. Managers at all levels are motivated to strive for cutting-edge developments in their particular area of responsibility. This strategy is implemented by an organization design featuring the centralization of the crucial scientific and engineering functions which feed products to the matrix line organization. An array of management controls and key committees constantly remind managers of the importance of prospecting. These controls are not free from the normal politics and careerism that go along with highly motivated and ambitious managers but they do provide a great deal of force and motivation for institutionalizing the prospecting spirit throughout the company.

A caveat is necessary here. Even though corporations achieve a good fit between strategy and management controls, this alone is not a surefire guarantee of continuing success. In CG's case, for example, their prospector stategy served them well over the years. In the late 1990s and early 2000s, however, when the telecomminications bubble burst and the industry suddenly went into disarray, CG experienced a drastic drop in demand for its major optic fiber line as well as other related telecommunications products. It had relied on a small handful of customers for these products. In the wake of these events, CG's sales plummeted resulting in a $7 billion loss over three years related to the writeoff of restructuring, impairment of assets, and goodwill accumulated on its acqusitions. Corning Glass's profit machine had turned into a disaster. By 2004, however, the company was slowly turning things around and sticking firmly to its prospector strategy. As James Harington, chairman and CEO, reported:

> Corning would continue to be a vibrant leader in its chosen markets. Our culture of innovation is remarkable—in fact it is legendary success, born of more than 150 years of creating products that have helped change the way we live. The tough material and manufacturing problems we solve for our customers are so complex that most other companies won't even try them—at Corning, we *thrive* upon them. (Corning Glass annual report, 2003)

The prospector's strategy involves competing in a broad product market domain, which it deliberately keeps in a state of flux by constantly introducing new products and developing new markets. These moves enable prospectors to keep a step ahead of the competition. Formal planning, vertical hierarchies, and tight controls give way to self-directed, often temporary, product groups. These product groups are run by specialists who rely on performance information with short horizontal feedback loops and self-evaluation. Sometimes the prospector may be riding high on a wave of innovation, at other times limping along in the doldrums. Defenders prepare meticulously, take careful aim, and deliberately fire. Prospectors fire first then take aim.

Analyzer Organization: Dual Control Systems

The next type of organization, the analyzer, is a hybrid of the defender and prospector. In one domain, like the defender, the analyzer competes with a stable core of products for a set of traditional customers. It does not, however, try to dominate the market for these products. Rather, it takes a piece of the action by developing clearly identified market niches. These are usually in the most lucrative corners of the market where it relies on its marketing expertise and strength in channels of distribution. It is a player in the market, but not the predominant one.

The analyzer also operates as a quasi-prospector in its other domain. However, instead of developing new products by investing heavily in R&D, the analyzer vigilantly monitors the environment for new products that competitors successfully introduce into the marketplace. When such a product is spotted, the analyzer's applied engineers spring into action and rapidly develop a good-value "me too" version. Then the product is marketed, posthaste, through its well-developed distribution channels. Market surveillance, product engineering, and distribution are all key skills in this dynamic domain. The analyzer never leads the market but will always be close behind those who do.

So the analyzer goes for the best of both worlds. It tries to skim off the cream in its stable market domain where it captures a small but lucrative niche rather than holding a commanding position. Simultaneously, for its other domain, it aims to minimize the risks of new product opportunities by never being first in the market but by rapidly developing a "me-too" copy of products successfully introduced into the market by prospectors.

The analyzer strategy calls for a unique kind of organizational design—one that can handle both the stable and the dynamic domains. The stable domain is best served by high levels of routinization, formalization, and mechanization. The emphasis here is on efficiency and strong functional departments such as engineering, manufacturing, and marketing. By contrast, the dynamic domain is best served by an organic, flexible organization design where the stress is on the effectiveness of getting new products into standardized production and through the distribution channels. The dual domains demand a dual organization.

The analyzer often resolves the tensions between its two domains by relying on a matrix organization. The matrix features the combined presence of functional groups housing similar technical specialists, and product groups, which are partially self-contained. This permits the functional specialists to hold sway in the stable core with the product engineering groups playing second fiddle. In the dynamic domain, the influence swings in favor of the engineers with integration needs handled by special product managers working in the crossroads of the matrix. Their job is to coordinate the tricky but very necessary integration of the production-oriented functional domain and the market-oriented development and engineering one. Even so, the analyzer can never be either fully efficient or fully effective.

The dual marketing strategy and the matrix organization places unique demands on the analyzer's MACS. The stable domain requires tight controls to monitor performance against standards and promote the cost-efficient production of standard products. The dynamic core calls for loose control systems which focus the effectiveness of adapting new products to existing technological skills. Controls must balance flexibility and stability.

Brothers Ltd: An Archetypical Analyzer

Brothers Ltd, the Japanese consumer goods firm, is typical of the successful analyzer.[9] Brothers competed in Japan and around the world in a variety of household products, including sewing machines, vacuum cleaners, typewriters, calculators, and personal computers. And more recently, its product line included laser multifunction office machines, printers, and all the peripheral equipment and supplies that go along with the electronic office. Its products are never the top of the line but they work well and are reasonably priced. The vice-president of marketing outlined the finer points of Brothers' strategy this way:

> We monitor our markets and competitors very closely, keeping a special eye on the prominent firms in each product area. When a product is nicely in the growth stage of its product life cycle, we like to enter the market with a pretty good copy of the best product on the market, one that we know we can manufacture efficiently. Because of our strength in distribution channels and dealership networks, we are able to quickly capture 5 to 10 % of the world market. You would be surprised at how much this amounts to in total sales.

In order to do this successfully we must watch the movements of the prominent firms as closely as a crane watches frogs in a pond. We know instantly when a new product hits the market and we begin at once to sketch out the design for a similar product. If the innovator's product starts to take off, we get down to serious business, finish the detailed design, get it into production, and push it out through our distribution channels.

We have a large group of dedicated engineers at headquarters who are very good at imitating products—without infringing on any patents—and who find this work very challenging and exciting. Our great strengths are in copy design and distribution channels. We feel it is better to be second with a good imitation, than to be first in unchartered waters. So far, the result has been very lucrative "frog catching." While many companies strived to follow the mantra of "excellence in everything we do", Brothers capitalizes on "being mediocre." And, we are very good at it!

Reactor Organization: Ineffectual Controls

The final organization in the typology is the reactor. A key characteristic of a reactor is inconsistency in the way it responds to change in its environment. For some companies this is due to a mismatch between strategy and technology. For others it is because upper management clings to clearly articulated strategy and structure when they are no longer viable. More frequently, it is simply a case of running blind rather than following an explicit strategy. In this case new products and technologies are introduced at random without the benefit of strategic planning, or systematic planning and control systems. In any case, the common factor is a misalignment of environment, strategy, and organizational systems.[7]

In a way, reactors are a residual type of organization. Such firms have fallen out of, or have been unable to shift into, one of the more stable patterns of defenders, prospectors, or analyzers. They seem to be continually playing catch up, so they chronically respond in an inappropriate way. They may, for example, move to a prospector strategy when a defender strategy is called for. Poor performance is frequently followed by a loss of confidence, highly tentative initiatives, and backpedaling on positions. Reactors become overcautious and shy away from acting firmly and aggressively in the face of environmental change and internal chaos. Luck may bring success to some reactors, but in the main they seldom prosper.

In reactor firms, politics and careerism frequently feature prominently. Decisions are made in secret and communications are often distorted. Management accounting and control systems tend to be ignored and financial managers are treated as bookkeepers. In such a situation, the disciplinary effects of planning and control systems, no matter how technically sound in design, are not much help. Not surprisingly, reactors make stressful workplaces.

Avignon Aviation & Fusele: An Achetypical Reactor

Avignon Aviation & Fusele (AAF), a large French aircraft and missile company with operations spread across Europe and beyond, provides a clearcut example of the reactor organization. Its Toulouse Avion (TA) division had won a large and potentially lucrative cost-plus incentive contract from the French government for various armaments for the

French Army. The division had not been profitable since being privatized in 1990 and so came under considerable pressure from AAF's president, George Cartouche, to become profitable. As a result, it was vigorously pursuing a formal profit-improvement program. The new contract was seen as the chance to make TA a major profit contributor within AAF.

One vital piece of high technology for the army, a sophisticated computerized air-to-air missile launcher (CML), was to be subcontracted to a sophisticated, specialty electronics firm. Henri Lagrange, the director of purchasing, identified three possible sources of supply including Alsace Cie (AC), an aircraft electronics subsidiary of AAF. He was reluctant, however, to do business with Alsace Cie because severe problems of quality, delivery, and changes in specifications on a previous contract had led to acrimony and bad feelings between the two divisions. He decided, after consulting other TA executives, not to ask Alsace to bid on the CML. Toulouse Avion managers felt deep down that Alsace should not even be in the aircraft electronics business and that the latter saw TA as a captive customer.

Lagrange had all but agreed to accept the bid by the Italian firm Casa Milani, an outside Italian company, when President Cartouche called a meeting of TA's division manager and AC's marketing director. Alsace Cie's marketing director was extremely upset at not even being asked to bid and reported that AC had recently put a great deal of money into R&D on CMLs claiming that, with this new technology and AC's reputation for technical proficiency and low cost, it was now the leader in the field. He also explained that AC needed this business to carry it over until its traditional missile launcher market recovered. He also stated that AC's good reputation in the marketplace had suffered badly as the word spread that TA had not even asked AC to bid, and that AC would be all but out of the CML business if TA did not give them the contract. In fact, he argued, this would either make or break AC. At this point, Cartouche ordered TA to let AC bid on the order.

Lagrange phoned Casa Milani's marketing manager, telling him to put the contract on hold. The contract had been sent to Casa Milani in final form but had not been executed. In the next several weeks, Lagrange tried without success to get a final bid out of AC, who claimed to need time to evaluate and price the highly technical blueprints. In the meantime, Casa Milani requested TA to pay a substantial amount of the anticipatory costs, stemming from short delivery dates, they had incurred on the project with Lagrange's knowledge and agreement before final execution of the contract. At this point Lagrange's liver acted up and he spent one month in hospital and another week in bed at home. When AC's bid finally came in it was nearly 40% higher than Casa Milani's with delivery one month later than required. Meanwhile, TA's divisional manager had received an angry phone call from the French Army Supply Department's contracting officer questioning the wisdom of subcontracting with AC at such a high price.

The case study ends there. Decisions were made in secret, communications became distorted, and political maneuvering ruled. So instead of managing on the basis of messages from the management accounting and control system, politics played a central role. Clearly, AAF's executives face an unpalatable and thankless situation. No miracle cure appears. At best, Cartouche can mandate that AC be given the contract and that, for internal management accounting measurement purposes, the transaction be recorded on AC's books at their bid price but on TA's books at the Casa Milani bid price with the difference charged to some headquarters special expense account. This way AC is not strategically finished in the CML business and TA's profit improvement drive is not undermined. Though not very satisfactory, it is, perhaps, the best that can be done in the circumstances.

The case, then, provides a dramatic illustration of those situations that occur all too frequently in reactor organizations. The lack of any clear-cut strategy makes it difficult to put into effect MACS that support the strategy. It is not surprising that AAF has not mapped out any explicit and logical procedures regarding how divisions should deal with each other nor has it put in place any explicit rules and policies for transfer pricing on interdivisional transactions. So instead of decisions being made by the appropriate managers involved at the divisional level in a rational way, they came to be dominated by internal power and politics, inevitably leading to the point where the president had to interfere to save the day. As stated earlier, reactor firms are not pleasant places in which to work.

Some Research Findings

The study of the relationships between strategy and accounting is one of the newest fields to emerge in the area of behavioral management accounting. These ideas have led to research designed to explain the interrelationship between strategy and management control systems. The central idea is that an organization's competitive strategy shapes and guides the key characteristics of its MACS. Recent research, however, has yielded the tantalizing idea that the relationship is a two-way street. Management controls are influenced by strategy but they can also have a profound influence on strategy.

One important study uncovered evidence that the use of different parts of management control systems seems to vary with the type of strategy being pursued (Simons, 1990, 1991, 1992; see also Chapman, 2005, and Chua, 2007). Today most organizations of any size have in place and use a similar set of management controls—operating budgets, long-range plans, strategic planning systems, standard operating rules and policies, performance evaluation systems, and nowadays activity-based costing systems. The research indicated that some controls were treated in a programmed way, handled in a mechanical and cursory fashion without a great deal of attention.[8] Other parts were handled interactively as the input data for debate, dialogue, and learning. The mix of programmed and interactively used controls differed between defenders and prospectors.

For example, in one successful defender organization, the controls included specific value-chain cost-reduction programs for nearly all its products. Value-chain analysis involves tracing vertical cost-effectiveness of products from suppliers' production via the firm's manufacturing to the ultimate customers. Top management closely monitored information reports regarding progress on these programs, scrutinizing them closely for clues about possible improvements. A great deal of learning took place and management made several changes in the production process along the chain as well as in the products themselves.

The controls had affected the organization's competitive strategy in an interactive way. In contrast, other parts of the management control system, such as the strategic planning and the operating budgets, were handled in a programmed and routine manner. In fact, the weekly review of actual and target cost reports for all its products was treated on a management-by-exception basis and completed in less than twenty minutes.

In one successful prospector firm, the mix of programmed and interactively used controls was different. The strategic business plan, the two-year forecast, and the operating budget, which was updated three times during the year, were the raw material for almost continual discussion and debate about products and markets by managers at all levels. As a result, competitive strategies were constantly revised and changed. In contrast, detailed cost and efficiency reports, also part of the regular management control system, were not an agenda item for top management. Instead, they were dealt with by staff offices and treated as programmable.

In sum, both the defender and the prospector had the usual assortment of MACS in place. Yet each treated different parts of the controls as either programmed or interactive depending on which were most relevant to the strategy. The interactive use of controls for both organizations led to dialog and learning, which in turn led to changes in their competitive strategies. The point to underline is that controls can feed back into and change strategies. This means that the relationship between strategy and controls is not simply static and one-way; it is dynamic and two-way.

The idea that MACS are used differently according to strategy and are also used interactively in a way that makes top executives focus their attention on matters of strategic importance opens up exciting new terrain for looking at the roles these systems play in organizations.[10] They can be thought of as strategic accounting and information systems. They go beyond the traditional job of providing financial information after the fact to monitor operational performance towards predetermined plans. And they can be explicitly designed and used to focus on strategic variables. One way to do this is to think about the strategy MACS link from a product life-cycle perspective. We now turn to a framework based on this idea.

6.4 Product Life Cycle, Strategy, and Controls

The key notion in the life-cycle idea is that products pass through four major stages in their journey from initial appearance on the scene to their extinction: introduction, growth, maturity, and decline. The central argument is that different generic strategies are compatible with each stage. It follows, importantly for our purposes, that key characteristics of MACS should also differ at each stage, as shown in Figure 6.2.

During the *introduction* stage of the product life cycle, the strategic focus is on research and development. The firm is looking for a new product or process that will eventually yield a competitive advantage. At this stage, controls should concentrate on identifying opportunities for such breakthroughs. Measuring performance, decision making, and problem solving, the traditional functions of MACS, must be set aside in place of assessing the prospects that appear promising. During the latter part of the introduction stage and the early part of the growth stage, a *build* strategy is appropriate. A build strategy is achieved by expanding

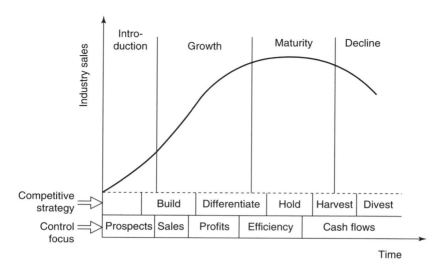

Figure 6.2   Product Life Cycle, Competitive Strategy, and Control

the product line, more R&D, investment in production facilities, vertical integration, joint ventures, and acquisition of technology. The strategic mandate at this stage calls for investing capital in projects that build strength. The prime concern of the management accounting and control system should be directed to getting advance signals from the market in terms of its response to the products being developed. Early market reaction is the bottom line.

During the *growth* stage, the focus of assessment and control shifts to profit performance and market share. Strategies begin to feature product differentiation, which must be supported by capital injections. As a result, especially in the late growth stage, measuring return on investment becomes a priority. So also does developing elaborate methods of calculating interest charges for different types of capital needs, such as cash, receivables, inventory, facilities and equipment. Control systems featuring residual income (volume of profit after an interest charge on invested capital) help fine-tune strategic choices.

As the life cycle approaches *maturity*, the focus of the management accounting and control system shifts to efficiency measurements and cashflow budgets. Management must tread a narrow path between replacing old production equipment with newer models and on getting caught with overcapacity as competitors follow suit in an attempt to reap the benefits of economies of scale available from the most recent technologies.

The clever response to this flux in the market is to rationalize product lines with an eye to concentrating on high-profit products while phasing out unprofitable items. Astute scaling down requires pinpoint accuracy in costing. Sophisticated product costing becomes a key competitive skill and management and control systems must introduce new accounting techniques such as activity-based costing and cost-driver identification. Costing information becomes the key ingredient for strategic choices about product pricing and product line pruning.

During the mature stage of the life cycle, the control side of management accounting systems also increases in importance. Budgets and standards must be tightened. Detailed analyses and responses to variances from standards become mandatory. And close coordination across engineering, manufacturing, marketing, and other functions is essential. General indicators of profit and growth appropriate during the previous stage give way to detailed analysis and pinpoint scrutiny of operations. Tight control and strict discipline are the keys to survival.

Finally, at the end of the maturity stage, the right strategy calls for walking a precarious tightrope between *harvesting* and *divesting*. Harvesting means minimizing cash outflows and maximizing cash inflows while keeping a close eye on the proper time to divest. Management accounting and control systems here take on a new function. They must provide estimates of breakup costs such as labor settlements, site cleanups, loss on liquidation of finished goods, and raw materials inventories as well as disposal prices for equipment, land, patents, and trademarks. There may also be unanticipated costs of experts, including lawyers, accountants, and appraisers.

Limitations

Do recognize that use of the product life-cycle notion to look at the strategy–control relationship is more like a sensitizing device than a solid theory and be aware of the potential problems of this approach. For one thing, the life-cycle curve, indicating progression from one stage to another, is never as smooth as the figure suggests. Further, it is never easy at the time to decide where particular products lie on the curve. Sometimes products skip entire stages. Moreover, many firms follow a strategy of concentrating mainly on products in one or other of these stages.

Some very successful companies, for example, concentrate on innovating in high-technology products at the R&D stage. When the technology is developed and the product potential spotted, the firm then sells or licenses it to a company with marketing skills—especially one that concentrates on products during the growth stage. Other firms concentrate on products at the mature stage of the life cycle, operating with a very lean organization. Still others, like most multinational conglomerates, try to have a portfolio of products spanning the entire life cycle. General Electric, for example, competes in electrical products ranging from kettles and light bulbs to highly sophisticated, secret, Star Wars products for the US Department of Defense. There are many possibilities.

Nevertheless, the framework can provide helpful clues about the appropriate strategic focus for MACS at each stage. Undoubtedly, strategic management accounting systems will be the subject of a lot more research attention in the future. Even now, it is much more than a tantalizing idea; the practical applications can be decisive to success or failure. And for us it provides a way to develop some insights into strategic management accounting systems.

6.5 Strategy as Ideological Control

This chapter closes with some speculations on the strategy–control relationship by looking at it from the radical humanist paradigm recalled in Chapter 3. Ideology is one of the most important and controversial concepts to emerge from developments in critical social theory, and from the radical humanist vantage point it seems to be vitally concerned with how individuals within any social system are controlled. Yet it has been by and large ignored in the conventional management accounting literature.[11] Its central argument is that a strategic plan is an organization's ideology and as such it acts directly as a powerful mechanism of control.

An ideology from the social theory perspective is a socially constructed worldview about what activities the participants in a social order should pursue, how they should be pursued, and why they are important. So individuals in a social order, such as a firm, are seen to have more than just a bundle of randomly collected beliefs, attitudes, career goals, professional aspirations, and aesthetic endeavors regarding their working life. Rather, they have access to some sort of coherent social knowledge whereby each piece fits into a coherent package in which the parts are related, albeit in a complex way.

This package of ideas is called an ideology. It has a characteristic structure, deals with the central issues of human life, is shared widely by the various participants, and has a deep influence on their behavior. It is a major factor in determining the patterns of social action and their routine reproduction. Thus we can conceive of a strategy as an ideology for a particular organization. When participants come under the sway of the precepts for proper behavior incorporated into the ideology, they are *ideologically controlled*. In this way, strategy acts as a very powerful direct control on the individuals in the organization. An example of the way strategy can act as ideological control may be helpful at this stage.

The Case of Tandem Computers

Tandem Computers, following a simple strategy, grew from sales of less than one million dollars to a place on Fortune's second 500 listing in less than a decade. Tandem's strategy was to build computers that were guaranteed never to fail or to garble data. These products were targeted at very precisely identified market niches, such as online systems for car reservations, travel booking arrangements, and bank transactions recording. The system consisted of two computers that worked in tandem, splitting the work load evenly. If one had a problem, work simply shifted automatically to the other computer, thus safeguarding the data and not interrupting the work flow. In short, Tandem would make foolproof systems for very special applications. Tandem constantly improved their products over the years.

Mr. Treybig, the founder and president, made sure that every employee clearly understood Tandem's strategy. He held meetings with employees where he explained the strategy and reviewed the five-year financial plans. He ensured that employees understood how one little mistake or oversight could affect profits in a big way, and so leave less money for R&D and, importantly, employee bonuses. He constantly preached his five cardinal points for running a company: all people are good; all employees, managers, and shareholders are equal; every employee must understand the essence of the business; every employee must benefit from the company's success; and an environment must be created where these rules are applied. This ideology was reinforced by giving every employee stock options.

New employees went through a mandatory two-day orientation where they studied and discussed the company book, *Understanding Our Philosophy*. Company newsletters and a glossy magazine repeatedly reminded employees of the company's business strategy and the need for loyalty, hard work, and respect for coworkers. At Tandem, the corporate strategy, acting in an ideological way, proved to be a powerful mechanism of control. The company prospered. Sales reached the billion dollar mark by the mid-1990s and Tandem was acquired by Compaq in 1997 and in turn by Hewlett-Packard in 2003.

Ideological control, however, does not always work in a way that enhances the lives of the individuals under its sway. In fact, it can have important negative consequences for them. More specifically, it can delude them about their real values and interests, their true position in the social order, and their notions about how the social order works. When this happens, ideology produces a delusion—a false consciousness—and a fettered existence whereby individuals are misguided, partly by themselves, as to their situation and life goals. The history of ITT provides a vivid example of strategy working in this reprehensible way.[12]

The Case of ITT

Sosthenes Behn founded ITT in 1920 as a tiny telephone business in Puerto Rico. Behn saw a great opportunity in the telephone—the newest form of instant communication—for expansion in Latin America and eventually around the globe. Early on he had a lucky break by acquiring Western Electric from ATT when the US Anticombines Agency ordered ATT to divest its network of telephone equipment manufacturing companies including its large UK subsidiary. From this new safe base in the US and the UK, ITT expanded to equip, install, and operate telephone systems in Central and South America as well as throughout Europe. Behn's mission and opportunity, as he put it, was to bring the telephone systems of the rest of the world up to US standards and to make a tidy profit along the way.

But Behn's plans to rival ATT by manufacturing and operating telephone systems around the globe constantly came up against a major hurdle. National governments were bent on controlling their own telephone and telegraph systems in the interests of national security. In consequence, Behn formulated his notorious chameleon-like strategy: do business in each country by enthusiastically supporting the local regime regardless of its political beliefs, aims, and methods, hire nationals as managers to run ITT's local subsidiaries and always retain a controlling interest. In pursuing this strategy, however, Behn ". . . gradually wove a web of corruption and compromise which left idealism in ruins, and his company with deep kinks in its character" (Sampson, 1974, p. 23). Subsequent chief executives at ITT, including Harold Geneen in the 1960s and 1970s, seemed content to carry on the chameleon strategy.

Since its inception in 1923 and through the 1960s and 1970s, ITT executives engaged in a litany of corruption and unsavory and illegal escapades around the globe. Of the many well-documented illustrations, a few stand out. For example, ITT colluded with the highest-ranking Nazi officials before and during the Second World War. Its factories in Europe and its communications networks and spy operations in Latin and South American pro-Nazi countries contributed mightily to the Axis war effort just as they had done for Franco's dictatorship in the Spanish Civil War. At the same time, its plants and facilities in the US and the UK helped the Allies in their battle against the Germans. Even so, ITT did not lose its German and Italian operations after the war. They successfully played it both ways.

ITT continued with its nefarious activities in the postwar era. During the Cold War, ITT engaged in considerable espionage and sabotage in Eastern Europe, which eventually led to the execution by local governments of some of its executives and life sentences in jail for others. It also collaborated with CIA officials in a plot to prevent the election of communist President Salvador Allende of Chile, and later on abetted in his subsequent removal from office. Allende was later assassinated under mysterious circumstances. And ITT has been accused of unsavory lobbying in Washington as well as giving huge "donations" to very high-ranking US elected officials and bureaucrats.

These are but a few examples of the scandalous activities carried out under the umbrella of ITT's strategy of operating as a sovereign global conglomerate transcending the control and aims of nation states, including even the most powerful. The mandate for its executives has been to do whatever is necessary for business and to maintain operations in the local host country. The consequences, early on and years later, were behind-the-scenes activities so reprehensible that ". . . ITT's record of mendacity and doubletalk . . . implies a deep irresponsibility: and the prospect of its being further involved in communication must be viewed with dread" (Sampson, 1974, p. 307).

The Tandem and ITT cases illustrate how a strategy acting in an ideological manner can have a powerful direct effect on its managers, motivating their behavior as much or more even than a firm's MACS. But in a sense, ideological control acts behind the backs of the participants. The strategy is taken for granted and participants' actions become second nature. This can be positive, as in the case of Tandem, or it can be reprehensible, as in ITT, where participants were deluded about their real personal interests and went against the grain of society and their own deeply held values.

6.6 Summary and Conclusions

This chapter described three frameworks for thinking about the strategy–control relationship. The first identified four distinct strategies—defender, prospector, analyzer, and reactor—and outlined the key characteristics of MACS for each situation. The second framework sketched out a scheme based on the product life-cycle notion and speculated on the appropriate focus of the controls for each stage. The third discussed strategy as a form of ideological control. These frameworks provide a focus for management accountants and controllers to go beyond the conventional ideas about cost accounting and control. They also enable them to develop strategic management accounting systems.

The single most important idea in this chapter is that there are important links between an organization's strategy and its MACS. A strategy determines how an organization enacts its environment, how it intends to arrange its organizational structures, and what sort of controls it needs in order to implement its strategy successfully. The relationship between strategy and control, however, is a two-way street. While strategy places unique demands on the important characteristics of an organization's MACS, they can be used interactively to help managers realign strategy. Moreover, strategy acting in an ideological way can be a powerful control in its own right over the actions and behavior of an organization's participants, even to the extent of pushing them into unsavory actions. Either way, strategy acts as a powerful means of control over organizational participants. In Chapter 10 we will see how management accounting and control system have a proactive role in strategy definition when discussing the idea of the balanced scorecard.

Endnotes

1. We will discuss Norton and Kaplan's idea of the balanced scorecard later in the book (see Chapter 10) as we want to focus on the rhetorical nature of this technique to explain why it is so succesful in linking strategy to management controls.
2. See Dent (1990) and Simons (1995) for overviews of the literature on the strategy–control systems relationship. Since 2000 a large number of studies (mainly case and field studies) have been reported. See Chapman (2005) and Henre (2006) for recent reviews of such research. It seems fair to say that this line of research has reached its mature stage.
3. Weick (1979) in his classic book, *The Social Psychology of Organizing*, brought the enactment process to the attention of scholars in organization and management theory. We will recall this concept later in Chapter 8 when dealing with issues of management accounting and control change.
4. The following summary is based on Chandler's (1962) detailed, historical research and documentation of the DuPont company.
5. For another careful and detailed analysis of the strategy–management accounting relationship in a UK conglomerate in the 1980s, see Roberts (1990).
6. This typology is based on the work of Miles and Snow (1978). Simons (1987, 1990, 1991, 1992) has pioneered the research in behavioral accounting, linking Miles and Snow's (1978) work to issues in management control.
7. Gordon and Miller (1976) describe in some detail the accounting issues in running-blind firms.
8. Simons (1992) also uses the term "interactive" to describe this style of using a management control system "when top managers use that system to personally and regularly involve themselves in the decisions of subordinates."
9. From the case study Brothers Ltd, Queen's University (1974) by N.B. Norman.
10. In addition to Simons's work cited above, Shank (1989) offers a highly readable and insightful article on this topic, as do Shank and Govindarajan (1989) who provide several case illustrations of the evolution from cost accounting to strategic accounting in various firms.
11. Notable exceptions include Tinker and Neimark (1987) who provide a careful analysis of the ideological control of women in the workforce at General Motors between 1916 and 1976. Also see Tinker (1980) for a theoretical exegesis of the ideology–control problematic. And Macintosh (1990) offers an ideology-based critique of IBM's annual reports in terms of the control of women in the information technology workplace.
12. Sampson's (1974) blockbuster book, *The Sovereign State of ITT*, provides a carefully documented and startling exposé of these activities over the years. The case details are based on Sampson's research. See also Hopper and Macintosh (1993).

Further Readings

We will come back to issues of strategy implementation and management control in Chapter 10. For further readings in the area of the relationships between management control and strategy you can usefully consult the following texts:

- Chapman, C. (ed.) (2005) *Controlling Strategy: Management, Accounting, and Performance Measurements*, Oxford University Press, Oxford.
- Chua, W. (2007) Accounting, measuring, reporting and strategizing—re-using verbs: a review essay. *Accounting, Organizations and Society*, **32** (4–5), 487–94.
- Henre, J.-F. (2006) Management control systems and strategy: a resource-based perspective. *Accounting, Organizations and Society*, **31** (6), 529–58.

MACS: Modes of Operation

In this chapter:

7.1 Introduction

This chapter continues the flow of thought from the previous chapter and looks at four frameworks that, in different ways, seek to establish a link amongst scorekeeping and control needs, the nature of MACS, and the nature of the uncertainty involved in the work done by the organization or organizational components. It tries to provide a solid understanding of the precise way in which a few different patterns of uncertainty influence how organizations handle these important functions. Whereas the previous chapter focused mainly on formal controls, such as budgets and statistical reports, this one expands the terrain to include informal, unofficial, and nonaccounting-based scorekeeping and control systems. It also explores how the lack of a clear link between information and decision making can lead to a mismatch between ideal and actual use of these systems. As an extreme case, the chapter also highlights how the rational aura of MACS in fact often hides more chaotic and conflicting teleologies. In this sense, this chapter also establishes a link with the symbolic use of management accounting and controls that we illustrated in Chapter 4 and anticipates some of the issues concerning the use of these systems in actual situations, which we will discuss later in the book. The basic premise is that the cutting edge of uncertainty affects the actions that organizations take to cope with these requirements.

More specifically, the chapter talks about different ways of keeping score (efficiency, instrumental, and social tests), different modes of control (bureaucratic, charismatic, market, collegial, and tradition), and the differences between ideal and actual uses of management accounting and controls, and it critically defines these controls as camouflages for other substantial activities taking place in organizations. It shows how variations in uncertainty result in systematic differences in these practices and how these can be used to exploit some gaps in control systems.

It will be helpful at the outset to make a distinction, at least in the abstract, between *closed-rational* systems and *open-natural* ones. The frameworks include a valuable mixture of the objectivist and relativist positions. For the closed-rational part of the organization, the objectivist position is adopted and scorekeeping control systems are treated as concrete social facts existing independently of social actors, whereas for the open-natural part of the organization, the relativist position is assumed whereby these systems are treated as social phenomena existing subjectively and intersubjectively in the minds of the managers and employees.

7.2 Closed-Rational versus Open-Natural Systems

Under conditions where certainty is pretty much the order of the day, organizations are amenable to the logic of closed-rational systems. By this we mean a system where the number of variables and the relationships between them can be comprehended and controlled in a predictable manner. That is to say, they can be effectively treated as rational.

We might ask a few questions in order to determine whether or not a component is amenable to the logic of rationality. Are the component's goals and mission known? Are the necessary resources to reach these ends on hand or available? Are the component's tasks well understood? And is the output absorbed pretty much automatically? If the answer to most of these questions is yes, then it is likely that organizations will treat such components as closed-rational systems and try to protect (or buffer) them as much as possible from environmental disturbances. In these circumstances, the rules of rationality can reign.

In fact, we are surrounded by such systems. Routinely they deliver newspapers, carry conversations over long distances, transport people back and forth to work, stock supermarkets, keep track of money, educate children, and even entertain us. These daily miracles are achieved through marvelously efficient action systems within organizations that are buffered from environmental disturbances which might upset their routines. Following the rules and norms of rationality, they perform with such precision that we are outraged if the morning paper is late or if the supermarket runs out of our favorite brand of food.

These circumstances do not pose large problems for the selection of organizational scorekeeping and control systems. Operations proceed smoothly according to the rules of rationality. This is the case, above all, in the technical core of large industrial enterprises (e.g., a factory, post office, or a mining operation), which are buffered and shielded from environmental shocks by such means as inventory reserves, production scheduling, and idle capacity. It is also true of clerical units, where large numbers of similar transactions are processed day after day as was the case for the finance company branches in Chapter 4. Predictable environments are congenial to organizational effort. Specialized units with repetitive tasks are established and operated according to plans and predetermined yardsticks.

For example, a mass-production factory operates under relatively certain conditions. Scorekeeping is straightforward and focuses on whether or not optimal results have been accomplished. Management accounting and control systems, backed up by inducements geared to ensure conformity to plans, provide accurate and timely information for performance assessment. They play a critical role in the relentless drive for efficiency.

Another example is the case of a national supermarket chain that recently restructured its retail arm. Under the new arrangements nearly all management decisions are taken centrally. Purchasing, advertising, payment of bills and employees' wages, personnel policies and records, banking, and special promotions functions are handled at the corporate and district offices. Even store layouts and shelf-stocking methods are dictated by a central blueprint. The individual stores are thus buffered from almost all environmental uncertainties.

The premise that components should behave rationally is reasonable enough when organizational goals are known, the necessary resources are available, tasks are understood (explicitly or intuitively), and output is absorbed automatically. Organizations go out of their way to operate their basic core technologies as closed systems by buffering them from environmental turbulence and then treating them as rational systems.

In contrast, when the answers are mainly "no," an open-natural system logic is called for. A natural system is not closed off from the forces and changes in the larger environment. Nor are the number of variables and their interrelationship fixed. Uncertainty is the order of the day and the system must adapt to environmental perturbations in order to survive. It must, as the rule of nature dictates, change and evolve.

These circumstances mean the organization is not amenable to rule by rationality. It is open to the uncertainties and vagaries of the environment. Many parts of an organization operate under such conditions. A marketing department, for example, has no way of knowing whether or not it has optimized operations. The same applies to accounting and computing departments; and for R&D units, optimizing resources is not even the goal. Survival overrides efficiency.

Turbulent environments, then, pose major challenges. Organizational structures and management control systems, so well-suited to closed-rational logic, are inappropriate.

Nevertheless, while it may appear at first that developing suitable scorekeeping and control systems is a random trial-and-error process, evidence is mounting that organizations faced with similar sources of uncertainty respond in similar ways. The major thesis is that systematic variations in uncertainty tend to lead to patterned, and therefore predictable, variations in scorekeeping and control needs and practices.

Following this line of reasoning, we can move on to describe our first two insightful frameworks which treat the kind of uncertainty in the component's ends and means as the driving force behind scorekeeping and control needs. We start with a typology of scorekeeping and assessment based on the above ideas.

7.3 Typologies of Controls: Uncertainty, Means, and Ends

Our first framework deals with the appropriate type of assessment and scorekeeping for different kinds of uncertainty.[1] Uncertainty is defined as the interaction of two antecedent conditions: whether task instrumentality is rational or nonrational and whether purpose is crystal clear or ambiguous.

Task instrumentality refers to the available means for task accomplishment. It is a continuum; at one end the ways of doing the work to get the desired output are believed to be known, either by calculation or through experience. Well-understood actions produce highly predictable results. In the machining department of a tractor parts factory, the correct sequencing of work through the machines is well understood, the precise technical tolerances are predetermined, and the exact quantities of raw materials, direct labor, and supervision are known with a high degree of precision. When task knowledge is complete, the effect of instrumental action can be traced to known results.

Sometimes, however, the effects of instrumental action cannot be predicted with any degree of certainty. At this end of the continuum, outcomes may be the result not only of actions taken inside the department but also of events and actions taken outside the department. Further, some consequences of actions may be known, others generally agreed upon but unproven, some suspected, some occurring in the vaguely far-distant future, and still others go entirely unnoticed. Task instrumentality is problematic.

In a marketing department, for example, sales results cannot be related to specific instrumental action within the department. The effect of pricing decisions, choice of distribution channels, selection of advertising media and message, and bonus schemes for salespeople cannot be traced directly to specific sales transactions. External actions of competitors, governments, and banks also have an important but undetermined influence over the outcome.

The other continuum concerns beliefs about the organization's ends, mission, and purpose. At one extreme, ends are rational—that is to say, they seem to be factual and objectively determined, one-dimensional, and with clear-cut preferences over other possible ends. Profit, for example, is preferred to market share. Health is preferred to illness, wealth is preferred over poverty, efficiency is deemed better than malingering, and world peace is clearly preferable to global holocaust. The direction for improvement is also obvious—from market share to profit, from poverty to wealth, from inefficiency to efficiency, and from hostilities to peace. When there is general agreement on one clear-cut end, goals can be treated as unambiguous.

But often ends and missions are nonrational; they are not always represented by a single unambiguous criterion. Sometimes they involve a choice between two or more dimensions. It is not merely a matter of health over illness, but a choice between health and wealth. Shades of health and shades of wealth may be involved in the choice. Ends are value-oriented and subjective. Much of the time we are dealing simultaneously with some degree of health and some amount of wealth.

To further complicate the issue, we may feel ambivalent if the choice lies between two roughly acceptable alternatives, such as long-run cashflows and short-run profits, or even between two equally repulsive alternatives, such as illness today versus poverty next year. Ends usually change with time too: one day we prefer wealth but the next we favor health. When ends and mission are nonrational the choices are agonizing; we are hard-pressed to decide. When there is no general agreement about which end(s) are preferred, goals can be treated as ambiguous.

Efficiency Tests

These two continuums, particularly their extreme values, can be combined to derive different assessment and scorekeeping situations, as depicted in Figure 7.1. When instrumentality is believed to be complete and goals clear and unambiguous, the optimum economic

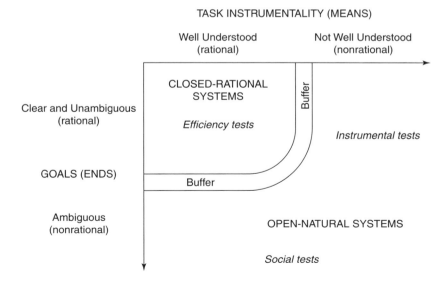

Figure 7.1 A Typology of Assessment and Scorekeeping

relationship between inputs and outputs can be derived. In such circumstances, efficiency is the appropriate test. Efficiency is achieved when the maximum amount of output results from a given level of input resources.

"Was the result produced with the least cost?" asks a scorekeeper for a closed-rational system. Alternatively, efficiency may be the minimum input resources for a given level of output. The scorekeeping question asks, "Was the given amount of input used in a way to achieve the greatest result?" Either way, a known scientific relationship exists between resources consumed and outputs produced. Perfection is the goal and the efficiency test measures relative perfection.

Instrumental Tests

When uncertainty enters the scene—nonrational means and/or ends—efficiency scorekeeping quickly loses its utility. One source of uncertainty is poorly understood task instrumentality. The relationship of inputs to outputs cannot be known with any degree of certainty and it is not possible to determine whether the desired result has been achieved efficiently. There is no way of knowing if the best instrumental action was taken because the possibility always remains that a better course of action exists.

We do know, however, whether or not the instrumental action achieved the desired state. So, the scorekeeping question should center on effectiveness. Did the action result in the desired goal? The robust efficiency test gives way to the more appropriate *instrumental test.*

Instrumental tests, of course, are widely used. In professional sports, for example, won–lost columns and which teams reach the playoffs are common ways of judging performance. Managers and coaches are well aware that their continued employment hinges on these simple instrumental tests. In the public domain, even though objectives for desired outputs such as levels of employment, inflation, and interest rates are less clear, voters and political commentators alike set arbitrary levels of satisfactory attainment. These are straightforward bottom-line assessments.

Most large industrial and commercial organizations aim for instrumental scorekeeping. They carve themselves into smaller components, each of which is relatively self-contained in terms of resources, products, and markets. Performance is deemed satisfactory if predetermined desired profit targets are met. But optimum profit levels are indeterminate because the possibility always remains that some other combination of resources, products, and markets would yield more profit. And we do not know whether or not factors outside the system, such as a spurt in the economy, influenced the result. We do know, however, whether or not the *desired* level of profit has been achieved. Instrumental tests are never perfect, but they can be appropriate.

Social Tests

Our third assessment situation occurs when both ends and means are nonrational. Here uncertainty reaches its maximum and assessment takes on a new dimension. Both efficiency and instrumental tests are unsatisfactory, so organizations must retreat to an even less sat-isfactory but more appropriate means of assessment, the *social test*. The idea of a social test may be foreign, even repugnant, to many accounting and control systems professionals, but the basic idea is to judge accomplishment and fitness by the collective opinions and beliefs of one or more relevant groups, not on the basis of efficiency or instrumentality.

A human resource department, for example, provides an organization with services such as hiring, firing, pay and promotion schemes, safety programs, and union negotiations. The collective opinions and beliefs of its client departments regarding these services are good indicators of its fitness for future action. Another good source of assessment comes from personnel associations that periodically award prizes for outstanding achievement in the field of human resources. In these examples, assessment leaves the realm of economic fact and enters the domain of social opinions, beliefs, and values.

If we pause and think about it, social tests are not so uncommon. In fact many of them are a regular and official part of organizational life. Scientists in R&D departments present papers at conferences where their research undergoes close scrutiny and criticism by col-leagues from other organizations. Students elect the teacher of the year. Panels of journal-ists decide best-article awards. Small groups of critics make artists, playwrights, and writers famous, or even infamous. A panel of expert accountants from industry, government, and universities judge the annual reports of corporations. Research funds are granted by groups of distinguished academics, who judge the fitness of applicants to conduct the research work. And for many, the ultimate social test is the Nobel Prize, which is awarded for outstanding contributions to science and the humanities. In each case the social tests are anchored not in organizational rationality but in the collective and subjective opinions and beliefs of relevant social groups.

Such tests, of course, have their problems. It might be recalled that when Giuseppe Verdi applied to the Academy of Music in Rome, he was turned away for lack of ability; the French impressionist painters were shunned by the Academy of Art; and several universi-ties rejected Albert Einstein's application for enrollment due to weakness of background and lack of promise. Still, in the absence of efficiency and instrumental tests, social ones, even though capricious and precarious, provide at least some information about fitness for future action.

Social tests, in fact, play a critical role in organizations. More often than not an organi-zational component, even if deemed to be a separate and autonomous subunit, is in reality highly dependent on several other components. A typical example is a parts and assembly plant treated as an autonomous profit center within an integrated home appliance com-pany. Transfer price systems and methods for allocation of joint costs are used to develop efficiency (costs per unit) and instrumental (profitability) tests for the plant.

Efficiency and instrumental tests, however, lose some of their bite and credibility since output is highly dependent on the performance of other interdependent components, such as engineering, purchasing, marketing, and sales. In such a case, social tests, although informal and even invisible, come to the fore. The expectations, beliefs, and opinions of the other managers in the network are the crucial test of performance and fitness for future action. Does the component fill its quotas? Does it deliver as promised? Does it follow the rules? Are its members good team players? The confidence expressed in a component by the other coordinate interdependent units is an important and relevant assessment test.

In addition to scorekeeping for individual departments, organizations also attempt to assess the overall performance of the entire organization. In stable environments, historical improvement, particularly growth, is taken as evidence of both current fitness and past performance. In dynamic environments, historical improvement is of little consequence and organizations turn to comparisons with similar organizations.

Business firms, for example, try to convince those they depend on, like investors, bankers, shareholders, suppliers, customers, and employees, that they compare favorably with competitors. To do this they point to increasing market share, amounts spent on R&D, the number of new products brought to the market, and concern for the environment. Historical improvement and favorable comparison with similar organizations are the vehicles for convincing relevant social groups of organizational fitness.

Assessment and scorekeeping, however, become even more difficult when there are several important external groups to satisfy. Organizations, realizing they cannot compare favorably on all criteria, try to hold some constant, and show improvement in other more crucial areas. A business firm needing a bank loan will attempt to score well on the balance sheet, especially working capital and liquidity ratios, by investing in inventories and paying suppliers quickly. Firms seeking new equity capital will attempt to score well on the income statement, particularly in the earnings per share category.

Universities must also respond to many external groups. They try to convince government funding agencies that their operating budgets are kept at a minimum consistent with some quality standard, while simultaneously demonstrating to alumni and prospective students that the already high quality of teaching is getting even higher. They also publicize the more rapid than average improvement in the quality of their students and the quantity of research done by their faculty. And they try to convince accrediting agencies and research funding committees that faculty scholarly output is better than ever. The trick is to hold some aspects of performance constant and show improvement in those areas important to critical external assessment.

Coping with the need to satisfy simultaneously many different elements is no easy matter, but the problem becomes all the more difficult when dependency on various groups fluctuates. Here the organization must adjust the relative weightings of the multiple and varying criteria. Although the scorekeeping task is difficult when critical elements change and weightings shift, keeping alert for clues about the shifting weights enhances flexibility and helps organizations shift to a different but more viable competitive stance consistent with changing demands.

The US automobile industry in the 1970s provides a concrete example. For many years the industry was motivated by shareholders' requirements for growth in earnings per share, customers' wants for bigger and more powerful cars, and managers' needs for large annual profit-based bonus and stock option schemes. The Big Three US automobile companies concentrated on the larger, accessory-laden automobiles, which produced the highest profits. In the interim, however, important environmental elements shifted the industry's concerns away from traditional performance criteria. Safety, pollution control, quality of working life, energy conservation, and eventually jobs for auto workers emerged as dominant criteria. The Big Three firms, spurred on by declining profits, the success of Japanese competitors, and government regulations, slowly but surely shifted their assessment criteria to stress factors such as safety tests, fuel consumption, improvement in working conditions, and the number of jobs at stake.

7.4 Styles of Controls

Our second framework, also based on the cutting edge of uncertainty, is concerned with the way organizations control their managers and employees. It deals with the way they keep their members in step with each other and keep them working towards overall organizational purpose. The ideas underlying this typology stem from Max Weber's classic and seminal work on the sociology of organizations (Weber, 1947). The framework, outlined in Figure 7.2, identifies five generic types of control—bureaucratic, charismatic, market, collegial, and tradition—and indicates the circumstances under which each can be used to advantage. It also brings into consideration the significance of authority and power, aspects of organizational life which most conventional treatments of MACS tend to ignore or push off center stage.

7.4.1 Bureaucratic Controls

The rise of the rational–legal bureaucracy (or hierarchy) to its dominant position in society today, is one of the most remarkable events of modern times. Bureaucracies, such as

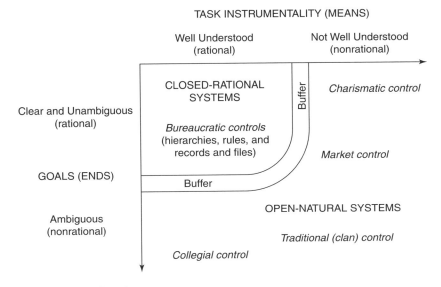

Figure 7.2 A Typology of Control

churches and military organizations, have existed for centuries. Today, however, the bureaucracy is ubiquitous throughout the world in public, private, and mixed organizations. Most of us spend all our working days, and much of our nonworking days, in bureaucracies of one kind or another.

The most outstanding feature of the bureaucracy is that authority is vested not in persons but in offices (bureaus). Thus, at least in principle, officials who are appointed to the offices act without prejudice or personal feelings. Governance is not by personality, hereditary rights, or tradition, as was formerly the case, but through offices. Bureaucracies rely on three major mechanisms to control their members: observational hierarchies, rules and procedures, and written records.

Observational Hierarchies

Bureaucracies feature a hierarchy of supervisory positions, each of which endows incumbents with the authority to oversee the work of others. Direct observation involves having superiors watch and guide the actions of subordinates. Supervisors, for example, watch the workers on an assembly line closely, knowing that if the work is done exactly as prescribed, the expected quantity and quality of product will automatically appear. Personal observation and the issuing of commands assume that superiors have a relatively complete understanding of the task instrumentality involved in the work. It also assumes that ends and values are rational and clear. When these conditions obtain, observation and command are appropriate.

Department managers in a retail store, for example, keep a watchful eye on the way sales personnel dress, approach customers, ring up sales, and wrap parcels. Apprenticeships for trades, internships for medical students, and training camps for aspiring athletes involve intensive training periods where neophytes work under the close surveillance of certified and respected experts. Supervisors observe the actions of individuals as they go about their activities and issue appropriate commands when corrective action is judged to be in order.

The acceptance by subordinates of this command hierarchy is an essential ingredient in hierarchical control. They exchange their talents for organizational rewards and must willingly give up their autonomy and submit to authority of superiors up the line to command and guide their actions. Such acceptance is made easier by the fact that observation and command is not necessarily hard hearted. In fact, it is more often than not exercised within a considerate, warm, and flexible relationship. Moreover, supervisors are also under the watchful eyes of superiors further up the line and they are obliged to follow the rules prescribed for their particular office.

Another key feature of bureaucracies is that they attempt to define each office as clearly as possible in terms of its jurisdictional boundaries: section, department, plant, and so on. Each component is specified in terms of its functional specialization and its functional relationship to all the other bureaus. And each office is assigned a place in the chain of command. Bureaus are specialized, serialized, and ranked in terms of hierarchical authority.

Rules and Procedures

Bureaucracies use formal rules to control their members. The rules outline the rights and duties of each office and position as well as, as far as possible, the proper procedures for getting work accomplished. They provide the impersonal codes for conduct at work as well as the criteria, based on technical competence, for promotion and pay. Rules and regulations are conducive to the development of impersonal relationships between superiors and subordinates and among members of the rank and file. They depersonalize the work environment and mitigate the effects of personality, whims, and nepotism. Importantly, rules are binding on *both* subordinates and superiors.

Records and Files

Bureaucracies invest heavily in keeping complete records and files. Such records include both standards and actual outcomes for inputs, outputs, and resource utilization. Management accounting and control systems are some of the most important types of records and files used by bureaucracies. Organizations make full use of accounting records and data files. Cost accounting systems, variance analysis reports, operating budgets, and profit–cost–volume charts abound in the bureaucracy.

Records and reports have one distinctive advantage over hierarchies and rules. Upper management does not have to be involved in direct observation of either the specific actions and the rule-following behavior of subordinates. Nor do they have to be knowledgeable about the instrument action used to achieve the results. They can merely rely on records and files, such as accounting reports, to know whether or not results conformed to expectations. They can control at a distance.

Consider some practical examples. For a chemical refinery, the actual yield of chemicals and consumption of feedstock are measured and compared with predetermined standards for quantities. Direct surveillance and issuance of instructions is not necessary. Upper management can afford to ignore the behavior of employees as long as outputs meet required levels. For a television show, network officials can rely on the ratings without knowing how the producer went about putting together a successful production. Teachers can use examination results to control students without knowing anything about the students' study or classroom habits. Formal, impersonal information is used instead of direct personal observation.

Accounting reports are an important part of these controls. They must, however, be used judiciously. In some circumstances they are a mixed blessing. At higher levels of management, for example, they are far from ideal. High levels of interdependencies obscure individual contributions; complexity is high, specific technical expertise about top-level jobs is thin, and role ambiguity is common. Yet ambitious upper-level managers often go overboard to provide evidence of their contributions. They seek out and even develop accounting-based measures.

A budget, for example, is welcomed since it appears to reduce role ambiguity, thus giving managers a sense of knowing where they are going and how they are doing, and, most importantly, providing them with objective proof of good performance. The temptation, however, is to treat accounting controls as unambiguous evidence of performance even when they contain only vague information.

But observational hierarchies, rules, records, and files, the distinguishing features of bureaucratic control, are not cost-free. Accountants, information system specialists, analysts, personnel people, lawyers, and a host of other administrative support staff are paid to design and administer the bureaucracy. They are, in effect, the costs of bureaucratic arrangements.[2] Despite the transaction costs, bureaucratic controls can be effective, especially when task instrumentality is well understood and ends are unambiguous.

This, of course, is not always the case. Sometimes accounting records do not contain reasonable performance standards. Standards are often only approximate representations of desired behavior and output levels. So they lose their effectiveness when they do not contain reasonable performance information. Standards are also prone to idiosyncratic interpretation by managers and employees alike. They become even more problematic when tasks are unique, when task knowledge is not well understood, or when interdependencies on the job are high. When standards no longer provide either the necessary motivational force or the direction necessary for goal congruence, accounting controls lose their effectiveness.

7.4.2 Charismatic Control

Charismatic control is almost the antithesis of the bureaucratic mode. It works best in situations where there is a clear-cut mission or calling but where the means of accomplishing it are uncertain. Certainty and routine are anathema to charismatic control. If bureaucratic control feeds on constancy, regularity, and order, then charismatic control thrives on radical change and promises of emancipation from the ordinary. If bureaucratic control conjures up a vision of faceless bureaucrats poring over records and files and looking up rules and procedures, charismatic domination brings forth a vision of a dynamic, heroic leader with personal magnetism, the gift of grace, and the capacity to perform superhuman feats.

Charismatic control works particularly well when purpose and the leader's claim to authority is in conflict with the claims of a well-established, fully institutionalized order. It requires some sort of revolutionary mission aimed at overturning the status quo. The leader's charismatic qualities, however, must be proven from time to time in order to be recognized as genuine by followers. In order to maintain support the leader must also provide gifts and share any booty and glory with followers, especially outstanding ones. Exceptional feats, revolutionary missions, and the sharing of spoils are the basis of the charismatic leader's legitimacy.

Charismatic control, importantly, means that the leader does not have to watch subordinates to see that they follow orders and carry out their *ad hoc* assignments. The leader simply tells them what to do (and sometimes how to do it) knowing it will be done. Duties are never taken as orders but are accepted as obligations, almost in the nature of holy missions to be carried out at any cost. Followers are disciples, not subordinates.

Thus the charismatic leader does not have to be concerned with gaining the consent of followers nor with trying to understand their will. Unlike the bureaucratic control situation, charismatic leaders frequently have no established legal rights over subordinates. Likewise, there are no rules and regulations spelling out subordinates' rights in terms of their protection from superiors. Instead, enthusiasm for the cause, hero worship, and personal loyalty to the leader guarantee compliance.

There are many examples in recent history. Early on in their reigns, Hitler and Mussolini, initially revolutionary and social democratic, were archetypes of the charismatic leader, even if they used this charisma for evil aims. Both exuded charisma and gained the overwhelming support of the citizenry when their countries faced economic crises and general malaise of enormous proportions. Similarly, Churchill and de Gaulle, also relying on charisma, rallied their nations against the Axis powers during the Second World War. Field Marshall Rommel, nicknamed "Desert Fox," was a prototype of the charismatic leader. During the Second World War, outnumbered and with inferior firepower, he kept the Allied forces on the run despite overwhelming odds. More recently, other public figures like Berlusconi, in Italy, and Sarkozy, in France, exert a kind of media charisma which seems to be difficult to resist. They possibly illustrated, more than all the other examples, how poorly people are equipped to resist charismatic leaders.

Formal accounting systems are little used in the case of charismatic control. Pure charisma is foreign to economic considerations (Weber, 1947, p. 302). Economic resources (often in the form of booty) are required, but only as a means to achieve the mission or calling. Accounting is concerned simply with keeping track of the assets on hand and relating them to the mission. Charismatic leaders, however, often maintain their own private information network (including informants and spies) to keep tabs on followers.

While charismatic control works well during revolutionary periods, it can rapidly lose its robustness if the mission remains unaccomplished over a long time or if it runs out of steam. It also loses its effectiveness if the mission is successful, when it usually gives way to bureaucratic arrangements and a more stabilized order. Large business organizations seldom have success with charismatic control. Instead, they pursue clearcut goals, such as profit maximization and rely more on market controls.

7.4.3 Market Controls

Market controls are based on the idea that victory in the marketplace is a key indicator of successful effort and that the information capacity of the market is a powerful vehicle for mediating among individuals. This is particularly so for spot markets where the goods or services desired are available and are exchanged and paid for immediately. Commitments and obligations are short-term and prices are the only information needed to regulate behavior. They enable individuals to pursue their goals in a wonderfully efficient manner.

The idea that organizations might use market controls may come as a surprise since this is not the main business of markets. Yet if circumstances are favorable it is possible to use them to advantage. The invisible organization of the market, as discussed in Chapter 5, is thought to capture and condense information about the sundry actors' wants and productive capabilities into market prices and so provides the disciplinary glove of the invisible hand. There seems to be no need for more complicated arrangements.

A practical example of the parts division of a major company may help to highlight the differences between bureaucratic and market controls.[3] In the warehouse, 150 overseers and supervisors oversaw the work of nearly 1400 pickers and packers. The overseers gathered information about the workflow from two sources. First, they watched the workers to ascertain who was doing a good job and who was not. They queried workers about the way in which they performed their tasks. If appropriate, they gave orders to follow proper procedures. The other source of information was records of daily output for each worker. The overseers used these reports to confirm their personal observations; they worked within the limits of normal rank and organizational authority, along with the informal limits bestowed on them by the workers. Surveillance, output records, and the organizational hierarchy ensured an effective and efficient flow of work.

In the purchasing department, by contrast, only a few supervisors and a dozen or so clerks purchased hundreds of thousands of items each year from thousands of suppliers. The purchasing agents received bids for each order from a handful of suppliers and accepted the lowest bid quoted on the condition that the supplier had a reputation for reliability and honesty. Instead of undertaking costly surveillance and monitoring of the efficiency, quality control mechanisms, and delivery systems of each potential supplier, the company used market prices and competition to promote efficiency and quality on the part of the suppliers.

Within the purchasing department itself, market controls were also at work. As long as the purchasing agents were getting competitive bids for each order and sampling delivered products for quality, there was little need for supervisors to watch over the employees or for accountants to prepare output records. The manager needed only to spot-check that the purchasing agents were accepting the lowest bids. Market control proved effective and efficient for controlling both suppliers and purchasing agents.

The profit-centering concept is a more familiar example of market control. In fact, it is almost ubiquitous in today's world of huge, widely diversified, global business enterprises. These firms simply carve up their operations, as far as possible, into self-contained businesses (subsidiaries, divisions, product centers, strategic business units, etc.), which are granted considerable autonomy and discretion in making decisions relating to products, markets, production, marketing, engineering and R&D. Then upper management monitors progress and tracks performance by means of simple measurements of profit and share of market.

Profit measurement, it is important to recognize, is a market control in the sense that it reflects the prices received from customers for products and services as well as the prices paid for costs and expenses expended to earn those revenues. So the profit earned by the component for the accounting period is an indication of how well it competed in the marketplace, while share of market indicates the possibilities for future profits. Market controls, however, are usually complemented by some form of bureaucratic control by head office staff experts over their counterparts in the business units.

Market controls also have their limitations. While the normal objective is to maximize profits, it is usually difficult, if not impossible, to determine the maximum amount. So organizations settle for a targeted amount, which becomes the standard for judging market performance. Comparisons are also made with previous periods and other comparable companies. As long as the prices used are truly competitive and targets realistic, profitability measurement is a reliable indication of market performance.

As with the purchasing department example, upper management do not have to monitor each and every employee in the profit center as they perform their tasks. Nor do they have to gather detailed information on daily output. They simply periodically review the component's profitability and share of market. As long as the manager of the component behaves like a self-interested entrepreneur, competing in an assigned marketplace, the invisible hand of the market will reach in to provide the necessary motivation and discipline.

While market controls work well when profit is the clear-cut goal, they lose their efficacy when goals and missions are nonrational. Then organizations look to other means of motivation and discipline, such as tradition and collegial controls.

7.4.4 Control by Tradition

The next mode of control in our typology is control by dint of tradition. Until the advent of the Enlightenment project it was the major means of nonviolent (physically) domination in Western society when the legitimation of social codes for authority and domination stemmed from the collective wisdom of ancestors and the revered customs of antiquity. The inherited right of clan chiefs, the divine right of kings, the authority given to fathers to discipline their wives and children, and the supremacy of the Church over souls were ideas handed down from ancestors to posterity. Embalmed in the orthodox of custom and belief, these codes become imperatives for all members of the social order.

While traditions were normally beyond reproach and questioning and could not be challenged on the basis of rational knowledge, they could be changed on the basis that new or altered codes were traditions that had only recently been rediscovered. Generally, however, the received order was beyond rebuke.

An extreme form of domination by tradition is known as "clan control."[4] Membership in traditional clans was highly exclusive, sometimes limited only to persons of blood or marriage. Members had to undergo a long period of indoctrination and subtle value training into the ways of the clan before they knew how to behave. Clans had their own jargon and special meanings, which were normally not understood by outsiders. Sometimes the only way out was death and this is still true for some Sicilian clans. Clans are insular and members have intense feelings of pride and loyalty towards them.

Clans stored blueprints outlining proper social behavior and their own means of communicating it to their members. Sagas and myths told of heroic deeds, almost superhuman abilities, and great achievements of ancient and legendary figures. Legends depicted dire events which befell the errant. Rituals and ceremonies reinforced the implicit but well-understood codes of correct conduct. Once these codes were absorbed, members knew precisely how to behave without being told or watched.

Relations of authority also took on special characteristics in clans. Leaders were neither seen as superiors nor considered as officials. A leader was simply the chief, the person designated by tradition as the ultimate authority. Similarly, the rank and file were neither considered subordinates nor subjects; they were simply members. Their obedience and loyalty was due not to the chief personally, but to the traditional authority granted to the chief. Nevertheless, members' obligations for obedience were essentially unlimited.

This does not mean that the chief's powers and discretion were unlimited. On the contrary, the extent of the chief's authority, as well as the content of any commands, were also inscribed in traditional codes. These usually left the chief some space for personal decision and prerogatives, such as sprinkling grace and gifts on favored subjects. Thus, while chiefs had some freedom for arbitrary imposition of their own will, they had to keep within the bounds of traditional limitations. The chief that violated these undermined the very source of his or her traditional status. While opposition to the chief could be legitimated by claiming he or she had violated or failed to observe tradition, it could not be sustained against the traditional system itself. The codes of conduct, etched in tradition, contained powerful obligations for both chief and subjects.

In Scotland, the Highland clans of the Middle Ages provide a dramatic example of clan control. Membership was by birth or marriage only. The selection of the chief was based on the hereditary rights of the chief's family. Clansfolk had a great love of their place of origin and a deep knowledge of the clan's genealogical roots. Songs, poems, and bagpipe laments encapsulated the tales of great feats, deeds, and battles in bygone years. Each clan had its own tartan, coat of arms, heraldry, and motto. The English invaders, as part of their efforts to eliminate the clans in the eighteenth century, outlawed the wearing of clan tartans. The annual gathering of the clan featured contests of strength and skill, dancing, bagpipe music, feasting, and the raising of the clan standard. Although they frequently fought internally about who should be chief, clansfolk happily followed the chief into battle against other clans or foreign invaders, even in the face of overwhelming odds and certain death.

Criminal organizations such as the Sicilian *Cosa nostra* and its multitude of equivalents in various other parts of the world also rely on clan controls. These prove to be especially effective because formalized methods of control based on written inscriptions would leave traces of what has been done and by whom. Traditions and recognized customs instead guarantee the secrecy that these organizations want to keep; they define a clear guidance for organization members and are a way of discriminating between those who adhere to it, and become members of the clan, and those who do not.

Clan controls are extremely powerful. Members hold the belief, legitimated by tradition, that their interests are best served by complete immersion of every member in the interests of the whole. A strong sense of solidarity prevails and commitment towards global goals runs high. The goal incongruence problem is minimized, or even dissolves. The needs of the clan swamp those of its individual members.

Clan controls are subtle and elusive; it takes a long time to learn the codes for proper behavior. Members share a profound agreement about what constitutes proper behavior and new members are not able to function effectively until these codes are absorbed. It takes newly elected senators in the US Senate, for example, several years to discover and assimilate its traditions. Performance evaluation is a continuous process of subtle signals from long-serving members. Yet once taken on board by the individual, clan controls are more powerful than either bureaucratic controls or market controls.

A striking example of control by tradition comes from the exploits of the Japanese *kamikaze* pilots who shocked and stunned the world with their certain-death attacks on US warships during the Second World War.[5] The name *kamikaze* was taken from the legendary "divine wind," which miraculously destroyed Kublai Khan's huge invasion fleet in AD 1281 and saved Japan from certain defeat and repressive colonization.

The force consisted of a special squadron formed spontaneously in the autumn of 1944 from pilots and officers of the Japanese First Air Fleet in a last-ditch attempt to slow down the American invasion forces. Its mission was to destroy as many enemy aircraft carriers and other warships as possible. Each pilot attempted to crash his plane, loaded with a 250 kg bomb, into a warship. The resources of the First Air Fleet were severely depleted and the chances of scoring a hit by a kamikaze attack were very high compared with conventional bombing. Each pilot fervently believed that his individual interests were served best by complete personal immersion in the needs of Japan and the emperor. It was implicitly understood that each flier would sacrifice himself and his plane by crashing into an enemy warship. National ruin without resistance was eternal ignominy. These beliefs were shared intensely by each pilot.

Rituals, ceremonies, and slogans played an important role in sustaining the organic solidarity of the force. Talks and memos from officers included slogans such as: "to the divine glory of his majesty," "win the Holy War," "save the divine nation," and "we are the imperial forces of heaven." On the evening before their fatal mission, chosen pilots meditated and then wrote a philosophical and cheerful letter to loved ones at home. Fellow pilots, not lucky enough to be chosen for that particular mission, sang the *kamikaze* song and, before takeoff, the pilots performed the Hachimaki ceremony of wrapping the traditional white cloth, with a red circle on front symbolizing the rising sun, around each other's helmets, all the while chanting patriotic slogans.

The history of the *kamikaze* force is a rich example of the awesome potential of control by tradition. All the necessary ingredients were present: sagas, ritual, ceremony, agreement on correct behavior, dedication to global purpose, and exclusive membership. Surveillance and output measures were out of the question. Not only were they unnecessary; they would have been seen as disgusting. These controls were more powerful than even the human desire to live.

The *kamikaze* force, of course, is an extreme example. Yet if we stop to think about it, control by tradition is widespread. It is used to some extent in nearly all our institutions: families, schools, universities, fraternities, clubs, athletic teams, corporations, public accounting firms, professional associations, and governments. It is obviously a powerful means of motivating individuals toward global goals. Although, according to the model, they come to the fore when ends and values are unambiguous and task instrumentality is not well understood, they are also used frequently along with other types of control.

7.4.5 Collegial Control

Collegial control is closely related to traditional control. It has its roots in the idea of *collegiums* (colleges) where one particular group (e.g., the professors) enjoyed special privileges regarding authority and domination. Entrance to a collegium was usually by way of election with each incumbent having a vote (sometimes in the form of a veto or a blackball) or selection by an elite committee of colleagues. Members of this elite group, the colleagues, were usually experts in their field of specialty, persons of high social status, or individuals privileged through education. Each colleague had a say in most important matters.

Collegial controls are much more common than is generally recognized. It is the dominant means of control in many of our most important institutions, including universities, churches, fraternal orders, and international organizations such as the United Nations and NATO. This lack of recognition may be due to its undemocratic veneer in that an elite coterie holds sway. Its strength, however, is that the best, brightest, and most capable individuals have the upper hand in important decisions.

The distinguishing feature of collegial control is that administrators are the subjects of control by the collegium. This differs from bureaucratic control where the incumbent officeholder has the upper hand and from clan control where the chief is the ultimate authority. In contrast, the collegium has a monopoly on both creating the rules that govern the actions of the administrators and in determining the means of checking to see that they adhere to them. In many cases the collegium also elects the chief administrator, or leaves it to a committee of colleagues, or the position is rotated among colleagues. Either way, the chief administrator (dean, Pope, secretary-general, etc.) and other officials owe their obedience and loyalty to the collegium. The final authority rests with the colleagues.

These arrangements frequently result in considerable tension between administrative officers and the collegium. The colleagues' antipathy towards the chief administrator stems from a deep suspicion in general about the intentions and motives of demagogues, charismatic leaders, dictators, and any type of strength. Colleagues resist monocracy of any kind. They also have strong apprehensions about the dilettantism of administrators in regard to important technical and social issues. The typical university president is often a distinguished scholar in a narrow field of specialty, but is almost totally ignorant of the technical, political, and social issues in most other academic areas.

Collegial control, on the one hand, can make decision making tedious and time consuming. It also leads to apparent inconsistencies in policy, because every important decision is made *ad hoc*. It tends to cloud individual responsibility. On the other hand, collegial control promotes objectivity and integrity in decision making. It also limits the power of any one individual to usurp power and it champions the need to reconcile different points of view and divergent interests of the sundry experts. Collegial control ensures that debate and compromise are possible.

Not surprisingly, administrators and the collegium coexist in a state of dialectic struggle. In this contest, budgets and accounting systems play a vital role. Administrators attempt to gain control of the financial strings and control reports. This is readily accomplished if the colleagues see accounting as merely bookkeeping; administrators use the budget process to garner command over resource allocation and exploit the financial reporting system as a way of controlling debate and discussion. The administrator's plea, "That would be nice, but we simply can't afford this initiative," masks the fact that other programs and projects are automatically funded without debate. Accounting systems are used to problematize some matters while simply taking others for granted.

In sum, collegial control can be used to advantage when means are well understood but ends are ambiguous. Although they are widespread in many of today's important institutions, they are generally not well recognized or appreciated. Collegial control is rule by those persons selected according to merit due to their outstanding abilities and accomplishments. Thus, it gives the impression of being undemocratic and elitist. Unless colleagues are on their guard, appointed administrators will frequently usurp the prerogatives of the collegium and use budgets and financial controls as a way to allocate resources according to their own priorities, not necessarily those of the collegium. When this happens, the benefits of collegial control, such as debate over important issues and necessary compromises over values and ends, can vanish.

7.5 The Teleologies of MACS: From Ideals to Practice

The frameworks that follow leave behind the objective realist presupposition of the structuralist position to embrace the interpretivist and relativist premises.[6] The former implicitly assumes that the meaning in a MACS pre-exists both its capture by the accountant and its semantic content for the manager. This implies that accounting systems objectively reflect and mirror (or at least seek to) some already-there reality, and so anybody who uses them can, if they try, discover that reality in the reports and take actions accordingly. We now take a radical turn away from these assumptions to concentrate on several frameworks that adopt the relativist presuppositions introduced in Chapter 3.

From this alternative vantage point, the meaning in any MACS is seen to be the product of the subjective experience and intersubjectively of the accountants and managers involved. The accountants and users construct a story about that reality using as materials the principles and theories that accountants and managers are trained in and skilled at putting into practice. This does not mean, however, that a world doesn't exist until the accountant or manager thinks it up. Rather it recognizes that accountants and managers subjectively construct the "facts" about an organization's reality even though they may then come to reify them, as if they existed independently of their subjectivity. It also gives full recognition to the subjective processes that shape and control meaning and to the fact that the realities of organizational life are *socially constructed.* Simply put, socially constructed means that the social structures and arrangements (e.g., who shall rule, how to speak, what is deemed to be ethical) are not given by nature but made by people, therefore they are potentially mutable. Later on this book, following the idea that "facts" are constructed in network of relationships, we will see how also non-human agents play a role in this construction. At this stage we will though mainly concentrate on subjectivist forces and worldviews.

In constructing meaning we must rely on a common medium such as language in order to communicate our subjectivity to others and to ourselves. One such instrument especially applicable to organizations is accounting; as the saying goes "accounting is the language of business." From the subjective interpretivist perspective, accounting is an important part of the material out of which reality is constructed.

A simple illustration may be helpful at this point. In accounting for an oil refinery the accountant has a lot of choices. It can be accounted for as a cost center, as a revenue center, as a profit and return-on-investment center, even as a discretionary cost center. There are lots of possibilities. But the responsibility center is not, say, a profit center until the managers and accountants construct it as such. It does not pre-exist as a profit center. Importantly, however, the social relationships of the center will likely vary considerably depending on which of these accounting meanings is attributed to the refinery. The "reality" is socially constructed.

Another example is the case of the health center discussed later in this chapter. It was originally set up to provide adequate preventive as well as therapeutic care, become a family centered source of healthcare for the local low-income community, and to act as an experiment to determine the impact of a community health center on the community and the parent hospital. The aim was to bring family oriented and preventive healthcare services to a community that traditionally was resistant to and suspicious of outsiders including social workers, psychiatrists, and, to a lesser extent, medical doctors. The new management accounting system, however, defined the center as a financial performance and efficiency center. The new financial discourse reconstructed the social reality of the center in a fundamental way.

We now look at two valuable frameworks which adopt this subjective interpretivist perspective. The first of these outlines the *ideal* way that MACS should be used in organizations and then contrasts these with the way they are *actually* used. The second takes the wraps off the notion of objective accountability to reveal how accounting systems are used subjectively by organizational participants in the invisible war of self-interest in the workplace. Each shows us how accounting and control systems, rather than providing an objective neutral mirror on reality, play an important role in the way reality is subjectively constructed by organizational participants, especially accountants and managers.

Our first framework is anchored on two familiar dimensions of work: the extent of knowledge available about the task conversion process and the degree of certainty in objectives.[7] The interaction of these two dimensions produces four types of problem situations; it also dictates the ideal way to use accounting and control systems in each situation and reveals how managers actually use them in quite a different manner.

Ideal Uses

The ideal uses are depicted in Figure 7.3. In the first situation the task conversion knowledge is believed to be complete and objectives are seen as certain. Under these conditions tasks can be programmed so that predetermined rules, formulae, and algorithms can be applied to the work and decisions can be made by computation. Accounting and control systems often provide answers on the spot. Examples are standard cost systems, economic order quantity inventory systems, credit inquiry systems, and linear programming models for transportation problems. For these situations, accounting systems can provide accurate, timely, and unequivocal answers.

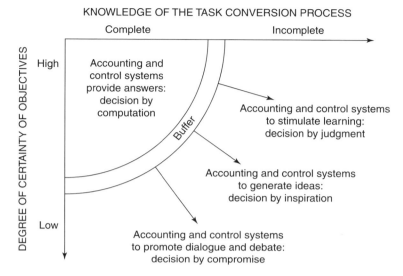

Figure 7.3 Ideal Uses of Accounting and Control Systems

Sometimes uncertainty arises; there may be disagreement over which objective is primary; managers may be ambivalent about the major choices amongst multiple objectives; or objectives may simply be unstated. Whatever the reason, uncertainty over objectives, spurred on by individual self-interest and rapidly changing environments, brings with it conflict over principles and perspectives.

In these circumstances decision making should be oriented towards opening up and maintaining channels of communications. Opinions and different perspectives need to be identified and debated in an open and lively fashion. Accounting and control systems can facilitate this by helping managers develop and argue points of view which are conflicting but consistent with the underlying facts, data, and context. In such situations, MACS should be used to promote dialog, to act as a catalyst for debate, and to help participants reach a compromise rather than to provide *the* answer.

They should also be used to bring conflict, power plays, and bargaining over objectives out into the open where discussion and compromise might lead to better decisions. For example, MACS can be used to initiate debate during the strategic planning process whereby two quite different but equally feasible strategic alternatives are articulated from the same data base. Dialogs, not answers, are called for.

Similarly, in the situation where objectives are clear but knowledge of how to complete the task correctly is low, MACS seldom yield a final optimal answer but they can be of considerable support in figuring out how to get the job done. The need here is for exploration of problems, investigation of the analyzable parts of the work, and the application of judgment and intuition as learning takes place.

In these situations MACS can, at best, only suggest a set of feasible solutions, provide data along the way, and help managers assess alternatives thoroughly. Budget variance analysis reports, inquiry systems for probing data bases, computerized models with sensitivity analysis capabilities, and simulations with what-if facilities are examples of systems that help managers learn more about the possible alternatives and their consequences before they make the final judgment. Learning takes precedence over correct answers.

In our fourth situation uncertainty stems from both incomplete knowledge of the task conversion process as well as from unclear objectives or disagreement about which ones are paramount. Accounting and control systems can be used to stimulate and trigger creativity during brainstorming sessions, where any idea, no matter how ridiculous at first glance, is given serious consideration. They can also be used as a supplement to the strategic think-tank sessions where possible critical events are listed and scenarios developed about the consequences of two or more occurring at the same time. It has even been suggested that, in extreme situations, semiconfusing accounting systems can be designed deliberately to shake organizations out of rigid behavior patterns in times of changing environmental conditions (Hedberg and Jönsson, 1978). While inspiration cannot be guaranteed, it can be given a boost with MACS that provide multiple streams of thought to trigger creativity. They can be valuable cohorts for idea generation.

Actual Uses

In each of the four circumstances depicted above, MACS can be used to construct the reality of the work situation in the most appropriate way. Yet when these systems are in actual use, they do not always mirror their ideal uses. Instead, they are used in quite different ways, as depicted in Figure 7.4.

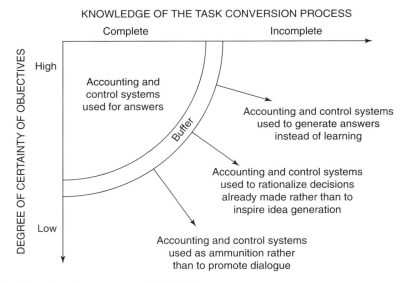

Figure 7.4 Actual Uses of Accounting and Control Systems

There are no problems when objectives are certain and task knowledge complete. Here MACS are used to generate answers. We find, however, that when knowledge of the task conversion process is incomplete, they are still used to provide answers instead of to promote learning. One reason for this may be that accountants are good at providing answers. They are trained and called upon to provide them even when circumstances are in reality fraught with uncertainty. In fact, techniques relying on probability and risk analysis are considered to be rational ways of coping with uncertainty and so work to camouflage the inherently uncertain situation. Either way, the result is that opportunities to stimulate learning and to exploit uncertainty are lost.

Further, we often find that when the degree of certainty regarding objectives is low, accounting and control systems are used as ammunition to win the day. So instead of promoting dialog, debate, and leading to compromise, they are invoked to support the vested interests and values of specific groups. They emerge from political processes where one side attempts to prejudice the criterion for selection of a solution and then proceeds to influence the other parties on the basis of that criterion.

Traditional MACS are undoubtedly employed as ammunition. Reports containing only financial information are used to reduce multiple objectives to a single financial goal when, in reality, organizational needs also include marketing, engineering, and human relations aspects. By focusing on only one objective, MACS can be exploited to further the political ambitions of particular vested-interest groups.[8]

The classic example comes from politics, where various political parties try to influence lawmaking in legislative assemblies. Using the same data base, provided by the Bureau of Statistics, one party develops an information system that supports a reduction in government meddling in the economy while another party develops information that indicates the need for an increase in government planning. Similarly, when accounting systems are used as ammunition, they are dangerous because they override the need for constructive dialog and compromise.

Finally, when task knowledge is incomplete and objectives are uncertain, instead of the necessary idea machine we often find MACS designed to act as rationalization vehicles to justify and legitimize actions already decided upon. Capital budgeting proposals, for example, are put together after the managers have decided that a particular long-term project should be pursued.[9] Task forces, established to investigate issues that have already been decided upon by top management, often use management accounting systems in this way.

Rationalization by management accounting systems can have legitimate uses. Sometimes it is necessary to create a rationale to justify decisions to others. Problems arise, however, when they overwhelm the creativity and inspiration necessary for uncovering new and unique decisions. Instead of interactive accounting and control systems, which promote learning and growth, they are used to rationalize and to rubber-stamp the status quo. When objectives and task instrumentality are unclear, accounting and control systems should be used more often than not to facilitate learning, not to rationalize predetermined decisions.

7.6 Control as Camouflage

The final set of ideas in this chapter presents a radical exposé of the *objective accountability* and *bottom-line* mentality so prevalent in today's organizations.[10] The basic premise of these notions is that what is presented as objective and rational is merely the camouflage over what is really a subjective, invisible war of self-interest that is endemic but inevitable in the workplace. As the developers of these ideas put it, "Each day we march off to an invisible war. We fight battles we don't know we're in, we seldom understand what we are fighting for and worst of all, some of our best friends turn out to be the enemy" (Culbert and McDonough, 1980, p. 3).

There are a couple of simple reasons for this state of affairs. First, organizations today feature a complex world of specialization and narrow expertise. Work must be delegated to a variety of people with different skills and interests who can get the job done. So organizations try to specify the type of responsibility and commitment needed in order to strike an agreement with employees who will stand accountable for what has been agreed upon. Then, after the fact, evaluators will be able to appraise objectively whether or not inputs and outputs lived up to expectations.

Second, and just as crucial, most employees have career ambitions. This is particularly the case with managers. They like to have their efforts recognized and their accomplishments rewarded. They like to get ahead and they want to know how they are doing. So organizations need objective accountability and subordinates look for it from superiors. Thus MACS loom large; after all, they are thought to contain neutral, objective information regarding plans and outcomes.

So objective accountability becomes a given. But one point is often overlooked: whose objectivity? As it turned out, getting the product out of the door as required (and most people do a pretty good job of this) is necessary but not enough to get a favorable appraisal. Success also depends on getting evaluators to recognize and value one's efforts and accomplishments—particularly to see how they contribute to the organizations overarching mission and purpose.

However, evaluators are also busy getting their efforts recognized and valued. And they have their own cherished ideas about what inputs, outputs, and commitments really count. This orientation, as it is called, usually consists of a self-serving ideal about global mission, an important accomplishment that matches their own interests and affinities. The evaluator's orientation seldom matches the evaluee's orientation. In consequence, the evaluee's orientation is discounted and his or her efforts and accomplishments become short-changed by the evaluator's "objective accountability" framework. Evaluators see the world from their own particular orientation, not that of the evaluees.

There are many plausible ways of defining organizational reality, so there are many self-convenient orientations circulating within an organization at any one time. It is no great feat, then, to find an orientation that puts one's own efforts in the best light while devaluing the contributions of others, especially those who are seen as rivals. Thus, even though most people in organizations do a good job most of the time (in fact it is ironic that evaluation systems are not at all necessary to identify those few who perform poorly, everyone already knows) it is easy to trivialize their performance. Evaluators select their own subjective orientation for this task and thus tilt the battlefield heavily in their favor. Evaluation never takes place on neutral terrain.

A specific example may be helpful to highlight these points. In a professional accounting firm most managers have the normal ambition of becoming a partner. The manager who treats client attention and billings (outputs) as the bottom line finds it easy to deprecate the performance of another manager who believes that training juniors (inputs) and service to the accounting profession (impact) are absolute organizational imperatives. Each have a genuine vested interest in establishing their orientations as dominant.

Yet the firm, in all likelihood, is well served by both. There are many plausible organizational realities for a professional accounting firm and this makes it possible for most managers to view performance from a position that most devalues others' contributions while highlighting their own. The astute manager is constantly vigilant for attempts by others to establish grounds of meaning that renders his or her own reality ineffective.

Furthermore, the selection of the particular turf within the evaluation terrain turns out to be pivotal to the outcome of the evaluation. Sometimes inputs are selected by evaluators as the turf for objective accountability. Inputs are the necessary materials, wages, capital, effort, and actions that go into producing outputs. Objective standards are struck for input levels and standard operating procedures defined for effort and action so they can be compared with actual levels and conduct. Evaluators are then quick to point out that input standards were not met, or that essential operations were neglected, or that proper procedures were not followed. Such attacks are mounted regardless of the level of output achieved or the overall impact of effort on global purpose.

This self-serving logic can be used, for example, by a divisional manager to explain why he fired the marketing manager for neglecting to train salespeople in the proper way to deal with customers, despite the marketing manager having consistently met sales objectives. At the same time, the divisional manager will make much of meeting the standards for inputs and meticulously following all procedures and rules; the manager will deny any blame for unsatisfactory profits (output) and a bad reputation (impact). Similarly, engineers fall back on the standards of inputs rationale when they are on the carpet because the bridge that they designed collapsed. Selection of turf is critical to the kind of evaluation given.

When the problems of input and activity accountability are recognized the objective accountability war is shifted to the level of outputs. Outputs are the tangible accomplishments, such as finished product, services provided, and profit and sales volumes, of the effort exerted on inputs. The rationale for output accountability is simple: hold people accountable for achieving agreed output objectives and do not interfere with how they do it; either they make it or a new crew is brought in. This is the essence of management by objectives (MBO). What counts is hard results, the bottom line of performance.

There are, however, major flaws in this way of managing. Agreed profit levels, for example, can be accomplished in the short run by neglecting machinery maintenance programs, reducing institutional advertising, cutting back on customer services, and ignoring the need for training programs for middle managers. When outputs are emphasized, managers can meet them by cutting back on inputs. This is done at the expense of the long-run impact on the health of the organization for future profits and accomplishments. The abuses of bottom-line accountability are legion.[11]

When it becomes difficult to win the day with objective accountability for inputs and outputs, evaluators can shift the evaluation turf to impact. Impact is the effect of effort and output on the higher order, overarching institutional objectives, such as the long-run health of the organization or its contribution to society and mankind. The television sponsor wants commitment to good taste, and not merely high Nielson ratings. Parents want schools to provide for the social adjustment of their children, not merely high scores on national mathematics or reading contests. High-minded values are invoked as more important than inputs and outputs.

As it turns out, the roughest and toughest objective accountability battles take place over impact. Evaluators try to find out in advance whether or not accountable managers stand for given organizational imperatives. They demand to know whether or not the manager will be ready to do whatever may be called upon as specific situations evolve in order to serve the overarching purpose. These mission standards are treated as absolutes even though in reality they are relatives, as they must be selected on the basis of subjective values and morals which, unlike input and output standards, can never be objective. As with the selection of the turf, objective accountability for impact is a subjective value-laden enterprise.

So the objective accountability game can be played at three levels: inputs, outputs, and impact. Wily evaluators, including rivals, know how to switch from level to level in order to further their own self-interest at the expense of the evaluee. A manager, for example, may be contributing mightily to agreed long-run missions but the evaluator merely points out that input standards, as shown clearly by formal management accounting and control reports, were not met. But if input standards were achieved, the evaluator points out that bottom-line outputs, once again clearly shown by the formal reports, have not been met. When both input and output standards have been achieved, evaluators shift the turf to the dubious commitment by the evaluee to the overarching mission.

Thus, it is the ground on which the war of self-interest is fought, and the orientation that best fits the self-interests of specific parties, that decides the winner. The key to winning is to keep the opposition debating within a structure that supports your own position, but be quick to switch the territory when your opponent begins to score well. Formal accounting and control systems provide plenty of ammunition for attacking opponents on either inputs, outputs, or impact.

Most individuals either explicitly recognize or intuitively sense the workaday world is awash with such self-serving definitions of organizational reality and that, more often than not, the orientation of significant evaluators is different from their own. In consequence, they tend intuitively to rely on some sort of distinctive survival tactic. Careful research has identified three such ways of coping: framing, fragmenting, and playing it both ways (Culbert and McDonough, 1980, 1985).

Framing

Framing is a means of meeting opponents head on by asserting an orientation that forces others to relate to the entire structure of one's position instead of to the individual parts. It involves subjectively constructing a self-serving reality on a foundation that is pretty much unassailable in general but with which others may reasonably differ in terms of its specifics. It means appealing to and aggressively promoting a set of lofty ideals while getting on with business as usual, in terms of specific practical endeavors and outcomes that may or may not be consistent with the overarching frame.

President Bush's handling of the situation in the Middle East just before the Gulf War is an example of a highly successful framing—one that easily swept aside different orientations of various politicians and citizens opposing armed conflict.[12] In getting Congress to vote for a war, the president (accountable to US citizens and their elected politicians) appealed to an interlocking set of lofty goals and ideals. He constructed his frame so as to put at stake many of the cherished imperatives of the modern world, not least of which were the democratic ideals of Western civilization (Saddam was a dictator along the lines of Hitler and with similar ambitions); the humanitarian values of civilized people around the globe (Iraq had used chemical weapons in the war with Iran and on its own Kurdish citizens, and had inflicted barbarous attacks on Kuwaiti civilians, including babies in hospitals); the violation of the international nuclear weapons limitation agreement (Iraq was developing its own nuclear weapons capability); the economic stability of the entire Western industrialized world (Iraq would get hold of the vast oil reserves in Kuwait and Saudi Arabia and hold the West up to ransom); and the future existence of an Israeli state (Saddam's real plan was to give Israel to the Palestinians as an Arab state). These and other lofty ideals were woven into an almost unassailable frame.

This framing was constructed in the face of and despite a host of contradictory specific facts and events (Kaplan 1993b; and Friedman 1994). Never mind that Kuwait and Saudi Arabia with their relatively tiny populations were in the hands of enormously wealthy totalitarian family dictatorships at a time when much of the Islamic world existed in a state of poverty and was moving towards democratic government; that the US itself played a huge hand in supporting and arming Iraq as a counterbalance to Iran; that Iraq had never acquiesced to the British carving up of the Gulf region in the 1920s, including separating Kuwait from Iraq when it drew up its arbitrary borders for the Gulf states; that the US had the largest stockpile of chemical weapons in the world and had used them in Vietnam; that Israel was armed with nuclear bombs and chemical weapons; that the continuing settlement of the Palestinian territories was in violation of United Nations declarations; that Israel was the biggest threat to any lasting peace in the Middle East; that Kuwait had continued to take the lion's share of the oil market with price-cutting tactics in spite of repeated requests from Iraq and other Arab nations to discontinue this practice; that US diplomats had indicated to Iraq that it would not intervene if Iraq invaded Kuwait and even seemed to encourage such action; and that economic sanctions by the US and its allies were beginning to hurt Iraq. These and many other specific facts and events did not count for much against the masterful framework constructed by the president.

The strength of Bush's approach did not lie in the facts he presented, many of which later proved to be inaccurate. Instead, he linked his position to the highly principled logic of doing what was needed to rid the US and the United Nations of the biggest threat to their way of life since Hitler and Mussolini. He also made it clear that he called out, not as a single voice, but as the trusted and rightful spokesperson of the president's office and, indeed, of the Western free world. His opponents did not have a chance against the highly principled logic of this overarching lofty frame.

Of course a similar argument applies to the crisis following the 9/11 attack and the response of president George W. Bush, based on the construction of facts such as the existence of weapons of mass destruction which were then revealed simply to be inaccurate if not completely false.

Fragmenting

Fragmenting is a survival tactic that becomes necessary when one is on the receiving end, not just of one evaluator's orientation but of several, each of which has been framed with someone else's best interests at heart. It is common, today, to be in situations where many people think they have a stake in what we accomplish and how we do it. It is as if we are in a fishbowl being watched and evaluated from a host of subject positions, many of which we are not even aware of until they suddenly appear on the scene to question whether or not our activities and efforts are in aid of their own particular causes. We are constantly in the midst of a host of evaluators and multiple evaluating frames.

In order to cope, it seems necessary and easiest to split the truth into pieces which can be dispensed on self-serving occasions. This permits us to continue to pursue our own orientation in the face of sundry evaluators, each of whom expects us to be immediately responsive to what they see as absolutes. While each piece is more or less accurate, in total they go against the grain of most evaluators' orientations. Unlike framing, where the overall picture works but the details don't, in fragmenting the pieces work but the big overarching story doesn't.

The public accounting profession can be used as an illustration of fragmenting. Shareholders could not fathom how savings and loan companies went bankrupt six months after the accountants had given them a clean audit opinion. Politicians questioned accountants' competence when they had not reported bribes to foreign politicians by US airplane and armament companies. Government agencies and academics wondered how public accountants could be independent and objective in auditing when consulting services to the same companies accounted for nearly half their fees. Financial analysts asked how public accountants could let clients issue favorable, unaudited, quarterly earnings reports that were suddenly wiped out in the annual audited report. Corporate accountants were puzzled by the obvious catch-22 of cooperating fully with the auditors in providing information and explanations that were later used against them in the auditors' reports to the Securities and Exchange Commission (SEC). These are only a few of the concerns by evaluators of public accountants, but they illustrate the point.[13]

The response by the public accounting firms is vintage fragmenting. They simply told different parts of the total story to different evaluators. Regarding the bribes, they invoked the generally accepted accounting principle of materiality as a more important guide for action than ethics. In response to the sudden bankruptcies the answer was that they diligently followed professional standards. As for the conflict of interest regarding consulting, they pointed to their code of ethics and their sacred concern for independence. Regarding the misleading quarterly earnings reports they pointed out there were no generally accepted accounting principles in this regard but they would nevertheless follow SEC guidelines if and when required. And in replying to the corporate accountant conflict, they assured them that they were on their side and only unwillingly used the provided information against them because of pressures from securities commissions and governments. The public accounting profession fragments its total story, invoking professional standards here, ethics there, friendship and collaboration here, and just following government orders there. Each piece makes good sense by itself and is a way of holding off multiple evaluators with different orientations. But the big picture doesn't wash very well: partners on huge salaries who are nonetheless objective, independent servants of the free-enterprise system.

Playing It Both Ways

Playing it both ways, the third tactic for dealing with multiple evaluators, involves telling a different big story to the different evaluators while getting on with the business at hand in the usual manner. It allows the evaluee to say the right things to the right evaluators while keeping the real story about effort and commitment under wraps, thus avoiding embarrassing and unproductive confrontations. In short, it means paying lip service in public to evaluators while going one's own way in private.

University administrators, as a striking example, are highly adept at playing it both ways. The story for legislative funding bodies is that excellence in teaching and turning out graduates who are useful to society is the university's prime mission. The story for the public at large is that the university is a sanctuary for civilization's store of knowledge and wisdom and the wheelhouse for moving society towards a better and more just world. The story for the students who can't find jobs is that the purpose of the university is to develop students' minds so they can enjoy a full and satisfying life. The story for local politicians is that the university pours money into the local economy, provides jobs and service to the community and so should be exempt from property taxes. The story to the support staff is that in spite of professors' high salaries and their occupying all the powerful positions, the university is one big democratic community where all are equal. The story to women's and minority rights groups is that the university is bending over backwards to accommodate their aims and make up for their previous exclusion while at the same time maintaining high academic standards. And the story for the faculty is that the aim of the university is to allow them to get on with their scholarly research and consulting careers with minimal teaching loads, ample support staff, and generous amenities. Each evaluator gets a different big story.

Disorientation and Alignment

While framing, fragmenting, and playing it both ways are common survival tactics, they nearly always lead to *disorientation*. Disorientation occurs when one's activities and efforts become disconnected from one's deep commitments. It happens, for example, when the young trainee accountant starts to acquire the nuts and bolts of computer auditing to please a manager or mentor, instead of following a real interest or aptitude in corporate taxation and tax policy. It also happens when universities move heavily into job-oriented training and privately funded practical research—consulting—when the role of the university is to be critical of the status quo of society and develop knowledge to change it. A fine, almost indiscernible, line is crossed and long-term interests and careers become subverted by the structure of evaluators' orientations.

Alignment is a better and more honorable way to engage in the invisible war of workplace self-interest. Alignment involves, first, being quite clear that self-interest and power games are an inevitable and not necessarily sinister part of the woodwork. It also involves realizing that organizations need many different skills and activities to accomplish organizational goals, so there is a wide variety of valuable orientations. But, most importantly, alignment means being clear about one's own aptitudes, affinities, ambitions, and how they align not only with one's activities, outputs, and commitments but also with the organization's mission and objectives. Finally, it is important to market this alignment to evaluators to see how it plays *before* formal evaluation takes place, not during it. Some fine tuning by appreciating the boss's situation may be necessary and valuable, but if the evaluator still doesn't appreciate how one's orientation serves the organization, it is time to look for a new place where it will be not only recognized but also valued.

7.7 Relating Models to Empirical Observations

The cases below provide a brief illustration of some of the frameworks that we have described in this chapter. The cases of the community health center and Knox Walter & Thomas are examples of the different typologies and styles of control. Then we provide an illustration of a private school that provides insights on how different ideal uses of MACS may well differ from what happens in practice and also provides material to reflect on the symbolic nature of these systems (as illustrated in Chapter 4) and on the opportunities for camouflage that they offer.

7.7.1 The Case of a Community Health Center

Case Information

The center was established under the auspices of a leading hospital as an autonomous unit in a separate location.[14] Its purpose was to provide a full range of preventive and therapeutic healthcare to the residents of a nearby slum district. The primary objective of the center was to be a prevention-oriented family centered source of healthcare, available to all community residents. The administrators also hoped that, in the long run, the center would become financially self-sufficient.

The mission departments included pediatrics, internal medicine, community mental health, nursing, dental health, social services, and nutrition. Each department was staffed by high-calibre physicians and practitioners who held joint appointments at the parent hospital and who incurred a substantial loss in earnings by working at the center. The quality of their work was controlled by careful screening and selection of physicians, continuing peer review by department heads, and random reviews of medical records by a review committee. The center prided itself on its competent, dedicated, and altruistic medical staff.

The center also had a good financial accounting system, as well as line-item budget controls. Feelings that costs were above average for this kind of establishment led the administrative director to have a consultant install a new MACS. The source data for the new system came from detailed forms, which reported the actual time spent with a patient, the total minutes available, and the salary rates for each practitioner. These data were used to calculate the cost per minute for each physician and to create a series of reports, including total costs for each department, average cost for each practitioner per visit and by type of visit, and average cost per encounter for each department. The reports included standard and average cost data and highlighted whether or not each physician had spent more or less time than average for each encounter, and whether or not direct patient care time had changed from the previous period.

The new control system soon became an integral part of the center's administrative activities. It was used to assess the monthly performance of each physician. The director met individually with each physician, and used the new control system as a focal point for reviewing their allocation of time. The data were also distributed to the department heads and discussed at executive and departmental meetings. A management accounting discourse became an integral part of the center's activities.

Reactions to the new system were mixed. The administrators were pleased with it and believed it had greatly increased cost-consciousness behavior on the part of the staff. Evidence of this was the hiring of low-salary people to relieve the physicians from routine tasks. The department heads allowed that the new system made them more aware of time constraints and costs but believed that it ignored important long-term effects of spending time out in the community. They also complained that the new system had brought about a philosophical change by the administration to increase the volume of direct patient care and a decreased emphasis on the quality of care and on family preventive medicine.

Analysis

Let us use some of the ideas in this chapter to analyze and highlight some critical problems with the new control system. For one thing, there are two quite different tasks involved, direct therapeutic medical care (TMC) and preventive-oriented, family centered healthcare (PFC). The TMC objectives are unambiguous: to effect a successful cure. Cause–effect

knowledge is complete for most patients (a broken leg) but incomplete for others (cancer). The new control system does a good job of measuring the efficiency of TMC activity. It is likely, however, that effectiveness is more important than efficiency. Yet the new control system pays no heed to it. The motivation of the new control system is strong and its message is efficient TMC.

Preventive-oriented, family centered healthcare is quite a different matter. Objectives and ends are more ambiguous. How to install an effective preventive/family healthcare system into the slum is not well understood. Clearly, the new management control system with its efficiency orientation is not only unsuitable but also counterproductive to PFC activities. Routine, programmable tasks have a natural tendency to drive out nonroutine, nonprogrammable tasks. When this tendency is strongly reinforced by the control system, with the physicians consequently spending more time on TMC than previously, the results could prove highly detrimental for PFC activities.

The ideas in this chapter also provide clues about the selection of more appropriate assessment and control. In terms of our first framework, when efficiency and instrumental tests are of only limited usefulness, we turn to social ones. There are three relevant social groups involved in the center: the slum community, the funding body, and the physicians themselves. Periodic surveys should be taken of the families in the community regarding the center. A key aspect of PFC is the acceptance of the center by this social group. Such social tests, not the efficiency ones, are appropriate for assessment and scorekeeping.

Turning to our second model, we can see that a bureaucratic system of records and files like the new management accounting system is unsuitable for controlling the physicians. Market controls are ruled out due to the inability and lack of inclination of the slum community to pay market prices for healthcare. But statistics should also be collected about increases in the number of families registered, the number of vaccinations, dental check-ups, fluoride treatments, and the like, to demonstrate to funding agencies that historical improvement has taken place.

However, it seems likely that a clan atmosphere could be readily fostered. Weekly meetings of all practitioners to discuss PFC problems and progress, formation of specific family-designated teams including nurses, circulation of research material on healthcare progress in poverty-stricken communities, and visits to the center by dedicated minority leaders and politicians could all lead to a sense of a working in a very special, dedicated, and loyal group of medical professionals. The physicians have willingly given up a higher income to dedicate themselves, at least for a time, to solving the health problems of the slum. Clan control, in fact, is remarkably well suited to the type of work necessary to achieve the major aim of the center.

Our typology also points towards the potential for collegial control. We already see evidence of the dialectic tension between the practitioners and the administrators. At the end of the case, it appears the administrators have gained the upper hand by invoking messages about efficiency in the new management control system. In order to restore power and control to the practitioners, it may be necessary for the most senior and respected practitioners to form a collegium to challenge and overturn rule by the administrators.

To summarize, we have a classic case of the skillful design of a technically sound control system that is, unfortunately, unsuited to the prevailing circumstances. The detailed cost accounting system was thoughtlessly designed and used without regard for the purposes of the organization or the nature of its work. Efficiency of TMC became the focal point for performance measurement. As a result, the new management control system started to have what could eventually be a profound effect. The practitioners have already shifted their efforts to TMC to the neglect of the center's fundamental purpose. A clan atmosphere and collegial control could effectively get the center back on the right track. While our frameworks do not provide a definitive answer, they point the way towards a means of redressing the balance.

7.7.2 Knox, Walter & Thomas

Our second case involves the introduction of profitability and efficiency management controls into Knox, Walter & Thomas (KWT), the Canadian subsidiary (a disguised name) of Walter Thomas & Associates, a UK-based advertising agency with operations in 37 countries. Agencies like KWT service advertising campaigns for brands marketed by existing clients. They also take on new clients after consideration of their long-run profit potential and possible conflicts of interest with their established clients. Agencies earn revenues through either a flat 15% commission on the gross billings by the media organization (television, radio, newspapers, etc.) where the media are placed and from cost-plus contracts and retainer fees. For cost-plus assignments the agency bills the client for the full cost of the work plus an agreed profit margin; in the case of a retainer, the agency receives a guaranteed fee for the job as well as reimbursement of expenses.

Case Information

Knox, Walter & Thomas was a full-service agency and most of its work involved creating and implementing advertising campaigns for major corporations as well as for the federal Progressive Conservative party. It also took on cost-plus and retainer fee engagements. Knox, Walter & Thomas had worked with most of its 20 major clients (involving over 100 brands) for more than 25 years and with some for over 50 years and took on a major new client every year or so. In order to prevent advertising programs from stagnation, KWT followed a policy of rotating clients among the account supervisors every couple of years or so. As well, it was common for clients to hire KWT account supervisors as in-house product executives.

Knox, Walter & Thomas followed the normal organizational structure (see Figure 7.5). Five directors reported to the president, John Knox, who reported to the board of directors. The account management group, the hub of the agency, worked with clients to develop the advertising approach and oversee the production process through the agency. Account executives and supervisors performed a dual role: consulting with clients on marketing strategies and plans and coordinating overall agency involvement with clients.

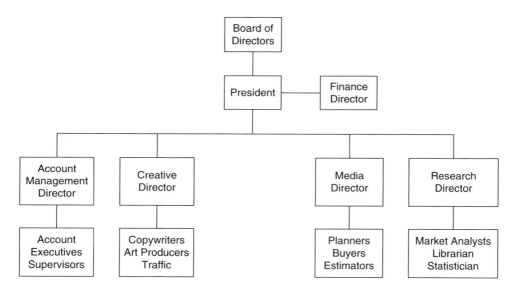

Figure 7.5   KWT Organization Chart

The creative group developed the communication concepts for the campaigns, sold the concepts to clients, and executed the creative work. This involved planning out the words and artwork and producing the printing advertisements and visual communication in keeping with the advertising objectives and strategy developed by the accounts people. The media group then developed the placement plan deciding which media to use, where and for how long. They also became involved in presenting media plans to clients and were responsible for buying media space. The research group provided basic market information to assist in the development of advertising objectives and strategies and also conducted market research studies for clients including pretesting, posttesting, awareness and recall testing, and opinion measurement.

Knox, Walter & Thomas took pride in its team approach to servicing clients. The president, acting on advice from the directors, formed teams from the four groups to work together on specific clients' advertising campaigns. Generally, a team consisted of an account executive, an account supervisor, an art director, a copywriter, a media buyer, and a media planner. Often the finance director sat in on team meetings.

Analysis

A full-service advertising agency seems to be very much in the nature of an open-natural system rather than a closed-rational one. Client's whims, customer's tastes, competitor's innovations, and the ups and downs of the general economy make for a highly uncertain and often turbulent environment. Agencies are very much open to the uncertainties and vagaries of the environment. This is particularly so for the technical core—the creative, media, and research groups—where there is little chance for them to know whether or not their efforts have optimized input–output relations. Survival, not efficiency, is the primary goal.

Analysis of the two antecedent conditions in Figures 7.1 and 7.2 helps define more specifically the nature of this uncertainty. The goals of an advertising agency are relatively clear-cut and unambiguous. The mission is to sell the clients' products. But creating advertising that works is anything but a rational, well-understood task. Successful advertising is very much a hit-and-miss creative process.

As David Ogilvy, the creator of the now classic Hathaway Shirt eye-patch ad and the recognized father of the image school of advertising, put it, "I've been in this trade for more than thirty years and written as much advertising as anyone alive. In those thirty years I had only nine big ideas. It's not many, is it? But it's more than most people."[15] *Advertising Age* summed it up this way: "Advertising is like electricity. We know a great deal about it and its uses, but we are not very successful in defining it or delimiting it."[16] Moreover, clients' sales of products are also affected by a large number of factors such as sales-force effort and pricing decisions in addition to those factors mentioned above.

More Case Information

The finance and administration group maintained the accounting records, handled treasury matters, and took care of the usual sundry office management duties such as personnel records and computer support for the other groups. They also developed a budget every six months for presentation to the board of directors. The budget included anticipated revenues, line-item expenses (salaries, rent, entertainment, supplies, etc.) and overall net income. In addition, the finance director kept a subsidiary client ledger in which expenses and revenues were recorded for each client and each client account.

Knox, Walter & Thomas's salaries and wages amounted to 63% of gross revenues while other expenses (travel, entertainment, rough-copy costs, general research work, pretesting, occupancy, employee benefits, telephone, stationery, etc.) ran about 22%, leaving 15% profit before taxes. All employees, with the exception of those in the finance and administration group, filed weekly time sheets indicating the hours spent on each client account. Nearly 90% of the payroll total could be traced directly to client accounts with the rest posted to the indirect expenses account. About one-third of the other expenses also were charged directly to specific client accounts. The remainder and nonchargeable payroll costs were allocated to client accounts on the basis of direct salary payroll.

This data base was used to put together a profit-and-loss statement for each client account showing: gross billings; commissions and fees; direct payroll by each group (account management, creative, media, and research) and the allocated amount of direct expenses, unbillable costs and indirect expenses. Each month, the finance group also produced client P&L statements, which included the above items for the current and previous year to date and for the current and previous month. These statements were bound in a package each month but were made available only to the president and the board of directors. While the other directors knew they existed, they were not routinely given copies, although they could, if they wished, come to the finance director's office and have a look at the numbers for specific accounts.

Recently, one of KWT's large and long-standing clients appointed a new chief executive whose mandate was to improve the company's sagging earnings per share. Historically, the company had budgeted 12% of total sales to advertising but was now considering cutting this back to 8 or 10%. In discussing advertising with KWT's president she stated, "I know half the money we spend on advertising is wasted but we never know which half!" And her new controller had initiated a detailed analysis of the company's advertising expenses. The controller reported that a sophisticated sensitivity analysis produced no statistically significant correlations of changes in sales for the company's 45 different consumer brands with changes in advertising dollars. John Knox responded with the traditional comeback, "advertising should be seen as an investment, not as an expense".

Nevertheless, Knox was concerned that the problem might be widespread. So he asked the finance director to undertake a study of the agency's MACS and to make recommendations for any changes that might help KWT maintain or improve its overall profit picture. The director commissioned a consultant from a leading professional accounting firm to assist him in this charge. Six weeks later, the director informed Knox that, on the advice of his wife whose tolerance for Montreal winters had fallen in recent years, he had decided to take early retirement and move permanently to his condominium on Long Boat Key near Sarasota in Florida. The director recommended that Knox appoint the consultant, who had been chief controller of Ford Canada's huge Oakville automobile plant, as his replacement. When Knox approached the consultant, he immediately accepted the position.

The new finance director, comparing the controls in the agency with those he was familiar with at Ford, became concerned with the lavish expense accounts submitted by account executives and employees in the other groups. As a result, he designed an elaborate budgetary control system, which collected expenses by every conceivable category, right down to individual taxi rides. He also introduced a new computer system including a network of online terminals. All the employees were on hand to witness the installation of the network and give a resounding cheer as the president pushed a button, which put the system on line.

The new director also initiated a series of monthly meetings during which he met with key employees in each group to review the profit statements with them. He soon came to the conclusion that account supervisors and executives should be held responsible for the profitability of the client accounts they handled. He also concluded that each of the directors of the four operating groups should become responsible for the profit performance of their particular group. The calculation of group profit involved allocating revenues and expenses among the operating groups on the basis of the amount of direct labor dollars each group charged directly to client accounts, as well as a cost-plus-profit-margin-based transfer price for services provided by the research group to the other groups.

A year after the expense contract system was installed the director of finance learned that the group executives and managers no longer bothered even to look at the reports. The numbers, they claimed, did not seem to help them very much so the reports fell into disuse even though they were happy with them. He also noticed that their interest had waned in the monthly meetings to review profit performance. While a few executives tried to make sense of the information and to understand the intricacies of cost and revenue allocations and transfer price calculations, most seemed bored and indifferent. Behind his back, the executives referred to the new expense and profit reports as so much "smoke and mirrors bean-counting." Shortly thereafter he left the agency, blaming the executives and managers for the failure of the new controls.

Analysis

The frameworks in this chapter indicate clearly that the finance director was a long way off base. He had treated the advertising agency as a closed-rational system instead of an open-natural one. Instead of efficiency tests, like the detailed expense reports and profit break-downs, the model in Figure 7.1 indicates that instrumental assessment and scorekeeping tests are much better suited to the work of an advertising agency. And, in fact, gross billings are a simple, yet highly relevant, instrumental test and are readily available. By focusing on expenses, which are recovered from clients in any case, instead of tracking gross billings, the new scorekeeping system was out of sync with the key factors involved in advertising work. Similarly, the model in Figure 7.2 indicates that market controls are better suited to the nature of work in advertising agencies than are bureaucratic controls such as account-ing reports. Moreover, market controls are readily available; executives can simply track the sales volume of clients' products.

Furthermore, the new accounting-based controls precipitated a number of dysfunctional actions. For instance, the account management, creative, and media groups cut back on services from the research group. So the research director, in an effort to show a profit, raised the transfer prices. This backfired as the other groups cut back even further on research services. In addition, intergroup squabbles broke out as each group tried to pin-point the blame for low profitability on other groups while taking the lion's share of credit for the high-profit accounts. Furthermore, executives found themselves spending a lot of wasted time trying to make sense of the accounting reports and going to budget meetings instead of servicing clients.

When the finance director left, Knox hired a newly qualified certified general account-ant as treasurer, *not* as finance director. She quickly dropped the comprehensive expense and profit reporting in favor of a system that simply tracked gross billings and direct costs for each account. The executives and managers reverted to spending money in their own way to increase gross billings. The control system once again matched the nature of the agency's environment.

7.7.3 An Illustration

We conclude this chapter with a real-life illustration that highlights some of the key con-cepts outlined above and recalls some of the arguments about symbolic controls examined in Chapter 4. The situation involves the development and distribution of a cost accounting information system in a private school.[17] The school's 80 faculties taught nearly 600 tuition-paying students in grades 6 through 12. The school was organized into eight departments each of which offered a variety of courses. The English department, for example, offered

12 courses with projected enrollments ranging from four students in a grade 12 advanced Shakespeare class to 120 students in introductory English literature sessions. As a rule of thumb it was thought that 12 students per class was the appropriate size.

The headmistress, impressed by a demonstration of a sophisticated, computerized cost accounting estimation system developed by an interstate education commission for long-range planning and financial decision making, developed a simplified system for her school. Input data included actual and projected enrollment by department and by course, as well as faculty mix by department and average salary for each pay step. Assuming an average of 12 students per class and 45 student contacts per day per teacher, the system produced eight exhibits including a schedule of teacher cost by department and per student contact hour, data for current work load per department, and projected staffing requirements. Table 7.1 includes selected data constructed from these exhibits.

In reviewing the output, the headmistress became alarmed about the apparent large range in costs and loads across departments. Even though she treated the numbers as only preliminary estimates, she distributed the eight exhibits to the members of the board of trustees, department heads, and key employees asking them to comment in writing. To her great surprise, she received a wide range of replies, some giving high praise to the new accounting system and some angrily attacking its accuracy and usefulness. Yet most of the reactions can be explained readily in terms of the frameworks described earlier in this chapter.

Some board members and the business manager saw the system as rendering clear-cut answers—this despite the problematic nature of both objectives and instrumentality in the educational process. As one board member put it, "This is the greatest management tool I have seen in this school in ten years. It raises questions that scream to be answered." Another board member stated, "It will help identify areas where excessively large classes are having a detrimental effect on the school's quality of education." And the business manager asserted, "It will serve as a decision-making aid in pinning down areas where our budget is taking a beating because classes are so small." Such responses implicitly assume, wrongheadedly, that knowledge of the teaching task is complete and that objectives of education are clear cut. Thus, answers are seen as forthcoming when instead the new system should be used for dialog, learning, and debate.

A few replies, however, did suggest that the data produced might be valuable for debate and discussion instead of providing instant answers. The head of mathematics, for example, commented this way:

> Our department's reaction is generally favorable to the ideas that seem to lie behind the model. We think they are potentially useful. But I personally fear that cost/effectiveness analyses are somewhat misleading for measuring the quality of a school and its departments for, ideally, we are not turning out a product for popular demand in quite the same sense as does General Motors. My apprehension is that these figures may eventually be misused at some level. But we are, at least, now getting some concrete data that ought to be taken into account in examining our operations. Also, if the data are used to draw questionable conclusions, we will at least have something definite to argue about.

Table 7.1 Selected Statistics from the Cost Estimation Model.*

Department	Faculty		Contact Hours Per Week Per Faculty		Average Salary For Faculty ($)	Cost Per Student Contact Hour		Student Enrolment in Hours Per Week	
Lower school	20	(18.1)	213	(204)	26,550	124.62	(130.14)	4,260	(4,080)
English	14	(11.7)	197	(189)	29,571	150.00	(156.81)	2,760	(2,640)
Mathematics	8	(8.8)	248	(247)	31,500	127.26	(127.26)	1,980	(1,980)
Social science	8	(10.9)	270	(308)	28,125	104.16	(91.49)	2,160	(2,460)
Natural science	8	(8.5)	232	(240)	47,500	161.28	(156.24)	1,870	(1,920)
Fine arts	7	(6.9)	223	(223)	29,142	130.77	(130.77)	1,560	(1,560)
Languages	6	(5.9)	220	(220)	27,481	125.01	(125.01)	1,320	(1,320)
Physical education	9	(9.1)	227	(227)	28,668	126.45	(126.48)	2,040	(2,040)
Total on average†	80	(225)	224	(225)	29,364	130.59	(130.50)	17,940	(18,000)

*Figures in brackets are projections for the next year.
†Figures are weighted averages.
Source: Assembled from data in various Exhibits in the St. Augustine School (A), case in Shank (1981).

Comments like this point towards the potential usefulness of the new system for dialog and learning. Importantly, however, the system depicts mathematics as a relatively low-cost department and so it is not surprising this department head viewed it in a positive light. Further, the well-balanced and carefully reasoned response is suggestive of symbolic posturing at the altar of rationality and perhaps some coyness on the part of the department head, since the model argues for more staff for mathematics.

Other department heads jumped at the chance to use the output as ammunition. The data indicated that social science was understaffed by three teachers and was the lowest-cost department in the school. The head of social science pounced on the data and quickly mounted an impressive offense.

> I knew we were overworked and overloaded, but, up until this point, we haven't had an objective way of demonstrating it. I never would have had the nerve to ask for three additional teachers, but the figures clearly show that that's what we need. I guess enrolment is up because of the new interest in urban affairs and environmental problems, which fall into our domain.

The head of languages, also a low-cost and low-salaried department according to the data, followed suit:

> It will serve as an independent forecast of faculty needs which will provide an objective yardstick for evaluating the hiring needs submitted by department heads. It will bring fairness and efficiency to an area that has previously known the influence of seniority and internal politics.

Thus, management accounting systems are frequently used as ammunition to support parochial positions, rather than as the raw material for dialog, learning, and ideas.

The new system also presented an excellent opportunity for some participants to display ritualistic assurance of their belief in rational decision making and intelligent choice. The chairperson of the board of trustees, for example, responded this way:

> I see tremendous managerial applications for the model. It can answer questions I've had on my mind for ages. I don't know how to begin to answer them, but this model provides an analytical framework for doing so.

Even though the data are of little help for any specific decisions facing the school, they provided the opportunity for the top executive to symbolize to the rest of the participants that he was indeed a true believer in intelligent, rational choice.

The situation also vividly illustrates some of the dynamics of the invisible war of self-interest in the workplace. The new management accounting system provides mainly data regarding inputs. This is the turf where departments like social science and languages look best while other units such as English and natural sciences score poorly. Thus, as the framework predicts, these departments were quick to shift the evaluation turf to outputs and impact. The English department head, for example, attempted to divert the struggle to the battleground of impact:

It is absurd to use a mechanical model to make decisions about a qualitative issue. I am hurt deeply by the prospect of using an adding machine to determine the quality of education that a student at St. Augustine will receive. To suggest that two teachers be dropped from the English Department strikes at the heart of the discipline that made St. Augustine strong, created its reputation, and currently serves as a main source of its pride and dignity. If there are "adjustments" to be made, let us bring the other disciplines up to the standards set long ago by the English Department.

The lofty turf of intangible impacts provides the English department with a much safer position for defending its current staffing levels and from which to attack the more mundane departments such as physical education and social science which look good on input measures.

Similarly, the department head of natural sciences (with the highest cost per student contact hour) attempted to shift evaluation to outputs:

I suppose the model is correct in pointing out that direct faculty costs per credit hour produced for the Natural Science Department are the highest in the school. The reasons for this are not very subtle or startling: we simply have a greater proportion of senior faculty than other departments. These senior teachers bring more experience and teaching quality to the classroom and therefore command a higher salary. The quality of instruction per credit hour produced in the Natural Sciences Department is higher, and so is the cost. The model yields no decision rules useful for management except that to get more experience and quality in the classroom, the cost is higher. We did not need a model to learn that.

By stressing the quality of the department's output and its more experienced staff, he hoped to shift objective accountability to a more favorable turf.

In summary, as our first framework predicts, instead of using the system to learn why natural sciences, mathematics, and fine arts need smaller class sizes, or to debate the objectives of a private school—whether, for example, to respond to apparently trendy developments like environmental studies or concentrate on the lifelong basic skills like math, science, and fine arts—the system was used as ammunition and to provide answers regarding staffing requirements. The framework also makes it abundantly clear that the system would not automatically give answers but could have been used to advantage to promote constructive dialog and learning. According to the framework, the headmistress would be wise to keep the data produced by the system to herself and perhaps use it only symbolically at board meetings to demonstrate that she believes in rational and intelligent decision making.

Finally, the new system, as the ideas in this chapter suggest, was not well suited for either scorekeeping or control. The appropriate scorekeeping for a private school would be to collect the opinions and beliefs of relevant social groups—parents, alumni, university and college admissions officers—regarding the quality of the school's graduates and its general reputation. As for control, one alternative is to organize a collegium of the department heads and eminent faculty to make key strategic decisions and advise the headmistress on policy and hiring. It also seems likely that building a clan atmosphere for the dedicated faculty would be a good option for control purposes. This might entail regular wine-and-cheese parties, faculty outings to cultural events, ritualistic dinners for new and retiring faculty, and a well-stocked faculty lounge with coffee, muffins, magazines and newspapers.

Ironically, the headmistress has done the opposite. Her new management accounting system not only precipitated a war of self-interest in the workplace but it also provided the ammunition for the battle. By initiating efficiency scorekeeping she has split the clan into warring factions and will be hard pressed to turn the faculty into a cohesive, proud, dedicated, and loyal social unit.

7.8 Summary and Conclusions

The four frameworks presented in this chapter provide alternative ways of thinking about the problems of designing appropriate MACS. The approach is based on the need to go beyond, although not to exclude, closed-rational systems, and the need to understand how patterned variations in uncertainty call for systematic differences in MACS. The rational approach is highly satisfactory for stable and predictable parts of the organization, particularly the technical core. Here efficiency tests and bureaucratic controls are a valuable and integral part of the drive to optimize the use of resources. Bureaucratic control is ubiquitous in today's world. It works by means of observational command hierarchies, rules, records, and files. These controls function reasonably well for those parts of the organization that can be treated as closed-rational systems because ends and values are unambiguous and the knowledge regarding means of getting work accomplished is well understood.

They do not work as well for open-natural systems where these conditions do not prevail. Here, organizations look to other forms of control. Bureaucratic controls, so well suited to the certainty of closed-rational systems, tend to lose their potency when means are not well understood and when ends are ambiguous.

Efficiency tests and bureaucratic controls lose their power in the face of changing and uncertain environments. The rational approach, so well suited to a predictable closed system, should give way to an open-natural perspective, which focuses on the mechanisms whereby organizations react, adapt, and survive in the face of an incessantly changing environment. Under these conditions, other types of control must be brought into play to supplement bureaucratic controls. These include charismatic, market, tradition, and collegial controls. Historical efficiency tests are replaced by criteria of instrumental effectiveness and ultimately yield to the opinions and beliefs of relevant social groups. Similarly bureaucratic controls give way to market, charismatic, tradition, and collegial controls.

The other basic element of this new perspective is that it rejects either the quest for universal truths, contained in generally accepted management accounting principles, or the preoccupation with detailed case studies with their exhaustive analysis of the uniqueness of the scorekeeping and control systems in a particular organization. Instead, a middle ground is advocated where the patterned variations in the uncertainty are linked with systematic differences in organizational action. Different kinds of uncertainty lead to different patterns of assessment and control.

By following these premises and looking for patterned variations, we were able to capture the full range of assessment and controls mechanisms used in organizations: efficiency, instrumental, social, bureaucratic, charismatic, market, collegial, and tradition.

When objectives and missions are clear and unambiguous and the means for getting work done are well understood, organizations can assess the performance of their components according to past efficiency. If, however, the means are not well understood, assessment must be based on instrumental tests dictated by goals and mission. But if components are internally autonomous, assessment must shift to extrinsic measures. And when ends and missions are nonrational, organizations must turn to the opinion of relevant social groups. Finally, under conditions of multiple criteria, organizations must be sensitive to, and quick to change the relative weightings of the various criteria as the importance of relevant social groups also shifts with the fluctuating environment.

This section outlined a typology of control styles that links Weber's general ideas with systematic variations in the uncertainty involved in the work and tasks of organizations or their components. Bureaucratic controls, consisting of observational hierarchies, rules, procedures, records, and files, are well suited to circumstances featuring rational ends and means. When ends are unambiguous but means are not well understood, market controls, which rely on the information content of prices, and charismatic controls, provided by a dynamic heroic leader, can be used to advantage. Finally, under circumstances where the means for task accomplishment are well understood, collegial and tradition serve as suitable controls.

Management accounting and control systems have a role to play in each of these types. They are a major part of the records and files needed for bureaucratic controls. They provide the necessary information about prices required for market control. In the case of charismatic and traditional control, they are less important but do provide information regarding the use of resources in terms of missions as well as indicating how resources are shared. Finally, in collegial control they become an important resource in the struggle between the collegium and the administrators.

These ideas, which put accounting and control systems into the wider and more realistic organizational context, can provide a richer understanding of the issues and problems of management accounting and control than the traditional textbook approach, which focuses on technical problems such as better cost allocations and more accurate profit measurements. They are not wholly theoretical. In fact, they can have very important practical applications.

That accountants should gather, store, and report information about social opinions and beliefs remains a novel and perhaps uncomfortable idea. The idea, however, is creeping into the accounting domain. Socially and environmentally concerned groups of citizens are forming mutual investment funds to purchase securities of only those firms with a good record in these areas. Their opinions count, even in the pocketbook. And assessment and scorekeeping in the public sector at the federal, state, and municipal levels have been working on this front for many years. It is a good time for MACS managers to take the idea seriously.

This chapter also introduced the idea that MACS do not simply objectively reflect some pre-existing reality. Rather, they are the raw material from which organizational participants subjectively "construct" reality, often a self-serving one. Under conditions of certainty, MACS can be relied on to provide answers. But when uncertainty enters the scene they can be put to better use for promoting dialog, stimulating learning, and generating ideas. But instead we often find them used by managers as ammunition to win the day or to rationalize decisions made unilaterally. These ideas take a radical turn from the traditional perspective. Accounting systems are revealed not as objectively reflecting some pre-existing reality, but as constituting organizational reality. They do not merely tell the score after the events, they shape them.[18]

The chapter also demonstrated how MACS often provide the ammunition for the objective accountability war during which organizational participants stress input, output, or impact performance, whichever turf favors their own orientation and contribution while degrading those of rivals. Thus the chapter took an important turn away from objective realist thinking to adopt the position of a subjective interpretivist. In the next chapter we look at a more comprehensive framework which incorporates both of these positions.

These ideas present a radical demystification of the objective accountability and bottom-line discourse so prevalent in the conventional accounting literature and in practice. They reveal how objective accountability is in reality a highly subjective and inevitable invisible war of self-interest. Evaluators subjectively construct self-convenient frameworks of reality and then, treating them as objective frames, use them as the structures to evaluate others. In the process, the evaluee's orientation gets pushed aside. Evaluators also subjectively select the specific turf—inputs, outputs, or impact—for the war and are quick to put the battle on the turf that shows themselves to advantage or which puts opponents in a bad light. They are also quick to shift to a different turf if opponents seem to be getting the upper hand. What is put forth as objective accountability is more realistically subjective framing and maneuvering.

In order to survive when on the receiving end of someone else's orientation and turf, evaluees frequently resort to framing, fragmenting, or playing it both ways. Framing involves constructing a master idealistic framework with an unassailable, highly principled logic while ignoring any specific ongoing activities and outputs which contradict the master frame. Fragmenting goes the opposite way. It involves pointing to different specific activities and outputs for different evaluators while hiding or ignoring the overarching frame. Playing it both ways consists of presenting a different master frame to each important evaluator.

Pursuing such survival tactics, however, frequently leads to disorientation and losing one's way. A better strategy is to make sure one's orientation is consistent with one's personal aptitudes, affinities, and aspirations, and to communicate that orientation to important others before formal evaluation so it is clear how one contributes to the organization's global mission.

Endnotes

1. This framework was developed by Thompson (1967), one of the great pioneers of organizational theory.
2. Williamson (1973), who developed an elegant theory of organization, calls these "transaction costs."
3. Ouchi (1977) describes the two departments in detail.

4. Ouchi (1977, 1979) popularized the notion of clan control. See also Ezzamel and Hart (1987) and Macintosh (1985).
5. See Inoguchi, Nakajima and Pineau (1958) for a detailed description of the *kamikaze* pilots.
6. We have already seen an example of this in Chapter 4 when we discussed of the symbolic nature of MACS.
7. This section is based on the work of Burchell *et al.* (1980), Earl and Hopwood (1980), and Thompson and Tuden (1959).
8. See Ansari and Euske (1987), Boland and Pondy (1983, 1986), Covaleski and Dirsmith (1986, 1988), Dirsmith and Jablonsky (1979) for careful and detailed case histories focusing on the political aspects of management accounting and control systems.
9. See Bower (1970) for a detailed exposition of the politics of the capital budgeting process and Chenhall and Morris (1991), who investigate the interaction of cognitive style and project sponsorship on such decisions.
10. This section is based on the innovative and enlightening work of Culbert and McDonough (1980, 1985).
11. See Dearden (1960, 1961) and more recently Dearden (1987) and Merchant (1985, 1990).
12. See Kaplan (1993b) and Freidman (1994) for detailed documentation of the Iraq-gate scandal and US involvement in the Middle East.
13. These instances and the following examples of fragmenting are outlined in Culbert and McDonough (1985).
14. See the Hyatt Hill Health Center case study in Anthony and Dearden (1981, p. 720).
15. Quoted in Wright, Winter, Zeigler and O'Dea (1984, p, 137).
16. World of advertising, *Advertising Age*, 15 November, 1983, p. 10.
17. The case is described in detail in Shank (1981, pp. 280–95). All quotations are from this case study.
18. This point is brought home in the well-known story about the two baseball umpires who were asked by a reporter how they saw their job. The first umpire gave the traditional objective realist response that if a pitch was in the strike zone he called it a strike, otherwise he called it a ball. The second umpire, in contrast, replied, "They ain't nothin' till I calls 'em!" It is the same, more often than not, with accounting. Organizational realities ain't anything until the accounting system and its managers "calls 'em."

Further Readings

You can usefully do some further readings in each of the following areas. On various styles of control:

- Ouchi, W. (1979) A conceptual framework for the design of organizational control mechanisms. *Management Science*, **25,** 833–48.

On how management controls vary according to some contingent variables:

- Chenhall, R. (2007) Theorising contingencies in management control systems research, in *Handbook of Management Accounting Research* (eds C. Chapman, G. Hopwood and M. Schields), Elsevier, Oxford, vol. I, pp 163–206.

PART III

MACS IN ACTION: ISSUES OF CHANGE AND INFORMATION TECHNOLOGY

MACS IN ACTION

CHANGE

INFORMATION TECHNOLOGY

8

MACS and Change

In this chapter:

8.1 Introduction[1]

Bruno Latour, a French sociologist, contends that ignorance of key concepts in scientific analysis is commonplace:

> We know very little about what causes sciences, technologies, organizations and economies. Open books on social science and epistemology, and you will see how they use the adjectives and adverbs "abstract," "rational," "systematic," "universal," "total," "complex." Look for the ones that try to explain the nouns "abstraction," "rationality," "systems," "universe," "science," "organization," "totality," "complexity," without ever using the corresponding adjectives or adverbs, and you will be lucky to find a dozen. Paradoxically we know more about the Achuar, the Arapesh or the Alladians than we know about ourselves. (Latour, 1991, p.116)

We wish to add "change" to Latour's list.

Organizational change is a central issue within organization theory, management and, increasingly, accounting. How accounting systems need to change has been one of the key dilemmas that managers and academics had to face in both their recent and more recent past. Since accounting has been said to have lost its relevance,[2] as it was too concerned with legalistic requirements rather than assisting decision making, debates on how it should change have proliferated. As we will see later, in Chapter 10, accounting practices succeed and spread across time, economies and societies because of their ability to change and adapt to, or foster, new information needs and requirements. Thus, whatever job you have, be it a consultant for small and medium-size enterprises or the CFO of a big corporation, you will always have to cope with issues of accounting change. Yet, you will face the difficulties typical of change management: to convince others to adopt a "new" accounting system or try to persuade them to resist this overpoweringly attractive temptation.

New management and accounting systems come in many different forms although, interestingly, they are always identified by a three letter acronym: ABC, ABM, BSC, and EVA are among the most popular.[3] Many firms have responded with alacrity, adopting them with varied results. In some cases this adoption caused people to miss the old systems. In some others, the implementation of these new systems brought benefits to the organization and contributed to better decision making and improved bottom lines. Whatever the effects, and despite the centrality of change processes in daily business life, change is often approached simplistically and still not well understood and managed.

This chapter will seek to shed some light on the models theorizing change and the issues that accounting change processes entail. It will first introduce quite a conventional notion of change and relate it to some of the studies that have sought to explain drivers of management accounting change and its effects. This notion leads to a fairly linear notion of change and is underpinned by a simple relationship between knowledge of the processes, actions required to change the organization and rationality assessing the validity of these actions. The resulting view of an organization is an ordered system that creates an illusion of control. This model may be appropriate for stable environments but complex organizational realities and processes require different approaches to the problem of organizational and accounting change. The current chapter therefore continues with more complex views of change and introduces frameworks that are inspired by the works of the British sociologist Anthony Giddens and the French sociologist Bruno Latour. We will introduce the main tenets of Gidden's structuration theory and link these to the ways in which management controls work in practice by illustrating the cases of General Motors and the implementation of a new management accounting system at the US Department of Defense. This will be followed by the illustration of the case of a large multinational implementing a new technology of management control. Insights from the case are then informed by Latour's approach on actor-network theory to redefine the notion of change as drift. Drift is seen as a process that combines serendipity with the purposefulness of managerial actions and controls. This case will also offer material that suggests a need to think differently about the role of information technologies in enhancing management controls, moving away from the conventional view that more information necessarily means greater control.

8.2 What is Change? A Commonsensical Definition

Let's begin our journey into the nature of management accounting and control change by asking a question which, at first glance, may appear trivial: what is *change*? The *On-line Encarta English Dictionary* defines it as "Making or becoming different, a shift from one state, stage, or phase to another."

This definition is commonsensical. Organizations "change" when they transform their structure and operations; or management control systems "change" when a new information system, such as an Enterprise Resource Planning (ERP) system,[4] is implemented; or cost accounting systems "change" when cost allocation bases are redefined from direct labor hours to activities. The definition can be represented graphically as in Figure 8.1.

Figure 8.1 shows how a given entity (be it an organization, an individual or a state of mind) passes from one state to another. From this viewpoint, as the object of change passes from state "A" to state "B" it is modified, i.e. it gains and loses identifiable features. Change happens in a fairly stable and linear spatio-temporal framework, where actions follow one another in an orderly manner and are linked to results by clear cause-and-effect relationships. Let us consider, for example, the case of the Cooperative Bank in Great Britain.[5] Like many other organizations in the banking sector, the Coop bank moved from a conventional accounting system to a new ABC accounting system. Before this, the volume of transactions related to the various banking products (current accounts, deposits, loans and so forth) was the key parameter to calculate their costs. Key decisions concerning, for example, customer profitability and staffing of various departments were based on these cost calculations. With the new system, costing information showed a different picture and the change led to the renegotiation of relationships with some customers, and to the reconsideration of customer categories and costing for each service provided. The system highlighted the existence of unused capacity in some of the bank departments and led to their reorganization. This was the logical consequence of the new costing knowledge gained thanks to ABC. Both the accounting system and the organization had changed.

The next sections analyze the tenets of this view of change and look into possible alternatives.

$$ A \quad \overset{t_1}{\underset{s_1}{\rule{12cm}{0.4pt}}} \overset{t_2}{\underset{s_2}{\longrightarrow}} \quad B $$

Source: Reproduced from Quattrone, P. (2001) with permission of Elsevier.

Figure 8.1 Modernist constitution I: a schematization of the concept of change

8.3 Perspectives on MACS Change: The Power of Individuals and Institutions

Academics have commended various theoretical frameworks to explain accounting changes.[6] Differences in how to conceive these changes have provoked epistemological, political, and ethical debates. Postmodernists and historical materialists,[7] and critical Marxists and Foucauldians,[8] have argued over whether accounting transformations represent exercises in rhetoric and ritual rather than practice. They have also debated the political implications of methodological choices for whether one is *for*, *against*, or *indifferent* to the *status quo*.

Roland Munro places change theorists into two categories:

> On the one hand, . . . there are those who lionize a "people" view of power . . . called methodo-
> logical individualism; individuals change the world. On the other hand are those who profess an
> "institutional" view. Here a motley crew of social structures, including class, genders, capital,
> the professions and even democracy, *reduce* the discretion of persons; and conspire to keep the
> world the same.[9]

Munro's grouping of the literature may be too schematic and oversimplified (as he concedes) but it captures how some research on organizational change, especially in accounting, has evolved—though not necessarily chronologically. An aspect that may need to be added to this grouping concerns the role of variables such as new operations and production processes, new technologies, muted market demand and product characteristics, and so forth. As with the functionalist perspective, which we saw in Chapter 3, in between individualism and the role of institutions in prompting change, there is also a functional response to some key events, which make a need for changing accounting systems pressing.

Managers and academics normally make sense of change in terms of its drivers and effects on the organization and the environment, and as organizational responses to external stimuli or endogenous forces. Thus, for example, perspectives based on individualism and positive belief in reality claim that organizations change when individuals identify some key problems which need to be addressed. Change is thus prompted and individuals' actions modify the organization with respect to some of its features. For instance, thanks to the intervention of a consulting team an organization may realize that its accounting system based on volume-driven allocation bases needs to be replaced by an ABC system. Or, as we will see later in this chapter, the IT manager of a multinational organization may realize that the corporation could become more efficient thanks to the implementation of an ERP system as this rationalizes billing and helps with moving from a multitude of legacy systems to a global and common system. This is, according to the words of the managers involved, the rationale underpinning the introduction of a new IT system in Think Pink, a case that will be discussed later in this chapter.

Other approaches based on contextualism and socio-contructivism view change as a process of institutionalization based on the adoption of rules, norms, and routines. For

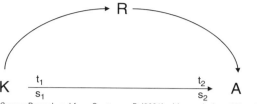

Source: Reproduced from Quattrone, P. (2001) with permission of Elsevier.

Figure 8.2 Modernist constitution II: relationships between knowledge, action, and rationality

instance, the very same introduction of the ERP system above may be seen instead as the result of a process of homogenization that leads organizations to adopt such technologies because of contextual imperatives. In other words, the majority of companies (or some key players in an industry) adopt an ERP system and other organizations have to follow, otherwise they will be seen as not keeping pace with innovation in management controls and will lose the confidence of the market. Our real-life experience with managers involved in the implementation of such systems shows that this pressure is not only an abstract theory of some scholar with an excessive liking for sociology but a concrete feeling shared by many in the field. They see decisions shaped more by fashions and legitimization issues than economic rationality.

If change is defined as in Figure 8.1, then relations between knowledge, action, and rationality can be depicted as in Figure 8.2.[10]

Here individuals (or organizations) acquire (or have imposed) *knowledge* ("K") about a unique reality "out there." This could be represented by a new technology, a new environmental or market condition or even an institutional pressure such as a social or legal norm requiring change in daily operations. This knowledge is followed by *actions* ("A"). Behaviour is *rational* ("R") if it complies with knowledge, i.e. with the reality which is perceived to be important. If there is a gap between actions and the desired situation then feedback controls try to bridge this gap.

An Illustration of the Model

Let us illustrate, with an example, the relationship between K, A and R in the context of an accounting innovation. The ABC system can easily be defined as one of major accounting innovations of the last decades. What is the rhetoric underpinning such innovation? It is a simple but effective one. Most conventional accounting practices were developed with the emergence of mass production and they reflect that production and market environment. Take the example of the famous Ford Model T and compare its features with those of a recent model, say the new Fiat 500. Table 8.1 illustrates the main differences between these two models and their respective production processes.

As the legend goes, the Ford T, the first mass-produced car, was a very standardized product as it had to serve an increasing demand for transportation at a cheap price. It thus was sold only in black, with no list of accessories available for customers to choose; it was manufactured on a linear production belt, which processed only few, simple components;

Table 8.1   Features of the production process of the Ford T and the Fiat 500.

Characteristics	Yesterday: the Ford T	Today: The new Fiat 500
• Production Process	• Simple, linear, rigid	• Complex, and flexible
• Product Lines	• Very few	• Many
• Cost Structure	• > Direct (production) costs	• >Indirect (support) costs
• Price Setting	• Cost-based (int.)	• Marked-based (ext.)
• Product Life Cycle	• Long	• Short

there was no postsales service, and the lucky owners of the Ford T had to be mechanics themselves when needed. The Ford T epitomized the philosophy of its times—a philosophy that would be unthinkable today. Nowadays cars have to respond to very different demands and production process have to follow suit. The new Fiat 500 offers an enormous list of accessories, which can generate thousands of combinations for a complete personalized car. It comes in different models (from basic ones with only 69 horse power to sporty versions with more than 150). The new 500 is small but it is not a simple car. It is a complex project, which shares components not only with other models from the same manufacturer (for example, the Fiat Panda) but also with other manufacturers (for example, the Ford Ka, which shares with the new 500 the chassis and other components and is manufactured in the same plant).

Two cars such as the Ford Ka and the new 500 will have a completely different cost structure compared to the Ford T, as illustrated in Figure 8.3.

The production costs of the Model T will be driven by the volume of production, with a relatively lower proportion of fixed versus variable costs. The cost of producing the new 500 will instead be driven by the complexity of the whole project. Even before beginning the production, Fiat engineers had to design a manufacturing system that was flexible enough to accommodate the most disparate requests from potential customers taken by the fashion for personalization. The situation became more complex when Ford joined the project and another car, sharing important parts, had to come out of the same production line as if it were a completely different product, and indeed it is. And of course marketing costs will be much greater than in the Ford T case. Even producing only two cars, one new 500

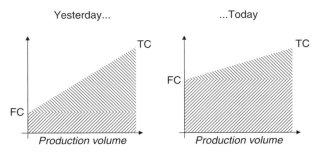

Figure 8.3   Cost structure of old vs. new production systems in the automobile industry

Figure 8.4   A straightforward contingency relationship: independent external variable, internal production and organizational processes, and accounting systems

and one new Ford Ka, makes Fiat and Ford incur considerable costs (engineering, logistics, marketing, etc.). As illustrated in Figure 8.4, external demands for more differentiated and complex products imply more complex internal operations, organizational solutions, and interfirm relationships. It is this complexity, and no longer the volume of production, which generates costs. Conventional accounting systems have thus to change in order to reflect these changes. The ABC system seemed the rational response to a shared understanding of changes in the external environment. Knowledge drives certain actions and if these go into the right direction the goal should be attained.

Recent research on ABC illustrates how the diffusion of this very successful management accounting innovation is far more complex than the story we have recounted here.[11] But complex stories are hard to sell.[12] It is much better to identify clear changes in the demand and environment (a reality "out there") and link them, in a linear way, to changes in the organization, which in turn have to be reflected in the accounting system monitoring the efficiency of operations. In a scheme such as that depicted in Figure 8.4, MACS change because of a change in some independent variable. For those who have a positive faith in reality, accounting simply has to be appropriately changed to calculate costs neutrally. It needs to change to stay tuned with changes in the market and production environment. We are fully in the realm of cybernetic and functionalist controls as we have seen them in Chapter 5.

For those perspectives drawing on socio-constructivism, the adoption of a new accounting practice would instead be guided by a social imperative: it reproduces a socially negotiated organizational reality. In both, behavior is teleological (i.e. it aims at individual or institutional goals) and sequential from a state in time and space (t_1 and s_1) to another (t_2 and s_2).

Both perspectives may have different epistemological underpinnings but they share the same view of change and the entities involved. They see behavior as adaptation (i.e. action is guided by knowledge). On the one hand, for those approaches that view the impetus for change coming from individual agencies, the managers are seen as being almost omniscient. They are able to assess the current situation in environments, markets, and production processes, and then respond with appropriate actions. The ideal of the *homo oeconomus* rules the organization in order to reach socio-economic equilibrium. On the other hand, those who view the impetus for change as arising from institutional pressures theorize organizational members as (consciously or unconsciously) mimicking reified institutionalized routines, rules and norms, as if these were clearly visible to them. Both approaches emphasize acts of compliance with objective (or objectified) rules and norms rather than the possibilities of escaping from them.

This view of change may be appropriate for stable environments where certainty about processes and goals is the rule. However, we have seen in Chapter 7 how this is more an exception rather than the norm. Uncertainty rules the world. The traditional view conceives of change as adaptation to external blueprints and prohibits an adequate understanding of the complex dynamics between stability and change and of the role of different actors' enactments (cf. Chapter 7) in defining what changes occur, how, why, where and when. It results in static, deterministic analyses.

A Modernist Constitution

The French sociologist whose quote we used in opening this chapter, would classify these approaches as belonging to what he calls a "modernist constitution"[13] where entities are supposed to be well defined and easily accessible and change is conceived as linear: a segmented passage from one unique location in space and time to another (see Figure 8.1). Models underpinned by a positive belief in reality (be it a hard external reality or a socially constructed one) interpret change but do not define or question it—what change is is taken as self-evident. A "modernist constitution" presents a uniform and unique worldview and organizational reality that precludes alternatives. It presumes that either actors (or academics in their analysis) can *see* technologies, accounting, organizations, market and institutions as if they were tangible things. Actors therefore adapt voluntarily to these demands for change, which mold them, generating little resistance. The process inevitably leads to equilibrium; no room is left for further change. Paradoxically models which define change as depicted in Figure 8.1 describe processes of stabilization and deny the possibility for change.

This modernist constitution also implies a very specific notion of organization and proffers an illusion of control. We will briefly discuss these in the following section.

8.3.1 Centered Organizations and the Illusion of Control

Imagine that you have to implement a new IT system in your organization to improve management reporting. Conventional (and rational) wisdom assumes that every action to implement this system follows a learning process to gain the knowledge necessary to perform this complex act. If so, then the design and implementation of a new software package would follow the logical sequence described in Figures 8.1 and 8.5. More prosaically, and expanding on what we illustrated in the previous section, to do *something* one has to know *how* to do it. The implementation is judged as "right" or "wrong" according to canons of rationality, i.e. whether the implementation (the *action* "A") followed the guidelines in time t_1 and space s_1 (*knowledge* "K") that makes the system work, thereby modifying organizational features (making it *change* "C") and resorting to the guidelines ("K") if this was ineffective. Rationality ("R"), aided and abetted by a control system, reigns sovereign: it acts as judge on whether the implementation ("A") reproduced the new information system in time t_2 and space s_2 by following this sequence of events. As we said, depictions of change as conformity to institutional requests share the same schematization. The difference is merely the socio-constructed nature of K, R, and A.

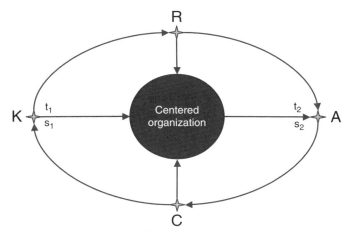

Source: Reproduced from Quattrone, P. (2001) with permission of Elsevier.

Figure 8.5 Modernist constitution III: the relations between knowledge, action, rationality and change entailing a centered organization

This conception of change implies a view of an organization as a flat space where actions follow a specific temporal sequence. We can say that this organization is centered on a univocal point of view, which makes everything ordered. It assumes that knowledge, actions and assessment of whether these actions are rational or not all happen in one clearly identifiable space (for example, the controller's office) and at one specific time (for instance, the end of the budgeting period when actual results are compared with budgets). It also assumes that change processes follow a linear path where, at a given point in time, organizational actors all share the same knowledge, actions plans, and notions of what is "right" or "wrong." Management theorists and change managers can see it all from their viewpoint and this knowledge is easily shared across the whole organization.

These homogeneous and linear relationships are depicted as in Figure 8.5.

We will demonstrate, in the following sections, that actual change processes only partially fit into this model and that a different, more complex, view of management is required for those organizations and environments where this clarity of objectives, processes and viewpoints is not the norm.

8.4 A Structuration Perspective: Change as Interplay between Structures and Actions[14]

Management accounting and control systems are seen as doing much more than providing information to decision makers for purposes of scorekeeping, directing attention, and problem solving. Many accounting scholars have recently warned that to leave relations of domination and legitimacy out of the equation and to view the world only in terms of a collection of individual actors is to miss some very important and essential aspects of accounting systems.[15] In consequence, the degree to which accountants and the systems they design are deeply involved in the social relations of domination and morality is beginning to dawn on most thoughtful academics and practitioners. When this notion really hits home, we will probably see a wholesale revolution in the way we think about MACS. Structuration theory distinguishes between structure, agency, and system. Social systems have structures that are the codes for social actions whereas agency is the actions of individual members of the system. Agents draw on structures during social action and as they do so they produce and reproduce discernibly similar social practices across space and time. So structuration theory, and this is the point to emphasize, in contrast with many social theories, includes both structures and agency. Thus it subsumes two otherwise fundamentally antagonistic positions: the contextualist position, where social life is determined by impersonal, objective social structures, and the individualist position, where social life is a product of the individual agent's subjective, existentialist choice making.

What follows draws on the work of Anthony Giddens and seeks to develop a comprehensive framework of MACS—one that incorporates issues of signification and communication, domination and power, and legitimacy and morality. This framework can be a very useful tool to understand MACS in action, that is, not thought of as abstract systems of norms and rules but as dynamic evolving systems where there is not a stable notion of rationality and efficiency that can serve for their design and assessment on how they work.

Structures

Structures are the abstract codes or templates that guide our behavior in social settings. They can be thought of as the DNA for agents' social action and interaction. These codes, however, never display the same internal unity as do biological systems, like those of ants and termites. For these and other insects, DNA programs their social roles. Human social systems are not nearly so deterministic. While structures provide for the organizing (structuring) properties of social systems and make for the ordering and binding of similar social practices across space and over time, they can and do change, sometimes gradually and at other times in astoundingly rapid and radical ways.

Structures exist, in a manner of speaking, outside and independently of any particular agent. But they are available to agents as a blueprint for action in specific time–space settings. Another way of putting this is to say that structures exist in virtual time and space and can be instantiated (made an instance of) by agents during social interaction in specific time–space settings. Nevertheless, they are the product of human invention. They are not biologically given by nature, as is the case for ants; rather they are grooved and regrooved by humans in social situations and they are potentially alterable.

An example may help to clarify the idea. The social codes of the Presbyterian Church direct its followers (agents) to be God-fearing, temperate, law-abiding, hardworking, thrifty, mind-your-own-business Christian folk. Anyone visiting Presbyterian communities in Scotland, California, and South Africa would witness a remarkable likeness in their social behavior, central beliefs, and key values. A return visit to one of these churches a year or two later would reveal a great similarity in the pattern of its congregation's social practices.

The Presbyterian templates are reproduced through space and across time to institutionalize patterns of behavior. This enables the Church as a social system to maintain its unique systemic characteristics.

Agency

Agency is the other major property of a social system. It is defined as the intentional actions of self-conscious individuals as they interact with others in social situations. Unlike our insects, agents can and do make choices in social settings. Agents are not merely social dupes pushed around by structures; rather they are capable of acting existentially. That is to say, they could have acted differently, if they had chosen. The point is that agents take part in social interactions in a way that presents them with the possibility of acting positively in such a manner that social codes are sometimes modified and at other times altered drastically.

For the most part, however, and as a matter of convenience, we respond *reflexively* in social settings, that is to say, without giving them much thought. We simply rely on our implicit store of knowledge about how to behave. In fact, it would be impractical for us to pause, monitor, and reflect about all the choices available. As with the mythical caterpillar who tried to think through the movement of each of its hundreds of legs consciously, we would soon be paralyzed. Nevertheless, agents take part in social interaction purposively and they know a great deal about why they act as they do at what Giddens calls the *practical* and *discursive* levels of consciousness.

At the practical level of consciousness agents monitor their own and others' social behavior by implicitly following the stocks of knowledge about how to act and how to interpret events and the actions of others. For example, individuals apply the laws of grammar and sound production when speaking, writing, or reading even though they cannot formulate these laws, let alone keep them in mind at the time, whereas at the discursive level, agents can give reasons for and rationalize about what they do in social settings. They use their linguistic skills to reflect on their involvement in social interaction. For the most part individuals respond automatically, but they can, if pressed, provide explanations for their own social behavior.

Structuration theory proposes that these two levels are influenced by an agent's primary need for ontological security lodged in the unconscious. Ontological security is grounded in the methods developed during the infant's prelinguistic stage to cope with the anxiety caused by the mother's periodic separation and return. At this stage, the infant has no conception of self and other (i.e., mother). The mentally healthy infant experiences no undue anger or anxiety when the mother is out of sight, develops a general state of trust, and grows confident of the continuity and sameness of outside providers. Conversely, the absence of trust can lead to a lifelong complex of trust anxiety.

Either way, ontological security lodged in the unconscious is seen as an essential ingredient later in life for action and interaction in social settings. It explains, to a large extent, why agents routinely reproduce social systems, even those they might readily recognize as excessively coercive.[16]

Structuration and the Duality of Structure

Structuration, and the duality of structure, are also central concepts in the framework. *Structuration* denotes that structure and agency exist in a recursive relationship. It is the process whereby social systems sometimes function to reproduce the status quo almost automatically, while at other times they undergo radical change. So instead of limiting the analysis to a snapshot, as in many of our previous frameworks, structuration analysis brings the dynamics of history and change onto the scene.

The *duality of structure* idea is closely related to the notion of structuration. It denotes that structures are both the medium and the outcome of the agents' conduct, which they recursively organize. As actors in social settings we produce (or reproduce) structures, but at the same time we are guided by them. Agency and structure presuppose each other.

To recapitulate, structuration theory is concerned with the interplay of agents' actions and social structures in the production, reproduction, and regulation of any social order. Structures, existing in virtual time and space, and are drawn upon by agents as they act and interact in specific time–space settings, which are themselves the outcome of those actions and interactions. Agents are not mere social dupes; they are purposive and they know a great deal about why they act in the way they do. They can provide rationales for their actions and interactions. In their reflexive monitoring of action in social settings, agents rely on both their discursive and practical consciousnesses, which are motivated by an unconscious need for ontological security. This picture of the agent's psychological makeup and its articulation to structuration, social structure, and agency is shown in Figure 8.6.

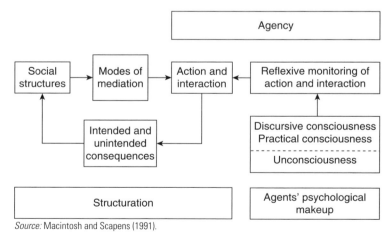

Source: Macintosh and Scapens (1991).

Figure 8.6   Social structures, agency, and structuration. (1) Social structures are not immediately available to agents but are mediated through modes of mediation drawn upon by agents. (2) Structuration refers to routine reproduction of existing social structures or production of radically different ones during a crisis. (3) Agency refers to actions and interactions of agents in social settings.

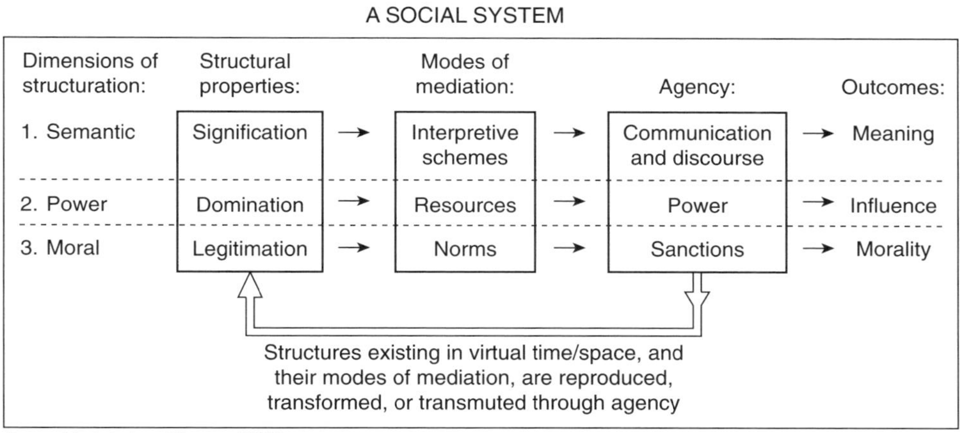

A SOCIAL SYSTEM

Dimensions of structuration:	Structural properties:	Modes of mediation:	Agency:	Outcomes:
1. Semantic	Signification →	Interpretive schemes →	Communication and discourse →	Meaning
2. Power	Domination →	Resources →	Power →	Influence
3. Moral	Legitimation →	Norms →	Sanctions →	Morality

Structures existing in virtual time/space, and
their modes of mediation, are reproduced,
transformed, or transmuted through agency

Source: Macintosh and Scapens (1991).

Figure 8.7   Structures and Agency in Social Settings

Dimensions of Structuration

Structuration theory also proposes that all social systems have three dimensions: *signification*, *legitimation*, and *domination*. Signification creates meaning in social interaction, domination produces power, and legitimation provides for the system's morality. These three layers, while separable in the abstract for analytical purposes, are intimately intertwined in reality. Meaning, morality, and power always come along as a bundle. Figure 8.7 outlines these dimensions within the duality of structure.

Signification

Signification is the abstract cognitive dimension of social life whereby agents communicate with and understand each other. It consists of abstract structures, interpretive schemes, and discursive practices. Signification structures are organized webs of semantic codes. Interpretive schemes are the stocks of knowledge, skills, and rules used by agents to draw on the signification structures in order to communicate with each other. They comprise the procedures that mediate between the (virtual) structure and the (situated) interaction. Discursive practices consist of speech, writing, and other forms of discourse used during social interaction. Language, for example, our most important signification structure, consists of the semantic codes (words and vocabulary) that agents draw on using their knowledge of the rules and syntax of language in order to speak, read, and write and thus communicate with other agents.

   In day-to-day interactions human agents draw upon interpretive schemes in order to communicate meaning and understanding. Interpretive schemes are the cognitive means by which each actor makes sense of what others say and do. The use of such cognitive schemes, within a framework of mutual knowledge, depends upon and draws from the signification structure, while it also reproduces that structure. During an individual speech act, for example, language (the signification structure) is drawn upon through cognitive schemes of syntax and semantics (the interpretive scheme) to create understanding (the communication of meaning). But language itself is the outcome of these individual speech acts.

Management accounting systems can be thought of as a major signification modality. For example, management accounting provides managers with a major means of making sense of the activities of their organizations and it allows them to communicate meaningfully about those activities. As such, a management accounting system is an interpretive scheme that mediates between the signification structure and social interaction in the form of communication between managers.

The signification structure in this case comprises the shared rules, concepts, and theories that are drawn upon to make sense of organizational activities. They include the various notions of finance, economics, and management science, as well as central accounting concepts such as income, assets, costs, revenues, and profits. These accounting concepts, moreover, have signification prior to the interpretive scheme. Managers will have shared understandings of their meanings, which, although mediated by the management accounting system, are presupposed by that interpretive scheme.

For example, the concept of profit is given a specific time–space location through management accounting systems, but it exists outside time and space. It is instantiated only through the use of those systems in practice and it can be changed through such use. Accounting is a major cognitive order shared by executives and managers to make sense of what they and others do. Accounting, as the saying goes, is the language of business.

Legitimation

Legitimation involves the moral constitution of social action. Legitimation structures consist of the normative rules and moral obligations of a social system. They are its collective conscience or moral consensus. They constitute the shared set of values and ideals about what is regarded as virtue, what is to count as important, and what ought to happen in social settings. They also designate what is considered immoral, what is to be trivialized, and what should not happen. Agents draw on these codes during social interaction by means of normative rules of conduct. In doing so, they sanction others (and themselves) in accordance with their compliance or noncompliance with the codes and norms. Compliance, however, does not necessarily mean commitment.

This moral undercarriage inculcates values into the minds of individuals and ensures a fit between the individual and the collectivity. The values and ideals define the mutual rights and obligations expected of agents across a wide range of interactional contexts, including work sites, schools, libraries, discos, sporting events, churches, and shopping malls. The norms specify how to operationalize the values, while sanctions make agents morally accountable for their actions. The legitimation dimension institutionalizes the reciprocal rights and obligations of the members of a social order.

Management accounting and control systems are vitally involved in the moral constitution of managers' actions and interactions.[17] They embody norms of organizational activity and provide the moral underpinnings for the signification structure. In most large complex industrial and commercial enterprises, for example, profit making is the paramount moral ideal.[18] Management accounting systems also legitimate the rights of some participants to hold others accountable in financial terms for their actions. This is widely recognized and accepted as the responsibility center concept.

Accounting systems, seen from the structuration framework perspective, then, are not merely an objective, neutral means for conveying economic meanings to decision makers. Rather they are deeply implicated in the production and reproduction of values and morality. They are an important medium through which the legitimation structure can be drawn upon by managers to produce morally meaningful action for organizational participants.

The structuration framework highlights how these systems can give legitimacy to the actions and interactions of managers throughout an organization. This is because accounting systems set forth values and ideals about what ought to count, what ought to happen, what is deemed fair, and what is thought to be important. They institutionalize the reciprocal obligations and rights of managers throughout the organization. "The giving of 'accounts' of conduct is intimately tied to being accountable for them" (Giddens, 1979, p. 85). Accounting and control systems can and do play a critical role in defining the moral constitution of an organization. "Accounting may be seen as a legitimating institution to the extent that it mediates the mapping between action and value . . . accounting fills this role by structuring relations among actors and acting as the medium through which control is exercised" (Richardson, 1987, p. 343).

Domination

Domination concerns a social system's capacity to achieve outcomes, to produce power. Normally power flows smoothly and its far-reaching effects go almost unnoticed in the process of social reproduction. But sometimes its effects are clearly visible and understood, as is the case in warfare or during strikes by unionized employees. While power works to constrain individuals and gain their cooperation, it is also a medium for emancipatory efforts.

Power is generated by drawing on the structures of domination, the blueprints for relations of autonomy and dependency. In feudal times the organization of relations of domination ran in descending order from God, to the king and royal family, to the barons and dukes, to the knights, to the vassals, and finally to the peasants. In a classroom, the power goes from state authority, to principal, to teacher, to student. In contrast to such hierarchical ordering, the domination structure of tke US government is one of equal power divided among the legislative, administrative, and judiciary branches. These blueprints are in the constitution.

Domination structures are drawn on by means of allocative and authoritative resources. Allocative resources involve the rights of some to hold command over material objects (mines, factories, computers, weapons, farms, etc.) as well as the knowledge of how to operate them (technology, techniques, technical skills, etc.). These are the property rights that some individuals hold regarding these resources. Authoritative resources are different; they comprise the rights of some agents to command others. This is the harnessing of human beings, not physical artifacts. It concerns the rights of some humans to have dominion over other humans. Both power resources provide for the coordination and control of things and people within social systems.

Management accounting and control systems are deeply implicated in relations of domination. They are a vital authoritative resource in the hands of upper management. Responsibility center accounting, a cornerstone of conventional management account-ing, involves much more than simply tracing costs, revenues, and capital to the sundry responsibility centers. Management accounting systems also carry the codes regarding who is responsible to whom and for what. They are a major discourse for the domination structure through which some participants are held accountable to others.

Moreover, accounting systems can play a vital role in domination structures. This occurs, for instance, during the ritualistic monthly review of a responsibility center manager's budgetary performances including written explanations of significant variances. It also happens when a superior uses budget performance as an important criterion in appraising the performance of subordinates. It takes place when the responsibility center manager participates in preparing the budget for the center. In each of these instances, the manage-ment accounting system is involved in the reproduction of the domination structure, even though for the most part the process goes unnoticed.

In sum, MACS are vitally involved in relations of domination and power. Command over them is a key allocative resource used by upper level executives to hold dominion over the organization's physical and technical assets. The master budget, for example, contains the detailed and all-encompassing blueprint for resource allocation for the entire organization and is a powerful lever in terms of ability to make a difference, to get things done, and to dominate the organization.

The Dialectic of Control

The concept of a *dialectic of control* is also an important building block in structuration theory. It signals that relations of dependence and autonomy are always a two-way affair. While superiors obviously have access to allocative and authoritative resources with which to exercise power over subordinates, the subordinates always have some power resources at their disposal to use over superiors. Superiors are always dependent on subordinates to some extent and the latter are never absolutely autonomous, no matter how much leeway superiors seem to grant them.

The dialectic of control is connected to a social system's primary contradiction, an essential aspect of the constitution of any social system. This is not so much a logical contradiction as a contradiction in the sense that some basic "structural principles operate in terms of one another but yet also contravene each other" (Giddens, 1984, p. 193). Each depends on the other while at the same time negating the other. The antinomy between the two basic structural principles is an intrinsic aspect of the social system in that the tension between them is basic to its systemic integration.

A specific illustration may help to bring this point home. Within a private-sector organization under the capitalist system of production, some members of the social order (the owners) are entitled to the private appropriation of any surplus value created by the system. This is a basic structural principle. At the same time, that surplus is produced by means of socialized (or public) production carried out by the rest of the members. Any capitalist organization, then, is intrinsically contradictory. "The very operation of the capitalist mode of production (private appropriation) *presumes* a structural principle which negates it (socialized production)" (Giddens, 1984, p. 142). These enterprises only exist as a contradictory form of social entity whereby the two intertwined forces always push against each other.

A striking example is the case of the meganational, conglomerate enterprise.[19] These firms can interject an abstract, impersonal signification structure, the MACS, into the local environment of a business component halfway around the world. This becomes the means by which executives at headquarters legitimate the appropriation of the profits produced by the social practices of local managers and employees. This paradoxical situation, where some parties produce the profits but others in a far-off land take the lion's share, must in some sense be seen as a double-layered, ambivalent experience at the local level.

The dialectic of control is one secondary contradiction that arises as a consequence of this primary contradiction. Top-level executives, by virtue of the structural principle of private appropriation, have the upper hand over subordinate managers and employees in the sundry business components, while subordinate managers and employees, by virtue of the structural principle of socialized production, have considerable power resources of their own within the dialectic of control.

For example, subordinate managers, such as the divisional general manager in a meganational firm, have authority over the material assets of the business component (an allocative resource) and command over the employees in the component (an authoritative resource). In addition, relative to upper echelons, they have privileged access to a great deal of knowledge and information regarding the component's business affairs, including the possibilities of its production equipment, the technical and administrative skills of its employees, and the strategies and tactics of its competitors. Although they lack authoritative resources with respect to upper executives, upper executives lack allocative resources with respect to component managers. Both parties have access to and can, through agency (in the structuration theory sense), draw on their resources of power in the dialectic of control.

One way this is done is through the annual operating budget process. During the budget formulation, subordinate managers participate in the setting of budget targets by submitting their estimates to headquarters for review and approval. Normally, a great deal of negotiation takes place before arriving at a mutually agreeable budget target and component managers are usually able to exercise their power resources to settle for a level they can be pretty sure to achieve.

In fact, evidence is mounting that subordinate managers are able to build considerable leeway into their budgets readily and deliberately. Careful research suggests that in most cases such bargained budgets include 20% to 25% slack.[20] Managers accomplish this in a variety of ways: underestimating sales volume and price levels, overestimating expenses, ignoring the effect of known planned improvements, and using discretionary cost estimates in a judicious manner. These actions are taken in virtue of their power resources. Management accounting systems are by no means as one-sided, tightly knit, and inflexible as is commonly portrayed in our conventional textbooks.

Routine and Crisis Situations

Routinization is another fundamental concept of structuration theory. Routine, a basic element of daily social activity, is defined as whatever is done habitually across time–space locations. In *routine situations*, activities undertaken are repeated in like manner day after day. So agents have no need to consciously think or speak about them or to devise and negotiate new social codes every time they meet. Social structures are paramount.

Moreover, in the enactment of social routines, individuals sustain a sense of ontological security. This helps them develop feelings of trust in conducting their daily affairs and staves off what otherwise might be the potentially explosive content of the unconscious. Under routine conditions, social action, including the reproduction of social structures, flows continuously. Routinization is both functional and economical.

In *crisis (or critical) situations*, structuration works differently. Crisis situations occur when the established routines of daily social life are shattered or drastically undermined. Under crisis, agency comes to the fore, often reshaping prevailing social structures. For example, the orderly crowd in a small town general store suddenly turns into a lynch mob, ignores traditional structures, and replaces law and order with vigilante justice. In such a situation members of a crowd can be easily exploited by leaders. Conventional social templates are abandoned, new ones emerge on the spot, or repressed ones re-emerge vigorously. A striking case in point is the re-emergence of sundry Christian religions during the recent breakup of the Soviet Union. In crisis situations, agency often brings different structures, even old ones, into existence. This often involves MACS.

This routine–critical demarcation merits further elaboration as it concerns the possibilities for changing social systems. Under routine conditions much, if not most, of the reflexive monitoring of action and interaction can be handled at the practical level of consciousness. Here the chances of a significant change in the existing systems through agency tend to be slim. In critical circumstances, by contrast, where there is a radical and unpredictable rupture that affects a large proportion of the individuals in the social system, it seems almost inevitable that the system will change through the actions of individual agents acting at the discursive level of consciousness. If these new social structures continue to be reproduced, a new social order will emerge through the process of structuration.

Change can occur, however, without such extreme critical situations. The intentional action of human agents, also taken at the level of discursive consciousness, can bring about gradual social change. Every act that contributes to the reproduction of a structure is also an act of production, a novel enterprise, and as such may initiate change by altering that structure at the same time as it reproduces it. While each of us has the potential to bring about social change, individual acts of themselves will not change social structures until they become institutionalized features of the social system; then new structures will have emerged.[21]

The English language, for example, changes routinely and without much fuss as time passes. The codes (rules) of basketball have changed in an evolutionary, piece-by-piece fashion over the years. Early on a center-jump ball followed each basket, whereas today the defending team simply puts the ball into play from its own end. More recent rule changes include the two-shot free-throw rule, the shot-clock, widening of the key, and the three-point basket. Social structures do change routinely and without radical disruption.

Perestroika (restructuring) in the Soviet Union is a much more striking case in point. In the late 1980s, General Secretary Gorbachev and his supporters faced an economic crisis on the home front and an untenable war in Afghanistan. The aim was threefold: first, to shift the social system of the nation towards more open and democratic processes; second, to reform and revitalize industrial, commercial, and agricultural productivity; and third, to reestablish the credibility and effectiveness of the Soviet Union in international relations and foreign affairs.

Gorbachev adroitly articulated the possibilities for change within the social structures. The substantive changes that took place under *perestroika* are a dramatic example of agency bringing about social change without the emergence of extreme conflicts. This contrasts vividly with the coming to power of the Bolsheviks in 1917, when a revolution proved necessary to secure radical social change.

The Apollo Computers (AC) case, discussed at length in Chapter 5, provides a practical illustration of the role that accounting can play in effecting organizational change. The MACS was a powerful resource in the process of making radical changes in social structures. Prior to the takeover by Dionysus, AC featured a centralized chain of command with a functional division of duties, and an ethical moral undercarriage emphasizing hi-tech computer and information systems innovations. The new owners effected a radical change in these social structures to transform AC into a social system featuring a decentralized chain of command and product group division of duties, along with a value system revering profits—lots of profits.

The new management accounting and strategic planning systems played a crucial role in this transformation. They acted as primary signification systems to show how managers and employees would make sense of organization events and activities. The new accounting discourse reinforced the new domination hierarchy of product center responsibility and accountability. Both control systems served to legitimate profit seeking over scientific creativity and innovation. They played a key role in producing a radically different social order. Once these new structures were institutionalized, the financial controls served to regroove these social templates every time participants drew on the accounting discourse in their daily interactions.

The two sections that follow put the structuration framework to work in a more extensive way by using it to develop detailed analyses of MACS at General Motors and at the US Department of Defense.[22]

8.4.1 Structuration in Action: The General Motors Case

In 1920, General Motors (GM) was on the verge of bankruptcy and faced a crisis of enormous proportions. William Durant, using the Chevrolet operation as a base, had acquired a huge empire of companies involved in the manufacturing, and distribution of automobiles and the supply of parts for them. He had, however, stretched GM's financial resources to breaking point just as a general slump in the economy hit the US automobile industry, reducing sales of new cars from a monthly high of 200 000 in March to about 50 000 in December. General Motors' shares plummeted on the stock market and Pierre du Pont, representing the majority of shareholders, retired Durant and surveyed the wreckage.

What du Pont and the remaining top executives saw was a crisis of formidable dimensions. First, GM operated under a vague and indecisive product policy. Second, GM's precarious working capital position featured a bloated inventory of raw and semifinished materials, an immense inventory of finished but unsold cars, and a short-term bank borrowing of $83 million. Third, since the production plans of the sundry manufacturing facilities were uncoordinated internally and unconnected externally to sales forecasts, the plants continued to produce parts and vehicles even though dealer lots were spilling over with unsold cars and trucks.

But the most pressing problem seemed to be the fact that headquarters lacked any sort of systematic management accounting system for control over the far-flung operating units. As Sloan, who was soon to become president, summed up the situation: "The corporation faced simultaneously an economic slump on the outside and a management crisis on the inside" (Sloan, 1963, p. 42).

Durant, the consummate entrepreneur, seemed oblivious to the need for a rational alignment of strategy with organization structure and management control systems. Strategic decisions (capital investment, acquisitions, product type and price, etc.) were made unilaterally by Durant, although on occasion he talked with the head of the relevant operating division. Organizationally, there were no clear lines of authority, no effective channels of communication, and there was virtually no accurate, timely, and systematic information about the performance of the operating divisions.

Further, some divisions were very large and highly integrated whereas others were small and managed a single function such as spark plugs. The company was little more than a haphazard, ill-coordinated, unsupervised, loosely built federation of operating enterprises. General Motors was running fast, but it was running blind.[23]

The board of directors appointed Alfred Sloan as the new president. Sloan, already a member of top management, had been president of a roller-bearing company as well as president of United Motors, a GM subsidiary. Sloan formulated GM's first real strategy, realigned the organizational structure, and put in place a sound management accounting and reporting system.

Strategy, Structure, and Controls

The cornerstone of the new strategy was the ingenious realignment of GM's product line. The implicit existing strategy has been to compete head-to-head with Ford in the low-price market segment by making better technological improvements than Ford. Sloan and the other top executives decided instead that GM would aim for quantity production of high-quality cars in all segments of the market, whether or not they were leaders in design within each segment. Sloan banked on attracting customers from below each segment who would willingly pay a little more for the extra quality in the next highest segment. This strategy eventually paid in spades.

General Motors had another important break. Before being appointed as chief executive officer of GM, Sloan had already worked out in some detail a thorough organizational blueprint to implement these policies. The blueprint, which he labeled "decentralization with coordinated control," involved the realignment of duties and responsibilities by separating the executive from the administrative function. Administrative offices were charged with responsibility for the operations of car divisions including the design, production, and marketing functions. The executive office concerned itself with formulation of long-term corporate strategy, developing critical competitive policies, and measuring and monitoring the efforts of the administrative offices. Key committees, including members from both offices, provided the necessary vertical and horizontal coordination and integration.

The lever to success for this blueprint, however, proved to be GM's new MACS. It consisted of sound and effective systems of operational controls including well-established techniques for controlling resources and activities such as cash, credit, inventory, production, orders, sales, and shipping. The management control system, built on this solid base, focused on the profit performance of entire responsibility centers, such as the various car, accessories, and parts divisions, each under the jurisdiction of one manager.

Financial Controls and Signification

This new accounting-based signification structure proved pivotal. Financial control was an integral part of Sloan's all-encompassing organizational plan, designed to bring order out of the chaos he saw running rampant throughout the company; a plan incorporating changes which ". . . though of an emergency nature, coincided with a sweeping reorganization of General Motors, going to the roots of industrial philosophy" (Sloan, 1963, p. 15).

In structuration terminology, Sloan's actions reshaped GM's signification structure as well as its domination and legitimation structures into a form that would serve the company for the next half century and provide a model of management for industry at large (Chandler, 1962). It was this signification structure that was to provide the dominant meaning system for action and interaction at GM. Upper management at GM, drawing on rights of domination given to them by du Pont, were able to impose the accounting discourse on the organization in general and on the managers in particular.

The new social order in GM involved a basic realignment of duties and responsibilities. The most important feature was the separation of the executive function from the administrative function. Administrative offices were charged with responsibility for the operations of the car divisions including the design, supply, production, and marketing functions. The executive office, assisted by appropriate staff offices, was to concern itself with formulating long-term corporate strategy, developing critical competitive policies, and measuring and monitoring the efforts of the administrative offices. Key committees, including executive, administrative, and staff officers, provided the necessary vertical and horizontal coordination and integration. But the fate of the restructuring of organizational duties and responsibilities, Sloan believed, hinged on the management control issue: ". . . if we had the means to review and judge the effectiveness of operations we could safely leave the prosecution of those operations to the men in charge of them" (Sloan, 1963, p. 140).

In structuration theory terms, the actions of Sloan and the executive committee were overturning the prevailing technical engineering signification system and replacing it with accounting and finance signification. Sloan had appointed Donaldson Brown as vice-president in charge of finance. Brown came from the DuPont company where, as we saw in Chapter 6, he had introduced accountants, statisticians, and economists into the finance office and successfully implemented detailed financial controls throughout the organization. At DuPont, financial and economic matters had been the main point of discussion in meetings of the executive committee and of the general managers in charge of the operating field units. Discussions during meetings involved mainly the language of accounting and finance. Executive at all levels used Brown's return-on-investment interpretive scheme to make sense of the operations of the business.

Brown successfully established a financial and accounting discourse at GM as the major means of communication, in place of the prevailing technical engineering discourse. This was no small undertaking. Prior to 1921, the meaning system at GM was that of engineering and technical innovation for the development of better engines, transmissions, suspension, steering, braking, tires, and so on. By 1920, as Sloan observed decades later, "Great as have been the engineering advances since 1920, we have today basically the same kind of machine that was created in the first twenty years of the industry" (Sloan, 1963, p. 219). The key component of Brown's new signification system was the financial control chart shown in Figure 8.8 that spelled out the specific relationship of the major

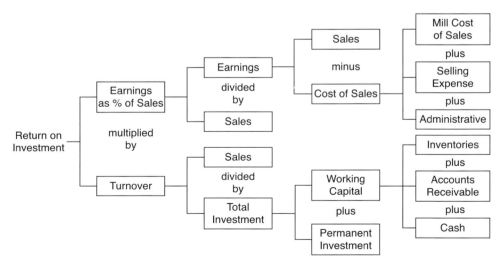

Figure 8.8   General Motors financial control chart

elements underlying and articulating return on investment. In terms of structuration theory, Brown's system was instantiated in practice through social action; and in turn it drew on a signification structure of finance, accounting, and control.

In Brown's scheme, standard volume was defined as 80% of practical capacity. In order for a division to earn, say, 15% per year on operating capital, the standard price for a product had to be set at a level that would yield 15% with the plant operating at 80% of practical capacity. Standard volume not only guided pricing decisions but was also used in determining *standard* costs and calculating *standard* burden rates. This concept of standard volume became an essential aspect of the new signification system. For the fixed costs, a burden rate was calculated as the amount needed to operate at practical capacity. For costs that varied directly with volume, a standard variable rate was calculated. Standard burden rates were also developed for cost centers, which were partially variable.

Once the degree of variability of all manufacturing expenses was determined, the total expense at the standard volume rate of operation could be established. This made it possible to develop a standard burden rate for allocating fixed, variable, and partially variable costs to products. Any underabsorbed or overabsorbed manufacturing costs were assigned to profit. The scheme, which took into consideration differences in product mix and the quantity and rate of use of machinery and working capital, was used in a very specific way.

The object was not necessarily the highest attainable *rate of return* on capital, but the highest return consistent with attainable volume, care being exercised to assure profit with each increment of volume that will at least equal the economic cost of additional capital required (Sloan, 1963, p. 141).

These new financial controls proved to be the means by which Sloan pulled GM back from the brink of disaster and established control over the far-flung divisions. Differences from standards could be attributed readily to either fluctuations in volume beyond the control of the divisional general manager or to inefficiencies in operations. Financial control arising as it did out of crisis "was not merely desirable, it was a necessity" (Sloan, 1963, p. 119). Each segment of the business could now be evaluated in terms of a common yardstick, standard return on investment.

In structuration theory terms, finance and accounting became integral to the signification system for GM's community of managers, with the return-on-investment chart an important element of the interpretive scheme. Managers at all levels in the organization made sense of what each other said and did by drawing on the language of accounting. The importance of financial controls in the meaning structure at GM is evidenced by Sloan.

> Financial method is so refined today that it may seem routine; yet this method—the financial model as some call it—by organizing and presenting the significant facts about what is going on in and around a business, is one of the chief bases for strategic business decisions. At all times, and particularly in times of crisis, or of contraction or expansion from whatever cause, it is of the essence in the running of a business. (Sloan, 1963, p. 118)

The new management control system, with its focus on purpose, policies, and operations, enabled Sloan to curtail the freewheeling divisions effectively and to put into effect decentralization with coordinated control. The question that arises, however, is how did the actions of Sloan and Brown successfully introduce an accounting and finance signification structure into GM? Why did managers throughout the organization begin to draw increasingly on the new signification structure and less on the previously paramount technical engineering meaning structure? It is precisely for these kinds of questions that structuration ideas can be valuable.

While it cannot produce a definitive answer, structuration analysis sensitizes us to the relevant dimensions of social structure, and particularly to the way that significant structures are always inextricably intertwined with structures of domination and legitimation. It also alerts us to the way social structures are reproduced, transmitted, or replaced under conditions of crisis and routine. As we will attempt to demonstrate later, Sloan and Brown would probably not have been successful in supplanting the technical engineering discourse without the existing domination and legitimation structures.

But these structures were themselves changed by the new accounting and finance discourse. As structuration theory stresses, the three structures are inextricably intertwined in practice and only separable analytically. The key to understanding the successful supplanting of the old technical and engineering discourse by the new accounting and finance discourse lies in the changes that took place *simultaneously* in the legitimation and domination structures during a crisis of enormous proportions.

Financial Controls and Legitimation

The accounting and finance signification structure at GM was intertwined with the company's legitimation structure. The moral undercarriage for the organization was profit seeking over the longer term. Sloan made the moral assumptions of the business process abundantly clear:

> We presumed the first purpose in making a capital investment is the establishment of a business that will both pay satisfactory dividends and preserve and increase its capital value. The primary object of the corporation, therefore, we declared was to make money, not just to make motor cars. (Sloan, 1965, p. 64)

The new moral code, endorsed by Sloan and the other top executives, was soon adopted as "a soundly conceived theoretical reference to guide us in the practical management of our affairs" (Sloan, 1965, p. 144). Thus the financial legitimation structure drawn on by the upper echelons of GM was a decisive step for Sloan in putting into effect decentralization with coordination control. As structuration theory states: "The level of normative integration of dominant groups within social systems may be a more important influence upon the overall continuity of those systems than how far the majority have 'internalized' the same value standards" (Giddens, 1979, p. 103).

At the time when Sloan took over the reins, the prevailing and deeply entrenched competitive strategy called for the development of a revolutionary car with an air-cooled engine to meet Ford head-on in the low-price market segment.[24] Sloan's idea, in contrast, focused on producing a quantity production line of high-quality cars in all segments of the market, whether or not they were leaders in design within their segment, and attracting customers from below each segment who would willingly pay an increment for the extra quality. This product strategy, now recognized as a crucial part of GM's recovery and subsequent domination of the US market, proved decisive. As Sloan put it: "Companies compete in broad policies as well as in specific policies" (Sloan, 1963, p. 65).

So profit seeking and growth in capital value came into being as the moral underpinnings for GM personnel throughout the organization. Managers at all levels were morally obliged to strive for, and deliver, a 20% after-tax return on their operations. Those who succeeded were rewarded handsomely; those who failed received well-deserved sanctions. Profit seeking, now formally and informally legitimized, came into being as the moral constituent of GM's collective conscience. The new moral undercarriage was, of course, inseparable from signification and domination.

Financial Controls and Domination

The new financial discourse was also intertwined with the domination structure. The administrative officers in charge of the operating units became responsible for the financial performance of their operations. They were held accountable to the executive committee for making a 20% standard volume return on investment. This enabled the executive committee to exercise power over the operating units routinely; power in the narrow sense of providing the medium for the domination of operating managers. It also provided the executive committee with the power to put into effect the new product strategy; power in the broad sense of command over resources to facilitate the transformative capacity of action.

> It was on the financial side that the last necessary key to decentralization with coordinated control was found . . . if we had the means to review and judge the effectiveness of operations we could safely leave the prosecution of those operations to the men in charge of them. (Sloan, 1963, p. 140)

The financial control system was a critical authoritative and allocative resource in the hands of the top executive team as they put Sloan's organizational model into place and exercised power within the organization.

Recapitulation

Prior to the reorganization, GM's package of social structures featured engineering and entrepreneurial signification codes as the sovereign dimension reigning over an accounting and finance dimension whereas, at the domination dimension, the blueprints called for the operating field units to command most of the authoritative and allocative power resources and to operate fairly independently from the small headquarters office. At the legitimation level, the morality of high-quality engineering predominated over profit seeking. Sloan, along with Brown and other key individuals, during a period of great crisis and relying on their practical consciousness, were able to replace these structures with a new set of social blueprints, whereby an accounting and finance discourse dominated the engineering and entrepreneurial discourse. The executive offices, now following the dictum of decentralization with coordinated control, ruled over the operating components, and the morality of profit making prevailed over engineering at the legitimation dimension. When the smoke cleared, organizational participants "talked that financial talk," "toed that profit responsibility line," and "walked that money walk." The old social structures were overturned and replaced by dint of reflexive and reflective agency.

At GM, the accounting and finance discourse provided a crucial resource in the hands of central office executives. It allowed them to enact decisions, such as product policy and organizational design, which they favored. It became the key resource through which Sloan and the executive committee routinely exercised power, it regularized relations of autonomy and dependence within the organization, and, through the moral component, it held managers of operating units responsible for their financial performance and accountable to the central office.

The philosophy of profit seeking provided the moral underpinnings of the domination structure embedded in the process of decentralization with coordinated control. Sloan, operating at the level of social practice, drew on the structures of signification, domination, and legitimation to transform GM from a loosely related group of autonomous, freewheeling operating units with a technical engineering orientation into a tightly controlled group of integrated operating units with a financial, profit-seeking orientation.

Financial Controls and Change

General Motors' history can also be used to illustrate the different dynamics of structuration under situations of critical proportions. It seems clear from both Sloan's and Chandler's accounts that managers at all levels readily accepted and adapted to the new management control systems. At first glance, this might seem to contradict the widespread view that new accounting and control systems tend to meet with stiff resistance. Structuration theory, however, offers a plausible explanation for the swift acceptance of the new controls.

Managers throughout the organization, facing a critical situation—a huge sales slump, a general economic downturn, a cash shortage pushing GM to the brink of bankruptcy, and chaotic organizational arrangements—may have experienced a heightened unconscious need for ontological security and so readily succumbed to the influence of the top executives. As Giddens states, "In such a situation, the members of a crowd are readily exploited by leaders" (Giddens, 1979, p. 125). So the operating managers, responding to their inner feelings, may have followed the mob rather than relying on cultivated reason.

Structuration theory also sensitizes the analysis to the forces that influence managers' conscious motivations. At the individual level it seems plausible that the managers, reflexively monitoring the critical economic situation and aware of the changes taking place in the wider social arena, as discussed above, would also have recognized at the discursive level of consciousness the need for radical changes in the accounting and finance systems and the organizational structure. They would also have perceived the power (through du Pont's shareholdings) of the top executives to bring about such changes. These understandings would be legitimated by the economic crisis and the general scientific management movement.

What we see is the working out of the dialectic of control in the context of a great crisis, one that enhanced the already powerful position of top management to effect a radical change in GM's signification structure. This, along with the managers' unconscious motivation for ontological security, reinforced by a working out of the need for change at the level of their discursive consciousness, all favored the rapid acceptance and assimilation of the new system of management control.

Agency and Structure

Finally, the GM case can be used to illustrate duality of structure. General Motors' new social order was a skilled accomplishment of its upper management, particularly Alfred Sloan, Jr. Facing a crisis of enormous proportions, the top management was able to overturn the existing structures and establish a new social order. According to structuration theory, GM executives were acting as self-conscious agents with discursive and practical consciousness; they put in place a new social order. During crisis agency overcame structure.

The ideas behind Sloan's conception of the new GM did not come out of thin air. His engineering training at MIT, great academic ability, penchant for orderliness, rational Methodist discipline, and experience as president of Hyatt Roller Bearing and United Motors were all drawn upon to conceive of and to put into place the new organizational design. Sloan's own words support this:

> I cannot, of course, say for sure how much of my thought on management came from contacts with my associates. Ideas, I imagine, are seldom, if ever, wholly original, but so far as I am aware, this study came out of my experience in Hyatt, United Motors and General Motors. (Sloan, 1965, p. 47)

Wider Social Structure

Sloan also drew on structures of the wider social order, which at the time were undergoing marked changes in the US. Sloan's label, decentralization with coordinated control, seems to mirror the metamorphosis taking place in the US in the ideal of individualism. Individualism, one of the cherished and founding beliefs of the American Revolution, was imported from France in the nineteenth century. In France, however, individualism had a pejorative connotation. It signified selfishness and blind instinct and denoted persons who had isolated themselves from other individuals and from society. In America its meaning was transformed to denote a condition of social equality. Individualism became an ideal for personal behavior and action. Ralph Waldo Emerson, the great author and philosopher, argued that the enlightened person exists in harmony with nature and has no need for the fetter of state or society.

Individualism, paradoxically, manifested itself in an unpredicted burst of entrepreneurial zeal and led to a world of engines, servomechanisms, levers, and assembly lines in great factories. Harmony with nature as an ideal gave way to the discipline of the machine. The new world of technologies, factories, and machines made organization, the rationalization of activity, specialization, and social interdependence absolutely essential. The ideal of the rugged individual, standing alone, believing no one to be more powerful or spiritually richer than himself, and holding his destiny in his own hands, seemed very much out of place in a social order featuring machines, organization, and interdependence. Public figures, such as the great entrepreneur John D. Rockefeller, began to make public statements to the effect that individualism had disappeared and in all likelihood would never reappear. In consequence, it seemed necessary somehow to recover individualism as an ideal, but change its substance.

The root metaphor for this transformation of individualism was the machine. A machine functions because of its organizing (structuring) principles. The blueprint for the machine articulates the interrelationship of the individual parts. The parts, however, have no meaning or function in their own right. They are subject to the higher order (organization) of the machine. Similarly, the individual, enmeshed in a world of assembly lines, machines, and factories, is subject to the organizing properties of society.

Frederick Taylor, acknowledged as the father of scientific management, saw clearly the nature of the tension between the ideal of the rugged individual and the ideal of the machine.

> Let me say that we are now but on the threshold of the coming era of true cooperation. The time is fast going by for the great personal or individual achievement of any one man standing alone and without the help of those around him. And the time is coming when all the great things will be done by the cooperation of many men in which each man performs that function for which he is best suited, each man preserves his individuality and is supreme in his particular function, and each man at the same time loses none of his originality and proper personal initiative, and yet is controlled by and must work harmoniously with many other men. (Taylor, 1911, p. 128)

The individual, formerly free from others and the social milieu, is now free to find his niche within a harmonious cooperative network. Taylor had recovered the ideal of individualism by enmeshing it within his metaphor of a cooperation machine.

This new construction of individualism also became embedded in the cooperation machine of organization. Like the parts of a machine, the individuals working in an organization have no meaning of their own apart from the master blueprint that articulates the relationship of each individual and department to the overall collectivity. The ideal organization, like the machine, has no extraneous parts and once set in motion functions as a coherent whole whereby all individuals work toward the greatest possible efficiency. The ideals of the machine became the blueprint for the best possible organization—one where each part became subjugated to the organizing and coordinating principles of the total organization.

Returning to the GM case, it can be said that this new formulation of individualism was an important component of the wider social structure in which GM operated. Durant and his organizing principles seem almost archetypes of the older ideal of the socially unfettered, freewheeling, rugged individual. In contrast, Sloan's organizational blueprint seems to be an exemplar of Taylor's cooperation machine of individualism.

Under Sloan's principle of decentralization with coordinated control, the individual managers of operating divisions were free to run their units as they saw fit with no interference from headquarters, but with the substantial caveat that they mesh their activities with GM's long-run strategic blueprint and policies regarding competitive factors, and that they follow the decisions and policies of the powerful interdivisional coordinating committees.[25] Sloan's organizational blueprint mirrored closely Taylor's ideal of the individual as free within his specialized niche but all the while enmeshed in a cooperative and coordinated social network.

Social Structures are Cemented In

Once institutionalized, however, GM's structures remained virtually intact for over 50 years. Successive executives routinely reproduced the prevailing social structure through the Depression years of the 1930s, the war years of the 1940s, and the postwar expansionary years of the 1950s and the 1960s. Sloan retired as chief executive in 1946 at the age of 71. He remained chairman of the board until 1956, when he became honorary chairman. Even then, he continued to serve as a member of the board of directors and on a few select and powerful committees, including finance and bonus and salary. In 1974 the four top executives of GM had served an average of nearly 40 years with the company. So it seems likely that the revolutionary structures of the 1920s were well guarded, preserved, and cemented in.

In fact, they became so entrenched that in the 1970s they resisted the attempts of some executives to change them. As a consequence, GM did not adjust to the very real threats posed by dramatic oil price increases, environmentalists' concerns for clean air, Ralph Nader's exposé of safety needs, and a dramatic increase in sales of smaller, cheaper, fuel-efficient, imported cars. It took almost a decade and a new generation of managers before GM, in the 1980s, slowly began to change the long-standing signification, domination, and legitimation structures.

8.4.2 The Weapons Repair Accounting System at the US Department of Defense

Our other empirical study involves the introduction of a system of uniform cost accounting (UCA) for weapons repair by the US Department of Defense (DoD).[26] The UCA was one of a host of new management projects introduced by Secretary of Defense Robert McNamara in the 1960s. Although the UCA concept emerged in 1963, it was not introduced until 1975 and did not become operational until 1979.

In 1985, there were 33 major repair depots located in the US and overseas, carrying out repair work on the entire spectrum of weapon systems and operated by the four military services: army, navy, air force, and marines. The lines of authority were complicated, but in general ran from the individual repair depots to intermediate command centers, to DoD, to the Secretary of Defense, and ultimately to Congress.

Motivation for UCA

The prime motivation for the introduction of UCA seemed to be an apparent lack of accountability for funds appropriated to the individual repair depots. Congress demanded some sort of accountability for how maintenance dollars were being spent. The introduction of UCA provided visible external evidence of the DoD's concern for controlling these expenditures: "From the depots' perspective, UCA was a means to demonstrate control over depot operations" (Ansari and Euske, 1987, p. 557). Previously, the depots had not been held "accountable" for their spending; they merely spent the monies appropriated to them and requested funding for the coming year on an incremental basis.

Each depot, however, maintained and continued to maintain a management accounting system that was used for budgeting, setting rates for work, and measuring efficiency. Consequently, most of the information gathered for UCA was duplicated in the depots' own accounting systems. Depot personnel viewed UCA not as a means of controlling their operations but, rather, as a way to demonstrate to outsiders that it had control of weapons repair expenditures, whereas DoD personnel viewed it as a way of increasing the visibility of the DoD in controlling depot costs and of enhancing their influence over the depots.

Management Accounting and Signification

The introduction of the new weapons repair management accounting system at DoD parallels the situation at GM, although it was played out over a much longer period of time and under more routine conditions. At GM the clash of discourse was between the parlance of engineering and the language of accounting but at DoD it was a clash of military and accounting vernaculars. The need for the DoD to demonstrate its control over weapons repair expenditures stemmed directly from the emphasis on economic rationality, quantification, and measurement that McNamara brought to the DoD in the early 1960s.

This emphasis prompted changes in the signification structure that was drawn upon in relations between the DoD and the Congress. The conventional language of accounting—reporting cycles, cost-effectiveness, efficiency, performance standards and capacity utilization—became part of the frame of meaning used to make sense of activities such as weapons repair, which previously had been understood only in military terms. At this level, accounting was seen in purely technical and rational terms.

Management Accounting and Legitimation

The new accounting system, however, played a crucial role at the legitimation level. As stated, the reason for the introduction of UCA was an apparent lack of accountability, which led Congress to demand the implementation of a system of accountability reporting on the maintenance-related expenditure. Ansari and Euske reported that, from the depots' perspective, ". . . UCA was a means to demonstrate control over depot operations" (1987, p. 557). Prior to this, the depots spent the monies appropriated to them and requested funding for the coming year on an incremental basis. They had not been held accountable for their spending.

While UCA was a system designed to control operations, the existent management accounting system was kept in use, with the same functions (budgeting, setting rates for work, and measuring efficiency) it had before. This resulted in a great part of the information gathered being replicated in the depots' own accounting systems. For depot personnel, UCA was seen not a means of controlling their operations but rather as a way to manage external relations with the public by providing the DoD with an instrument to demonstrate some degree of control over costs. DoD personnel, on the other hand, believed their implementation of UCA would increase their visible influence, thereby enhancing their authority and making the depots more accountable.

The signification structure is always implicated in both the structures of domination and legitimation. Signification, in terms of an accounting discourse, was the basis used to legitimate the actions of the DoD in controlling the budgets of its individual activities without the direct involvement of Congress. The introduction of accounting systems, such as UCA for weapons repair, gave legitimacy to claims by the DoD to congress that they were exercising control over the defense budget.

Management Accounting and Domination

The new UCA also played a key role at the domination level. It seems clear that UCA influenced the relations of power between the DoD and Congress. Visible controls, such as UCA, were an important resource in attempts by the DoD to resist direct involvement of Congress in the details of defense budget spending. Signification, in terms of accounting discourse, affected the relations of power between the DoD and Congress.

The effect of UCA on the relations of power between the DoD and the individual depots, however, is not so clearcut. The personnel at the depots interpreted and continued to interpret, their mission as the provision of facilities for quality repair work. Where this mission conflicted with economic efficiency they would emphasize quality over efficiency. Within the dialectic of control, the depots had considerable resources at their disposal, which they could use in resisting attempts by the DoD to impose controls through an accounting discourse.

These resources included the complex command structure that channeled responsibilities through the four military services; the lack of common work among the depots; the absence of clearly defined measurement systems; and the control of local information. These factors gave the depots considerable opportunities for controlling their input to UCA. Furthermore, the DoD had restricted authoritative resources to draw upon, because of the complex command structure. Consequently, UCA was not effective for DoD control over depots, nor was it used by depot personnel to control their expenditures.

Uniform cost accounting, however, proved to have an important role for the depots. Compliance with UCA's information requirements provided a space within which the depots could work without the direct involvement of the DoD. Uniform cost accounting gave a level of visibility to DoD attempts to control depot expenditures without significantly constraining the depots. As such, the new accounting system proved largely symbolic. In contrast with GM, where upper management drew upon the existing structure of domination to impose the accounting discourse on the organization in general and on the managers in particular, the weapons repair system gave individual depots sufficient resources to resist such an imposition, as signaled by the dialectic of control.

Nevertheless, the accounting discourse did affect depots. Depot personnel became more sensitive to the financial aspects of their activities and they made some technical improvements in their own management accounting practices. Although UCA provided a resource for the DoD to impose controls, because of the resources available to the depots, the introduction of the accounting discourse did not have much influence on the depot personnel.

Summary

In the weapons repair case, signification, in terms of an accounting discourse, proved to be the basis used to legitimate the actions of the DoD in controlling the budgets of its individual activities without the direct involvement of Congress. The introduction of accounting systems, such as UCA, gave legitimacy to claims by the DoD that they were exercising control over the defense budget. These systems also influenced the relations of power between the DoD and Congress. Visible controls, such as UCA, were important resources in attempts by the DoD to resist direct involvement of Congress in the defense budget. Consequently, signification in terms of accounting discourse affected the relations of power between the DoD and Congress.

8.5 A Relational Perspective on Change: Insights from the Think Pink Case*

Let us now explore an alternative definition of change. Let us see whether the process of change can be thought of and represented in a form that, at least partially, represents the degree of complexity that every organizational change implies. We will conduct this exploration with the help of a case story. What follows is an account illustrated through the words of the managers and controllers interviewed while they were coping with the difficulties of changing their IT and management controls.

Think Pink, a name chosen to disguise the identity of this company, is a firm that operated in three related industries: building materials, pipes, and fiberglasses. Its headquarters is in the US Midwest and it has subsidiaries across the world: from the Americas to Europe, from East Asia to South Africa.

---

*Quotes from interviews by P. Quattrone.

As part of the new strategy of the corporation and to improve management and financial reporting, Think Pink started to implement SAP[27] in 1995, initially in a UK subsidiary acquired the year previously. A member of Information Systems Business Relationships at US headquarters[28] explained in more details the rationale of this choice.

> We put together the proposal to the board (for the information technology strategy) of which SAP is a big component . . . Our original sales pitch to company leadership was that . . . having a common, global, simple set of processes and system support was the right thing to do . . . In parallel . . . we are going to spend . . . money taking all of these legacy systems and making them year 2000 compliant . . . We might have sold it first on, we have got this year 2000 problem, we have got all these disparate legacy problems that need to be modified, but I think a close second was, it was the right thing to do anyhow.

The company decided to adopt what was then believed to be a preconstituted information package—SAP. However, contrary to common beliefs amongst users of business software packages, SAP is not ready-to-use. It needs a long process of customization to meet business requirements of specific companies. This may be because the standard SAP "is designed having in mind how a German company works" (Information Systems Business Relationships, US Headquarters). Whatever the reason, the implementation of such a complex system offers a perfect occasion to study change as a major reorganization of processes, roles and tasks come with SAP. As the financial controller of the UK subsidiary testified:

> There was a two year program where our people . . . were basically living in the States to develop a business engineering plan . . . It wasn't just a case of changing IT systems . . . we are changing the way we do business. And it meant that there was far more devolved responsibility. So guys now on the shop floor who are keying in GRN's [Goods Returns Notes] are actually posting into the ledgers. Now they don't necessarily know that is what they do but that is the effect that it has . . . I don't have accounts people anymore either here or at [a UK plant] who are making sure those GRNs are going to the right account. The system does that for us.

After the initial implementation of the system the greater part of the corporation was managed through SAP (in the year 2001 it managed 90% of the $5 billion turnover). Doing business in Think Pink was revolutionized—from finance to customer service, and from management control to logistics. The use of SAP was described as one of the major changes the organization had undergone in the last decade. For example, conventional reporting procedures were dramatically changed as HQ and other plants could now access key financial indicators for all plants across the globe virtually in real time. Control from multiple locations was possible with SAP. A plant analyst in the UK subsidiary described the consequences:

> There are three plants which are the same: [A, B and C]. And we are constantly compared . . . [A] is seen as . . . an exceptionally good plant, very simple, low stock levels, good production, and clean. And often we are compared against [A] and obviously unit cost is a key indicator.

Benchmarking was easier and available almost instantaneously. Yet, it was not necessarily and exclusively done at HQ: plants could compare performance across manufacturing sites. This was one of many *changes* that SAP brought into Think Pink but they cannot be represented merely as technical exercises to learn how to use SAP. The shift to SAP precipitated a complex process of change accompanied by shifts in beliefs and practices about conducting business. SAP's rationale was integration, real-time visibility of actions and controls—the opposite of what people were used to and the design of Think Pink's traditional management control system. For example, in the "good old times" (as managers often said), reporting procedures were clear and simple (the controlled, typically the subsidiary, produced regular reports for the controller—typically at HQ). Now, following SAP, managers at HQ could run performance reports on a subsidiary unbeknown to that subsidiary and possibly *before* its managers had bothered to do so.

People may not have understood how SAP ran but its implementation certainly brought a lot of change in the way in which MACS and financial reporting were used. The organization was restructured, too, both in terms of processes and also physically, with changes which spanned from reduction of personnel to the layout of the central finance office.

Let's try to understand how managers made sense of these dramatic changes.

8.5.1 Enaction

Every implementation of a new system requires staff to learn how to use it and SAP was no exception: its introduction was accompanied by a long and hard training period on its rationale and consequences. However, this was not successful initially and SAP had disruptive effects as is testified below:

> The business units . . . had a very simplistic business model . . . they can't have much sophistication in their systems world . . . We could go in and say: "Here is what you have, here is what we can deliver with SAP . . . and can you live that way?" And the answer was "Yes, we can." So we got prepared for deployment . . . through until March the next year in 97. . . We put all the business rules in place, we put all the systems in place, and we fired everything up. And we struggled mightily . . . Even though we went through all the right steps, no one was really checking to see whether the folks out in the field really practised on the system and that they really had used the training window appropriately and that they were ready to go live. We assigned the accountability for training and monitoring training to someone in the . . . field. So a representative for the plant would have that accountability and he or she made sure that the folks that were going through the training process attended the class. But they did not follow up and make sure that they truly understood what was there. So they put in their time but there was no real confirmation . . . Actually what we ended up doing was what we call certification. We really had no certification model in place or acceptance in very limited areas. And we really, really struggled. It was a very dark time for us, those of us that had worked very hard for the year to the point of being able to pull the trigger and then discovered that the system is very, very stable but the processes to wrap around it were very, very chaotic. And we ended up with customer disruption

issues and, I mean, could have very easily been to the point of saying, "Wait a minute, let's go back to what we have and figure out a better way to do that." Fortunately we had some very strong executive support at that time and we worked our way through those issues. (Director of Electronic Business, US Headquarters)

The instigators of SAP had to check the learning process to ensure that SAP's functionality was understood. Controls were introduced to prevent a subsidiary going "live" without personnel understanding the implications of the new SAP philosophy. However, the learning process was more complex than just testing whether specific instructions on using SAP (i.e. knowledge about the system, "K") had been correctly transferred to its users so they could operate it (i.e. act, "A"). As the business relationship IS support team leader at US HQ stated:

Another lesson learned was that we needed to require the plants to demonstrate through use that they knew what they had been taught. It's not good enough to have people go to training, pass a test, and be proficient enough when the system goes live. We train people now and then put people through . . . several iterations of integration testing leading up to their deployment, so that they can demonstrate to us that not only were they trained but they can put that training into use. We didn't do that in our early deployments . . . When we went live we had a bunch of confusions, which led to a lot of support and a lot of people actually travelling to that remote site to carry out that integration experience . . . The last couple of deployments we have forced the sites . . . to go through with these iterations for the three or four weeks leading up to the deployment and the deployments have been much more successful as a result.

The initial learning strategy was consistent with the modern constitution of change in Figure 8.1: before acting (using SAP) you need to learn how to use it (follow a set of guidelines). This assumes certain knowledge (a packaged set of instructions on what SAP is, what it does, how it can be used, its features, etc.), which must be transferred to prospective users. This relation between knowledge and action did not work in Think Pink and training had to be reconceived.

An analysis of the implementation through the theoretical lenses of Figures 8.1 and 8.5 might attribute the initial problems to bad training (the package of knowledge) resulting in a bad implementation (set of actions). However, the explanation could be different and more consistent with managers' recollections. The implementation of this new system was part of the overall strategy to reorganize business processes and relationships between HQ and subsidiaries. This was summarized in a three-word slogan: "Common, Global and Simple." They wanted to have common systems and processes, which could work globally for the entire corporation, and wanted to have this through a system that was simple to understand and operate. However, managers suggested that the revolution implied by SAP's underlying philosophy of "Common, Global and Simple" made little sense outside the daily context of tasks putting into practice the abstract knowledge from training sessions. This is different from "learning by doing" where skills are acquired by practice, which assumes the transfer of fixed skills is implanted through rehearsal. In Think Pink what people learned

was constantly defined and redefined during daily business activities. The SAP system was often described as evolutionary, hence difficult to grasp and define. Three examples illustrate this:

> SAP is so powerful that you can't just go to one person and say what is the best way of doing this. It really is evolutionary. (Financial Director, UK subsidiary)
>
> It has changed a lot . . . since I first saw it. People discover new features and new ways of doing things every day. There is very much an onus on looking into the system: into what you actually can do. I don't think there has ever been a limit put on the system. (Plant Analyst, UK subsidiary)
>
> So we have had to re-engineer further on as we have discovered the other things that SAP can do for us rather than just the basic order processing. Again it is coming out of reports. Once you understand what the system can do for you in terms of reports, you then look at, "Is that a useful report, to whom is it useful?" In this case we are saying: "Yes, we know it is left . . . hang on! We can use that for the customer! We can advise him it is on its way" . . . The re-engineering is still taking place . . . as we are discovering . . . what the system can do for us. [For instance] I'm going to start something called Pricing Management because we have now discovered how we can predict price, look at price, analyse price and its effect on stages in the pricing process, off invoice rebate etc. So we are reorganizing ourselves to get a firmer control on price . . . it is only recently that we can do these things. (Customer service leader of the UK subsidiary)

The functionality and features of SAP changed with use. Rather than having specific predefined characteristics, its features and functionality were defined through a long, complex and tiring process.[29] Daily activities defined the features of the system (what it is and does)—not the ideas of the software engineer and consultants who originally designed and sold it.

External knowledge about what the system is and what it becomes cannot be separated. Managers immediately realized that there were no "best practices" that could help them with the implementation. No single best way to implement the system existed because SAP's features were codefined by the implementation itself. Managers and SAP users defined SAP's features through its use *in practice*—by enacting, understanding, and enriching the abstract and sterile knowledge imparted during training.

Remember the example of enactment we provided you with in Chapter 6. Here we face a similar situation. Daily acts using SAP and customizing it defined its functionality and made it intelligible. Without this, organizational members could not have understood or internalized the new philosophy of control proffered by SAP and the transformations it wrought.

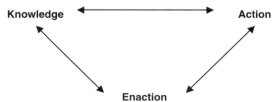

Source: Reproduced from Quattrone, P. (2001) with permission of Elsevier.

Figure 8.9 The "a-modern" constitution I: relations between knowledge and action—the notion of "enaction"

Change under the modern constitution, which we described in the previous section, is based on a dichotomy between knowledge and action. This can be avoided by the concept of "enaction," which assumes that knowledge and actions are inseparable. An example inspired by research in the natural sciences may help to further clarify the concept. A group of scientists studying how the brain learns once did an experiment.[30] They took two kittens, each a few weeks old. They put the first on a trolley that was towed by the second and they left them like this for a week in a room full of obstacles (feeding them— don't worry!). After a week they put both of them on the floor, freeing the second kitten from the harness. This kitten trotted around the room with no problems. The first kitten, however, was bumping into every single obstacle. What did they make of this experiment? The kittens had the same visual experience, they both saw the obstacles. However, only the second, towing kitten learned how to avoid them. The first had not enacted the environment around and had not learnt properly. Its understanding was limited to the visual experience but not actual experience.

This experiment teaches us that individual actions within organizations do not flow from a preordered framework of facts and laws but are part of complex learning processes during which individuals create knowledge by doing things (i.e. actions). As is illustrated in Figure 8.9, knowledge and action are interdependent: *knowledge is a form of action* inseparable from the activity of doing. Individuals make sense of abstract forms of knowledge—such as that taught on training courses—through practical activities that eventually become codified into managerial practice. Analogously, *action is a form of knowledge* because acting requires learned practices to make it possible. Actors wishing to use SAP, understand it, and define its characteristics and reports, must rely on categories created through previous processes of fabrication, for example, defined and agreed notions of cost, transactions. Previous objects of black boxing give a common meaning to SAP.

8.5.2 Poly-rationality

Arguing that a unique form and notion of rationality does not drive human and organizational behaviors is trite, at least for those who have some real-life experience of how organizations work. Refuting the idea that universal best practices of management exist has become common wisdom (except for those who sell these, such as ABC or TQM). Many studies of management control[31] demonstrate how individuals and groups within organizations have different interests and objectives and are in a continuous struggle to attain them.

Organizational behavior resulting from such struggles has been defined as "multirationality." Multi-rationality recognizes a variety of interests, valid sets of knowledge, and best organizational practices. As Jones points out "there are differences in interests which attach to the different positions in the social structure occupied by individuals or groups" (Jones, 1992, p. 244). Distinctions between functions, hierarchies, and groups of allegiance within organizations help classify the rationality within which they are bound. Organizational behavior and the definition of organizational practices are thus an emergent rationality from whatever organizational divisions prevail. However, slicing the organization into factions and then adding these up in order to represent the whole reproduces structural dichotomies and linearity that we would like to avoid. It would set individuals against organizations and create hierarchical orders for which consensus is to be negotiated at each level and then brought to a level up.

In Think Pink, achieving consensus on best practice was not easy. Theories of multi-rationality would attribute getting agreement on best practice for implementing SAP as individuals initially defining what should be done, followed by group discussions, for example within the Information System Development Group at HQ. Once this group reaches agreement after arguments and compromises, this definition of best practice will be negotiated with other hierarchical levels, such as the subsidiaries. Thus what is defined as best practice and rational for, say, an accounting system to implement within SAP, passes through progressive aggregations from the individual to corporate HQ levels. Ultimately the entire company agrees on what is best, although everyone knows that this has been negotiated.

However, observations from the case study contradict this way of constructing best practice regarding what SAP is and does. The multi-rational process follows a spatio-temporal sequence that is unique because spatial and temporal distinctions stem from categorizations and orderings of the observer and have no essence of their own. Multi-rationality cannot interpret events in Think Pink because notions of time and space were multiple and neither linear nor progressive. This is illustrated by the examples of different consequences of implementing SAP.

Further Case Illustration

Managers in Think Pink often referred to the evolutionary nature of SAP but this was not linear in space and time. Notions of best practice and roles played by different spaces within the MNO changed in complex processes, as the finance director of the UK subsidiary testified:

> If I am honest [SAP] is almost evolutionary, it doesn't stop. What typically happens is that you roll it out in a business and they make the first sort of beachhead and then they roll it out in another business and the lessons that they have learned in that first business get transferred to the second business, but in doing so they actually add something to the piece. And the trick is that as each business gets rolled out, to bring the businesses that are already on SAP up to the new level of knowledge. It's actually quite difficult . . . And so there is this constant retraining almost, not just of the new business but of the old business, saying we have learned something else and you need to come up to speed. It's a great idea.

Managers' descriptions of how SAP continuously evolved and changed its features did not follow linear paths. Nor was it driven by the center (HQ) or any ideal model of best ways proselytized by HQ, although the support of the US HQ for SAP was important. As the customer service leader of the UK subsidiary remarked:

> We are constantly looking at how each other works and . . . it took some time for (HQ) particularly, to have to admit that the way that they operate only works for the US, right. What we have had to learn is that we can't impose an organization around the same system. The organization is going to change as market situations dictate.
>
> [The vice-president of customer operations globally] goes around, talks to people, looks at good ideas . . . When I talk to her, we sit and talk . . . like we are doing now. She will pick ideas from me, she will say, "Well, we have tried this" and she will send me e-mails and presentations that they have done. If I've got a problem that I can't sort, either I will contact her through Customer Pride [a unit set up to solve SAP user problems] if it's a system thing, or if it's a process thing I will just ring her or send her an e-mail and say, "Look we have got this, have you any ideas?" And she will come back to me and say: "We have got it." That sort of chain. We tried to formalise it.

The center or focal point leading innovations for improving the functionality of SAP changed constantly: it could be in Europe, Asia-Pacific, or Africa. For many organizational members where this center lay ceased to matter—Think Pink was becoming a-centered.

The exertion of control after implementing SAP denoted a movement away from a "centralized" view of control (with some identifiable *locus* in space and time, say the controller at the reporting period end, defining what is "good" and "bad" management performance) to a multiplicity of *loci*. Here spaces and times competed and collaborated to redefine good practice without cumulative and linear learning processes. The "a-centeredness" of Think Pink, something we will discuss later in greater detail, was apparent in how the SAP philosophy transformed ideas and practices of control.

Before implementing SAP, control in Think Pink traditionally resided with the accounting function. The accountants reproduced centralized control from specific spaces in time and space, i.e. the accounting function was represented at each hierarchical level where it enacted accounting reports periodically, for example, monthly cycles. This ceased once SAP was in place. Control became dispersed across many business functions (spaces) at indiscriminate intervals (times).

The Director of Finance of the UK subsidiary described the accountants' ensuing roles as follows:

> We are seen as not so much controllers but very much as within the process, trying to drive efficiencies, trying to reduce costs, trying to enhance revenue growth . . . My financial team is almost not my financial team . . . for instance I have a team of plant analysts and they work on a day-to-day basis far more closely with the manufacturing people than with me. So I set up a framework for them from a financial management point of view but in day-to-day relationships they are far more embedded in the manufacturing team. Similarly I have a sales analyst who on a day-to-day basis deals with the sales leaders rather than with me.

The accountant's role changed from a bookkeeper (and gatekeeper) to an analyst.[32] Accountants lower down the hierarchy recognized this, as a plant analyst recalled:

> With SAP the days have gone where if you are the maintenance leader you come to me and say "How much money did I spend this month?" because you can just get to your terminal and look.

> And obviously it is your responsibility to control that cost and part of the job expectation is to (1) forecast how much money you are going to spend, let's say on repair materials and (2) also track . . . the costs, how much you are spending, whether you are going to meet your plan and your forecast in the budget. And I think that it is because the information is there.

He continued:

> A good example is the plant that I work at. It used to be . . . totally isolated and it didn't have SAP . . . I had been at (that plant) from September of 1999 and it went live on SAP in July but before July it was a stand-alone business. It had its own sales team, it had its own internal sales. People now call here [UK HQ] and order [that plant's] products, but before they were used to calling directly to the plant. But with [Think Pink] having absorbed us now it's a manufacturing unit, so a lot of the duties that were required . . . they used to have a couple of accountants because they used to need to reconcile the balance sheet . . . that is now not happening because that is managed centrally and other people are doing . . . typically accounting things. The maintenance manager is responsible for his costs. There is no requirement for the cost analyst or the plant analyst to track those other than to give the final numbers, consolidated for the plant.

Paradoxically, centralizing the accounting function decentralized control to people previously controlled by accountants. After SAP, people became "hybrid accountants," as some authors have pointed out.[33] Even the traditional core activity of accountants, posting the books, was delegated to myriad centers. The Director of Finance added:

> The other issue with SAP is that people have had to get used to new ways of dealing with money, a new way of working almost . . . it's almost outsourcing the financial recording to this shared services organization. And there is a process that you go through where you check everything that you do and . . . most of the things that they do until you are happy that, yes, they know what they are doing. Eventually . . . you just accept the result. My analysts do very little conventional posting. They may post the odd correctional entry. In fact some analysts aren't allowed to post. They generally are analytical people rather than analytical accountants.

The changed beliefs and practices emanating from centralizing records (now kept virtually on a central server far away from plants) and decentralizing accounting analytical work, marked a transition from centralized controls exerted by accountants to "an orgy of controls" where everyone in the business might act as a controller. Previously, good business practice (the relationship between knowledge and rationality) was, at least ideally, defined and controlled centrally. Now this has gone. Like an orgy, everyone participates in it for the same reason (pleasure) but the meaning of pleasure may vary for individuals and be achieved differently. Everyone has access to SAP and can obtain information and exert control as they wish, slicing and dicing the organization and information, and defining what should be controlled, how and why, differently. Ostensibly, integrated business functions decide what is best for each business area and accountants analyze how this can be attained. In Think Pink there were different centers and ways of defining good practice, knowledge, and what is rational. There was a move to a definition of rationality no longer linked to a center. Traditional views of rationality and "weak" versions of multi-rationality have always looked for a center to discern where different rationalities can be mediated. Now multiple centers exercise control and define discretional activities. The more people are involved in control, the less control is reducible to a common and shared view. Where and how many centers should exist is becoming less important than looking at how they interact. This is part of the journey towards a-centered organizations and poly-rationality.

Think Pink was not a uniform universe but a mélange of partially connected spaces and times that SAP helped connect.

Different categorizations, be they reporting times, or distinctions between HQ, subsidiaries and functional areas, differ according to the perception of the organizational actor making the categorization—for example, defining membership of an interest group. Nor can individuals and groups be segmented into conflicting camps with homogenous interests and beliefs, as multi-rationality implies—conflicts and mediations extend to individuals and the groups they are attached to. Homogeneous forms of rationality do not drive organizational actors (whether individuals or groups); rather they are driven by *poly*-rationality.[34]

Poly-rationality is intrinsically and reflexively related to space(s) and time(s). As is illustrated in Figure 8.10, knowledge and rationality are reciprocal. *Knowledge is a form of rationality* (in a synchronic and linear context) because it provides coordinates giving value judgments on organizational activities such as implementing SAP. Treated as such, knowledge is the product of a given spatio-temporal framework. *Rationality is a form of knowledge* because it is enacted through daily practices across time and space. What is rational at one point in time and space may not be so elsewhere as new categories (new and different orderings) are rendered giving rise to a multiplicity of spaces and times. Times and spaces are also reflexively linked in a "complex" and nonlinear manner. The definition of "before," "now," and "after" is a codefinition of all three terms (e.g. we cannot conceive of a "before" without a "now" and an "after"). Analogously, constructs in a space ("here" and "there") can only be defined through their codefinition. This process is tautological but it is impossible to escape. A word in a dictionary, for example, can be only defined through other words that in turn are defined by the word they seek to define. Current daily use gives sense and shared meaning to abstract words in a dictionary. Analogously, organizational practices construct and make sense of abstract notions of knowledge, actions, and rationality to create "best practices." Practices or "doing things" shape abstract forms of knowledge and rationality by enacting them and delimiting the time and space where these forms and the orderings that they entail make sense. This is analyzed below.

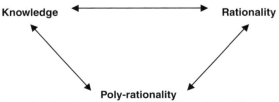

Source: Reproduced from Quattrone, P. (2001) with permission of Elsevier.

Figure 8.10 The "a-modern" constitution II: relations between knowledge and rationality—the notion of poly-rationality

8.5.3 Praxis

Academic accountants often view practices as an inferior form of knowledge compared to theories. Consequently, academic attention has been deflected from the practical activity of enacting and fabricating knowledge that becomes judged as rational.

The difference of what counts as "right" in an organization and in another can be surprisingly high. The adjudication of whether an accounting statement is "right" or "wrong" cannot be made against an abstract and general model but only from a practical and contingent definition. Thus evaluations of SAP and its implementation unrelated to contingent practices and local meanings lack significance. This is evident in the different experiences of Think Pink with respect to another company when implementing SAP.[35] We will call this company, for convenience and to disguise its identity, Sister Act. The rationale for SAP in Sister Act was based on the company strategy known as "the three Gs"—Global, Group, Growth. However, Sister Act's attempts to use SAP to become more Global differed markedly from Think Pink's efforts towards the same ideal. Sister Act markets office automation products, and industrial and domestic sewing machines. It has manufacturing and selling and distribution facilities in Japan, the Far East, Europe and the US.

The MNO held SAP workshops for its European subsidiaries to determine the best practice for each business process. This would then be incorporated into the SAP program for all subsidiaries. In the words of the Director of Finance:

> We have brought a lot of these good ideas from Europe into the specification that we are developing. And we are giving the consultants and SAP some headaches . . . but we didn't promise them an easy life . . . We are, after all, told that what SAP can do is provide the solution for the best practice for the business and if we are sure that getting everybody together will get us the best practice, then surely that is the goal that we should be aiming for.

He continued:

> That is what these workshops are all about. It is not just saying this is the way we do it, but what we do is we say, "Let's find out all the different ways that we do it and see what SAP has to offer and then choose between them." So a group of accountants will get together and agree what is the best approach so that we can get the best out of what SAP can do. In other places we are saying, "Let's do it that way and that is good and efficient and SAP will work." There are others where we disagree. I've got a meeting later on this morning to fight the argument for [weighted] average and FIFO stock accounting and control . . . moving averages is the way that [SAP] does it and therefore they say that that is the best practice. I maintain that that may be the way that you do it but it is not best practice.

Best practice was the aim but what was best for the consultants acting as spokespersons for SAP and its German designers was not necessarily best practice within Sister Act. Differences were fundamental: they extended to what SAP could and should do. The ideal of integration driving SAP in Sister Act was different from that in Think Pink. In Think Pink, SAP was described as "a cost cutting exercise" (International Business Controller, EU

Regional Headquarters), and a stimulus for new, improved practices, whereas in Sister Act the ERP project merely sought economies in current practices.

Sister Act's organization chart was left untouched by the implementation of SAP. For example, manufacturing remained separated from selling and distribution throughout the corporation. The SAP design was expected to reproduce this differentiated structure: integration was not a priority. There were also three SAP projects running concurrently (a European one, one for US manufacturing, and another for HQ in Japan directed at manufacturing). It was accepted that this would result in three different SAP systems running on three different servers.

The SAP projects in Sister Act were not expected to alter intercompany transactions. A complicated web of flows of goods and orders linked the various segments, areas and levels within the MNO. For example, typically an order received by a selling subsidiary would be passed to its regional sales HQ. This HQ would transmit its orders to relevant manufacturing facilities that would direct finished goods to the sales subsidiaries. The Japanese HQ, which directly owned the plants, would bill the regional sales HQ, which would bill the respective selling and distribution subsidiary! When the researcher contrasted the complexity of this exercise in Sister Act to Think Pink's methods, a manager in Think Pink exclaimed, "Oh my goodness!!!" (Account Receivables Manager, Shared Service Centre, UK subsidiary). Sister Act chose an evolutionary rather than a revolutionary approach to SAP.

This preference was not shared by all, especially the ERP project team members within the European HQ, but it was how the (Japanese) manager responsible for the project and other key figures (members of the project steering committee and the Director of Finance) wanted it. This may be informative about the reflexive relationship between power and knowledge but, more importantly for the analysis here, it illustrates how relations between rationality and action, especially established routines, create path-dependencies for future actions. The taken-for-granted way of doing business in Sister Act was not challenged by the eruption of SAP's philosophy. Ultimately, the design of practices and their enactment within the activities of managing the business determined what was deemed rational, even if they ran counter to initial judgments. Daily management practices created a paradigm for organizational members to judge what is "right" or "wrong." Such value judgments could only be made if members had experience of different situations that enabled them to draw from different coproductions of knowledge and action. Value judgments only made sense if related to a specific spatio-temporal context and had no significance outside it.

This brief comparison of Think Pink and Sister Act illustrates how rationality and action are codefined. This is illustrated in Figure 8.11. Here actions and rationality are interdependent.

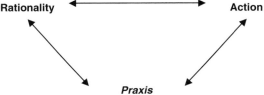

Source: Reproduced from Quattrone, P. (2001) with permission of Elsevier.

Figure 8.11   The "a-modern" constitution III: relations between rationality and action—the notion of praxis

Actions reflect what is considered rational in a specific location in time and space. The practices of Think Pink associated with SAP incorporated notions of best practice and integration that were different from those within Sister Act (although both were using the same system). We refer to this codefinition of action and rationality as *praxis*, an act permitting individuals to make sense of organizational practice and judge its rationality. In turn, abstract notions of rationality and abstract judgments on the correctness of a given practice assume tangible value and meaning only if referred to concrete *praxis*—specific tasks and operations that organizational actors carry out, such as the implementation and usage of SAP.

We will return to the importance of these shared meanings in the next chapter where we will discuss in greater details the meaning of "practice" and how it is linked to specific training regimes and worldviews as anticipated in Chapter 3. Now let us see what effects this alternative view of change processes has for its definition and for the nature of management controls.

8.5.4 Drift

With the description of the Think Pink case we have reformulated relations between knowledge, action, and rationality, introducing the categories of enaction, poly-rationality, and *praxis* to redefine change. A central argument has been that abstract (and abstracted) forms of knowledge, rationality, and action have little meaning and hence influence upon behavior in organizations. Actors attribute meaning through enaction and everyday *praxis* in a context of poly-rationality. The two case studies indicate how action made abstract claims such as "Global, Common, Simple," tangible. Everyday activities of problem solving, mediation, and displacing abstract objectives and knowledge defined SAP as an entity and a working system: its potential could only be realized through practice. Making an idea operational is not a simple, practical conversion of managerial prescriptions but a creative and artistic act emerging from partial connections. What, then, is change given these claims about enaction, poly-rationality, and *praxis*? Do the transformations in the cases correspond to modern definitions of change in Figure 8.1, i.e. an ordered path from a clearly defined entity A to another, B? The answer is "No."

Change in Figure 8.1 is teleological, operating in a unique and linear spatio-temporal framework. In the cases there was teleology (however constructed) symbolized in the slogans of the SAP projects (*Global, Common and Simple* and *Global, Group and Growth*) but, above all, there was serendipity and a displacement of objectives. New practices defining the organization were casually stumbled upon. Conventional notions of knowledge, action, and rationality could not explain the SAP implementation stories because a modernist view of change requires a single set of criteria whereas in practice there were multiple right(s) and wrong(s). There were many centers defining SAP. This led the researchers to view control not as a hierarchical, ordered and centered practice but rather an orgy of controlling embracing multiple times and locations. External (and unique) knowledge coming, for instance, under the form of the implementation manuals or advice from the consultants, was not a template for implementation, nor were accounting and accountability practices creating

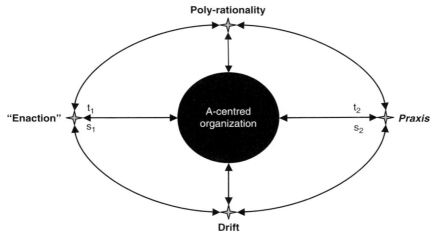

Poly-rationality

"Enaction" t_1 s_1 — A-centred organization — t_2 s_2 *Praxis*

Drift

Source: Reproduced from Quattrone, P. (2001) with permission of Elsevier.

Figure 8.12 The "a-modern" constitution: relations between "enaction", poly-rationality, *praxis*, and drift entailing "a-centered" organizations

single and unique benchmarks for assessing the validity of actions. Figures 8.1, 8.2 and 8.5 had to be reconceived to incorporate this multiplicity. Figure 8.12 is the result.

In the cases there was not adoption but *enaction*. There was no direct implementation of the SAP package because there was nothing to implement—rather SAP's features and functionality was constructed through *praxis*. Thus there was no change from one state to another, as expressed in Figures 8.1 and 8.5, capable of being judged as rational from a single perspective. Rather there were multiple worlds in multiple spaces and times giving rise to *poly-rationality*. The modern definition of change needed replacing by an a-modern definition of *drift* to act as a proxy for change.

When things are drifting (say castaways in a boat in the ocean or friends lost during an excursion in a wood), they may have no devices such as maps or a clock to give them a conception of time or space. They cannot accurately define their location or the time though they are likely to continually try to do so. This does not mean that they will not act purposefully—they may try to create a shared idea of the "right" direction with the available instruments and the enacted knowledge of the situation. Nor are they doomed to perish under the waves or in the perils of the wood. They may reach a safe beach or a village and get help. If they are unlucky they may return to where they started. But in both instances purposeful actions involve and are intertwined with serendipity and chance, i.e. drifting.

The idea of drift is preferred to change for several reasons. First, it has no connotation that individuals are sufficiently conscious of space and time to transcend the contingent factors facing them. Secondly, there is no assumption that people move from well-defined situations A or B in a linear, predictable and ordered spatio-temporal framework. Finally, it recognizes contingent factors (such as currents, in the sea metaphor) that actors may be aware of, and seek to respond to, but which carry them along in unpredictable ways. In organizational terms, drift recognizes the existence of some knowledge of what an organization is, where it is and where it should go (for instance, implementing SAP because of the pressures of global markets and automation). However, possession of such knowledge does not transcend actions or outcomes to unknown destinations.

Drift does not imply or equate to chaos and complete randomness, as some have observed. It leads us into the realm of relativism where, by this, we do not mean that anything goes but that processes such as change, and entities such as organizations, need to be viewed through the lenses of the relations that these establish and mobilize. Drift processes in fact relate to how knowledge is enacted (thanks to human interpretation but also to the technologies available and various other artifacts), how poly-rationality emerges and is mediated and how *praxis* leaves sediments which are constantly renegotiated.[36]

Drift better represents the change (and SAP implementations) than modern definitions depicting change. The "modern constitution" does not recognize the number, complexity, and scattered distribution of states in an organization. How a new system (be it SAP or a new accounting system) modifies doing business and its emergence from complex processes of mediation is more complicated than conventional models of change imply. In the cases above, mediations determined what SAP was, what it drew from, and what it did, but this was not simply the result of compromises between hierarchical spatial configurations such as subsidiaries and HQs as in the conventional model. Rather the new technology brought new and unstable spatio-temporal frameworks of control where various streams conflicted and co-operated in an orgy of controls to produce organizational drift, rather than simply change. It cannot be claimed that these streams transformed the organization, as this presumes the existence of the problematical before and after dichotomy within conventional ideas of change. The organizations studied did not change from point A to B but drifted—paradoxically they could find themselves back where they were five years previous, which indeed happened in the Think Pink case where after five years a division went back to the old system (SCALA) and dismantled SAP.

8.6 A-centered Organizations and the Power of Relations

We are now in a position to offer a different notion of organization in tune with the new definition of change that we have provided.

Figure 8.12 illustrates the relations between enaction, poly-rationality, *praxis* and drift and introduces the idea of "a-centered" organizations. Figure 8.5 was built around a simple and clear viewpoint. Managers could see the need for change and act accordingly. Everything was centered on this assumption and belief. The two cases we have briefly recalled in this chapter call for a different notion of organization and control. While we leave the implications for management control for the next chapter, we are now in a position to view how organizations change under a different light.

Contrary to what was described in Figure 8.5, the model illustrated in Figure 8.12 recognizes that homogeneous viewpoints are unlikely to emerge within organizations. It recognizes that, despite the fact that shared meanings and worldviews do occur within organizations, there are always gaps left for alternative views. These are ready to subvert taken-for-granted positions and influence change processes in directions that go against, or influence, converge and modify, the main stream. For example, in Think Pink, SAP was enacted and defined through its usage in doing business in various parts of the multinational and at various times.

In Figure 8.5, establishing whether an organization has changed always requires value judgments because what counts as knowledge, rationality, and action is not self-evident but requires choice and categorization by managers and employees (i.e. the observer) who in turn define criteria for judging the effectiveness of the process. In contrast, Figure 8.12 has no stable vantage point in space or time for observing and assessing change. Instead there are attempts to organize across multiple spaces and times but these are not necessarily linearly ordered. There is no neat linear flow of instructions from s_1 to s_2, hence the lack of a pre-ordered pathway (in space and time) in Figure 8.12 for defining what an organization *is* and how it *changes*. Instead it depicts how many attempts at *organizing* happen in many locations of the organizations, in ways which can be both contrasting and aligned depending on the perspective chosen. The result though is not simply change but a more complex organizational *drifting*.

This has also implications for the notions of rationality and control. That is, notions of improvement, progress, and advancement have strong temporal connotations of movement from one time period to another, from one stage to another which is considered to be "better." However, in the MNOs studied, multiple times coexisted. Consider the example of Think Pink. After five years of struggles to implement SAP, a division went back to the old and well-known software (SCALA). Hence the arrow of time in Figure 8.12 is no longer linear but multiple and reversible ($t_{1/2}$, $t_{2/1}$). What one organizing space in the MNO considered a more *advanced* IT system (again SAP rather than SCALA) was not necessarily considered as such in another location. What appears more advanced could also change under different circumstances. This normally occurs when there are sudden changes such as mergers, acquisitions, joint venture and the like. Some organizational actors may recognize as "best practices" what others categorize as less advanced, for these local practices prove more suitable for locally enacted information needs. Equally controllers may assess positively some performances which in other contexts could instead be judged negatively.

Under such circumstances notions of centralized organizations do not reflect the experiences of different worlds partially connected.[37] Such notions do not illustrate adequately how multiple centers and points of view attempt to order and control events, and how each attempt is incomplete and unable to center the organization around itself. This is why the organization is "*a*-centered." This concept recognizes that notions of knowledge, rationality, action, "best practices," are never set in stone but acquire meanings in networks of relationships.[38]

In this "*a*-centered" view, there is no room for adaptation and isomorphism that make actions identical to an ideal "reality" (whether socially constructed or "real"). Instead organizations are conceived as in a continuous state of flux where multiple activities of categorization intersect to create different notions of "best." The path of this drift (and associated value judgments) cannot transcend the contingent praxis in which it is constructed.

Thus there is no problem of closing the gap between knowledge and action, for example, through "appropriate training." Determining the correct training to ensure that SAP is correctly used becomes irrelevant, as there is no single knowledge to provide a benchmark. It is instead more useful to provide occasions to enact the nature and the functionalities of the new systems and processes which have to be implemented. This is what we will explore the following chapter where the role of MACS is discussed in relation to issues of innovation and change management.

Before moving to that we have to explore how information technologies, and especially ERPs, are changing the nature of MACS.

8.7 Summary and Conclusions

This chapter has reviewed the main approaches to organizational and accounting change and has proposed a view of the role that information technologies have in changing the nature and functioning of MACS. We began from a conventional view of the process, involving stable and centralized ideas of organization and controls. In what we have called a "modernist constitution," change is a linear process, organizations are homogeneous entities and control is exerted from an identifiable space normally coinciding with the top management and the controller's office. We have analyzed this view of change in terms of the relation between knowledge (of the variables prompting change, the subsequent process and outcomes), actions that follow, and the rationality assessing the overall process and providing the basis for feedback controls. This has led us to question some of the assumptions of this centralized view of organizations, which is shared by both positivist and (some) institutionalist perspectives drawing on contextualism.

In this way we have shown that structuration theory is a valuable way to expand our understanding of MACS beyond a focus on technical efficiency and beyond many of the ideas in previous chapters to include social, political, and moral phenomena. The analyses in this chapter demonstrate the potential power of the structuration framework to sensitize our understanding of how MACS contribute to the *maintenance* of the existing social order (the DoD case) as well as to *changes* in that order (the GM case). At GM, managers relied heavily on the accounting discourse to make sense of the firm's activities. And DoD participants at all levels drew on the accounting discourse to legitimate particular actions. In both organizations, it was an important resource for the exercise of power, both in the broad sense and the narrow sense. A structuration approach reveals the ways in which accounting is involved in the institutionalization of social relations. It is a focused, integrative, and comprehensive way to analyze case studies of management accounting. It also focuses on the importance of relationships and the need for a relational view of change and the role that MACS play in these dynamic processes.

This led us to introduce the Think Pink case and compare it with another case (Sister Act), which provided the empirical material to reformulate the relationships between knowledge, action, rationality and change. The resulting principles are enaction, poly-rationality, *praxis* and drift. Change as drift is no longer a linear and easily identifiable process but is one that recognizes the complexities of change management and change processes where the drivers of change are never clear to all the actors involved, or shared by them. Rather, the cases have illustrated that change happens in various loci, for different reasons, and that it produces different value judgments. This implies an a-centered view of the organization and control. In contemporary organizations, as much as in contemporary societies, a view of control and order needs to leave space for a perspective in which diffused controls better illustrate how organizations work. This approach seems far more fruitful for understanding and managing change processes, as we have illustrated with the case material from Think Pink.

Endnotes

1. This chapter draws on and expands the arguments in Quattrone and Hopper (2001).
2. See Johnson and Kaplan (1987).
3. Respectively, Activity-Based Costing, Activity-Based Management, Balanced Scorecard, Total Quality Management, Economic Value Added. See Cooper and Kaplan (1988), Johnson and Kaplan (1987), Kaplan and Norton (1996).
4. The ERP systems have been defined as "enterprise wide packages that tightly integrate business functions into a single system with a shared database" (Newell *et al.*, 2003, p. 26, drawing on Lee and Lee, 2000).
5. See the Harvard Business School Case (195196-PDF-ENG) by Robert S. Kaplan and Srikant M.Datar, Co-operative Bank, 1995.
6. For example, Briers and Chua (2001) commend actor-network theory whereas Burns and Scapens (2000) proffer Old Institutional Economics. Research is divided over whether and how management accounting changes bring success (Cobb, Mitchell and Innes, 1992; Shields, 1995), and whether clear-cut definitions of success versus failure exist (Malmi, 1997). Change has been examined across different geographical and temporal spaces to find variations (Lukka, 1994). Resistance to accounting change (e.g. Ezzamel, 1994; Scapens and Roberts, 1993) has been identified alongside models of how to implement change (Innes and Mitchell, 1990; Vaivio, 1999). Since Hopwood's frequently quoted claim that "very little is known of the processes of accounting change" (Hopwood, 1987, p. 207), studies on change have proliferated.
7. See Arnold (1998), Froud *et al.* (1998), Miller and O'Leary (1994a, 1994b, 1998).
8. See Hoskin (1994) and Neimark (1990).
9. Munro (1999, p. 430); emphasis in original.
10. This representation of relations between knowledge, action and rationality may appear very schematic but very broadly it reflects the evolution (not necessarily chronological) of theories of rationality and their use in accounting. It is not the aim here to review all the studies of relations between knowledge, rationality, and action in organization theory, economics, sociology, and accounting. However, it is worth noting that following Simon's (1976, 1983) delineation of bounded and procedural rationality, two divergent streams of studies developed that had significant effects upon the accounting literature. The first draws on bounded rationality and is followed by the so-called Chicago School, e.g. Hogart and Reder (1987), Tversky and Kahneman (1981), and, in accounting, Hogart (1991, 1993). The second draws on procedural rationality and was followed by the "Scandinavian" school, e.g. Brunssonn (1985) Cohen, March and Olsen (1972) March (1988) and in accounting, for instance, Brunsonn (1990), Cooper *et al.* (1981), Malmi (1997). This may

be see as the "weak" version of Simon's approach, leading to social constructivist views of the organizational world and the use of Berger and Luckmann (1966) and neoinstitutional sociology in accounting studies (Carruthers, 1995; Meyer, 1986; Vamosi, 2000, to name but a few). It is the latter stream of studies that are deemed to fall within the socioconstructivist approach in accounting. They close the "Arch of Knowledge" (Oldroyd, 1986) by reifying the subject (and the context) rather than reality (and the object).

11. See, for instance, Jones and Dugdale (2002).

12. Especially in a society where knowledge is defined more by the media than anything else: it is difficult to illustrate complex stories when TV forces us to think in blocks of 30 seconds!

13. See Latour (1999).

14. This section is based on articles by Macintosh and Scapens (1990, 1991), who based their research on Giddens (1976, 1979, 1984).

15. See Burchell *et al.* (1980), Cooper (1980), Tinker (1980), Tinker, Merino and Neimark (1982) for pioneer articles making this point. See also Covaleski, Dirsmith and Jablonsky (1984), and Covaleski and Dirsmith (1988) for the importance of relating accounting to relations of power.

16. See Willmott (1986) for an insightful critique of Giddens' notion of ontological security.

17. See Roberts and Scapens (1985) for an insightful discussion of this point.

18. See Lukka (1990) for an excellent discussion of the socially constructed meaning of profit.

19. See Lowe (1992) for a fascinating, highly readable, and revealing exposé of the power and workings of the meganational conglomerate.

20. See Ansari (1976), Otley (1978), Schiff and Lewin (1968, 1970).

21. See Giddens (1976, p. 128) for a detailed explanation of this idea.

22. The General Motors analysis relies on Alfred Sloan's (1963) classic book, *My Years With General Motors*, and Chandler's (1962) seminal book, *Strategy and Structure*, on the history of the emergence of the divisionalized structure in US industrial enterprises, and Chandler (1977). The Department of Defense analysis is based on Ansari and Euske's (1987) careful, exhaustive, and in-depth study of the new weapons repair management accounting. The analyses are based on Macintosh and Scapens (1991).

23. See Gordon and Miller (1976) for a valuable description of the running-blind firm and its accounting and information systems problems.

24. The idea of an air-cooled revolutionary car was not permanently snuffed out. It surfaced 40 years later in the form of the Corvair, built by the Chevrolet division. The Corvair, with its air-cooled, rear-mounted engine, went into production in the early 1960s, but proved to be a great embarrassment to GM and the subject of Ralph Nader's famous campaign, "unsafe at any speed."

25. These included the general purchasing committee, the institutional committee, the general technical committee, the general sales committee, and the operations committee, composed of high-ranking executives from both headquarters and the operating divisions.

26. Ansari and Euske's (1987) study is the source for this case study.

27. SAP is an acronym for *Systeme Anwendungen und Programme in der Dataenverarbeitung* (or in English, *Systems, Applications and Product in Data Processing*), a German software package that claims to integrate operations across different business functions and remote geographical areas. See Jazayeri and Scapens (1999), Newell, Huang, Galliers and Pan (2003) and Scott and Wagner (2003).

28. This team was, and still is, responsible for informing personnel about the support they can receive about information technology—it initially proposed the SAP project to top management.

29. Latour defines this process as "black boxing"— "An expression from the sociology of science that refers to the way scientific and technical work is made invisible by its own success. When a machine runs efficiently, when a matter of fact is settled, one need focus only on its inputs and outputs and not on its internal complexity. Thus, paradoxically, the more science and technology succeed, the more opaque and obscure they become" (1999, p. 304). See Quattrone and Hopper (2006) for an interpretation of SAP as the emerging result of black-boxing activities.

30. See also Varela, Thompson and Rosch (1991).

31. See, for example, Bryman (1984), Dermer and Lucas (1986), Weick (1979).

32. See Jazayeri and Scapens (1998).

33. Burns and Baldvinsdottir (1999) and Caglio (2003).

34. Our preference for the term "*poly*-rationality" (rather than "*multi*-rationality") is not based on an etymological analysis. However, the prefix "poly" denotes a variety of abstract *poles* that define notions of "best knowledge" and modern dichotomies such as knowledge and rationality, controller and controlled. The term is also adopted to signal differences between our concept and what is in the extant literature.

35. A fuller comparison is in Quattrone and Hopper (2005).

36. Chua and Baxter have indeed talked of "situated drift." For control as drift see Ciborra (and associates) (2001).

37. See Law (1997).

38. This is what for Latour (1999) constitutes an "a-modern" constitution.

Further Readings

You can usefully do some further readings in each of the areas below:

On various perspectives on management accounting change:

- Burns, J. and Raivio, J. (eds) (2001) Management accounting change, Special issue, *Management Accounting Research*, **12** (4).
- Busco, C., Quattrone, P. and Riccaboni, A. (eds) (2007) Management accounting change, Special issue, *Management Accounting Research*, **18** (2).
- Wickramasinghe, D. and Chandana, A. (2007) *Management Accounting Change. Approaches and Perspectives*, Routledge, London.

On institutionalist and structuration approaches to management accounting change:

- Burns, J. (2000) The dynamics of accounting change. Inter-play between new practices, routines, institutions, power and politics. *Accounting, Auditing & Accountability Journal*, **13**, 566–96.
- Burns, J. and Scapens, R. (2000) Conceptualizing management accounting change: an institutional framework. *Management Accounting Research*, **11**, 3–25.
- Granlund, M. (2001) Towards explaining stability in and around management accounting systems. *Management Accounting Research*, **12**, 141–66.

On actor-network theory approaches to management accounting change:

• Andon, P., Baxter, J. and Chua, W. (2007) Accounting change as relational drifting: a field study of experiments with performance measurement. *Management Accounting Research*, **18** (2), 273–308.
• Preston, A., Cooper, D. and Coombs, R. (1992) Fabricating budgets: a study of the production of management budgeting in the National Health Service, *Accounting, Organizations and Society*, **17** (6), 561–93.

MACS and Information Technology

9.1 Introduction[1]

Information technology (IT) has always been attractive to management controllers. Bloomfield and Combs (1992, p. 459) observed that:

> When computers first came into common use within organizations there was an expectation shared among many observers that they would centralize organizational power. Information was equated with power and the potent information processing capacity of computers was seen as an extension of managerial control.

However, if possessing a computer is equated with having access to greater information, and thus managing greater power, then the diffusion of IT within organizations could be said to increase decentralization rather than centralization. In short, the effects of new information technologies on management controls are contentious.

This chapter will explore these effects and provide a view of the relationships between IT and management control and accounting systems that deviates from the common idea that IT necessarily brings benefits to the organization and that it necessarily centralizes controls in one specific space, typically at the top of the management hierarchy. We will deal with these issues by looking at a very basic constituent of every control activity which is the establishment of a distance and a hierarchy between two poles: the controlled and the controller. We will explore how managing information flows is key in setting this distance and thus in exerting control, and we will highlight how the introduction of new IT systems does not necessarily produce linear effects on controls. In other words we will try to explain that the relationship between knowledge, IT and management control is more complex and also entails issues of power, as we anticipated in Chapter 4.

The chapter is organized thus. The next section interprets management controls as a matter of distance and action at a distance. We will draw some parallels between MACS and cartography as both deal with issues of the representation of distant and remote areas. We will then draw on further case material from Think Pink to illustrate that IT projects are becoming key strategic imperatives for controllers. The case will help us to understand how complex the process of ERP systems implementation is and their effects on management accounting and controls.

9.2 MACS and the Distance Making Controllers and Controlled

We noted in Chapter 1 that the word "control" has an interesting etymology coming from the Latin *rotulus*, that is, a roll on which the script of a play is written and that actors had to follow, and *contra*, which means "to be opposite." In that sense, the word gives an embryonic idea of what control is: a mechanism through which actors' performances are guided and monitored. This basic feature of every form of control becomes even clearer when the word was first used in French, where it expresses a clear opposition between two poles: a *rôle* (role-player) who acts to a script, and a *contre-rôle* (counter-role) who monitors the role player's compliance.[2]

Thus control always implies a separation between controller and controlled, who both act in the clear spatio-temporal framework that exists between these two poles, as depicted in Figure 9.1. There we see a sequence of fragmented but well-defined spaces (s_1 and s_2) and times (t_1 and t_2), which rupture what otherwise would be a seamless flow of organizational life. Quarterly reports, annual budgets, functions, processes, cost centers and business divisions, for example, are based on and reproduce this simple idea.

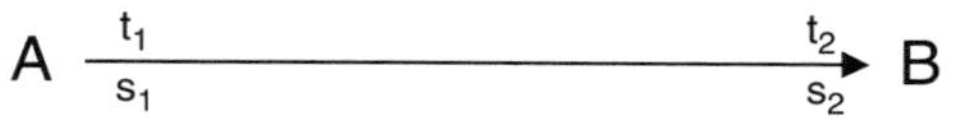

$$A \xrightarrow[\;s_1\;]{\;t_1\;} \qquad \xrightarrow[\;s_2\;]{\;t_2\;} B$$

Source: Reproduced from Quattrone, P. (2005) with permission of Elsevier.

Figure 9.1 A schematic interpretation of the conventional spatio-temporal framework of "modern" control

This dichotomy is the cornerstone upon which hierarchical accountability is built. This is, for example, what is needed at the individual level within the Society of Jesus' accounting for sins, as illustrated in Chapter 2 (see Figure 2.3)—an elementary mechanism of recording sins that allowed the constitution of a simple but effective dichotomy between "me" and "I." This visualization permitted self-control and allowed a Jesuit member to look at his self as in a mirror.[3] Thus, control activity implies the establishment of some kind of distance (virtual or actual) between controller and controlled. This distance has a spatial and temporal dimension. For instance, a distance, say between the HQ of a multinational organization (MNO) and its subsidiaries, is articulated in "space" (i.e. the space separating the center from the periphery), and in "time" (i.e. the time lag between devising plans at HQ, their execution in the subsidiary, and reports of accomplishments by the subsidiary to HQ).

Information technology innovations, especially ERPs, are interesting sites for examining relations between distance and management control. Shared data bases, simultaneously accessible from many locations, fulfill the dream of many management controllers— remote and instantaneous control by real-time performance information. Some MNOs adopt information and communication technologies believing that they create a virtual vista of corporate activities that eliminates distance between the controller and controlled, and hence provide quicker, integrated control.

Information flows and technology certainly alter perceptions of distances.[4] Internet, e-mails, Skype, Facebook and the like are all examples of how communication flows may make physical distance change or disappear. However, assumptions that distances between the two poles of the control relationship seen in Figure 9.1 are homogeneously and linearly reduced by more information may be too simplistic. The world is certainly "shrinking" through quicker transportation and communications. However, it is not clear whether it does so following the linear path depicted in Figure 9.2, where it is assumed that greater information inevitably leads to smaller distances.[5]

The perception of distance may be made more complex by the introduction of the very same information technologies that were supposed to eliminate it, and to reduce and comfortably manage the separation between "center" and "periphery," between "HQ" and "subsidiaries." This is because intermediaries, information technologies, and people continuously redefine what counts as information and hence perceptions of distance in space and time. As we saw earlier, the enaction of information, of the related functioning of management controls and thus also of the idea of distance makes the relationship between information and control more complex.

It is also certain that information is intertwined with issues of power. The power of somebody to control somebody else can emerge for several reasons. For example, it can originate from a law that assigns to the state the task of monitoring public security and thus exerting control over citizens. It can derive from institutional arrangements as, for instance, in family structures where a family member is assigned the role of head by social norms, and has thus relatively greater power than the others. It can derive from organizational structures and governance rules that assign the board of directors a leading role within a corporation. Whatever the origin, control and, more specifically, management controls have to rely on very practical instruments, techniques and mechanisms in order for them to become operative and effective.

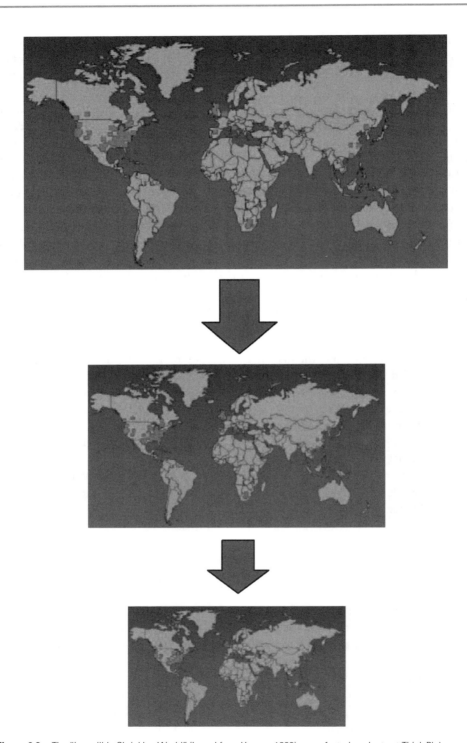

Figure 9.2   The "Incredible Shrinking World" (based from Harvey, 1989): manufacturing plants at Think Pink

Accounting systems are crucial in this respect. But how do they operate? What makes them so important in providing knowledge about the performance of an organization and its members and therefore granting power to those who have the possibility to access accounting information?

Let us compare MACS to maps and try to understand how accounting produces knowledge and therefore power. Some examples from cartography and design may help us to understand what the issues at stake are and introduce the notions of inscriptions and action at a distance.

9.2.1 MACS, Maps, and Inscriptions: Control as Action at a Distance

Management accounting and control systems rely on what in sociology (but also in semiotics) has been described as an "inscription." An inscription, "refers to all the types of transformations through which an entity becomes materialised into a sign, an archive, a document, a piece of paper, a trace" (Latour, 1999, p. 306). A double-entry record in an account, for example, is an inscription.

Why are accounting inscriptions so important? An example may help to clarify the issue. According to an Oracle advertising campaign, Dell handles 125 000 transactions per hour with Oracle's ERP system. Figure 9.3 is an illustration of the centrality of the

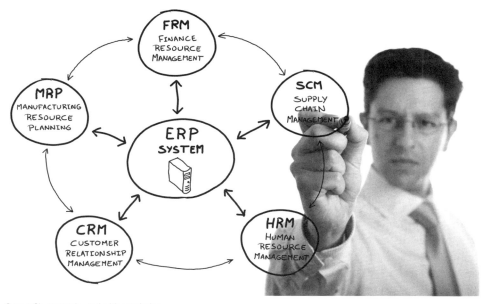

Source: Shutterstock, used with permission

Figure 9.3 Enterprise resource planning

ERP system. What the Oracle's system does is to make a record (possibly in double entry) on a virtual ledger for each of these transactions and it does so every hour, every day, every month, 12 months a year. These transactions, of course, are not collected randomly—they are ordered according to a chart of accounts, which defines the role and function of each account and their possible groupings. There will also be internal guidelines and external standards giving guidance on how to book each entry. These will have to be complemented by some subjective choice concerning, for example, how to allocate overheads, whether to book a transaction as a revenue or work in progress, and so forth. Accountants are there to make such choices and operate the system. If everything goes well, at the end, the CEO of that corporation can pretend to know what happens in a manufacturing site in China without having to leave his comfortable leather chair in the HQ in Europe. He could be there in the Far East without catching a transcontinental flight.

Nowadays what MACS do, especially thanks to the help of information technologies is what cartography did in the past for emperors, kings and chief commanders: they allow the CEO to control the battlefield without necessarily having to be there. Latour, the French sociologist, recalls the case of an explorer sailing over the East Pacific who did not know the island he was about to discover. Once landed on this remote island, he drew the contours of the coast on a piece of paper and brought that map back to Europe. This allowed other sailors to know the island and avoid the perilous waters around it without having been there. Using Latour's words, they could now know the island sitting at leisure in the admiralty office. What this example tells us is that knowledge (and therefore also power) cannot be known without knowing how knowledge *is gained*, without knowing that recursive and accumulative process of collecting pieces of information, bringing them back to the admiralty office and storing them somehow thanks to inscriptions.

You may now think that this activity of mapping is neutral and that, therefore, the world is really shrinking uniformly. You could not be less right. Think of the Tube map, the map of the London Underground (see Figure 9.4).

Now imagine that you are a tourist in London for the first time and that you have to travel from Queensway to Bayswater. What will you have to do? Given that you are in the UK you will first have to stand in an orderly queue to buy a ticket. Once you have the ticket you can go towards the Central line and get on the train. Then you will have to alight at Notting Hill Gate and catch the Circle line heading north. You will finally reach your destination. To make this journey, you will have spent at least 10 minutes of your life, according to the London Tube journey planner, and, above all, a few pounds. Once you get out of Bayswater station, if you look at the opposite side of the street towards the south, you will be greatly surprised to see the entrance of Queensway station, which is only a few yards away from where you are standing, astonished: the two stations are in fact opposite each other on the same road! How could Henri Beck's famous and beautiful piece of design betray you so badly? In fact what the Tube map has done for you is exactly what it is supposed to do: it simplifies reality to make it manageable in a beautiful piece of design. This is why the genial Beck made the city center portion of his drawing relatively larger than the rest of the map: you gain in clarity and ease of use but you lose in the

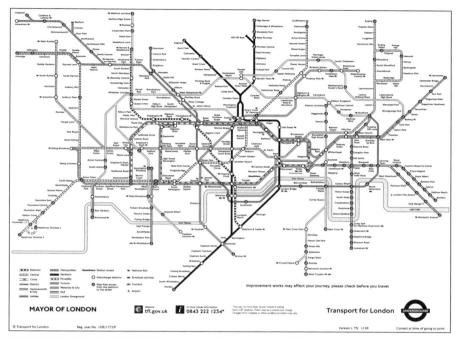

Source: Registered User No. 10/E/1772/P, reproduced with kind permission of © Transport for London.

Figure 9.4   The London Tube map

accuracy of representation. As commentators say, the tube map is a graphic representation of the London Underground. It is not exactly a map as the only geographical sign on it is the Thames. In a similar way, management accounting is a graphic representation of cost centers, subsidiaries, production processes and the like. What this analogy is telling us is that every act of representation works in the same way: you gain something and you lose something else. If you believe that what you gain is greater than what you lose then the map or the graphic design works well for you.

Do you still have doubts on whether this relates to MACS? We would argue that it does quite a lot. According to the Oracle ERP advertising campaign mentioned above and given that Dell works on a 24-hour circle across the globe, what you will have is an average of 125 000 transactions per hour, multiplied by 24 hours, multiplied by 365 days a year: this makes 1 095 000 000 transactions to take into account. It is certainly an ocean of transactions and you will need a map to safely navigate across this vast sea. This map is the management and financial accounting report.

In order to construct this accounting map you need to be aware of three things. The first is that, as with the sailor on a journey to discover a new island, maps and knowledge production require a process of accumulation: someone needs to be sent there and to come back with some news in order that others can be sent there again and travel in safe waters. The same applies to accounting: accounting inscriptions have to be accumulated in physical or virtual ledgers so that feedback controls can be provided. This process of accumulation is what defines the distance between controller and controlled. It allows the controller to access greater information than the controlled and thus, for instance, the distance between HQ and subsidiaries is established and managed. What this process does is to create a center of calculation from which controllers can act at a distance on the controlled, without leaving their comfortable and expensive chairs. Like cartographers who make the indigenous people's *local* knowledge of the island *universal* and accessible, accounting systems accumulate inscriptions, such as records in accounting books, for those with access.

The second important thing that Beck's graphic design teaches us is that representations are always partial. Management accounting and control systems select and represent only a subset of the information that could be collected. Accounting representations of reality are not reality: they speak for it but cannot ever speak the truth. Depending on what accounting includes and what it leaves out, you will get different pictures, different distances between controllers and controlled, different centers and peripheries. This picture is made more complex (as we will see below with some further information on the Think Pink case) by the introduction of another instrument of communication and representation—IT.

The third element that you will have to take into account is that this process of selection is not neutral. In order to be recorded, transactions have to be modified into forms that make them recordable. The process of inscribing these transactions on your ledger acts as a translation from one linguistic code (e.g., goods that are exchanged) to another (accounting numbers). The greater the distance between center and periphery, the more translations are required.

This reemphasizes the immateriality of distance. What constitutes information, how this information flows, from where, and when, is crucial for establishing centers, subsidiaries, and action at a distance, and how they change. In order to understand MACS we cannot limit our analysis to static examinations of structures and how controls operate, for this does not acknowledge that knowledge, and therefore power and control, can be understood only through the study of what constitutes it.

We will now illustrate these issues and explore the effects of changes in how MACS operate due to the introduction of new information technologies by going back to the Think Pink case. We will look at some more case material to illustrate how more information does not necessarily mean greater knowledge, control and power.

9.3 MACS, IT, and Minimalist Controls: Further Insights from the Think Pink Case*

"Location doesn't matter anymore . . . You don't need to be physically close to the plants [and] . . . the customer, you just need good connections within the different systems you operate" (International Business Controller in European Regional HQ of Think Pink).

---

*Quotes from interviews by P. Quattrone.

This was one of many benefits that managers in Think Pink believed they gained from implementing SAP. Typical judgments were positive: "[SAP is] A superb transaction processor—it is very good at dealing with millions of transactions" (UK financial controller) and "[it is a] common data base of information" (Director of Accounting in US HQ). Many managers valued its contribution to establishing visibility, clarity, and order: "SAP has helped us . . . to see the problem, to come up with a solution. It is giving me data. Instead of working on instinct, gut feel, 'This looks right,' 'That looks right,' I can actually quantify it and say, 'That is what is going on'" (UK customer service leader).

Overcoming distances between the corporate HQ and its periphery was crucial:

> SAP will allow you to slice and dice however you want to see it. So if you want to see the consolidated corporation, you look at all companies, all business areas, and it all goes together. If composites [a business division] wants to look at their global composites then they take all company codes and key on the business area, and that gives them all composites . . . They select certain company codes . . . and that gives them composites Europe or composites North America or Brazil . . . You can see what companies or what part of the world you are dealing with and so you can do different things. (Accountant, US HQ)

Coupling the new ERP system to traditional MCS tools increased visibility and enhanced control. However, this apparent feeling of control was only achieved after a long and difficult SAP implementation. The managers' evaluations of SAP were made late in 1999, when SAP already managed four-fifths of the MNO's activities, and was expected to manage them entirely by November 2000 ("4.7 or 4.8 billion dollars of business," Director of Electronic Business, US). Implementing SAP, reconfiguring the spatio-temporal framework, habituating Think Pink employees to this, and establishing new organizational routines were beset with trouble. The search for a real-time information system to minimize distance by globally integrating activities disrupted norms of control by action at a distance schematized in Figure 9.1. As in Sister Act, control and discretion coexisted but in Think Pink these were amplified and had no stable endpoint.

9.3.1 Information Technology Projects as a Strategic Management Control Change

The International Business Controller from regional HQ in Belgium summarized why Think Pink implemented ERP: "We had, before we took the decision to go on SAP, dozens and dozens of different legacy systems all over the world [211—according to managers interviewed]. [This] is very expensive . . . The second reason was that we were not Y2K compliant and SAP was."

Senior managers believed a new MIS would cut costs[6] but, above all, they emphasized how it promoted Think Pink's strategy to be a global corporation with integrated solutions for customer needs. They wanted an integrated system for an integrated strategy (Annual Report, 1998): ERP became the centerpiece of company globalization aims encapsulated in the slogan "common, global, and simple" (global development leader of ERP project).

Centers of excellence \ Divisions	Division A	Division B	Division C	Division D	Division E	**Process results**
A						⊕
B						⊕
C						⊕
...						⊕
N^th						⊕
Business Results	⊙	⊙	⊙	⊙	⊙	

⊙ = Financial targets for the divisions ("P&L bottom line")

⊕ = Nonfinancial targets for the "Centers of excellence" (or "Process organizations").

Source: Reproduced from Quattrone, P. (2005) with permission of Elsevier.

Figure 9.5   The matrix organization and the new accountability system in Think Pink

Integration through ERP became the theme for reengineering business processes (although *"not as much as I think anybody would have liked"*—IS business relations manager), and adopting a matrix structure (illustrated in Figure 9.5) where "centers of excellence" served different divisions and geographical areas.

The SAP system appeared to collapse distance with commercial benefits but, as an IS support team member observed, "The good thing about [SAP] is that it is integrated; the bad thing about [SAP] is that . . . it is integrated!" Integrating daily operations produced unexpected forms of control, accountability, and responsibility.

Chaos, the Collapse of Distance, and Multiple Controls

Conditions at the start of integration were often described as chaos. The leader of ERP deployment in the UK (now European Continental Business Financial Controller in the European HQ) commented how: "We underestimated SAP . . . it is so huge to implement . . . We were the pilot for the corporation and we were overwhelmed . . . It took time to understand and to manage SAP."

Managers needed time to digest the implications of ERP and the new organization structure as information and controls between the periphery and the center were no longer based on one-to-one relations (as in Figure 9.1). However, initially people continued as if nothing had changed. An accountant at the US HQ commented: "People didn't realize how unforgiving the system is . . . you put in bad data and you have got to whip that bad data out and put proper data in . . . When we rolled out some of the businesses there were problems with getting the bills . . . In the sales area there was a problem in getting the sales properly recorded and the invoices out the door. There were problems with inventory valuations in that some of the numbers inputted as the units of measure were wrong. So instead of having a thousand dollars of material you had a million dollars' worth. All kinds of things like that— you had a lot of scrambling."

The ability to understand the effects of direct accounting entries was missing during the initial stages of implementing ERP.[7] According to the corporate budget analyst, accounts intended for one (global) purpose in the uniform chart of accounts had been used for different (local) purposes in subsidiaries. Events in a cost center of an US manufacturing plant illustrate this:

> The cost center is really a sort of an internal control. It is like their control and I know there were some plants that were doing certain things in accounts that we weren't doing over here. They wanted to include certain cost elements . . . there are accounts out there that you are not using. You find that it is a very good way to segregate some of the costs you want to keep track of. If in a plant you want to keep track of a cost for maintenance—of your tow trucks—and there is no account for that in the corporate ledgers, the real temptation is to say, "Well I will use an account here and no-one else is using it for anything." Well YOU aren't using it but someone else may be using it . . . We at the corporate level get crazy looking at numbers. [For instance] we go to [SAP], to an account to get certain information. We assume that that account is what it is supposed to be . . . One of the things that you have to watch is if you get, especially in a plant location, someone using that account for something else because they want to control costs. [The uniform chart of account] tells them NOTHING. They know that account means: "This is my lift truck special maintenance account!" However, it might be something else over here in the corporate structure . . . that was their universe.

Accounting inscriptions used prior to SAP had temporarily created a local "universe" with its own space and time at odds with that in HQ post-SAP. Discretion to create accounting categories locally allowed the plant cost accountant to treat an account as, say, "my lift truck special maintenance account." S/he had had up to a month's grace prior to closing the books to adjust the account if so desired. Thus the subsidiary could, to a degree, control the controller by exploiting temporal and spatial gaps in Figure 9.1. In turn, the controller at the center knew (if s/he was aware) that at the month-end the account would revert to its shared meaning. Under the old regime the local cost accountant could balance local and global pressures simultaneously. The dichotomy between t_1 and t_2, and s_1 and s_2, in Figure 9.1 permitted mutual control and some local discretion within a shared notion of order. The Financial Director of the UK subsidiary fleshed this out, stating how under the "old" regime:

> We could put our spin on things and they weren't really able to challenge us, or not without a great deal of effort . . . When I worked for GEC I had to go to management meetings once a month and that was the game that you played. You held on to the good news that you didn't want to give them because you knew that there was bad news coming . . . So you could always tell lies and they couldn't prove it. What you have got to be careful with the type of systems that you have got now is that these people rely on you to tell the truth but you better understand that they have got ways of checking out that information because they have got that information.

The SAP system made dichotomies between controllers and the controlled, and local and global, disappear. Controllers could access data now, *before* those controlled, if they wished. As the Director of Accounting in the US HQ stated:

> A couple of accountants had been there [senior accountants at European regional HQ]—for over 30 years. They were very good . . . they were the gatekeepers . . . of their data. There was no way when I was sitting here in Toledo as Director of Accounting for the whole company that I could see anything in their ledgers previously. So I had to rely a lot on their abilities and their integrity to do the right things in their ledgers . . . [Now] I can tell you how the plant in Batisse is running today and . . . how they keep their accounting in Brussels. So we have totally taken that gatekeeper role out and it's really uncomfortable for folks in the field who are used to being able to do what they want with their own data. So from a control standpoint I like the change a lot because I have an ability to control from here.

The collapse of s_1 into s_2 and t_1 into t_2 in Figure 9.1 made boundaries between "here" and "there," and "before" and "after," confused and fuzzier.

This could imply that the MNO became an ultra-modern form of control.[8] However, this was not so, as technologies and management controls do not only constrain but also empower people to do things that were not possible before or envisaged by the designers of the system. This was evident in Think Pink. The collapse of "A" into "B" after implementing SAP did not lead to totalitarian controls; rather, it replaced a sequential and ordered fragmentation of space and time with a more chaotic framework. Multiple roles and counter-roles emerged enabling virtually everyone to create a space and time within which to act.

Prior to SAP the accounting function was responsible for all accounting—from data entry and discipline to preparing reports to managers. Thus accountants were masters of the accounts for which they were responsible. Integration through ERP changed conventional accounting systems and the roles of accountants. Post-ERP someone selling products, say in Belgium, could instantaneously and materially affect the books of subsidiaries. Multiple posting points created problems:

> The guy on the shop floor who's doing the shipping document, he's the accountant now. When he does the receipt, he updates the accounting records. We didn't realize what that really meant . . . If he messes that up, which is going to happen from time to time, my ledger is messed up immediately . . . That was a pretty big change, not one that we expected. (Director of Accounting in the US HQ)

Everyone became a potential "accountant"—and the repercussions extended beyond technical matters of inputting data to how control was enacted. After implementing ERP the Financial Director of the UK subsidiary noticed how:

> People begin to access things that they shouldn't be given access to . . . We got this new organisation and we got this new system and we [were] not really sure who should have access to which part of the system. I know, "We will give everybody access to everything" [is a] GREAT IDEA! to get you off the ground.

This freedom had consequences. For example, plant financial analysts could try to improve their unit's performance by benchmarking its costs against those of factories across the world without the center intervening or the other factory knowing, i.e. there was no common hierarchically ordered referent (a common "counter-role"). A more chaotic form of control replaced the linear one. It was difficult to know who was controlling whom, and when.

Shifting information flows and increased access to data created problems. Employees could not connect what they were representing (and creating) when posting accounting entries to how SAP used them to represent events. A manager responsible for ERP in the North American roofing business stated how:

> People knew how to do their task because they were trained . . . What they didn't understand was what the variation was upstream and downstream. So it was really a lack of overall understanding of how things fed into each other.

This goes to the heart of action at a distance as a workable control practice. The modernist project assumes a correspondence between reality and its representation. It assumes that information flows unchanged from the center to the periphery and vice versa. This was not the case in Think Pink: employees could not retrace their "footsteps." They no longer had familiar references (e.g., a transaction or a task to perform) with a referent (e.g., an entry in the accounting system or a controller who checks them) that made organizational events visible and meaningful. Information flows between the MNO's center and periphery (A and B in Figure 9.1) were no longer ordered within a sequential spatio-temporal framework: now centers and peripheries (the "As" and "Bs") and roles and counter-roles proliferated. This made tracking events back by tracing information flows difficult. Coupling accounting to the ERP ideology of integration replaced modern notions of control (linear, segmented and univocal) with a new form (complex, boundary-less, and multiple) alien to organizational members.

9.3.2 Information Technology Implementations: When Grand Objectives are Translated into Minimal Targets

Enterprise Resource Planning necessitated rethinking what was "local" and "global." In the "good old days" accounting inscriptions may have had different meanings for different people but they granted local discretion and people had shared meanings when accounts were consolidated monthly. Then "globalization" was just a fashionable word for many employees—now it was a pressing problem. Most managers deploying SAP recalled their efforts to regain control of even simple activities in heroic terms. The UK customer service leader's comments were typical:

> The first couple of months weren't too bad. The next six months were horrendous, and then slowly, slowly, we started to get things back . . . An implementation that on paper should have taken from conception to delivery twelve months ended up taking nearly three years to get right.

Re-ordering—to make things tidy again—was hard. Learning the advantages of controlling by ERP and how to track mistakes back took time. Employees responsible for posting data found they became visible if they made mistakes. "Everything that is done has a tag on it . . . It has got my name on it" (accountant at US HQ). Consequently, managers trans-lated the integration ideology into something more familiar. For example, they restricted access to data entry and information: many areas became accessible only by passwords (an example was the corporate budget analyst's table defining access to the budgeting system). The financial director of the UK subsidiary insisted that anyone inputting data affecting "his" books must e-mail him first. Thus managers made new "inscriptions" defining who could do what. Returning to the analogy of maps and journeys across the ocean or on the London Tube, organizational members tried to bring order into the unknown mass of entries in ERP by creating threads of responsibility for the new multipostings. However, the resulting ensemble of devices (passwords, e-mails) to reestablish linear time/space relations were largely frustrated by continuing multiple access to information and the different ways people used it.

Only three years after implementing ERP could the situation be defined as under control. Two years after this the CEO could proudly announce that Think Pink had had a tremen-dous year. However, his depiction of a tidy, more ordered corporation, more easily control-led by the new IT system is misleading. The matrix organization in Figure 9.5 depicts how new "centers of excellence" (customer services, accounting, shared services, logistics, etc.) and operating divisions should interact. Like many matrix organizations, managers expe-rienced conflicts between the service divisions' objectives (set horizontally) and financial targets (set vertically) by managers responsible for profits. The international business con-troller based in Belgium stated:

> In theory you have one general manager who has full responsibility for one P & L . . . for opera-tions, and in theory he has responsibility as well for the cash flow and the balance sheet. But some pieces of that P & L are out of his control, sure. But yes, that is the process organisation. The matrix organisation is sometimes a beauty on paper but sometimes it is difficult to manage.

The European financial controller reinforced this, arguing that people in process organi-zations:

> Can affect our business but they have a different perspective because they look at the proc-ess. "How many transactions per hour?" . . . They are measured by the processing [but] we are measured by . . . the P & L results. . . . So that's the permanent conflict we have in this matrix organisation.

It is difficult to depict relations and controls wrought by the new ERP ideology in the matrix structure in Figure 9.5 on a two-dimensional sheet of paper as it cannot represent their multidimensionality.

Even new centers of excellence, established to cut costs, found action at a distance difficult. The ordered matrix structure of Figure 9.5 could appear to make them centers of calculation. In practice this was impossible because they were not the only depositaries for SAP information: virtually everyone could now access this. As we saw earlier in the chapter, the organization became a-centered,[9] i.e. there was no single center (or series of centers) for accounting inscriptions—they were no longer accumulated to permit action at a distance, and they no longer had universal meanings and functions. Those with access to the system experienced a dilution of control. The new ERP system supplanted a unique vision of order with multiple versions. Accounting inscriptions within SAP exacerbated the intrinsic multiple nature of accounting.[10] Their meaning now depended on who accessed, downloaded, organized, and interpreted the data: this created disorder.

Veering responsibility and accountability lessened individual feelings of responsibility. Some interviewees recalled the "good old days" when:

> I knew much more who was doing what, and who was responsible and can get something fixed, whi e now there is an aggregate of people doing a process. I don't know who is responsible and maybe they don't know themselves where their responsibility goes. I think we are losing the sense of responsibility that we had before. (Continental European business controller)

It could be argued that unifying and ordering the matrix structure just requires someone to determine what is best for the organization and then subdivide and allocate the necessary tasks to departments. However, the matrix structure's conflicting demands frustrated this, as a manager explained:

> They [leaders of departments] are measured on their process so they are tracking what they consider to be their key deliverables . . . You are relying on other organisations to deliver for you. So you don't feel like you are in control and you have a much more difficult time setting their priorities . . . Their priority is to do the best for [Think Pink]. In their mind, if they are working in another division and generate lots of savings and then neglect you, it is because you are not as important overall—[Think Pink] is better off. They feel they have done their job. I have a more narrow viewpoint. We all want to have improvements . . . so there is a dilemma there. (Financial leader at the US HQ)

Each division and process organization (centers of excellence) has its own idea of what is best for Think Pink, and there is a seemingly infinite series of "locals" and "globals." Managers of service organizations may believe they control processes, and the director of accounting can say "I have an ability to control from here," but interactions between people temporarily accessing information for contingent and emergent aims are no longer controllable. The SAP system allows centers of calculation to emerge momentarily and disappear even before a manager responsible for a division knew they existed.

Thus, paradoxically, an implementation to integrate business functions, and to increase control and accountability, had the opposite effect as it became difficult to match responsibilities to accountability. Now there is a different representation of the business where accountability is unclear. Modern double-entry bookkeeping systems create one-to-one relationships between the controller and the controlled. Figure 9.1's representation of time and space in modern control matches accountability and responsibility: B is accountable for its actions to A, who should, according to the system's architect, understand the entire recursive control process. This was lost when Think Pink implemented

ERP because A collapsed into B and loci of control multiplied. The SAP system marked a shift from one center and one periphery with heterogeneous interests *but* shared intents to multiple centers and multiple peripheries, with heterogeneous interests *and* intents. Now no one could construct a universally accepted map of operational control. The idea of a center has less significance because responsibilities are diffused ("I have at least six bosses now"—shared service center leader in the UK). The collapse of conventional assumptions of space and time transgressed beliefs about how control between the center and peripheries should be exercised and left managers with a minimalist attitude and beliefs that they had partially lost control. Some employees struggled to preserve traditional control by restricting postings and access to data in their area of responsibility but these were pyrrhic victories. More often, order was reached within apparently isolated islands temporarily black-boxed by accounting inscriptions from SAP.

Thus it is more pertinent to trace continual changes in loci of control rather than trying to identify a specific center that exerts action at a distance based on modernist presumptions of a dichotomy between the controller and linear and uniform time and space. This is why studying accounting change is important and this is what we mean when change is an intrinsic feature of MACS. They deal with information and this is relative to the network of relationships in which it is produced. A network made of accounting regulations and choices, and information technologies, enacted distances between controller and controlled and power shifts.

9.4 Summary and Conclusions

In this chapter we explored how the introduction of IT, and specifically ERP systems, is affecting management accounting and controls within organizations. In contemporary organizations, as much as in contemporary societies, the idea of total and full control and order is tempting. However, we have argued in this chapter how this is simply an illusion. This illusion needs to leave space for another view where diffused controls better illustrate how organizations work and change. This minimalist attitude seems far more fruitful for understanding and managing change processes, as we illustrated with further case material from Think Pink. It promotes an understanding of the processes of knowledge production within organizations through the ideas of action at a distance and translation.

This emphasis on a-centered organizations and minimalist control does not mean that we want to surrender to the irrationality that seems to surround certain situations. On the contrary, assuming the irrationality of actors and organizations can help us understand how to make sound and knowledgeable decisions in change management.

Endnotes

1. This chapter draws on and expands the arguments in Quattrone and Hopper (2005).
2. See Hoskin and Macve (1986, p. 114) and Lipari (1984) for the French and Latin etymologies respectively.

3. See Quattrone (2000, 2004), Roberts (1991, 1996) and Willmott (1996).
4. See Bingham (1996), Clark (1985), Schields (1991), Soya (1989), Taylor and Thrift (1982).
5. See Kirsh's critique (1995) of Harvey (1989).
6. The International Business Controller claimed after implementing SAP, "The IS cost in Europe has been cut by 50% in three years. We went from, let's use a rough number, 20 million to 10 million dollars in three years because we got rid of all the legacy systems that we had before."
7. As commented by an interviewee, training had little effect until employees encountered SAP in practice. A manager responsible for deploying ERP in the US roofing business described the situation during 1997: "We put all the business rules in place. We put all the systems in place and we fired everything up. And we struggled mightily . . . Even though we went through all the right steps, no-one was really checking to see whether the folks out in the field really practiced on the system, and that they really had used the training window appropriately, and that they were ready to go live . . . We assigned the accountability for training and monitoring training to someone in the . . . field . . . But they did not follow up and make sure that they truly understood what was there . . . we really, really struggled. It was a very dark time for us . . . We ended up with customer disruption issues and, I mean, could have very easily been to the point of saying, 'Wait a minute, let's go back to what we have and figure out a better way to do that.'" The quotation illustrates how learning is more than memorization. Learning to perform a task cannot be dichotomized from practice because learning is not just following rules but is a creative and constructivist act: see Varela, Thomson and Rosch (1991). This is investigated further in Quattrone and Hopper (2006).
8. We will discuss of these disciplinary practices resembling Bentham's Panopticon (Foucault, 1977) in Chapter 10.
9. The definition, description, and illustration of the characteristics of an a-centered organization is elaborated more fully in Quattrone and Hopper (2006).
10. See Chapman (1998), Miller and Napier (1993), and Quattrone (2004).

Further Readings

On the relationships between management control and IT:

- Bloomfield, B. and Vurdubakis, T. (1997) Vision of organization and organization of vision: the representational practices of information systems development. *Accounting, Organizations and Society*, **22** (7), 639–68.
- Chapman, C. and Kihn, L. (2009) Information system integration, enabling control and performance. *Accounting, Organizations and Society*, **34** (2), 151–69.
- Ciborra, C. (and associates) (2001) *From Control to Drift. The Dynamics of Corporate Information Infrastructures*, Oxford University Press, Oxford.
- Dechow, N. and Mouritsen, J. (2005) Enterprise resource planning systems, management control and the quest for integration. *Accounting, Organizations and Society*, **30** (7–8), 691–733.

PART IV

MACS AS PRACTICES: ISSUES OF ACCOUNTABILITY, GOVERNANCE, AND ETHICS

Making Sense of MACS Practices

10.1 Introduction

Let us return for a moment to the Jesuit case in Chapter 2. The Order was clearly a very complex organization. While presenting some common features across the various geographical areas in which it expanded and throughout its history, the Society of Jesus also displayed considerable differences both in terms of its members' actions and of those of the organization as a whole. It is not by chance that, as the saying goes, Jesuits became mandarins in China and natives in Latin-America. Historians have thus questioned interpretations of the Jesuits' nature and mission as an indistinct whole—interpretations that view it as a monolithic organization geared up to act in the name of the Catholic Counter-Reformation. If anything, the Jesuits expanded even more diffusely exactly where the Catholic credo was alive and kicking and in no need of an institutional defense. The historians have therefore asked themselves: how shall we study this organization? What was the Jesuit Order about? What was its nature and organizational mission? What drove the actions of its members and of the Order as a whole, given the significant geographical diversity in colleges, membership and so forth? These questions can easily be asked of any kind of organization that shares the Jesuits' complexity.

Solving this puzzle requires a methodological innovation: in order to understand complex organizations one needs to look at their everyday practices, what their members do and how, which shared formal and informal rules of conduct inform their behavior and how these customs vary across time and space. This is a different approach from that of those who see organizations as stable and well defined entities with clear goals, strategies, and plans. Organizations are not "given" but result from everyday practices—from a network of actions that are linked in various degrees to each other through shared norms of social conduct. This is the kind of approach that we will illustrate in this chapter in relation to MACS.

Management accounting and control practices are an important *locus* to participate *in* and to reflect *on* these actions. They are not only a set of techniques to assess the efficiency of an organization seeking to pursue profit. They are also a way to study organizational and individual identities through the variations that management control systems present when observed as practices. They act as mirrors that help us to understand the individuals who use them and the organizations that deploy them. One cannot see the original picture reflected but one can study it from this reflection. Studying what organizations do is a way to understand what they are and the complexities associated with this. With this approach, it is through practice that knowledge recursively reproduces itself within processes of learning and knowing.

However, organizational knowledge cannot be conceptualized simply as a mental substance residing in individuals' heads. It should instead be seen as a form of distributed social expertise, situated in the historical, socio-material, and cultural context in which it occurs. If we look, for example, at the balanced scorecard (BSC), we will see how different organizations implement and define the scorecards differently. This is because when the abstract ideas that the BSC conveys (i.e. the overall vision and the four perspectives) are operationalized they become intertwined with a network of material (for example, other technologies such as ERPs) and immaterial elements (such as the company's tradition). This causes the BSC to vary as it travels from one organization to another. And it is only in this operationalization that those participating in the BSC exercise learn about the company's mission, how it can be pursued, and how related results can be measured. In a sense, this mission does not exist outside the practice of defining it and of measuring its performance. As we have already noted with regard to issues of change (in Chapter 8) and of system implementation (in Chapter 9), this process of definition is a reflexive exercise through which identities are not discovered but are constructed through a recursive cycle of organizational mediation, which implies a translation of abstract ideals into concrete actions. A practice view of management control and accounting systems assumes that it is only through participating in this reflexive and practical exercise that knowledge about organizations and their performance is created, circulated and/or redefined.

This attention to practice and to practicing is gaining an enormous relevance in accounting and control studies and beyond. Strategy is now seen as "strategizing," organizations as "communities of practice," and, of course, accounting is now seen as "practice" too (see Ahrens and Chapman, 2007a, 2007b). In this chapter we want to illustrate some of these contributions and concentrate on a specific notion of practice that refers to precise (albeit diverse) ways of doing certain things and not others. These differences may be due to some form of common context, discipline, or some form of classifying and gathering knowledge. In other words, we believe that what is done "in practice" is important but that it becomes theoretically relevant in terms of how MACS affect people and organizations if these practices are studied as part of some specific apparatus of control, socially constructed context or training regimes and *forma mentis*. These all contribute to shape MACS features, *modus operandi*, and how they emerge and evolve through appropriation by organizational users.

The following section begins with an analysis of approaches that see accounting as a way of disciplining the workforce that creates organizational and social order through the financial knowledge that accounting metrics generate. Knowledge gives power to those who have access to it and enables them to take decisions affecting others who do not have such access. In a similar vein, but at a different level, the argument can be translated to society as a whole: MACS of all kinds become a way to construct, embed, and maintain order using general discourses of efficiency concerning the whole economy and society. They become a form of governmental control, a way in which, through various financial and statistical information systems, order is brought into what would otherwise be a chaotic system. These power-knowledge relationships and governmental controls are inspired by the work of the French historian Michel Foucault and have been explored, for example, by some of the works falling under that stream of research named "new accounting history" (Hopper, Laughlin and Miller, 1991).

Section 10.3 also looks at how daily practices are informed by shared norms of social conduct that act at the organizational level. We will introduce the work of the French sociologist Pierre Bourdieu and how some of the concepts he devised (*field, illusio, symbolic violence, capital* and *habitus*) are useful in understanding formal and informal organizational control systems. After having introduced Bourdieu's concepts we will illustrate them through the case of the collapse of Enron and the practices that led to its inauspicious ending. Bourdieu's theoretical lenses will also help us, in Chapter 11, to illuminate the failure of Enron's management control and governance system.

Section 10.4 will speculate on the training regimes that accountants go through. In other words it will propose a journey into the *forma mentis* of those who are trained as management accountants by recalling the historical emergence of accounting and how it is linked to rhetorical forms of knowledge classification and communication that originated in the Middle Ages and are nowadays embedded in the ways in which, in Western societies, we classify and order otherwise chaotic organizational and financial relationships. You will be surprised to see how much accounting owes to these old forms of knowledge production, which share features with meditation and religious practices. We will argue that the more accounting and finance seek to become "scientific" forms of knowledge the more they go back to their original roots in religion, meditation and mysticism!

10.2 MACS, Governable Persons, and Power-Knowledge Relationships

Accounting practices do not only concern profit-seeking firms. It is now clear that most of what nowadays pass as MACS have emerged in organizations that did not have profit as their main objective. Michel Foucault (1926–84), a historian by profession, was very aware of the power of organizational and control practices and most of his research has been concerned with the impersonal, but pervasive apparatuses of power in society's central institutions— hospitals, insane asylums, prisons, factories, military, schools. Foucault was interested in the appearance in the eighteenth and nineteenth centuries of the so-called human sciences and how these treat the human subject as an object to be studied, examined, diagnosed, and corrected. He was interested in the various techniques and apparatuses that generated knowledge about the individual and how these were a form of bringing order to society.

Foucault argued that knowledge became power in that it was used as a blueprint to discipline individuals who seemed to deviate from what the knowledge deemed to be normal. His famous neologism, "power/knowledge," subsumes the will to know the true nature of what it means to be a normal human being and to use that knowledge to correct individuals along the lines of that knowing. Thus, Foucault saw the appearance of various institutions, including the medical clinic, the insane asylum, the military academy, Victorian-age sexuality, the factory, and the prison as a result of human power struggles—not as the discoveries of some timeless, primordial or pure presence that always existed in dazzling pristine form waiting to be discovered so that society could progress. If translated into issues of management accounting and control this means a destabilization of the neoclassical economic ideal that management techniques are neutral instruments in pursuing an obvious rationality. Using Foucauldian lenses helps us to see that what counts as "normal" performance within organizations is always the result of power struggles amongst various organizational parties. The very ideal of standard costing can also be seen as a form of disciplining the workforce through the gaze of costing techniques. So you should not be surprised to see a historian quoted in a book on management accounting and this is why Foucault has gained so much currency in some of the recent sociological literature on management and accounting.

This section draws on these ideas to look at accounting as a disciplinary formation and illustrates some of the key principles which Foucault identifies as the disciplinary drive that became ubiquitous during the modern epoch.[1] In Foucault's work three general principles underlie the way the disciplinary society functions: the principle of *enclosure*, the principle of the *efficient body*, and the principle of the *disciplined mind*. These achieve the maximum effect within the architectural arrangements of the panopticon, which will be described below.

Discipline proceeds initially by the careful distribution of individuals in general-purpose, self-contained places of confinement. These include monasteries, poorhouses, prisons, schools, universities, factories, hospitals, office buildings, military bases, asylums, and so on. This distribution is the first step in the discipline of the monk, the pauper, the criminal, the pupil, the scholar, the worker, the sick, the clerk, the soldier, or the mentally deranged, who can now all be isolated and controlled.

General enclosure by itself, however, is not sufficient to achieve disciplinary spaces. It is also necessary to partition the enclosure into smaller, self-contained locations, partitions or cells in which it becomes possible to know, master, and make useful each and every individual. This cellular principle can be traced back to the monastery of the classical era where each monk had his own cell and it is also related to the manner in which knowledge (and accounting knowledge in particular) is created. However we will return to this point later in the chapter when describing accounting training regimes. The point here is that partitioning also makes it possible to effect the rule of functional sites, whereby each location is defined in terms of the specific, regular, useful function to be performed therein. In a factory, for example, each workstation is assigned a particular task. A university library contains various rooms, each with a particular function: reserve reading, periodicals, archives, and study cubicles.

Partitions are also arranged horizontally and vertically. In the first instance, each is serialized within the general enclosure in a perfectly legible fashion and its usefulness is identified in relation to all the other partitions in the functional chain. In a factory, work moves from one workstation to another in serial fashion. Similarly, in a university, students are shunted from one building to another and from one class to another. Each partition is also defined in terms of the rank it occupies in the hierarchy and by the space that separates it from the partitions immediately above and below it. The result is the formation of a relatively permanent grid of functional, useful, serialized, and ranked spaces. The crucial consequence is that each individual becomes defined by the physical space he or she occupies.

The enclosure principle disciplines space and paves the way for the efficient body principle, which dictates the individual's time within any specific partition. The efficient body principle works according to three practices: the *timetable*, which programs the individual; the *maneuver*, which defines the precise timing of body movements; and *dressage,* which produces automatic responses to signals.

The timetable has a long heritage as a disciplinary practice. Religious orders such as the monasteries of the Middle Ages employed it to great advantage to establish a meticulous timetabling of the monk's daily life. Vespers, lessons, Bible study, chores, and contemplation time were ritualistically scheduled to ensure regular cycles of devout activity. The timetable later came into use in schools, hospitals, poorhouses, prisons, and workshops, where it established rhythms of actions, regulated cycles of repetition, and effected a clockwork repetition of useful activities. Since time was now measured and paid for in the factory, it "must also be a time without impurities or defects! A time of good quality, throughout which the body is constantly applied to its exercise." The individual was enmeshed in a constraining chain of detailed minute actions.

The rules of one factory, for example, required all personnel to start the day by washing their hands, thanking God for their work, and making the sign of the cross. Such pious exercises gave legitimacy to the timetable. Sanctions were invoked for being 15 minutes

late for work, for talking or joking with coworkers, or for leaving one's workstation. Even during meal breaks, no conversation was permitted that might distract workers from their duties. Every attempt was made to "assure the quality of time used: constant supervision, the pressures of supervisor, the elimination of anything that might disturb or distract: it is a question of constituting a totally useful time." Time penetrated the worker's body, rendering it docile, obedient, and efficient.

The maneuver, which also became widespread in early modernity, emerged as a technique to intensify time even further by articulating the body with the work object. The maneuver links the individual's body and the pen, rifle, wagon or machine into a man-object-machine by specifying the precise way to perform the task, as well as the exact timing required to complete the job. Taylorism is a clear example of this principle in a factory-like environment. In schools, for example, the correct technique for handwriting was spelled out in detail. The position of the feet and arms, the movement of the hand, fingers, eyes, elbow, and even the chin were rigorously prescribed. Each movement was assigned a direction, a range, and a duration within a prescribed sequence until handwriting resembled microgymnastics. The result was a systematic and meticulous meshing of the body with the pen.

Along similar lines, the French Army prescribed the precise body movements for various maneuvers such as marching and shooting. In the sixteenth century, the orders simply called for the troops to march in file, raising their feet in unison to the rhythm of the drum. In contrast, 100 years later, the regulations detailed four different sorts of marching steps: short, ordinary, double, and oblique. The oblique step had to be 18 inches, measured from one heel to the other, and had to take slightly longer than one second. The instructions for firing fusils contained precise details for various stages of preparing, aiming, and shooting. The user-friendly instructions and software of today's ubiquitous personal computer, although more subtle, can be seen as a present-day maneuver, tying the individual to the computer keyboard and screen.

The emerging factories also called for intensive discipline and control. Previously, the master in the workshop worked alongside the apprentices and helpers, keeping a close eye on them. And government inspectors checked occasionally to see that laws and regulations were followed. But, as the size of the workforce, the complexity of the workflow, and the sophistication of machinery grew significantly, a different kind of surveillance was necessary. This gave rise to a new cadre of supervision composed of overseers, supervisors, and clerks. They also kept a close watch over inventories, machines, tools, and quality of output but their major function was to provide an intense and constant surveillance on each worker's skill, zeal, promptness, and comportment on the job.

Thus, a new regime of surveillance came into existence alongside the physical system of production. Although running parallel to the actual workflow of machines, inventories, locations, and workers, it remained separate from the latter. This cadre of watchers, who looked on from raised stands over the heads of the workers (thus the origin of the overhead account) treated the employees with severity and contempt. Hierarchical surveillance worked as an uninterrupted, anonymous, automatic, and indiscreet disciplinary gaze, which played out over the entire organization.

Yet, it is not by chance that the word "supervision" has a clear link to the visual aspect of the superintendents' work: they are placed above the workers to see whether they are behaving according to the norm. It was this knowledge that gave them power, not the hierarchical position per se. In order to make their presence felt more deeply, incumbents in the supervisory hierarchy relied on systems of normalizing sanctions, that is, meting out various rewards and punishments in accordance with a set of arbitrary rules (like the confessional in the Catholic Church). These rules and sanctions were created without reference to any philosophical ideals; they constituted, in effect, a private system of justice that operated outside the state's legal judicial system. Together, hierarchical surveillance and normalizing sanctions functioned as a miniature penal mechanism.

The practice of normalizing sanctions spread throughout society in the eighteenth and nineteenth centuries. Schools, military establishments, prisons, hospitals, factories, state bureaucracies, and so on, all developed their private systems of justice. Regulations covered timeliness (lateness, absences, task interruptions), attentiveness (negligence, laziness, lack of zeal), comportment (disobedience, impudence, rudeness), speaking (idle chitchat, insolence, rudeness), appearance (dress, cleanliness, gestures, posture), and sexuality (lewdness, impurity, indecency). Even the smallest departure from correct behavior, or not measuring up to a certain required level, became the basis for a subtle range of penalties, including petty humiliation (standing in the corner or wearing a dunce cap), minor deprivations (no recess), or light corporal punishment (a tweak of the nose). The individual was enmeshed in a network of disciplining sanctions.

So that sanctioning appeared objective, masters, overseers, sergeants, wardens, and so on, came to rely on examinations. Previously, the scholar or apprentice worked alongside the master and after a long period of tutoring presented a masterwork for examination. If the master deemed it worthy, the novice became a fully fledged member of the academic community or guild.

This intimate ritual changed when the examination emerged as a constant and pervasive procedure in schools, workshops, prisons, military establishments, hospitals, asylums, and professions. The examination combined with normalizing sanctions was an integral part of the principle of correct comportment.

An important part of the examination process was the writing and numerical grading of each individual. The keepers (teachers, sergeants, physicians, psychiatrists, wardens, supervisors, etc.) administered the examination, assigned a numerical grade, and made out a written report, thus accounting for the individual. Moreover, each individual's performance became written in a permanent archive of records, results, files, report cards, and so on. Collectively, this array of documentation formed a grand register and a total field of comparison, thus making it possible to calculate averages, create categories, designate classifications, and establish norms and stages of development. Anyone and everyone could be defined in terms of these norms and located at a particular stage of development. Compulsory objectification and perpetual examination became a natural part of the social fabric. Embedded in a cumulative system of observation, examination, writing, and grading, the individual had no place to hide.

The records and archives also made it possible for the various human sciences to accumulate large and ever-growing fields of knowledge, each of which made the human being knowable in terms of the special attributes, characteristics, and capabilities measured by the examinations. Moreover, any individual could be treated by the expert professional of a particular discipline as a case study, an object to be measured, described, compared, and judged according to the norms and averages of the general population. Knowledge about the individual became power—power over the very individuals from whom it was extracted. The individual existed as a thing to be corrected, normalized, and treated in accordance with the discursive practices of that particular discipline. Hierarchical surveillance, normalizing sanctions, and the examination were most effective when applied within the panopticon.

10.2.1 "If I Cannot See It, I Cannot Manage It!"—MACS and the Panopticon

A brief prolog can help us understanding the importance of visibility and the visual in managing organizations and the role that MACS have in this exercise.

On a typical rainy afternoon in the UK, Paolo arrived at the site where he had to meet the plant analyst of a large American multinational company. He went to the reception where the porter welcomed him with a friendly and warm "Hiya!" This made him feel less embarrassed for leaving his car with Italian number-plates, illicitly and badly parked next to the reception. He had been reading stories of order and respect for rules in my English grammar books. On entering reception he signed the visitors' book and got his badge. Recognized as a "visitor," he could then go to the car park and, by following the direction signs, leave his car in a designated parking slot.

Back at reception, he met the guy he had to interview. This guy was a visitor too, being the analyst of a plant near the UK HQ of this American multinational, so both had to look for a place where they could chat about SAP and management control systems in multinational organizations. After a small detour around the site, they found a small office casually left empty by a secretary who was ill that day. Once in, they saw written on the notice board: "IF I DON'T SEE IT, I CANNOT MANAGE IT!!"

Making things visible, calculable and in the end controllable, is a key feature of a MACS. The notion of "panopticon," as used by Foucault, can provide a further perspective from which to understand the role and power of such systems.

Panopticism refers to the unique architecture of Jeremy Bentham's (1748–1831) renowned panoptic prison (see Figure 10.1). The geometry of the prison called for a central tower in the middle of a peripheral-ringed building, which was divided into solitary cells, each one facing the tower. Every cell had two large windows, one at the rear to light up the cell from the outside, and one in the front, facing the tower. Thus, the prisoner stood out against the back-lighting of the peripheral ring while the sidewalls prevented any visual contact with fellow prisoners. The cells acted as tiny theatres, putting each inmate on the stage, alone and individualized, but constantly visible from the central tower. Unlike the dungeon, which hid prisoners in a dark hold, the panopticon brought them out into the light, where they could be observed and corrected.

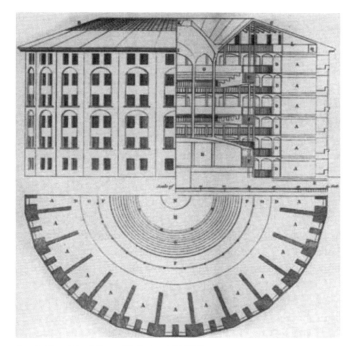

Source: *The works of Jeremy Bentham* vol. IV, 172-3.

Figure 10.1   Bentham's Panopticon

Panopticism also called for a constantly visible but unverifiable gaze. The central tower, always clearly in sight from each cell, was designed so that the occupant could never tell whether or not someone in the tower was gazing in. This was accomplished by installing Venetian and zigzag openings so that any small noise, movement, or ray of light in the tower seemed to indicate the watcher's presence. A petty clerk, a janitor, an inspector, a visitor, or even a tourist moving in the tower was enough to instill in the occupant's mind the feeling of being constantly watched. Under the power of an all-knowing, all-seeing gaze, the prisoner's anxiety rose, making him or her amenable to normalizing sanctions and prescriptions.

The panopticon design had further advantages. After various treatments of correction had been administered to the prisoner, their effects could be readily observed. Criminologists discreetly experimented with different punishments, work regimens, and drugs. Moreover, wardens and administrators could easily monitor the guards and watch correction workers with an eye to devising more efficient methods. The panopticon, in its ideal form, was a highly efficient and effective laboratory of power. It could be put into place in schools and military encampments and, importantly, in factories and business enterprises. Electronic surveillance in the workplace can be seen as a postmodern electronic panopticon with its constant watching.

But how does all of this help us to view differently accounting and management control systems? An economic view of these systems would explain their power and diffusion as a response to an economic need for an efficient allocation and distribution of resources. We have explored the underpinning of this approach in Part One of this book. An alternative view, based on Foucault's work, would instead see this diffusion as the result of a series of pedagogical practices, which, by the eighteenth century, would have informed behavior and world views of the first managers developing management accounting and control techniques during the Industrial Revolution.

From this perspective,[2] accounting is first and foremost a technique that, through writing, inscribes economic values into a set of accounts in order for them to create a space for grading, examining and therefore disciplining the workforce. Exactly as in current pedagogical practices, human actions are translated into standardized written records so that an examination of their behavior is possible and therefore discipline can be exerted through sanctions.

Take the emergence of accounting techniques in the US railway industry during the Industrial Revolution. According to a Foucauldian perspective, managers did not invent a new system of control because they faced new economic pressure for efficiency. Instead, being trained at the military academy of West Point, where training was based on pedagogical practices based on writing, examining and disciplining, they just applied this method to a different realm, that of business. As for Foucault, practices based on the ideals of enclosure (think of how accounting segments organizational realities), an efficient body (think of standard costing and how it can be used to normalize workers' behavior) and a disciplined mind (think of how through incentive systems individual and organizational objectives are sought to be aligned) were translated into management techniques. We thus witness the birth of a new disciplinary regime, based on the same principles, leading to the emergence of standard costing and the like. In a sense, it is this *forma mentis* that creates efficiency and not a need for efficiency that creates this *forma mentis*!

Let us examine why the combination of writing, examining and disciplining is so relevant for MACS. As we have seen, the etymology of the word "control" comes from the French *rôle* ("role-player") who acts to a script, and a *contre-rôle* ("counter-role") who monitors the role player's compliance. This in turn comes from the Latin *contra* (opposite) and *rotulus* (the roll; that is, a script that actors have to follow when they act). The inscription through writing on a *rotulus* is the first condition for the exercise of control: only when something is objectified on a piece of paper and made permanent thanks to the ink on this paper do we have a benchmark that can guide our behavior. However, this is not sufficient as we need to understand to what extent such behavior adheres to the standard set by the *rotulus*. Here is why various forms of classification and grading have been devised at school, first, and in organizations in the Industrial Revolution later. Thanks to the invention of "zero" double-entry bookkeeping it was already possible to discriminate between profit (good) and loss (bad). With the widespread grading mentality brought in by the education of the university elites later in the seventeenth and eighteenth century we were also offered the possibility of discriminating between various shades of good and bad. And if the grade was alarming, a disciplining sanction could be established in order to bring behavior back to normal.

The ideal of the panopticon comes into play as, once this system is in place, the workforce self-disciplines itself for the fear of incurring a sanction. Discipline and control are internalized thanks to the power of MACS.

These systems do even more (see Miller and O'Leary, 1987, 1994a, 1994b). They are "technologies of government," where the search for efficiency in individuals' behavior within the firm is inserted in a general societal and economic discourse. Management accounting and control systems, far from being neutral techniques for representing financial transactions, are instead perceived as forms of government, and technologies of social control and order.

10.3 The Logic of MACS Practice[3]

In this section we draw on Bourdieu's theory of the practical logic of everyday action, and on its central concept of *habitus*, to understand how MACS are intrinsically social matters. Thus, in order to comprehend how they operate in everyday organizational situations, both management scholars and practitioners need to develop a sound understanding of how apparently neutral techniques and tools are in fact deeply interconnected with how human beings interact.

The work of Bourdieu is very congenial to this aim. Bourdieu (1998, p. 85) identified habitus, field, illusio, and symbolic capital as indispensable in thinking about action.[4] He depicts social systems first and foremost as fields of power relations, where the agents (the field's inhabitants) compete for power resources in the form of cultural, social, symbolic, and economic capital as a valuable way to understand the field's "logic of practice" including its *opus operatum* of social structures and its agents' *modus operandi* for social action. Following Durkheim and Weber, he adopts the dualist agency/structure relationship as central to the flow of social action and incorporates both into his comprehensive conceptual schema.[5] Bourdieu conceives of any social/cultural arena as a contested field (*champs*) of power relations. The individual agents in the field compete for, accumulate, exchange, and exploit the kinds of capital (discussed later) that are valued and therefore scarce in their field. They invest their time and energy in developing the skills to compete in the field's capital economy and they draw on their accumulated capital in the struggle to dominate the field from their particular power positions (*postes*). Bourdieu thus applies economic theory concepts to areas of social life, abandoned by neoclassical economics when it narrowed its theoretical net to the production and exchange of material commodities, emphasizing the relations of power in the field of interest.[6] We will now examine his central concepts of *field, illusion, symbolic violence* and *capital*. Following this, we consider Bourdieu's frequently used concept of field in further detail, and examine the idea that each field has a unique habitus, doxa, and hexis.

Field

Bourdieu likens a cultural field to a game played on a sports field or on a board. Such games have a set of rules, a designated space, and time limits. The players voluntarily enter into a quasi-contract (often only implicitly) with the field's inhabitants to play the game fairly. And if the stakes are high enough, the game may be monitored by a referee of sorts thus assuring that the players play by the prevailing rules.[7] While a social cultural field is a lot like that, it is also different in one important aspect: it can be a whole way of life. For example, the inhabitants might be born into the game, or they may take it up later in life as a vocation, or they may be physically coerced into it as in mandatory military service, or incarcerated in it as a prisoner. They develop a feel for the game. Individuals (often unaware that the game is an arbitrary, socially constructed artifact and not a thing of nature) invest in the game, get caught up in it, take it seriously, and believe it is worth playing. Bourdieu calls such a belief *illusio*.

Illusio

Illusio, an inherent part of belonging to a field, is the ingrained idea in the mind of agents in a particular field that the game is worth playing. Bourdieu illustrates illusio by referring to the sculpture in the Auch cathedral in the Gers, depicting two monks fighting each other for possession of the prior's staff. The staff's value exists only for the two monks who are caught up in the game of the monastic field (see Bourdieu, 1998, p. 78). Even adversaries in a field, who seem at odds over many matters, have a tacit, hidden agreement that it is worth the effort to struggle over the field's capital. Illusio is at once both the result of the functioning of the field and the condition of its game. Moreover, "What is experienced as obvious in *illusio* appears as an illusion to those who do not participate in the game" (Bourdieu, 1998, p. 79). For them, as the adage goes, "The game is not worth the candle." Others are possessed by the game. They agree that the stakes of the game—its capital—are worth competing for. And in playing the game they make moves in anticipation of where the payoffs will be. Illusio, however, can cause agents to suffer from what Bourdieu calls *symbolic violence*.

Symbolic Violence

Symbolic violence comes into being when the holders of unequal stores of capital use them as power resources to alter and control those agents with less capital. It occurs when subordinate agents internalize the discourses of the dominant agents and come to perceive the conditions of their existence as self-evident, inevitable, and natural, regardless of how intolerable they are. "Symbolic violence is the violence which exhorts submission, which is not perceived as such, based on 'collective expectations' or socially inculcated beliefs" (Bourdieu, 1998, p. 103). It occurs when subordinate agents take on board and submit to the doxic attitudes of the dominant agent(s) and without hesitation or thought instantiate the injunctions of the later. "It goes without saying" that this or that is the right thing to do. Symbolic violence occurs when the disadvantaged themselves internalize this discourse. Such dispositions become lodged in these agents' durable principles of judgment and practice so that they treat the discourse as natural and self-evident. They do not challenge it but rather embody it as being just.

Capital

Bourdieu employs the term *capital* for those properties, attributes, capacities, skills, knowledge, etc., which agents deem to be of value in a particular field and that they labor to acquire. "In order for a field to function, there have to be stakes and people prepared to play the game, endowed with the *habitus* that implies knowledge and recognition of the eminent laws of the field, the stakes, and so on" (Bourdieu, 1995, p. 72). Agents in a field are situated in a particular position (*poste*) from which they compete for the field's capital.[8] Individuals not invested in the game often see it as irrational, and its stakes and capital as absurd.

Capital comes in several forms including economic capital (money, property), cultural capital (family upbringing, education), social capital (networks of friends and colleagues), and symbolic capital (ceremonial exchange of gifts, honorific awards). Such properties are deemed to be valuable, because they are in short supply. So agents compete for, accumulate, and exchange their stocks of capital. They mobilize them as power resources and draw on them in order to dominate the field or to change it to their way of thinking. The idea of economic capital is relatively straightforward: money can buy power positions and people, as well as material goods and services. The notion of cultural capital is also readily grasped. It consists of expertise in activities that are highly valued in a particular field and which some members' skills and abilities make them stand out from the crowd. Cultural capital, importantly, can be exchanged for economic capital.

Symbolic capital is more subtle and comes in many different forms and differs from cultural capital in one important way: it can be a whole way of life. Bourdieu also observes that cultural and symbolic capital usually circulate only within restricted markets. A gifted scholar's exceptional academic skills and academic awards attract no cultural or symbolic capital in the field of professional football or in the field of the classical musician. Symbolic and cultural capital can be exchanged for economic capital and vice versa. In addition to its unique mix of capital, every field also has a unique habitus, doxa, and hexis.

Habitus, Doxa, and Bodily Hexis

Habitus is the hallmark concept in Bourdieu's theory of social practice. It consists of the general dispositions, inclinations, attitudes, and values of any particular field that are embodied by the field's inhabitants (i.e., agents). As such, habitus is a form of innate capital that encompasses the logic of the field's social practices.

Bourdieu was also particularly concerned to introduce the idea of agency into structuralist analysis without recourse to volunteerism or existentialism. The individual agents in any field of cultural production acquire the dispositions of its habitus. Agents "absorb" the field's dispositions, inclinations, attitudes, and propensities in much the same way that children learn to speak and think in the language of their mother tongue (Bourdieu, 1990, p. 67).

Agents, however, are not merely robots rigidly programmed by the habitus. While the habitus provides the general templates for social action, it does not dictate how agents put them into practice. The way they instantiate the habitus takes on unique, personal characteristics. "Habitus are generative principles of distinct and distinctive practices" (Bourdieu, 1998, p. 8). Importantly, Bourdieu is not proposing a grand universal theory of any kind. Instead, he sees the habitus as reflected in the daily habituated, practical, tacit, dispositional actions of a particular field's habitants. A habitus also includes a unique doxa.

Doxa

A doxa is the field's correct, right, dominant vision, and orthodoxy that appear as self-evident and exist beneath consciousness. It consists of a set of core beliefs, fundamental principles and acquired skills, techniques, tastes, and references that are unique to a particular field. Adopting the "doxic attitude" means mental submission to the established order and its conditions, which are historically contingent and arbitrary but appear to the agents as natural. Doxic submission ties agents, usually unconsciously, to a symbolic, immaterial form of domination. Doxa also influences an agent's bodily hexis.

Bodily Hexis

Bodily hexis refers to the particular physical attitudes and dispositions that are adopted by agents. The process of internalization of the habitus's objective structures is a corporeal process as well as a mental one, and is incorporated in bodily form as well as in cognitive dispositions. A trivial example is the way a person holds and uses his cutlery during a meal. And, individuals who have spent a lot of time in a military institution have a recognizable posture and bearing. They stand tall and straight, shoulders back, chest out, stomach in, and march rather than walk. Bodily hexis is highly charged with social meanings and values.

10.3.1 The Enron Scandal

We will now use Bourdieu's concepts to illuminate the now infamous demise of Enron—one of the major corporate scandals in recent times. This will also serve to give practical meaning to these concepts and render them intelligible.

We begin with a description of the wider energy and regulatory field in which Enron was embedded. The habitus of this wider field influenced in no small way the development and changing nature of the Enron habitus. We then describe the Lay/Kinder leadership era (1986–96), which experienced a habitus arguably coherent with Enron's business model and its management control systems. We then examine the change of the Enron habitus during the Lay/Skilling era (1996–2001). During this time, this habitus vitiated the company's governance and control mechanisms, rendering them ineffective, thus playing a major role in Enron's demise. We draw upon Bourdieu's concepts to specifically analyze Enron's then governance control mechanisms: the Peer Review Committee (PRC), Risk Assessment Control department (RAC), Board of Directors and Code of Ethics. In doing so, we expose the social practices that ensued at Enron during its 16-year existence and show how Enron's governance and control systems were neutralized and perverted under the Lay/Skilling habitus.

The Historical Emergence of Enron

Between 1978 and 1986, the US gas industry underwent a series of momentous changes. In the 1970s the industry was highly regulated and government rules stipulated the wellhead price of gas sold to pipelines. The pipelines shipped gas at regulated prices and sold it to utilities and others, again at rates set by the government. The unintended result proved to be a shortage of gas. Producers had little incentive to explore for gas or to increase production from proven reserves. In 1978, the wellhead price regulation was lifted and by 1980 production soared, incurring a glut of gas. To make matters worse, at the same time many utilities and industrial customers were switching to oil. These were not easy times for gas pipelines. The hard times precipitated a merger of companies and a shakeout of smaller pipelines.

In 1985, a new government order drastically changed the gas industry. The Federal Energy Regulatory Commission (FERC) issued Order 436, which allowed utilities and other users to buy gas directly from producers and pay the pipelines government-approved fees for transporting it. The result was that gas traders now negotiated freely (and frenetically) over the phone for gas that would be transported between pipelines at centralized gas hubs. The gas industry was slowly but surely being transformed from a closely government-regulated industry into loosely regulated, free-market business.

In the wake of these developments, the consolidation and merger trend increased. At this time, Lay (who was to become the future CEO of Enron) was CEO of HNG. In order for HNG to survive as a separate company, Lay negotiated a merger with InterNorth, a much larger pipeline with headquarters in Omaha, Nebraska. InterNorth paid $2.3 billion for HNG. The new company, renamed Enron, owned 36 000 miles of pipelines across North America and, as a result of some financial maneuvering, InterNorth's CEO Irwin Jacobs's shares were bought out and Lay emerged as CEO and chairman. The new company emerged in 1985 with $12.1 billion in assets, 15 000 employees, the nation's second largest pipeline network, and a towering amount of debt. It reported a first-year loss of $14 million.

The next two years were precarious ones for Enron as it teetered on the verge of bankruptcy. At the time Enron was a typical natural gas firm, owning mainly hard assets including pipelines, refining equipment, and gas-producing properties in Texas, Oklahoma, California, Florida, the Rocky Mountains, and western Canada. However, this was not viewed positively by the stock market. It had all the traditional trappings of a highly leveraged, "old economy" firm competing in the regulated energy economy, although this would change rapidly in the next few years.

Enron Evolves

In the late 1980s, Enron became involved in trading gas derivatives in addition to its physical gas trading. While some of Enron's financial instruments at the time were standardized contracts traded on an exchange, many were not. In fact, Enron was also trading customized derivative contracts (options, hedges, swaps, collars, and other sophisticated financial instruments) in unregulated markets. This business grew so rapidly that in 1989 Enron entered into a joint venture with the Wall Street firm Bankers Trust (BT), which had derivative expertise, to open a financial trading desk in Houston. Bankers Trust proved highly profitable and, in 1991, Enron dissolved the joint venture and set up its own trading operation.

Enron's financial trading came on the heels of the 1990 opening of a regulated gas futures trading exchange by the New York Mercantile Exchange (NYMEX). This meant that traders who didn't own or want physical gas could buy and sell gas contracts (only money, not gas, changed hands). The year 1991 also saw the introduction of Enron's "Gas Bank," a development that would cement Enron's position as the leading company in this new market for gas financial instruments.

At the time there was no wholesale market in electricity, but a crude form of financial contracts market for electricity was emerging. Enron executives sensed a large market, almost three times the wholesale gas market, one that seemed a natural complement to their success and expertise in the gas trading business. In 1993, Enron obtained one of the first "power market" licenses issued by the FERC to foster a wholesale power market. Electricity trading, like gas, involved sophisticated risk-management techniques requiring basis risk management expertise regarding the fluctuating differences, due to weather and supply patterns, between energy prices in different areas of the country. In this regard, the electricity wholesale trading business offered higher profit potential than gas due to its greater volatility. Nevertheless, Enron's success in gas trading led Lay and Skilling to believe that they could be just as successful in electricity trading. In June 1994, Enron North American (ENA) staffed by a separate team of power traders, executed its first electricity trade. The idea of remaking Enron into a gas *and* electricity company led to its acquisition of a large electricity utility company, Portland General in 1996. Enron was the first gas pipeline company to acquire an electricity utility and the acquisition made Enron the seventh largest seller of electricity in the USA. By the mid-1990s Enron controlled nearly 25% of the US electricity market.

Expanding Beyond Energy Trading

In addition to gas and electricity trading, Enron Capital & Trade (ECT), the successor to Enron Gas Service (EGS), with Skilling as president, was diversifying into other investment banking businesses. During the second half of the 1990s, Enron in the US and Europe also expanded its trading into a variety of fields including mining, forest products, chemicals, weather, stocks and bonds, and bandwidth fiber optic networks. In 2000, ECT brokered over 300 bandwidth trades. Enron applied its highly sophisticated financial engineering expertise to this market. It bought and sold bandwidth options, swaps and hedges, and advised companies on how to manage their bandwidth risks, price changes, and availability of capacity. Although still not profitable, Enron executives announced to the capital market that its broadband services business would be worth $29 billion by the mid-2000s (at the time Enron's market capitalization was $50 billion). Bandwidth trading, however, proved to be small, growing only slowly. It was very competitive, and new to Enron.

During the 1990s another phenomenon occurred that would affect Enron in important ways. This was the appearance of the Internet business in general and online stockbrokers in particular. A task force began designing EnronOnline, which enabled Enron to take one side of any trade rather than merely charging a user fee for traders. The task involved a great number of highly technical, legal, and safety complications. Nevertheless, EnronOnline went live on November 29, 1999, offering 20 different contracts for gas. By January 29, 2000, Enron Online had completed over 10 000 transactions and was trading contracts worth $100 million a day. Over the next few months Enron gradually added products such as coal, metals, pulp and paper, and bandwidth. Enron also used the system for its retail business, to operate its pipelines, to develop and manage overseas projects, and to structure more complex financial deals that were unsuitable for regular Internet use.

Thus, with Skilling leading the way, Enron's business model shifted over the 1990s from a gas trading and pipeline company to become a full-scale sophisticated financial engineering trading platform. In 1996 (the year Kinder departed from Enron), trading operations (wholesale and retail) already accounted for 91 % of reported revenues, 54 % of income before tax and 62 % of identifiable assets. By 2000, trading operations accounted for 99 % of income, 88 % of income before tax and 80 % of identifiable assets, while reported revenue increased from $12 billion in 1996 to nearly $100 billion in 2000.

Lay/Kinder Habitus (1986–96)

During its first ten years Enron operated with a traditional businesslike management control system administered by Richard Kinder. He joined Enron in 1986 bringing with him a large store of cultural capital regarding the gas business. During this era, Lay was "Mr. Outside" focusing on institutional and big-picture matters. He worked the corridors of power in Washington and Houston (Enron at one time had over 100 employees in its Washington lobbying office) and was a personal friend of many powerful politicians, including the Bush family. Lay enjoyed a large store of social capital, which he used over the years to influence the deregulation of the gas industry.

Kinder, who joined Enron in 1986, was "Mr. Inside." He came with a large store of cultural capital in the gas industry. "He mastered the details of every business, from trading to natural gas liquids, and his knowledge fostered truth inside and outside the company" (Bryce, 2002, p. 114). He immediately took on responsibility for Enron's financial affairs, including a cost-reduction program in the face of Enron's heavy debt position and shortage of cash resources. He was known as Enron's "master money man" and personally dealt with bankers, investment analysts and dealers, and credit rating agencies. His cultural capital included a detailed knowledge of, and vast experience in, financial matters. Kinder was known as "Doctor Discipline" throughout the company. He met with the business unit managers every Monday morning in the boardroom to review and grill them on their updated numbers, plans, and strategies. He had a talent for recalling facts and figures from previous years and current budgets and strategies were routinely challenged and debated. One former executive recalled, "Kinder would sit in that room with his yellow pad and he knew every god-damned thing happening in that company."[9] He closely monitored cashflows, expenses, and employee levels. Kinder's control style was tough minded and dynamic but he was well liked and respected throughout the company. He was known for maintaining a collegial atmosphere and going out of his way to show respect for and loyalty to employees (Bryce, 2002, p. 114). And "he commanded respect in the (gas) industry and on Wall Street" (Fox, 2003, p. 99)—symbolic capital in Bourdieu's terms. Lay and Kinder then proved to be an ideal top management team.

In sum, Enron's habitus featured a tough-minded, business-oriented environment tempered with a family like, collegial atmosphere. The business managers readily absorbed its predispositions, inclinations, and doxic attitude regarding business and management. They readily took on board the illusio that Kinder's game was worth playing. Kinder's cultural and symbolic capital at the time, however, was attuned to a "hard assets" business model. As Bourdieu warns, there are always competitors seeking to overturn or to maintain the dominant position of the status quo, as illustrated in the struggle between the three Enron top executives.

In the early 1990s, Enron's upper-echelon level was a contested field of power relations, with Richard Kinder, Rebecca Mark and Jeffrey Skilling as the main combatants. Each had large stores of cultural and symbolic capital and each believed firmly that getting the top job under Lay was very much worth pursuing. The stakes were high, especially in economic capital but also in symbolic capital associated with becoming president when Lay planned to relinquish it to become CEO. The field's game mattered greatly to each of them. That they were caught up in it is a prime example of Bourdieu's illusio concept.

Mark proved to be a powerful competitor. She had a goodly store of cultural capital including a masters degree from Baylor University and she was by all accounts charming, sophisticated, and likable (social capital), but not arrogant. She came to Enron in 1985 as part of Continental Resources that was folded into Enron in the 1984 merger. In 1990, she went to the Harvard Business School for a MBA degree thus adding to her store of symbolic and cultural capital. And in 1998 and 1999, she was listed in *Forbes* as one of the top 25 most powerful women in the US (evidence of symbolic capital).

Skilling came on board with a substantial store of cultural and symbolic capital to draw on in the competition for the CEO position. He went to Southern Methodist University where he earned an applied science and business degree and then took a job at the First City National bank. But finding it boring, after two years he went to the Harvard Business School, where he excelled as a top scholar, thriving on the highly competitive, tough-minded, give-and-take of the classroom case method discussions. Upon graduation in 1979 he joined the McKinsey & Company consulting firm in Houston, where his intellect and tenacity impressed many clients, including Ken Lay. For example, while working in the 1980s as a consultant in the gas industry, he noticed a paradox in the gas market. Although the demand for gas was strong and gas reserves were plentiful, the short-term demand and supply situation was chronically out of balance. He proposed forming what he called a "Gas Bank," which was simply a trading ledger that facilitated buy and sell orders for gas contracts. It proved an instant success, adding to Skilling's store of symbolic capital. The three contestants used their large shares of cultural and symbolic capital to compete, not always without wile, for the CEO job. In 1996, when Lay picked Skilling to replace him as president, Enron's habitus experienced a radical rupture and reformulation.

Lay/Skilling Habitus (1996–2001)

What we will now describe is the change in habitus at Enron, described as occurring with the management change from Lay/Kinder to Lay/Skilling. Enron's habitus was to shift from

one that was business-like, tempered with a family atmosphere, to a Wall Street-like mercenary traders' one, featuring ruthlessness, callousness, arrogance, deception, and false pride.
This mercenary habitus ran roughshod over the governance controls, virtually nullifying
their efficacy. To illustrate this change in habitus we will also rely upon Bourdieu's concepts
of doxa, bodily hexis and types of capital in examining the corruption of specific governance elements of Enron—the Peer Review Committee (PRC), the Risk Assessment Control
department (RAC), the Board of Directors and the Code of Ethics.

In 1976, Enron had 7500 employees. This increased to 15 500 by 2000 as Skilling
went on a hiring campaign recruiting "the best and the brightest." He hired numbers
of younger but seasoned Wall Street traders, investment bankers, and information and
computer experts who were put through his associates program. He also hired hundreds
of top-of-their-class MBAs (many of whom had a couple of years' experience in Wall
Street firms and investment banks) from prestigious business schools as well as physics, mathematics and engineering undergraduates from top-tier universities. Skilling
also flattened the management hierarchy from 13 layers to four in order to empower
employees to come up with new ideas. He also set up a performance review committee
(discussed below) whereby all employees had their performance reviewed twice a year
and those coming in the bottom level were dismissed. Enron's field of social practice was
fast paced and exiting as employees competed vigorously for its symbolic and economic
capital.

The nature of Enron's doxic attitude was like "a religious tract from a New Age mega-
church" (Swartz and Watkins, 2003, p. 103). Cruver (2003, p. 37) reports that the prevailing climate of visible conformity extended to dress and appearance (bodily hexis): "The
first thing I noticed about Enron traders is that they all looked very similar: A goatee was
fairly common; otherwise they maintained a clean-cut yet outdoorsy look; and if they
didn't wear some version of a blue shirt every day, then it was like they weren't on the
team." Swartz and Watkins (2003, p. 193) note that this also extended to language: "No
one at Enron would ever 'build consensus,' they would 'come to shore,' as in 'We have
to come to shore on this' . . . Everyone (used) the term 'metrics' and anyone who used
the term 'numbers' or 'calculations' was a 'loser', the most popular Enron label of all."
Making a very big and profitable deal was called "swinging a big Dick" and cashing out of
a loss deal was called "puking." This socialization process was referred to "Enronizing,"
with people who didn't fit in called "losers," "damaged goods" or "shipwrecks" (Roberts
and Thomas, 2002). These behaviors reflect Bourdieu's bodily hexis concept. The logic
of social practices that emerged during the Lay/Skilling era would prove to nullify and
pervert Enron's governance and control systems, including the performance evaluation
review committee.

Peer Review Committee (PRC)

A key element in Enron's logic of practice was the PRC. All employees received a formal
performance review every six months. Each employee selected five coworkers, superiors,
or subordinates who would provide an evaluation to the PRC, along with the person's

boss, as well as anyone else who wanted to. These data (as well as a photo of the evaluee) went into a web site used by the PRC members who assigned a mark of 1 to 5 to each evaluee. The ratings were arrayed on a bell curve and the bottom 15%, regardless of how good, of each department or unit, were automatically assigned to a special department (known as Siberia) and given two weeks to find a position somewhere in the company. If not, and most did not, they were dismissed. The PRC became known throughout Enron as "Rank and Yank."

Managers and employees alike quickly learned how to game the PRC. For example, they "cut deals" with other employees whereby they gave each other the highest score possible. The Rank and Yank PRC led to "an environment where employees were afraid to express their opinions or to question unethical and potentially illegal business practices" (Fusaro and Millar, 2003, p. 52). The PRC also had a large negative effect on Enron's risk assessment control process.

Risk Assessment Control Department (RAC)

The RAC was designed to play a crucial role in Enron's governance and control at the operational level. It was responsible for approving all trading deals and contracts and for overseeing the company's risk management. All deals were required to be presented in a Deal Approval Sheet (DASH), which included a detailed description of the proposed deal, its economic data, a cashflow model, the deal's value, its internal rate of return, a risk component, its net present value, a financial approval sheet (FASH), and an authorization page requiring signatures from legal, accounting, finance, and, depending on the size, top management and even, in some cases, the Board of Directors. At its peak in 2000, Enron was making 1200 types of trades every day worth billions of dollars in notional value. A major enabler of this was the EnronOnline computerized trading platform, which came onstream in November 1999. Enron needed an ever growing volume of deals in order to report quarterly increases in revenue and profits that would support its stock-market price. In consequence, top management, especially Skilling, vigorously pressured the business units to push through deals as fast as possible. Risk management experts who tried to stop dubious deals were transferred out of the RAC by Skilling. The doxic attitude became "volume, volume, volume."

The business units eagerly responded, pushing through deals as fast as they could. Their individual volume of trades could mean large bonuses and pay increases. (Enron was well known for its high salaries and large bonuses.) Deals, however, were valued in terms of mark-to-market accounting, which in most cases meant a great deal of subjectivity and involved sophisticated Black and Scholes modeling, especially in unregulated markets and where deals were one-offs. In consequence it was very difficult for RAC members to verify the DASH details. Moreover, rejecting deals meant making enemies in the business units as the latter would lose their bonuses and take revenge during the PRC proceedings by rating RAC personnel low, and would also bring the wrath of Skilling on their heads. As a result of these factors, the RAC controls were systematically rendered futile, useless, and perverted. The Board of Directors was similarly tainted.

10.4 Praising Numbers as Sacred Figures: MACS Training Regimes

Let us begin this section with an episode involving one of the authors of this book. Imagine a lecture theater of a business school packed with MBA students hungry for more knowledge and the latest techniques to master the turbulence and volatility of financial markets. You can feel excitement in the room. People rush into the theater to get the best seats. Students prepare their notepads to take notes. The chair is anxious to obtain order and silence. He attracts the audience's attention and introduces the distinguished speaker. Once the lecture begins, the clarity and beauty of the formulas shown on the screens thrill the fantasies of dozens of people and you can almost see ideas on how to exploit this new knowledge floating in the air. The lecture is a cauldron of interest and the speaker is frequently interrupted with questions. His witty replies prompt peals of laughter. The Q&A session lasts longer than the time available and the chair has to tempt people with the promise of a glass of champagne in the foyer of the school to make them leave the room. The lecture ends with long applause and everyone is now ready for the drinks and new adventures in financial markets.

That day the guest speaker was a finance guru who made millions managing a hedge fund. A week after the lecture, he was charged with serious misdoings and resigned. A Reverend who was invited to attend the lecture recounted this experience and compared it to a priest rousing the masses with the idea of a new God: finance. The Reverend asked the business scholar how these finance formulas were so powerful that they attracted the interest of an army of MBAs? How could a multitude of people, with diverse interests, backgrounds, aims, training, histories, families and lives see in these formulas something that was appealing to them all? How could finance numbers seem so right one day and be discovered so wrong only a week later?

The answer may be relatively simple: numbers *are* figures, as the Benedictine Angelo Pietra astutely pointed out in his 1586 accounting treatise. Words have a history, although this is often forgotten, and this imaginative nature of numbers has old roots. Visualization practices are closely related to the historical development of accounting, rhetoric and the art of memory: the word "inventory," comes from *inventio* (the first canon of rhetoric), "record" comes from *recordor* (to remember), and "formula" comes from *forma* (a visual shape). The word "calculation" is not exempt from this visual nature either: *calculus* (calculation) is a synonym of "account," and accounts are those loci, those places, those visual spaces where transactions are stored in order to do their inventory.[10] Thus, to make calculations and prepare inventories relates to the ability to reconfigure these loci, these spaces, these accounts in forms that respond to practical and changing calculative problems. This is why these numbers as figures are important: they do not have a specific and intrinsic meaning to convey, a specific and inner truth. This is left to the user to find out through practices and performances. And when this truth is found, it appears as a *theoria*, that is, an illuminating and direct vision of a lay God,[11] of business truth and utility.

Even the most loved word by those who believe in the *homo oeconomicus* has a visual nature. "Rationality" comes from the Latin word *ratio*, which meant more than "reason"—it meant "schema," "ordering device," or an "account": *Il libro delle ragioni* was not the book of rationality but the ledger.[12] All of these words today refer to the human ability to make objective calculations but more interestingly they reveal how these rely upon very relativist forms of visualization and imagination. Thus, those who believe in the power of rationality should never forget that accounting techniques and finance models are "forms" and as such their validity is relative to a context, to the nest of relationships of which they are part.

The Reverend was right in pointing out how the supposedly neutral techniques and practices associated with the Stock Exchange markets and religious practices share the same regimes of truth and are based on complex ritual and performances. These truths may differ, but the processes of engagement and attraction may be similar and allow the coexistence of different usages, and meanings with the sameness of forms and methods. Understanding how this happens is a key theoretical issue for academics, but also a very practical task to perform to make sure that business succeeds, i.e. happens, as the Latin etymology of the word teaches us.

10.4.1 The Balanced Scorecard: Performing Measurement Systems[13]

The Middle-East Gas and Oil Company (MEGOC) is a large corporation operating in the oil and gas industry with operations in exploration, production, refining and marketing. It employs over 55 000 employees and an additional 100 000 outside contractors. The company is owned by a national government in the Middle East and the revenues generated constitute a large part of the GDP of that country. The company is divided into seven major divisions (or business lines). In addition, support functions such as corporate planning, information technology, human resources and management services also report directly to the company president and CEO.

Recently, the deterioration of some indicators concerning the socio-economic conditions in the country along with the need to achieve better organizational integration (". . . each business line is a kingdom on its own, we know that . . ." emphasized an engineer) suggested to MEGOC's executives that they should redefine the management systems of the company and, in particular, the mechanisms and the tools through which strategy is identified, communicated, and executed. Thus, in 2002, following an appeal from the country's government, it decided "to significantly increase its contribution to the country's revenue needs and consistently promote the development of the local economy" (MEGOC's mission statement). The Balanced Scorecard (BSC) was chosen as the framework to communicate this mission. It was intended as a means for managing strategic performance expectations and helping the company to translate strategies into key objectives and initiatives that could inform behavior and drive performance.

The Visual Appeal of the BSC

The government appeal translated into six imperatives: (1) transform corporate performance; (2) optimize the corporate portfolio; (3) maximize revenues by capturing oil growth opportunities; (4) protect the future market for oil; (5) leverage the oil and gas resources to expand the national economy; (6) prepare the workforce for the future. Once these imperatives were identified by the Board, several divisions, functions and departments began the implementation of the scorecard—see Figure 10.2. "These are our cornerstones to fulfill management expectations," a senior engineer suggested. He continued: "the balanced scorecard became the hub around which the 12 months plan (Operating Plan) and the 5 years (Business Plan) were structured and developed . . . Every initiative and action in the plan has to find its path in the Business Line Strategy Map to contribute to one of the six corporate strategic imperatives."

We are all familiar with the visual appeal of the BSC. It comes with four boxes and the circle in the middle (Figure 10.2). But these are more then simple representations. First, being graphical visualizations, they construct a simplified view of much more complex processes, visions, actions and targets. This kind of visualization offers something to which controllers and organizational employees can relate. Implementing a new system, be it the BSC or an ERP, is a painful exercise and often it deviates from the ideal roadmap. However, these visual representations can be mobilized to generate discussion, identify problems, and often solve them. They offer a starting point, something to play with and to help invent new ways of solving old and new problems.

Engineering & Operation Services Scorecard

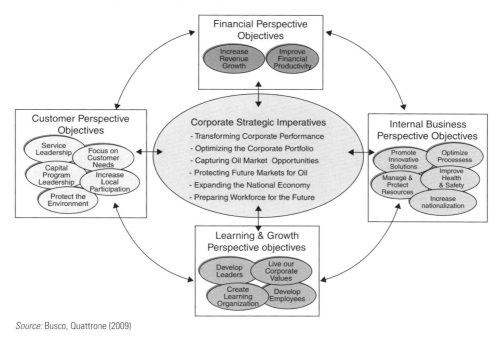

Source: Busco, Quattrone (2009)

Figure 10.2 Balanced Scorecard at MEGOC

Secondly, these boxes are classificatory devices, as they provide an order through which visions and strategy are made intelligible. They move from abstract statements to real measures of performance. Every controller and manager in charge of defining a strategy knows that organizational missions, visions and strategies are difficult to identify and define. Often they have to be left vague enough to then be changed and adapted once environmental conditions become clearer and organizational members realize how they can profit from and adjust to changes. In this sense, as good old rhetoricians know, the BSC's circle and boxes offer a space where these abstract (and sometimes vague) visions, and the measures that will help companies to monitor their organizational performance, can be progressively defined and become a tangible element of organizational lives. These spaces help vision and performance measurement to become real.

How the BSC Methodologically Engages the User

If we have to think of the oldest management technique still in use for performance measurement we would think of bookkeeping and accounting. They also rely upon visual representations (the account) where one can store transactions. However, the power of accounting lies in its method and how it offers a way to understand what goes well or not within organizations rather than providing definitions of what this "well" is. Management accounting and control systems are procedural in nature and offer protocols to be followed to interpret business operations in terms of variations in equity and earnings. Accounts are visual spaces, which require a lot of effort from accountants and controllers before they become meaningful. They have to choose how to organize the chart of accounts, how to post the entries, how to aggregate accounts in ways that produce meaningful results. Accounting systems are typically very analytical—that is, they break organizations into cost, revenue and profit centers, and these in turn are then analyzed further. Accounts, and the journey across them that accountants experience daily, offer a framework that allows managers to 'see' various parts of the organization. Accounting in this sense is a powerful training regime for if the procedure is followed slavishly, it makes managers to find a way to experience a vision and come to believe in strategies that would otherwise remain abstract and empty.

The BSC also can be seen in this manner as it provides methods and templates that help to establish analytical connections that eventually lead to an understanding of the performance of the whole business. Following the Board decision to clarify MEGOC's strategy by releasing the six imperatives to be pursued, a number of BSC implementation teams proliferated within the organization both at the division and department level. Each team was urged to identify the mission, vision and strategic imperatives of the area, and link them with the corporate strategic direction and its six imperatives. The BSC provides a method, a form of organizing and making sense of the vision it aims to enact through performance measurements, which can travel rapidly throughout the organization. Being malleable, the BSC can thus be adapted to different organizations; being a method, it provides a simple but powerful way of defining visions and implementing strategies. Calendars, diaries, and posters were some of the means used to diffuse the idea of MEGOC as a strategy-focused organization around four clear and balanced perspectives: these became the instruments of a common liturgy that MEGOC's members had to experience. Walking along the corridors of MEGOC it was quite common to find statements that were trying to communicate the "spirit" of the BSC. The following flyer was posted in several corners of a leadership development center:

> The Balanced Scorecard will help us translate our strategic imperatives into real action . . . The foundations of the scorecard are the mission, the vision and the strategies. Any participating business line develops a Strategy Map that describes the way in which objectives are linked in line with the strategic imperatives. It helps us understand our strategy by looking at it from four perspectives: Financial, Customer, Internal Business, and Learning and Growth. It provides a snapshot of the way in which activities are linked to and support each other. By studying this map, you will be able to identify where you fit into the company's plan for realizing its vision. (Source: P.Quattrone)

Like in the plan of the abbey, the BSC shows us the way to reach our goal.

In several divisions of MEGOC the BSC(s) and the associated strategy map(s) (shown in Figure 10.3) soon became templates used to visualize and communicate the division's objectives and key performance indicators, as well as the specific initiatives that were about to be undertaken over a certain business plan period.

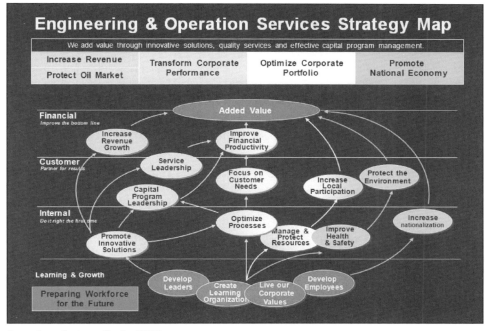

Source: Busco, Quattrone, Riccaboni (2007)

Figure 10.3   Strategy map at MEGOC

"As you can see," advises the senior manager pointing at a chart on the wall

> our key goal is to focus on customers' needs . . . Like a good strategy for a winning soccer club, our strategy map is strong up the middle: goalie—midfielder—center forward. Therefore we have these nine objectives [again, pointing at the chart] locked within cause and effect relationships with the aim to improve productivity and achieve "best-in-class" performance. Then, there are seven more supporting objectives to achieve increased revenue growth, to protect the oil market, to optimize the Corporate portfolio, and to support the national economy. Altogether these sixteen objectives complete the high-level view of the strategy map of the division. (Source: P.Quattrone)

If one focuses on the content of the circles on this map, they all ask for a performative act: they never tell how to focus on customer needs but ask the user to reflect on this issue and find a way that then can be transformed in some KPI. Successful management practices, and the BSC amongst these, are not simple and neutral techniques that store and represent facts: they help innovative processes of knowledge creation. They help to establish connections that were not there before or that were there but in a different guise. They engage by offering the user the possibility of experimenting with the ways in which various performance measures affect and generate managerial effects such as an organization's shared vision, mission or culture. "Successful" practices engage through the possibility of being appropriated by multiple users, by remaining at a very superficial level of abstract principles and linear visual forms. The metaphor of the soccer field is understandable by all and cause-and-effect relationships are familiar to many. Of course the BSC does not tell us explicitly how to play on that field or what kind of cause-and-effect relationship to privilege. All of this is down to the user.

The massive introduction and usage of the BSC(s) did not please everybody, though. Several members of the finance organization perceived the scorecard as an "operational tool" which *some* business lines were *eventually* implementing to measure *other* kinds of performances under the supervision of the Corporate Planning area. The mediation capacities of the BSC needed to pass the most difficult test.

The BSC as Medium (and Mediator) of Business Communication

Within MEGOC the deployment of the balanced scorecard(s) and the associated strategy map(s) relied on a number of media and platforms, such as the technology-driven Enterprise Resource Planning systems (SAP, in this case), the traditional and formalized budgeting practices as well as the innovative and informal café process (see below). The introduction of SAP in MEGOC required a significant process of customization that involved a complex (and expensive) adjustment of the software to manage existing processes and systems effectively. The BSC implementation benefited from such processes of organizational restructuring as it progressively established a growing connection to the budget. Such connection was mediated by SAP. Interestingly, the E&OS division of MEGOC also relied on informal platforms at work to diffuse the BSC framework within and outside its boundaries.

During 2002, as several balanced scorecards and associated strategy maps started to proliferate within MEGOC, the E&OS senior vice-president attended a seminar on organizational learning, and "eventually experienced the possibilities of informal mechanisms at work to align employees' aspirations with the company's strategic direction," suggested a senior E&OS manager. In particular, the E&OS senior vice-president engaged in a *Café*, a method for fostering collaborative dialogue among large groups (see Figure 10.4). The Café methodology creates focused networks of conversation around critical questions, and tries to maximize a small group's ability to focus, think together, and come up with creative possibilities and collective action.

The BSC and the *Cafés* acted as media of communication (of vision, strategy, objectives, measures, etc.) but also offered a space where mediation could happen. The word "medium" is an interesting one as it emphasizes not only the function of communication that, for example, many best practices have, but also the possibility of mediation that they offer. "To transfer" is "to transform" and management practices "happen" on some platforms, be this a piece of paper, an internal workshop or modern information technology, which makes this transformation possible. Therefore successful management tools are performed (practiced) through (and as) a series of media where meanings are not given but are prone to be discussed and modified. It is through these media that best practices come to life, not only thanks to those who design and implement them but also thanks to those who participate in these mediation processes.

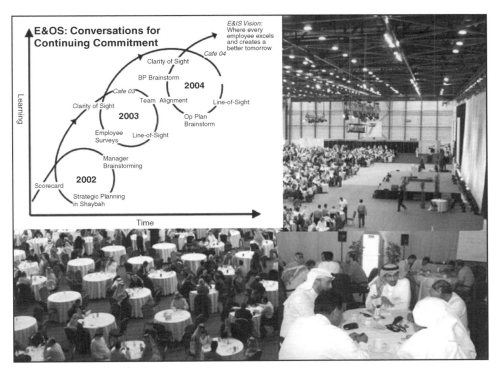

Source: Busco, Quattrone (2009)

Figure 10.4   The Café meetings at MEGOC

The BSC: Performing Management Measures

We have seen how, in order to become something to which people can refer, the BSC needs to offer a possibility for engagement and a space for action where mediation can allow this engagement. The BSC's simplicity was "marketed" within MEGOC so as to offer a space to practice the technique and to make it suitable for everybody's needs. Managers at E&OS were not trying to make everything clear and rigid, and they were not forcing anybody "to fall in love with the initiative of the month." Rather, they were trying to engage potential future users who could eventually come to see the BSC as an opportunity for action. The BSC became popular because it offered the impression that its method of looking at organizational strategies and performance could offer a solution to current organizational and countrywide imperatives. It was able to instill hope in the users: hope that they could solve the various problems that MEGOC's members at different levels and in different functions and divisions had. Within the Café conversations, the logic, jargon and rhythm of the BSC infused the dialogs, and helped the groups identifying and communicating the potential solutions to the country's challenges (local economy development, unemployment rate, low income, etc.) and corporate challenges (processes of sustainable value creation, need for integration, etc.).

It is the methodological simplicity entailed by the four perspectives of the BSC as well as the visual clarity of the strategy map that made such techniques *performable* within

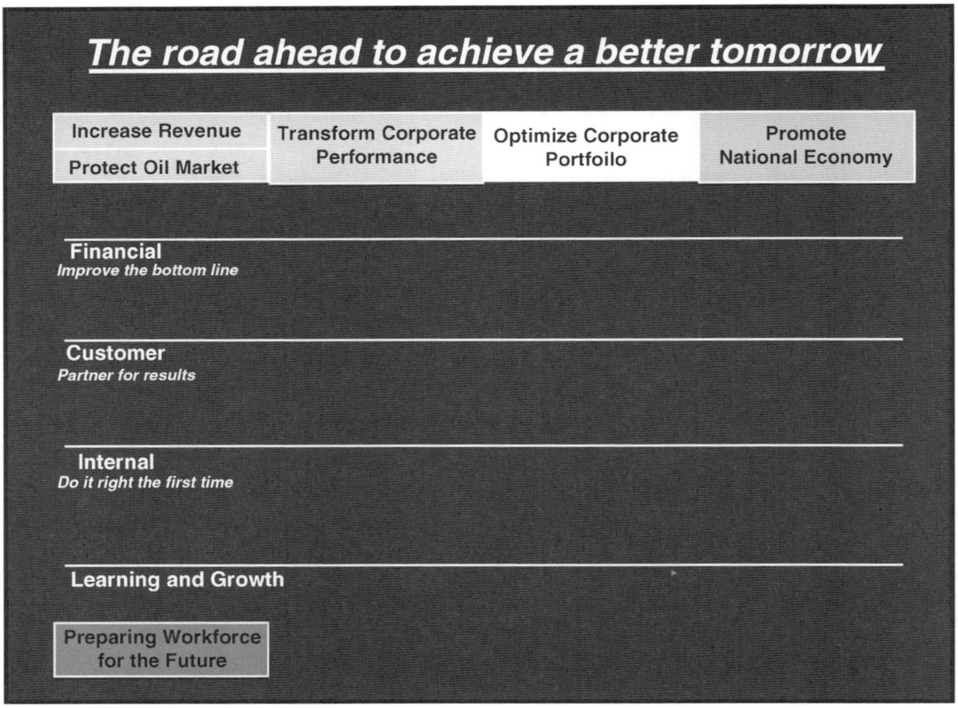

Source: Busco, Quattrone, Riccaboni (2007)

Figure 10.5   Performing management measures at MEGOC

MEGOC. The BSC is performable not because it forces users in certain directions but because it leaves the potential adopters free to enact the space which is offered within it. A member of the E&OS BSC team ended an internal workshop with these words (pointing at the chart reproduced in Figure 10.5): ". . . and now it is up to you, and your department leaders to find the proper objectives and measures to make sure you can orient yourselves on the (MEGOC) strategic map, and show how you can add value along the longitude and latitude of the company strategy map."

10.5 Summary and Conclusions

In this chapter we highlighted the importance of looking at MACS as practices that are inserted in specific apparatuses of control (e.g. Foucault's power-knowledge regime), social context and customs (e.g. Bourdieu's logic of everyday practice), and training regimes (as in our insights inspired by the work of Mary Carruthers and others on rhetoric and the art of memory).

Of course space was too limited to give a full account of what the literature in accounting has produced based on the idea of practice and thus we have to refer you to the references in this chapter to make sure you can appreciate the power of such an approach. Having said that we believe that we have given you sufficient information to enable you to understand the implications of the approaches we have dealt with and to understand how accounting can be seen in ways that are far from a conventional economy-based view of it.

In this respect, the work of Foucault (and of the Foucauldians) is crucial in understanding how, for instance, "the economic" may only be a dependent variable, rather than the main driver, in the evolution and diffusion of management accounting and control practices. The link to the pedagogical practices of writing, examining and disciplining helps us to understand that the genesis of these practices does not necessarily draw on what profit-seeking organizations have done—that they are, in fact, linked to broader societal factors and long-nurtured *forma mentis*.

Bourdieu's theory of the logic of social practice is attractive in that it can be operationalized in a valuable way at two levels. First, his concepts provide (as with Giddens's structuration framework and the actor-network theory of Latour and Callon) sensitivity to specific characteristics of the social properties and practices of the particular field under investigation. This would include the specific mix of stakes (the capitals) that are deemed to be precious, highly valued and worth struggling for, as well as the power relationships peculiar to the field. Second, his theory also works at the universal level. Every field includes secondary variables or generic mechanisms that are present in all fields, such as the struggle between the established dominant actors and their challengers.

Bourdieu's large corpus of works is noted for being formidable, challenging and often seemingly arcane. In the Enron case, we found it difficult to decide the boundaries of the field of interest—whether this should just be the trading operation, or whether it should include the physical asset part of Enron, or whether the field should be considered as that of the wider financial capitalist institution of which Enron was an important part. The boundaries between fields are often blurred, not sharply drawn, and so it is up to the researcher to define the limits of the field of interest. Thus, our interpretations of the concepts and their mobilization must of necessity be idiosyncratic. However, we hope that our narrative drawing on Bourdieu's concepts illuminates important aspects of the situation that might otherwise go unnoticed.

Building on the Foucauldian pedagogical apparatus, the focus on rhetoric, the art of memory and related training regimes leads us to reflect on how we come to know and make order in otherwise confusing organizational missions, strategies, and ways of assessing their effectiveness. We have seen how successful management (and accounting) practices work as methods that allow the user to solve practical and diverse problems. Management accounting and control systems have often been interpreted as neutral and passive techniques that convey a given result; they have been seen as orthodoxies, or as systems that contain a certain truth. Thus, for instance, it is not surprising that financial reports are believed to enable readers to see the "true and fair view" of a firm's financial transactions. However, moving away from this perspective allows "successful" techniques and solutions to be viewed as "orthopraxis"—as spaces (virtual or real) to be performed. The validity of accounting knowledge is thus not given by the inner meaning (an optimal equilibrium or the maximization of profit) they supposedly seem to pursue but rather by how they generate performances and are thus practiced. Interestingly the BSC appears homogeneous, i.e. as an identifiable technique with given features, not because it is the result of a process of isomorphic adherence to a template or a set of content rules but rather because, due to its malleability, it is able to attract and generate (rather than reduce) diversity and heterogeneity.

This interpretation of the BSC (and of accounting *tout court*) as a rhetorical form of ordering and creating knowledge shows us that words have a history and it is time for us all to rebuild this collective memory about what accounting has done for centuries—a memory that, in business, is made of economics as much as of art, design, anthropology, sociology and literature, the ignorance of which can indeed lead to mystical beliefs and collective frenzy camouflaged as science.

Endnotes

1. What follows is based on what is systematized by Foucault in his celebrated book, *Discipline and Punish: The Birth of the Prison.*
2. See Hoskin and Macve (1986, 2000) and Macve and Hoskin (1994).
3. This section is an adapted version of Macintosh and Free (2008).
4. Bourdieu's work has been used in accounting research in a few cases: see, for example, Cooper, Everett and Nue (2005), Kurunmäki (1999), Lee (1995), Lee and Williams (1999), Oakes, Townley and Cooper (1998). However, it is rare to see these notions mobilized in a related manner, and this section intends to fill this lacuna, in order to show the potential of Bourdieu's work in understanding the realities of MACS.
5. We illustrated Giddens' (1984) duality of structure concept in Chapter 8.
6. Bourdieu's writings are sprinkled with economic theory constructs including exchange rates, monopolies, economies, competition, self-interest, and the laws of exchange.
7. The US SEC can be thought of as such a referee for the field of financial capitalism.

8. This idea is similar to Giddens's (1984, p. 83) idea that social systems are, "organized as regularized social practices, sustained in encounters dispersed across time-space. The actors whose conduct constitutes such practices are 'positioned' . . . living along what Hägerstand calls their time-space paths, and they are positioned relationally . . . A social position involves the specification of a definite 'identity' within a network of social relations."
9. *Wall Street Journal*, 26 April 2002.
10. See Quattrone (2009).
11. See Carruthers (1998), p. 172.
12. Carruthers (1998).
13. The case is an extract from Busco and Quattrone (2009) and we refer to this publication for its more extensive description.

Further Readings

You can usefully do some further readings in each of the areas below.
   For those interested in a Foucauldian approach:

- Foucault, M. (1977) *Discipline and Punish*, Allen Lane, London.
- Hoskin, K. and Macve, R. (1986) Accounting and the examination: a genealogy of disciplinary power. *Accounting, Organizations and Society*, **11** (2), 105–36.
- Hoskin K. and Macve R. (1988) The genesis of accountability: the West Point connections. *Accounting, Organizations and Society*, **13** (1), 37–73.
- Hoskin K. and Macve R. (2000) Knowing more as knowing less? Alternative histories of cost and management accounting in the US and the UK. *The Accounting Historians Journals*, **27** (1), 91–149.
- Miller P. and O'Leary T. (1987) Accounting and the construction of a governable person. *Accounting, Organizations and Society*, **12** (3).
- Miller P. and O'Leary T. (1994) Governing the calculable person, in *Accounting as Social and Institutional Practice* (eds Hopwood, A. and Miller, P.), Cambridge University Press, Cambridge, pp. 98–115.

For those interested in Bourdieu's notions of practice:

- Bourdieu, P. (1977) *Outline of a Theory of Practice*, Cambridge University Press, Cambridge.
- Bourdieu, P. (1990) *The Logic of Practice*, Stanford University Press, Stanford, CA.
- Bourdieu, P. (1998) *Practical Reason*, Stanford University Press, Stanford, CA.

For those interested in training regimes, rhetoric and art of memory:

- Carruthers, B. and Espeland, W. (1991) Accounting for rationality: double-entry bookkeeping and the rhetoric of economic rationality. *American Journal of Sociology*, **97** (1), 31–69.

- Carruthers, M. (1990) *The Book of Memory: A Study of Memory in Medieval Culture*, Cambridge University Press, New York.
- Carruthers, M. (1998) *The Craft of Thought: Meditation, Rhetoric and the Making of Images: 400–1200*, Cambridge University Press, Cambridge.
- Nørreklit, H. (2003) The Balanced Scorecard: what is the score? A rhetorical analysis of the Balanced Scorecard. *Accounting, Organizations and Society*, **28** (6), 591–619.
- Quattrone, P. (2009) Books to be practiced. Memory, the power of the visual and the success of accounting. *Accounting, Organizations and Society*, **34**, 85–118.
- Thomson, G. (1991) Is accounting rhetorical? Luca Pacioli and Printing. *Accounting, Organizations and Society*, **16** (5/6), 572–99.
- Thomson, G. (1998) Encountering economics and accounting: some skirmishes and engagements. *Accounting, Organizations and Society*, **23** (5/6), 283–323.

CHAPTER 11

MACS, Accountability, and Governance

11.1 Introduction

Corporate governance and accountability, like auditing, have become ubiquitous. They are global phenomena. There are many reasons for their increased relevance and their diffusion across the world: the diminishing role of the state in regulating vast areas of the economy and society; the deregulation of financial markets; the growth of the multinational corporation as main engine of the largest economies in the world. These are only a few of those factors that the literature has highlighted as relevant to explain the phenomenon.[1] Their growth has been accompanied by the enlargement of the boundaries of what is meant by governance and accountability. This has happened to the extent that these two words nowadays encompass a vast, if not endless, range of regulatory problems faced by organizations, economies and societies. Furthermore, corporate governance has expanded beyond corporations to reach hospitals, schools, universities and public utilities. Interestingly, corporate governance systems, originally designed to protect shareholders' interests, are now used in organizations where shareholders do not even exist. In universities and schools, for example, boards of directors have supplanted more collegial governing bodies, researchers' and teachers' behavior is driven by incentives, and a new generation of entrepreneurial citizen is coming out of education. The effects of these changes are not entirely beneficial.[2]

For the purposes of this chapter, a meaningful (and short) definition of governance is the following: "Corporate governance is the system by which companies are directed and controlled."[3] From this definition it is clear that MACS are crucial in ensuring good governance as they contribute to providing most of the tools that make this governance possible, from financial information to performance indicators.

There are various theoretical approaches that deal with the problem of governance.[4] We cannot deal with all of them in this chapter. We will instead limit our attention to the approach inspired by agency theory: this approach views managing the relationship between shareholders and management as the key problem of governance. The reason for this choice relates to the relevance that agency theory has gained in academic and policy-making circles. In other words, when systems of governance have to be designed and discussed, solutions inspired by agency theory are always tabled and very often adopted. In these circles, it seems, the belief in its neoclassical economic underpinnings has gone unquestioned for a long time, despite the recursive cycles of crisis that have affected capitalism, notions of shareholders' value and governance. The other is that critiquing this approach (an easy task in these current times, we acknowledge) will allow us to question the ideals of transparency and independence, which are key to governance as much as to many other important accounting and control tools, and propose some ideas to rethink not only issues of governance but the whole accounting approach to financial reporting and organizational controls. And we think this is an appropriate way to conclude our book.

But what are the inspiring principles of contemporary systems of corporate governance?

The list below is only indicative (and you can go back to Chapter 4 for a discussion of the tenets of agency theory) but it helps us to introduce the issues we would like to discuss in this chapter:

1. *The separation between ownership and control.* Since the rise of the modern corporation, especially in the Anglo-American context, we have witnessed the increasing separation between shareholders (who provide finances to corporations) and management (which is supposed to make the most out of these resources). This creates two problems: information asymmetry and the need to align the interest of these two parties.

2. *The problem of information asymmetry.* Once ownership and management are separated, there is a need to control the relationship between them and make sure that managers act in the interest of those who provide them with capital. However, the (social or legal) contract governing this relationship is by definition incomplete as it is impossible to design a contract that covers the whole range of what is possible.

Managers are in a better position to gain from this situation as they, through their daily actions, will inevitably obtain greater information than shareholders and can use this to their own advantage rather than in the interests of shareholders.

3. *The need to align the interest of rational managers and shareholders.* It has been noted that since the separation between capital and management, the whole corporate governance discourse has been permeated and driven by the need to limit the self-interest of managers. Both parties are assumed to be rational and have clear and consistent objectives, and thus there is a problem of aligning the interest of managers and shareholders. Corporate governance has been viewed as a system to constrain and direct management's rationality and self-interest and to make sure shareholders' rather than managers' interests are pursued. Corporate governance systems have been devised with the intent of answering these questions: How can management act in interest or shareholders rather than their own? Is there a way of controlling this behavior if it is not possible to align these two sets of agencies?

4. *Technical forms chosen to produce alignment.* Various forms of (internal and external) controls have been devised in search of this alignment. Certainly stock options and the constitution of a board of directors with supposedly independent nonexecutive members can be enumerated as the two most common. The first should assure that, in working for their own interests (e.g. the increase in the value of the stock option) managers would also implicitly work in the interest of shareholders. The second inserts in the relationship a further mechanism of internal control represented by the presence on the board of external and independent members (although it has been noted that this duplicates the problem of agency). However, for the economist, the ultimate and automatic mechanism of control would be a firm belief in the regulatory power of financial markets: if managers do not perform well, share prices go down with a subsequent takeover. They would thus lose their jobs, a new management will be brought in and the abstract category of the shareholder would be safeguarded. Of course this presupposes a strong belief in the efficiency and transparency of financial markets.

The remainder of the chapter offers an alternative view of governance in a double sense. It does not assume that organizations can be seen as a nexus of independent contracts (between two parties only) and, secondly, it aims to show that, as always is the case, the world of practice differs significantly from the theory supposedly representing it.

11.2 Governance, Accountability, and Trust: From Societies to "Socie-*ties*"

Words have a history, someone said. This is why sometimes the etymology of a word can tell us many things that have been forgotten because of the passing of time. The word "society" is one of these. As we recalled in Chapter 3, "society" comes from the Latin *socius*, i.e. a companion, an ally. Thus "society" can be understood as a "friendly community of companions," and to study this community also means to study the ties that link these companions and make them "allies." Hence, as Bruno Latour has argued, we have to study societies as "socie-*ties*"—that is, we need to study how these various *soci* are linked together in stronger or looser networks of relations.

Governance and accountability are possibly the most diffused modes of establishing and regulating these ties, these relationships between various agents who then give birth to communities that have gained so much currency in modern and contemporary societies: organizations and firms. They can be seen, for the purposes of this book, as mechanisms through which various organizational members attempt to behave in an orderly way in organizations. Management accounting and control systems are very much concerned with this order and thus studying governance and accountability issues is a way of understanding how control systems work, or do not, in organizations. However, it is also a way through which we can reflect on what it means for them to work and function correctly or dysfunctionally.

This is why, in the following part of this chapter, we will illustrate two famous accounting scandals. One of these has already been introduced when we discussed MACS as practices: the Enron scandal. The other, possibly even more relevant in terms of its disruptive effects, is the infamous Parmalat affair. Discussing them will offer us material to reflect on two issues.

The first concerns the principles and assumptions underpinning contemporary views on corporate governance. These are relevant for accounting and financial reporting as they attribute a specific agency to the various agents/stakeholders interested in that kind of information, and assume that financial reporting plays one specific function, i.e. providing these agents with useful information. One of the key tenets of these views is that various stakeholders taking part in the game of corporate governance are clearly defined and have a clear and stable set of objective to pursue (e.g. shareholders are to maximize profit and their actions are driven by this idea).

These principles are also relevant for MACS as corporate governance systems suggest a clear framework of incentives that are supposed to work uniformly upon individuals. This should guarantee shareholders' interests and, if this happens, the welfare of other organizational stakeholders is guaranteed (at least in the mind of the corporate governance designer). The Enron case, and even more the Parmalat scandal, both create a series of insurmountable obstacles to those who believe in such simplicity and therefore question the validity of their approaches on governance from their foundations. These two cases are also useful for assessing the validity of internal and external controls in management control systems. In the case of Parmalat, given the institutional context in which that corporation operated, internal controls were preferred and failed miserably. In the case of Enron, external, or market, controls were supposed to be at work and unfortunately failed too.

The second issue relates to the possibility of thinking[5] of other mechanisms to guarantee the functioning of a society as a "friendly community," as the etymology of the word reminds us. In line with the idea of "socie-*ties*," if one thinks of individuals as complex social animals, then the idea of reducing them to rational agents driven by simple maximizing principles may be appealing but it is utopian. Knowing that individuals need a long process of socialization to make sure that they develop effective and durable ways of living together, another way of guaranteeing this governance would be to go back to those socializing practices that build strong, long-term ties. Rather than a short-term nexus of contractual relationships driven by an immediate return, perhaps systems of corporate governance should be devising organizations that work as long-term "socie-*ties*." The two cases desperately call for a different kind of control system, which guarantees civil cohabitation. Perhaps there is a need to go back to education rather than thinking that incentives are the way to control people's behavior. In this sense, the aim of this chapter is simple: it aims to instill doubts about the effectiveness of incentive systems as guarantees of good governance and civil cohabitation.

11.3 A Tale of Two Scandals: The Failure of Internal, Institutional, and Social Controls

11.3.1 Parmalat[6]

14.5bn euros. This is the hole that Parmalat left in the financial market when it became clear that it was insolvent in December 2003.

How could this happen? And whose fault is it? This is of course something that magistrates in Italy and elsewhere are still trying to understand but the picture is becoming clearer although, as often happens with scandals of this size, the whole truth will possibly never emerge. As an Italian comedian commented, Parmalat is in the dairy business and so the truth at the end of the story will very likely be much skimmed.

The Parmalat scandal is an interesting case of failure of organizational, institutional and social controls. The whole top management of the multinational was implicated with shareholders, employees and other parties in appropriating and "redistributing" funds for years. It is a case of the failure of institutional controls as neither the market, nor the regulators, nor others tasked with checking on Parmalat's financial robustness (auditors, rating agencies, and stock exchange authorities) managed to raise red flags. When they did, it was too late. It is also a case of the failure of social controls as there are many grey areas of connivance amongst those who should have conducted themselves in an ethical manner, or who should have checked the firms, banks, auditors, accountants, and regulatory bodies. As we will argue later, the lack of effectiveness of controls in Parmalat is possibly a metaphor for the failure of an entire worldview—that is, the idea of financial markets as spaces where transparency should guarantee effective internal and external controls on managers' behaviors and the efficiency and fairness of the whole economy and society.

But how did Parmalat get there? How was it possible to dig a hole as big as 1% of Italy's GDP? What follows is a partial reconstruction of what happened. It is partial in a two senses. Firstly there are space constrains (a book would not be enough to tell the whole story). Secondly, the dust has not settled yet, and trials are still taking place to ascertain the role of shareholders, auditors, banks and regulators in the story. But let us begin with some history about the company.

Parmalat's History

Parmalat was founded on the 15 April 1961 as the result of the division of a family business dedicated to the production and commercialization of salami and tomato sauce. Calisto Tanzi (with other members of his family) saw an opportunity in the dairy industry, thanks to two Swedish innovations: the first was the now famous aseptic pack developed by Tetra Pak to contain all sorts of liquids; the second was the ultra-high temperature (UHT) milk quasi-sterilization process, which allows milk to last for far longer than fresh milk. Mr Tanzi had the idea of combining these two developments and this is how Parmalat began to grow: first commercializing fresh milk in Tetra-packs and then filling the packs with UHT milk. Parmalat's headquarters was, and still is, in Collecchio, near the city of Parma: hence Parmalat, as "latte" is the Italian for "milk."

Things went extraordinarily well for the first two decades. Turnover grew at a rate of 50% per year and jumped from 260 million liras (125 000 euros) in the 1960s to 635 billion liras (310 million euros) in 1984. Parmalat was growing fast both in economic terms and in terms of image. Its brand became famous all over the world with Parmalat sponsoring Formula One teams, and ski champions. Like many Italian tycoons, Tanzi could not resist the attraction of soccer and TV and in the 1990s he bought *Parma calcio*, Parma's local team which also managed to play at the top level in *Serie A* (the Italian Premier League), and *Oden TV*, with the idea, so they say, of competing with Mr Berlusconi's *Mediaset* group. By then Parmalat was already a big multinational, one of the few in the Italian milieu, with commercial subsidiaries all over the world, and large investments in Italy, Europe, Latin America and elsewhere.

However, from the late 1970s, the fantastic growth in revenues and investments was accompanied by an equally extraordinary growth in debt. This is not bad per se. As Tanzi himself stated when asked how he felt sitting on a mountain of debt, he replied that debt is a substantial part of the strategy of growth of a firm. It is then top management's role in making sure that this does not exceed a certain proportion of the equity and that interest expenses do not go over a certain percentage of the revenues—an answer that any professor of financial management would have given.

Let us therefore look at the Parmalat scandal through the eyes of an accounting framework (financial reporting in this case) to see how theory and practice may diverge quite substantially.

The Efficiency of Market and Institutional Controls: Theory

If you open a manual of financial reporting, Chapter 1 will very likely provide you with a representation similar to Figure 11.1.

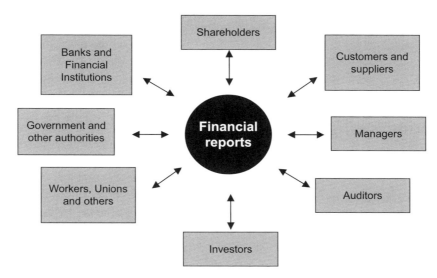

Figure 11.1   Stakeholders' interest in financial reports: *theory*

Figure 11.1 enumerates various stakeholders who are interested in financial reporting information. Typically the manual will state that each of these categories (shareholders, investors, etc.) will have one very specific interest in reading financial statements:

- *Shareholders*, especially those who can exert control through majority of shares, given the growing separation between ownership and management, look at financial reports to understand how managers are performing, and whether they are creating shareholders' value.
- *Managers* also want to get information on the company's performance to improve shareholders' value and make sure that their performance is adequately rewarded.
- *Banks and financial institutions* want to know from financial statements whether the company is financially solvent and liquid so that they can get their capital back and interest paid at regular intervals.
- *Government and other authorities*, by looking at these reports, want to ascertain whether companies are paying a fair amount of taxes, and whether profits are rising due to consolidation and lack of competition in the industry, so that they are able to intervene.
- *Customers and suppliers* will have a similar interest to banks and workers as they want to be sure that guarantees and payments are honored, respectively.
- *Auditors and rating agencies* are there to check on the validity of these accounts and the financial reliability of the company.
- *Workers* want to know whether the company that employs them will be stable and healthy enough to be able to pay their salary and continue to do so in future.
- *Other investors* share with majority shareholders a need for information on value creation and return on their investment.

In this picture financial reports contribute to the transparency needed for the efficient and effective functioning of financial markets. This framework also indirectly guarantees internal controls and good management/shareholder relationships as, if managers do not perform well, the market will realize it and share prices will go down. Poor share-price performance will force shareholders to intervene to put the situation back on track, possibly by firing managers and substituting them with better ones. The idea is that, in guaranteeing and protecting the interest of shareholders, the system also helps to regulate relationships with all of the stakeholders and, magically, acts in the interest of the whole economy and society.

Too good to be true. Let's look at what happened in practice with Parmalat.

The Efficiency of Market and Institutional Controls: Practice

Real life is always richer than simplified models. The Parmalat scandal, though, is a case of reality going beyond imagination. Let's look at the behavior of the various agents involved, revisiting the various familiar categories illustrated above, following the same order, but filling each box with some real personages.

- *Shareholders*. Parmalat's main shareholders were Calisto Tanzi and his family. Mr Tanzi had a dream that is difficult to fulfill without huge financial resources: to build a big multinational by buying and selling milk, a product with relatively low margins and returns. While Parmalat stayed within its core business (i.e. until the end of the 1970s) things were not going badly and margins were as high as 9%. However, with the expansion into other noncore businesses such as bakery products (biscuits, snacks, etc.) and as far away from the core as TV, tourism and sport, things began to be problematic. One may interpret this expansion as a strategy of diversification and one may be right. However, Tanzi was also driven by other objectives, which would not strictly fall into the aseptic agency of a shareholder/entrepreneur as described in economics, finance and accounting manuals. These will become clearer later but certainly Tanzi has entertained close relationships with politicians, and members of the Opus Dei amongst others, and, so they say, has always had the tendency to please them all (see Cappolino, Massaro and Panerai, 2004). We will see that Parmalat's expansion was possibly driven by, or somehow related to, these relationships more than to a pure interest in profit. The objective of expansion also provided a rhetoric to sustain the growth of debt, for any expansion needs finances.
- *Managers*. Many of Parmalat's managers were involved in the scandal but one has become more famous given his key role in the expansion of Parmalat debt and in arranging the mechanism through which this debt could be sustained. His name is Fausto Tonna. Fausto Tonna became Parmalat's MD in 1987 and then CFO in 1991. Under his administration Parmalat debt rose from 164.32 million euros in 1987 to 6340.15 million Euros in 2002. Interestingly, and this is the key to the whole scandal, cash and liquidity grew at a similar pace: from 8.95 million euros in 1987 to 3363.56 million in 2002. Cash and liquidity jumped substantially in 1990, when Parmalat was quoted

on the Borsa di Milano, the Italian Stock Exchange. The question that many analysts asked themselves during those years of growing debt was why did Parmalat resort to financial markets, issuing various kinds of bonds, and paying an increasing amount of interest when it could have slashed its debt by reducing this enormous liquidity? The answer was always that Parmalat wanted to be ready to take buying opportunities on the market and thus needed liquidity for these eventualities. This could have been a convincing answer in the first years of the expansion but not when debt increased to unsustainable levels. Merryll Lynch analysts were the first and only ones who looked with suspicion at this liquidity and suspected that it was fictitious. Unfortunately, they were right, although their analysis arrived too late. Mr Tonna and his collaborators had devised a series of techniques to boost revenues (for example, faking invoices of powdered milk sales to Cuba), increase assets (for instance, through the sale of nonexistent intellectual properties and technologies amongst offshore subsidiaries) and to reduce losses and debt (for example, by shifting uncollectable receivables sometimes artificially created to offshore subsidiaries in the Cayman Islands and other fiscal events where accounting controls were virtually nonexistent). These are only few examples from a list that is, sadly, much longer. Parmalat was growing debt to repay its debt: in the absence of a sufficient cashflow generated by genuine sales, the only way to repay the debt was generating more debt. This went on and on from the early 1990s with no one raising substantial doubts about the situation until early 2000. At one point, though, and we are close to the end, a bond needed to be repaid and some cash was to be found. Tonna turned once again to banks for help.

- *Banks and financial institutions*. Many of the most important world banks had business relationships with Parmalat (for example, Citigroup, Morgan Stanley, Deutsche Bank, Bank of America) and of course so did all of the main Italian ones (for instance, Banca Intesa, Capitalia, San Paolo-IMI, Unicredito). Some of these banks were overexposed and tried to reduce their credits to Parmalat. In a sense, and this is why some of these banks have been brought to court by the new Parmalat administrator, they could not be in a position to ignore Parmalat's situation and they must have been aware of the situation. Despite this they endorsed Tonna's idea of continuing to buy Parmalat bonds and then reselling them to the public and small investors who were unaware of the situation. Of course banks, like all organizations, are a coalition of different agencies and it could therefore happen, for example, that the same bank (such as Banca Intesa) was trying to reduce the exposure towards Parmalat in one office and buying Parmalat's bonds in another. Some argue that the Italian financial authorities should have intervened. Mr Tremonti, then Treasury Minister in the first Berlusconi government, fiercely attacked the then Governor of the Bank of Italy, Mr Fazio, for the lack of action on the whole matter. Some defended the Bank saying that its role was to invigilate on the banking system, not firms, and that the CONSOB, the Italian equivalent of the US SEC, should have intervened. There were certainly too many institutional and personal lapses[7] to allow Parmalat's irregularities to emerge before it was too late. These relationships did not exclude politicians and members of the various governments in power throughout the Parmalat saga.

- *Government and other authorities*. Parmalat's expansion strategy went in many geographical directions. One in particular exemplifies the rationale underpinning the expansion: a factory in Nusco, a small village in Campania, a region in the south of Italy. The reason for that investment is not to be found in abstract economic rationality but in public relations considerations, as Nusco is the electoral district of Ciriaco De Mita, former Italian Prime Minister and high profile member of the Christian Democrats (DC), politically close to Mr Tanzi. Other politicians benefited from their closeness to Tanzi. Apparently Mr Cossiga, Emeritus President of the Italian Republic, could travel on Parmalat's jet. It is also said[8] that he intervened to make sure that Parmalat bought a *de facto* bankrupted orange-juice producing company in Sicily; the reason being that this company was close to a local but influential member of the DC (Mr Calogero Mannino). Mr Tanzi was also close to Mr Alemanno (former Minister of the Agricultural Policies and Rome Mayor as we write) who was charged with the allegation of having allowed Parmalat to market *Lattefresco Parmalat*, a new high-quality milk sold as "fresh" although the milk did not technically fall into the definition of "fresh" (milk that is a maximum four days old; *Lattefresco* could instead be sold as fresh even if it was eight days old). Alemanno has been recently acquitted. Parmalat is also said to have supported Mr Massimo D'Alema (also former Prime Minister) through publicity in the magazine of his Foundation ItalianiEuropei, and Mr Romano Prodi (former Prime Minister and President of the European Commission). Both of them deny the charges or admit only those that have legally been recorded in the accounts. In this respect, as noted by a magistrate investigating these relationships, sponsoring political parties is not illegal, if this is done transparently. And if politicians do not know of the illegal provenance of the money received, they are not responsible so long as this money is correctly accounted for on the receivers' books. Tanzi also sponsored Forza Italia (now People's Freedom, Mr Berlusconi's party) and some argue that Parmalat diverted TV publicity to Mediaset preferring it to RAI not claiming the discount that that volume of ads would have generated. In summary, could the Government, as a party with an interest in the reporting of financial information, solve this intricate nest of relationships and make things more transparent? Well, it depends on what the objectives of a government are.[9]
- *Customers and suppliers*. The relationship with suppliers, for example, was not as clear as it should have been. Tetra Pak, for instance, was officially paid by Parmalat at the full price for its supplies but in fact offered a discount based on volume. The difference between the price paid and the price recorded on Parmalat's books was a way of diverting money from Parmalat and accumulating it in a Swiss bank account held by Mr Tanzi, apparently for his personal use (see Cappolino, Massaro and Panerai, 2004).
- *Auditors and rating agencies*. Were the auditors (mainly Grant Thornton) aware of this situation? According to Mr Tonna's declaration to the magistrates they not only knew but they helped to set up various offshore operations, and constitute offshore subsidiaries such as Bonlat, which had the role of absorbing losses generated by the industrial divisions, and also incorporated two other companies that had played that role in previous years (Zilpa and Curcastle). Interestingly the two auditors involved (Mr Penca and

Mr Bianchi) had worked also for Hodgson Landau Brands when they audited Parmalat's accounts and moved to Grant Thornton when they audited Parmalat. There is therefore a clear example of conflict of interest here.

• *Workers and other investors*. Those who do not appear in this web of relationships are those in whose interest, theoretically, Figure 11.1 was drawn: small investors who were unaware of the situation. They, along with workers, are the only ones who do not appear in this scandalous story and it will be they who pay the price for it. The forecast is that only four out of every 100 small shareholders and bond holders will get a partial refund.

This incredible network of relationships and fraud was discovered in December 2003 when Mr Tanzi was forced to resign under the pressure of the CONSOB and various banks. Mr Bondi was appointed as administrator of Parmalat and soon discovered that, for example, the bank statement of an account held at the Bank of America worth $3.5 billion dollars was in fact faked in a small office with a color printer. The entire paper castle constructed by Tanzi and his accomplices collapsed in a matter of hours.

What the Parmalat scandal teaches us is that theory illuminates some aspects of managing a business (including financial transactions and relationships) but also, and at the same time, casts a shadow on many other relationships. What Figure 11.1 does is to assign a clear and unique agency to various economic and institutional actors. It black-boxes them and, in doing so, it makes invisible what is not contemplated by that theory. A shareholder is interested in his own return. But Tanzi was interested in many other things, possibly including financing a large part of the Italian political apparatus, and this was not only for reasons of economic self-interest. The result is that we do not imagine and thus do not expect what could happen in practice, where the boxes in Figure 11.1 are in fact networks of relationships.

Paradoxically, a model that was thought to ensure transparency of markets, institutions and transactions ended up making these opaque. It is much better to believe that this transparency is not achievable and instead to seek constantly to unveil what happens in practice, without relying on a tick-box mentality.

This mentality is what we very briefly recall in the next section, which returns to the Enron scandal.

11.3.2 Back to Enron

The Enron case constitutes an illuminating example of the failure of internal controls, due to the poor effectiveness of conventional systems of corporate governance. But it also illustrates, like the Parmalat case, that there is something more fundamental that should be taken into account in order to understand how the Enron mentality led to a situation in which no one dared to stop what was going on. This "something" clearly relates to how certain values inform "socie-*ties*," i.e. "friendly communities of companions." It is thus also an example of a failure of social (and socializing) mechanisms, which should guarantee the functioning of organizations and societies. It is also clearly a failure of institutional controls, for all of those institutional mechanisms that had been put in place to ensure that the ordered functioning of businesses could enrich the whole economy failed miserably, at all levels.

Board of Directors[10]

At the time of its collapse in 2001, Enron could boast of the high quality of the 19 nonexecutive directors, most of whom were hand picked by Lay. Nonexecutive directors also sat on and chaired key Enron governance committees such as audit, finance, compensation, and nomination. All directors received a generous fee and were granted stock options and some bought Enron stock. Not surprisingly, then, the Board failed in many instances to exercise its governance duties. Perhaps the most telling neglect of duty involved the Board's approval of the highly publicized LJM, Raptors, and Rhythms SPE scandal, which brought Enron down. In 1999, the Board gave its approval to a top Enron executive (CFO Andrew Fastow) doing business with Enron as manager of a putatively independent entity (LJM) of which Enron was the major owner. The LJM arrangements were a clear violation of Enron's Code of Ethics. However, the Board approved a suspension of that part of the Code for these transactions. In regards to this matter, the Powers *et al*. report[11] later concluded that, "The Enron Board approved Fastow's participation in the LJM partnership with full knowledge and discussion of the obvious conflict of interest that would result" (p. 9). The US Senate Permanent Subcommittee on Investigations found that the Enron Board had breached its fiduciary duties, was embroiled in clear conflicts of interest, regularly approved excessive compensation for company executives and failed to monitor the effect of such on the company, and lacked independence due to financial ties between the company and several board members.

Enron's bankruptcy filings in 2002 elicited a series of investigations and class action suits against Enron's board of directors alleging securities fraud among other misdemeanors. In January 2005, ten former outside directors agreed to a $168 million settlement, without pleading guilty. The directors themselves paid only $13 million, the rest coming from insurance proceeds. None of these directors then or since have admitted to any wrongdoing. What is particularly disturbing about these events and the actions of the outside directors is not so much the amounts of money involved, nor that the directors got off nearly "scot free," but that such pillars of the corporate world would respond this way in carrying out their duties. It would seem that the board members were not immune from the pejorative Enron habitus, which we discussed in the previous chapter, nor was Enron's Code of Ethics, another important governance and control mechanism.

Code of Ethics

Enron's highly touted Code of Ethics, which every employee had to sign every year, stated in part:

> Ruthlessness, callousness, and arrogance do not belong here. We work with customers and
> prospects openly, honestly, and sincerely . . . Every employee is expected to conduct business

with other employees, partners, contractors, suppliers, vendors and customers keeping in mind respect, integrity, communication and excellence . . . relations with the Company's many publics—customers, stockholders, governments, employees, suppliers, press, and bankers—will be conducted in honesty, candor, and fairness.

The predispositions, inclinations and propensities of the Lay/Skilling era habitus, however, ran counter to these moral injunctions on many fronts.

Egregious Activities and Callous Trash Talk

During 1999 and 2000 Enron electricity traders in California engaged in a litany of egregious activities. These included "round tripping" (artificially running prices up by selling the same electricity back and forth with other Enron traders), congesting transmission lines by overloading them and deliberately shutting them and power plants down, thus artificially boosting demand and driving prices up, and falsifying information regarding standby power plant generation capacities. Trash talk by these traders, recorded on taped transcripts, include statements like, "We just f----- California to the tune of a million or two bucks a day."[12] Insiders gave these initiatives names such as Death Star and Get Shorty. These traders, some of whom later were found guilty of criminal fraud, contributed in no small way to the California electricity "blackouts" in 1999 and 2000.

Enron executives and managers engaged in a litany of actions that violated the Code of Ethics. There were widespread suspicions and accusations that Enron officials engaged in bribery and corruption in its overseas operations, including money laundering by means of its nearly 900 SPEs and subsidiaries in sundry tax havens. On many occasions accounting officers, collaborating with investor relations department managers, manipulated quarterly earnings reports to meet analysts' estimates. Enron's dubious accounting practices are legendary with several accounting officers pleading guilty to accounting fraud.

Enron's habitus also included flagrant sexist dispositions and inclinations. Many top executives were involved in widely known extramarital affairs with other company employees. The "sexual misconduct" at the executive apex set the tone for the rest of the company and became an important part of Enron's habitus. "You couldn't get away from it. It was like a humidifier. It was in the air."[13] The general attitude regarding women is illustrated by the trading floor's imaginary "Women of Enron Calendar" consisting of the twelve "sexiest Babes" working at Enron. Male chauvinism and sexists attitudes permeated Enron's habitus.[14]

Another matter that had a profound effect on Enron's habitus was the move, at Skilling's insistence (and with the approval of the SEC), to switch its corporate accounting from traditional *historical cost* to *mark-to-market* accounting, a method that was already in widespread use throughout the banking and finance industries. Skilling also demanded a bonus scheme for himself based on reported profits (measured with mark-to-mark accounting) of Enron Finance Corporation (later the Enron Gas Services Group). This meant that profits would be reported at the time deals were made rather than during the terms of the deals. While mark-to-market accounting provided better asset values for its contracts, more importantly, it permitted recording profits from long-term deals immediately rather than, as for traditional accounting, at the culmination of the contract. This meant that profits were recorded in the quarter in which the deals were signed, even for 20-year contracts. This had the effect of emphasizing short-term results since Enron's financial traders now had to start each quarter with a blank trading book and a new profit target.

> By mid-2000, Jeff Skilling had achieved his goal: Almost all the vestiges of the old Enron . . . were gone. In its place, Enron had become a trading company. And with that change came a rock-em, sock-em, fast paced trading culture in which deals and 'deal flow' became the driving force behind everything Enron did. (Bryce, 2002, 215)

Between October 1998 and November 2001, Skilling sold 1 307 678 Enron shares with a gross proceeds value of $70 687 199.

11.3.3 When Utility Meets Morality: The Ethics of Finance[15]

What can we learn from Enron's story? Possibly the most important lesson is that we cannot treat issues of control as if economic and social matters were disjointed. Believing that people are driven by single economic goals and that these can be viewed as separate from the social nature of human beings in order to model their behavior is, at best, naïve. Economic, social, political issues and, as the Parmalat and Jesuit cases teach us, even religious credos are all at stake when dealing with matters of control. These links cannot be ignored and truncated, or treated as "add ons" to consolidated economic frameworks, even when they are viewed in isolation. The consequences of doing so can be devastating. Economics and "socie-*ties*" are faces of a multifaceted coin.

What we witness at Enron is the evil translation of money seeking into a new ethic for Enron's top management. This new morality is powerful exactly because people do not realize how it makes them see certain behaviors as appropriate. Paradoxically, this moral regime is powerful because people do not see how powerful it is.

But how does this translation happen? Is it the result of people behaving badly or is it intrinsically related to the financialization of their behavior?

Perhaps going back in history and looking at religion helps us to answer this question as, in the end, what religion has done for centuries is to define and help followers to find the ultimate truth.

Some say that there are two ways in which truth can be achieved: through *orthodoxy* and *orthopraxis*. The orthodox believer seeks the truth in the text: "An orthopractical adept, by contrast, seeks to achieve an imminent experience of the divine equivalent to that of the founder, usually by following a devotional practice presumed to be similar."[16]

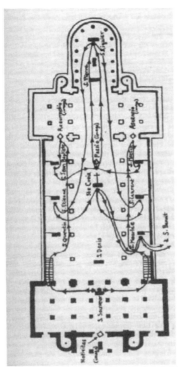

Source: Mary Carruthers, The Craft of Thought, p. 267 (Fig C), Cambridge University Press.

Figure 11.2   Route of the liturgical procession in the Abbey of Centula-St.-Riquier

Now, look at Figure 11.2. It reproduces the plan of the Abbey of Centula-St.-Riquier with a description of the liturgical route that the faithful had to follow to reach an illumination, the truth, a vision of God. You may ask yourself why we are asking you to look at this picture. In order to understand, let's see how this liturgical process works. This procession led the faithful in different spaces (the chapels, the choirs, the altar, etc.) in each of which they were asked to experience an image, either in the form of paintings on the walls of the church, or through imagination prompted by praying. As in the Ignatian Spiritual Exercises of the Jesuits, the devotee is asked to do certain things and experience certain ideas (sin, God, etc.). If the liturgical experience is well performed, i.e. all the steps and procedures are followed slavishly, then the faithful are likely to experience an illumination, a vision of God: the absolute truth.

The plan of the Abbey works as a meditation machine, as a practice that helps to create order in confused thoughts and helps one to *see* clearly what is "right" and what "wrong." If Norman and I visited that Church, we could follow the path, but without being trained in what to do, when and how, we could at best see columns, altars, frescos and the like. They could appear beautiful to us but they would not lead us to a vision of God—we would not even get close to that mystical experience leading to an illumination. The procession has a chance of working to make or reinforce people's beliefs only if it becomes a practice inserted within a specific, although not superimposing, training regime.

Reflecting on this liturgical procession brings us straight to questions on which we would like you to reflect. These are: How is that one comes to believe in something, be it God, an idea, a formula, science, values, economic rationality, profit, the correctness of a behavior and, broadly speaking, something that is worthwhile working and living for? What are those practices and trainings that allow the emergence and endurance of organizational, economic, and social beliefs? In what manner do these beliefs affect, and have effects on, individuals, given that most of these practices are always taken for granted and are thus invisible and forgotten? And, if we relate these questions back to the case of Enron and the issue of "good" governance, how is that what would everywhere else be seen as a repugnant behavior is instead seen at Enron as right?

The plan of the abbey exemplifies the concept of orthopraxis we have introduced above, where the altars, the porch and the various other spaces in the church are markers of a liturgical procession. It is this performance (and not merely the text in a book) that contains the spiritual experience of finding a way. And, in order to achieve this vision, one requires detailed and not random actions. It is thus this training, and to the practices that enact it, which one needs to look at to understand what is constituted as belief.

Contemporary organizations, economies and societies are pervaded by visions of this kind, which people clearly believe in strongly, given that these visions are able to mobilize individual and collective action. As contemporary examples of this new form of worship, of this form of lay religiosity and spirituality, one may think of possibly two of the most widespread and pervasive practices in contemporary capitalist economies and societies— finance, which provides the backbone of corporate governance theorizing; and accounting, which provides the numbers to judge whether management is augmenting shareholders' value or not.

You may say: "maybe, but how does this relate to the problem of Enron?" Well, it does. Think of your experience as a student. Especially if you are a student of accounting and finance, think of your daily training during, say, a Master in Financial Economics course. You are asked to take a class, say "economics," and this means that you have to go a specific place at a certain time, and if you mean to be a good student, you go there with your cases and exercises read and, possibly, during the class you refrain from look at your Blackberry and surfing the Internet. Then you are led by the lecturer through a series of steps and procedures (often maths and stats), which will make you find the right solution to the problem of maximizing profit under rational choice hypothesis. Then you abandon this "chapel" to move to the next one, say "financial econometrics," where you are introduced to more esoteric stuff and taught how to do financial modeling. Then you go back to your SPSS training course to make sure you are able to crunch a significant amount of data, and this equips you to then go on an internship and prepare the final project for your course (we have skipped a few steps but the idea is clear). If you follow all the steps slavishly then "Eureka!"—you have tested the truth of a theory. An incontestable vision of truth has emerged, normally in the shape of a formula such as Black and Scholes! You now believe that we are all profit seekers! And even if you resist this belief, you assume that this is the only way in which financial issues can be looked at. These things are true, and even if they are not, this is as close to truth as you can get.

In this hypothetical example resembling the training in a finance course, you, the unfortunate and unaware student, are asked to take part in what can easily be compared to a collective liturgy—a procession that has been refined so much thanks to mathematical modeling and statistical analysis that at the end of it you and your classmates think in similar ways and experience the same form of belief. A belief, though, that you all enact differently: you all are there to make money, but what this money means to you differs. The belief in the market ideology, which drives many neoclassical economists and finance professors, is possibly the strongest example of all. So strong is this belief that not even the evident failure of market mechanisms in the recurrent financial crises affecting capitalist economies make them doubt for one single instant that the market one day will rise again and reign as the ultimate form of financial regulation.

In fact, a theory (and a finance theory more than others) does not differ so much from the medieval monastic practice of meditating images which leads to a *theoria*—an illuminating and direct vision of God.[17] In accounting, finance, and, broadly, in contemporary economics, one witnesses the equivalent mystical belief in *numbers as figures*, as images to be praised, which, for their simplicity and apparent objectivity, are supposed to provide access to a privileged business truth and utility (and this seems to be increasingly the case in contemporary times). Numbers such as 10 000 or 1 000 000 000 are not even imaginable, they are a multitude rather than precise measures. This is even more the case when numbers come under the form of mathematical symbols: they assume an iconic and aesthetical value.[18] Accounting and finance[19] thus embed a specific training regime, which constructs a sort of renewed alliance between education and morality, where what is *just* is mostly what is *useful*, as referred to in the beautiful (but empty) aesthetics of their formulas, the etymology of which, not surprisingly, shows a clear relationship to a visual and schematic understanding of the world (from Latin *forma*, form; a term used in medieval classroom teaching to identify schema to aid the memory of students).

Let's go back to the initial question that we wanted to address. Is what happened at Enron (but it could be World.com—you name it) the result of people behaving badly or is it intrinsically related to the financialization of these people's behavior?

In broader terms, business practices all produce various theories, various *theorias*, various visions which manage to attract and engage individuals. The problem is that these theories, these visions, do not emerge and are not believed to emerge in the context of a religious liturgy, but in the context of scientific and rationality-driven praxis. The parallel with the liturgy in the plan of the Centula-St.-Riquier Abbey seems to suggest that they instead share many of those mystical and liturgical features that medieval and early modern *orthopraxis* presented.[20] Financial worldviews are not the result of evil in human beings. They can instead be traced to a certain view of what corporations (and people who run them) are supposed to be and do.

Training managers and instilling in them certain practices, which allow them to make sense of the world around them, is crucially important not for what these practices make them see but for what they make them ignore. This is why we need principles that do

Figure 11.3 On the power of numbers!

not purposefully (albeit unconsciously) make them blind. Numbers are powerful in making people acritical. The wisdom of Dilbert's cartoon illustrates this humorously in Figure 11.3. A critical education is the only antidote to make people see beyond the limits of transparency.

11.4 In Praise of Doubt: From the Tyranny of Transparency to a Search for Ethical Knowledge in Accounting, Accountability, and Governance

Parmalat and Enron are just two instances of a pressing need for redesigning financial reporting, MACS, accountability and governance systems. This difficult task has a multifaceted nature. It is an epistemological matter of how accounting produces knowledge about financial transactions in an economy (i.e. what principles underpin accounting frameworks). It is an institutional issue concerning how various bodies and actors govern this production (think of the role played by bodies such as the IASB and FASB and their related power networks). Finally, it is a question of how these complex issues are translated into technical financial reporting principles and theories, management accounting and control techniques, accountability and governance mechanisms (think of how the formats of different financial statements contribute to the definition of what counts as relevant in the context of financial information). For the sake of space, in this chapter we will concentrate our attention on what epistemological principles could underpin new frameworks for accounting, management controls, governance and accountability.

A difficult task, we said. Where could it begin? Given that a picture is said to be worth a thousand words, maybe a picture is what we need to make sure that accounting students do not have to go through decades (if not centuries) of philosophy of knowledge to understand how accounting is not different from philosophy when dealing with its foundation principles.

Many of you will be familiar with Escher's works. They are beautiful examples of how often irreconcilable opposites and illogical patterns are made to appear real and logical in

Figure 11.4 *Print Gallery,* M.C. Escher, lithograph (1956) Copyright The M.C. Escher Company B.V.

front of your eyes. *Print Gallery* (see Figure 11.4) is one of Escher's works that may help us to find new principles for representing accounting transactions in "socie-*ties*." What we see in the lithograph is a young man in a gallery. He is looking at a picture of a ship in a harbor of a town where there are various buildings, turrets, and finally a window where a woman is gazing out from her apartment. This apartment is above a picture gallery in which a young man is looking at a picture and . . . What?! He is within the picture he is observing![21]

This seems to be contrary to all logic but, as will soon become clear, there is nothing truer than what this picture tells us. When we are observing something we are never neutral in making this observation: we are always *within* what we are observing, as we observe by carrying with us a baggage of experiences, which are mediated by the various technologies and other material artifacts that we use in this observation. *Print Gallery* also teaches us that every observation is incomplete. The hole in the middle of Escher's lithograph is unavoidable. You can move it around within the frame, and this will help you to see what the hole had previously made invisible, but it will modify the other parts of the picture. The hole can be reduced to the infinitely small but, as with every dot, it can never be considered finite or closed: it cannot be filled (and Escher shows this mathematically) and the picture thus will never be complete as one can never have a full picture of reality.

The way in which this hole has been filled in *Print Gallery* is by the imposition of the author's signature. That signature is Escher's statement that this is the way in which he views knowledge. It is the author's authority: an act of faith, if you like.

Does this relate to MACS, accountability and governance? The answer is a resounding "yes." It does. Let's see how.

Roles that Accounting Can Play in Organizations

What roles does accounting play in organizations? Like every good textbook, we will refer to a two-by-two matrix (see Figure 11.5). On the two axes we can place the degree of uncertainty of management's objectives and the means to achieve these objectives, respectively. This degree can be relatively "certain" or "uncertain." Crossing these two dimensions you have four different roles that accounting plays in organizations. If degrees of uncertainty are low, a rare but possible event, then accounting works as an *answer machine*. It gives you answers: it tells you, for example, the "right" cost of two production lines so you can understand whether to push one line or the other; it tells you whether managers are acting in the interest of shareholders by measuring variations in shareholders' value, and so forth. This ideal situation, where knowledge is easily attainable (or it is thought to be attainable) is the default situation assumed in many dominant views of what role accounting is supposed to serve in organizations. However, it seems quite obvious that this situation is quite rare, if not impossible. Most likely, there is a high degree of uncertainty in at least one of these two dimensions. So accounting becomes an *ammunition machine* when there is uncertainty over the means to be used to achieve a given objective. It is then mobilized by different parties to promote their vested interests. If instead there is also uncertainty

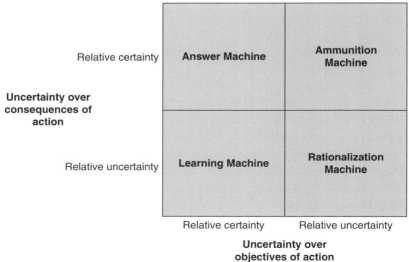

Source: Burchell *et al.* (1980).

Figure 11.5   The four roles of accounting

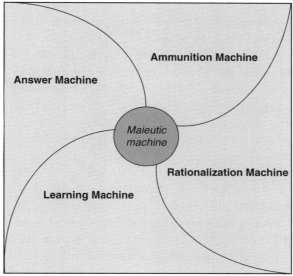

Source: Burchell *et al.* (1980).

Figure 11.6 Accounting as a maieutic machine

over the objectives, then accounting is used as a rationalization machine, as it can justify organizations' actions *ex post*, i.e. after these actions have taken place. When objectives are pretty clear but no one is sure of how to get there, accounting plays the role of a *learning machine*. This is the case, for example, for budgets and how they are often used to explore the future, to understand what actions realize the yearly targets.

In addition to these four roles of accounting, we would like to add a further one (see Figure 11.6). This new role can be constructed departing from Escher's picture. But let's proceed step by step and let's delve into issues of representation of financial transactions before moving too fast.

What Figure 11.4 teaches us is that accounting is not just about representations and true and fair views. Accounting rarely, if ever, works as an answer machine that truly represents the financial situation of a company. As has been noted, if representations could be a transparent image of the represented they would not be needed: representations exist (and can be conceived of) only if there is a gap between the represented and the representer, if the transparency that representation aims to achieve is, in fact, impossible to achieve. A true and fair representation of accounting transactions is impossible as accounting signs cannot represent the financial world: they speak of it in its absence. This is why this world needs to be made present again through accounting inscriptions: it needs to be "*re*-presented."[22] It is this absence that the hole in Escher's *Picture Gallery* exemplifies and it is from this impossibility that the possibility of representation emerges. It is thus from here that we need to depart when rethinking what accounting is all about. The same goes for accountability and governance.

The tyranny of transparency, as it has been described,[23] is quite ubiquitous in contemporary societies. So we live in "orgies of calculations," all directed to make our actions auditable and to make us accountable.[24] However, these attempts all work backwards—that is, they assume what needs to be represented and account only for this limited range of possibilities. Let us illustrate this with an example related to the Parmalat case. In the Parmalat scandal, Mr Fausto Tonna was theoretically accountable to Mr Tanzi for the way in which he managed Parmalat's resources. In fact, he was accountable to a much broader system of interests, which expanded beyond the border of Parmalat. This is why accounting and finance were not theoretically (and epistemologically) equipped to deal with scandals such as Parmalat and Enron. These theories assign a specific role and functions to various stakeholders (and to shareholders in particular) and whatever deviates from this view is obscured by the accounting framework and marginalized. In a sense, the various accounting scandals that cyclically affect our economies and society can be seen as a result of greater calls for accountability, as these always presuppose what needs to be accounted for and make us ignore other important and influential issues. These calls have the arrogance of knowing what is right, what needs to be done to make financial markets efficient, and this is why they fail cyclically. No one is God and it would be useful to be periodically reminded of this small detail.

We therefore would like to view accounting, accountability and governance as instruments that, rather than giving answers and providing checklists to be ticked, raise questions about what is not known, about the rationalities that drive shareholders and managers but do not fit within the simplistic notion of maximizing profit. They have to be seen as maieutic machines, in honor of the Socratian practice of producing knowledge by asking questions rather than giving answers. This would alert us to the possibility of actions which have nothing to do with maximizing profit, and if they do, this principle would alert us to the infinite range of possibilities (ethical and nonethical) that are offered to those who are truly driven by this objective.

This praise for doubt should not supplant transparency altogether as we definitely know that some actions have effects that are hazardous and noxious. But devising accounting, accountability and governance systems based on the idea of the impossibility of representation will force us to seek for more, not less, information.

An example may help to clarify why this is the case. During the financial crisis that we have recently experienced, regular savers (i.e. not the institutional investors but common citizens) in search of a secure bank in which to deposit their money began to look at the statements of the banks where they thought of spreading their saving. They did not stop at the superficial indicators of the rating agencies and were certainly not driven by the attractiveness of the interest rates offered on their deposits. They wanted to know whether these banks were fundamentally solid. It was precisely because they doubted official truths and understood that reaching the truth was an impossible task that they at least tried to know more. If they were reassured by the official truths of auditors and rating agencies that they had trusted until the beginning of the crisis, they would have stopped at the level of the credit score of those banks rather than digging in depth.

We thus need to modify Figure 11.5 and put at the center of it Escher's hole as in Figure 11.6. This hole testifies and reminds us all of the impossibility of representation and of the need to always try to understand what is shadowed by preconceived notions of transparency. If you like, our call is for more critical knowledge and for a critical role not only of academics but also of managers, financial controllers and experts in accountability and corporate governance. Someone needs to be responsible and accountable to those investors in Parmalat who could not speak or who could not be heard as they were not part of the network of power relations in which Calisto Tanzi swam like a fish in the water.

What are the implications of this new epistemology for accounting, management accounting and control, accountability and governance?

As we said when opening this section, they play at different levels and we can only sketch them in concluding this closing chapter of the book. Institutionally, we should abandon the idea that independent bodies, external nonexecutive members of boards of directors, controllers and various kinds of emerging agencies created to act in the name of some transparency are independent. Independence, as much as representation, transparency, accountability and the like, is another utopian supposition. It is better to assume that it is not possible and seek to discover why certain bodies are not independent and to whom these are linked rather than assuming that they are. To do otherwise would paralyze our critical action.

In terms of techniques, accounting and controls need to be profoundly rethought. If financial reporting cannot rest on the assumption that numbers are an expression of objectivity, it is much better to take the relativity of these numbers seriously and devise techniques that draw upon this relativity rather than pursuing the chimera of objectivity. And there are already tentative examples in this area such as providing financial statements that make this relativity less obscure. In terms of controls, it is obvious that prescriptive approaches are doomed to fail as there is no prescription that can foresee the entire range of possibilities. Rather than designing management accounting and controls systems that purport to provide sets of performance measures and incentives that indicate where the right direction to go is, it is better to leave people free to act within a clear range of shared values, the ultimate one possibly being civil cohabitation in organizations and societies.

We wanted to make this call in a book that is mainly directed to management accounting students because it is from business and accounting education that we need to begin to devise different forms, "socie-*ties*." Those who were expecting an answer to the problem of accounting, control, accountability and governance will be disillusioned but we would have contradicted ourselves if we had provided answers. In this phase of the development of capitalism we believe that we need to instill doubts in our students, knowing that it is not more transparency that we need, it is not greater accountability. Or, at least, not of the kind we are used to. Only by abandoning the dream of a true and fair view one can know more. Moving away from the idea that a reality exists and can be represented forces us to look for more reality. Only by renouncing the arrogance of knowing what is "best" and what is "right" can one expand the realm of our ethical knowledge. With Ludwig Mies van der Rohe: *less is more*.

11.5 Summary and Conclusions

This last chapter has dealt with issues of accountability and governance to critically review the underpinnings of most contemporary theories in accounting, management control and indeed accountability and governance. These theories take the possibility of representing financial transactions and organizational relationships as the aim of their theorizing. With the discussion of the Parmalat and Enron scandals we wanted to highlight how this approach can lead to disaster.

The case of Parmalat provides us with an example of how organizations, and even individuals, are "socie-*ties*"—that is, they cannot be taken in isolation; they cannot be granted precise agencies and black-boxed in fixed categories such as "shareholder," "manager," "bank," "the State." Even when such attempts are made in the name of simplification and for the sake of scientific analysis, one risks casting a shadow over the most important aspects of their conduct. Reality always resists such attempts, and ignoring this has serious consequences for those who are not allowed to see behind the veil of rationality, transparency and independence.

The critique of these key principles has been expanded through the discussion of the Enron case. The point we wanted to make through its analysis is that what happened at Enron is not the result of a dysfunctional use of the ideal of profit maximization. Instead it is intrinsic to the assumption about the rationality of economic agents which, even in its bounded version, modern theories of accounting and finance share.

A similar critique applies to issues of accountability and governance. We have tried to convince you that all kinds of expert knowledge always carry a tacit component and therefore the ideal that greater transparency will make us all experts is a chimera. Knowledge, including that of our disciplinary space, is always nested in organizing attempts from which the observer is by default excluded. We have argued that it is therefore better to renounce this dream as this allows us to remain alert and possibly become aware that some esoteric governance and accountability solutions cannot deliver what they promise.

In this sense, Enron is not an example of malfunctioning of the idea of the economic man: it is the result of it. The notion of economic rationality is not the solution to the problem of ethical and useful behavior but its main complication.

The discussion of these two cases has thus allowed us to question contemporary training regimes in accounting, management controls and indeed accountability and governance. This is why we think that there is a need to go back to education and go back to textbooks that make students think about problems that have difficult solutions rather than providing them with easy answers. This is the spirit in which this book has been written.

Endnotes

1. A useful analysis of the emergence of these phenomena can be found in Clarke (2007) and Power (1997).
2. See Shore and Selwyn (1998).
3. Cadbury (1992, p. 15) quoted in Clarke (2007, p. 2).
4. See Clarke (2007, p. 27, Table 1.4).
5. And possibly devising, but this requires another book!
6. The story of the Parmalat scandal is still in the making as we write. The case we describe here is based on the book by Capolino, Massaro and Panerai (2004), *La grande truffa*.

7. Institutionally, the Bank of Italy's equity was subscribed by the banks involved in the scandal, but we do not think this is a specific area of concern, as this is the way in which the Italian banking system was organized (although a recent reform has made the Bank of Italy institutionally independent from the banks it should supervise). It later became clear that the Governor entertained personal friendships with most of the bankers whom the institution over which he presided should have controlled . . . but this is another story.

8. At least, this is what is stated in Capolino, Massaro and Panerai (2004), *La grande truffa*.

9. Views on whether Berlusconi has a conflict of interest or not are varied and too numerous to be reported here.

10. This section draws on Macintosh and Free (2008).

11. Report of Investigation by the Special Committee of the Board of Directors of Enron Corp. William C. Powers Jr., Chair, Raymond S, Troubh, and Herbert S Winokur, Jr., Counsel Wilmer, Cutler & Pickering, 1 February 2002.

12. Recorded in taped transcripts and e-mail files published by the Federal Energy Regulatory Commission in 2004. On February 3, the Snohomish County Public Utility Department (SCPUD) in Washington State released material detailing Enron's flagrant manipulation of the power supply in California. The evidence was released as part of an effort to convince the Federal Energy Regulatory Commission (FERC) to void a $122 million termination fee Enron was demanding from the Washington State public utility.

13. Ibid. p. 145.

14. After Enron's fall in 2001, *Playboy* magazine's August issue featured "The Girls of Enron" selected from the 50 ex-Enron women who answered a call for a photo shoot. Several executives were known to have "their own harems" (Fox, 2003, p. 146).

15. This section draws and expands the arguments of Quattrone (2009).

16. See Carruthers (1998).

17. Carruthers (1998, p. 172).

18. See Espenland and Stevens (2008).

19. At least in schools where this book is not considered for use!

20. We would also argue that they share a few features with rituals that witches, magicians, and psychedelic techniques such as "astral trips" use (see Luhurman, T., *Persuasions of the Witch's Craft*, Harvard, 1989), but this requires a little more research before it can be believed!

21. The picture is repoduced and commented on in Hofstadter, 1979, p. 776, Figure 142. Its relationship with accounting epistemology, theory and practice is explored in Quattrone (2000).

22. Paraphrasing a passage in Latour (1986).

23. Strathern (2000).

24. Meyer (1986).

Further Readings

You can usefully do some further readings in each of the areas below.

For issues of accountability and governance:

- Roberts, J. (2009) No one is perfect: the limits of transparency and an ethics for "intelligent" accountability. *Accounting Organizations and Society*, **34** (8), 957–70.

- Strathern, M. (2000) The tyranny of transparency. *British Educational Research Journal*, **26** (3), 309–21.

For alternative views on how to conceive of markets, economies, organizations and societies:

- Czarniawska, B. (2008) *A Theory of Organizing*, Edward Elgar Publishing, Cheltenham.
- Guyer, J. (2004) *Marginal Gains: Monetary Transactions in Atlantic Africa*, University of Chicago Press, Chicago, IL.
- Latour, B. (2005) *Reassembling the Social. An Introduction to Actor-Network Theory*, Oxford University Press, Oxford.
- Mckenzie, D. (2006) *An Engine Not a Camera. How Financial Models Shape Markets*, MIT Press, Boston, MA.

For the rhetorical power of numbers and how they are inserted in powerful training regimes:

- Espenland, W. and Stevens, M. (2008) A sociology of quantification. *European Journal of Sociology*, **49**, 401–36.
- Quattrone, P. (2009) Books to be practiced. Memory, the power of the visual and the success of accounting. *Accounting, Organizations and Society*, **34**, 85–118.

References

Abdel-khalik, A. and Ajinkya, B. (1979) *Empirical Research in Accounting. A Methodological Viewpoint*, American Accounting Association, Sarasota, FL, vol. 4.

Abdel-khalik, A. and Ajinkya, B. (1983) An evaluation of "The Everyday Accounting and Researching his Reality". *Accounting, Organizations and Society*, **8** (4), 375–84.

Abernethy, M. and Stoelwinder, J. (1991) Budget use, task uncertainty, system goal orientation and sub-unit performance: a test of the "fit" hypothesis in not-for-profit hospitals. *Accounting, Organizations and Society*, **16,** 105–20.

Ackoff, R. (1986) *Managing in Small Doses*, John Wiley & Sons, Inc., New York.

Ahrens, T., Becker, A. and Burns, J. *et al.* (2008) The future of interpretive accounting research—a debate. *Critical Perspectives on Accounting*, **19**, 840–66.

Ahrens, T. and Chapman, C. (2007a) Management accounting as practice. *Accounting, Organizations and Society*, **32** (1/2), 1–27.

Ahrens, T. and Chapman, C. (2007b) Theorizing practice in management accounting research, in (2007) *Handbook of Management Accounting Research* (eds Chapman, C., Hopwood, A. and Shields, M.), Elsevier, Oxford, vol. 1, pp. 99–112.

Alchian, A. and Demsetz, H. (1972) Production, information costs and economic organization. *American Economic Review*, **62**, 777–95.

Alleman, R. (1985) Comptrollership at ITT. *Management Accounting*, May, 24–33.

Amey, L. (1979) *Budget Planning and Control Systems*, Pitman, London.

Amey, L. (1986) *A Conceptual Approach to Management*, Praeger, New York.

Andon, P., Baxter, J. and Chua, W. (2007) Accounting change as relational drifting: a field study of experiments with performance measurement. *Management Accounting Research*, **18** (2), 273–308.

Ansari, S. (1976) Behavioral factors in variance control: report on a laboratory experiment. *Journal of Accounting Research*, **14** (2), 189–211.

Ansari, S. and Bell, J. (1991) Symbolism, collectivism and rationality in organisational control. *Accounting, Auditing and Accountability Journal*, **4** (2), 4–27.

Ansari, S. and Euske, K. (1987) Rational, rationalizing, and reifying uses of accounting data in organizations. *Accounting, Organizations, and Society*, **12**, 549–70.

Anthony, P. (1977) *The Ideology of Work*, Tavistock, London.

Anthony, R. and Dearden, J. (1981) *Teacher's Guide to Accompany Management Control Systems*, Irwin, Homewood, IL.

Anthony, R., Dearden, J. and Bedford, N. (1989) *Management Control Systems*, Irwin, Homewood, IL.

Anthony, R., Dearden, J. and Govindarajan, V. (1992) *Management Control Systems*, Irwin, Homewood, IL.

Anthony, R., Dearden, J. and Vancil, R. (1965) *Management Control Systems: Cases and Readings*, Irwin, Homewood, IL.

Antle, R. and Eppen, G. (1985) Capital rationing and organizational slack in capital budgeting. *Management Science*, **31**, 163–74.

Argyris, C. (1952) *The Impact of Budgets on People*, Controllership Foundation, Cornell University, Ithaca, NY.

Armstrong, P. (1987) The rise of accounting controls in British capitalist enterprises. *Accounting, Organizations and Society*, **12,** 415–36.

Armstrong, P. (1991) Contradiction and social dynamics in the capitalist agency relationship. *Accounting, Organizations and Society*, **16**, 1–25.

Arnold, P. (1998) The limits of postmodernism in accounting history: the Decatur experience. *Accounting, Organizatons and Society*, **23** (7), 665–84.

Arrington, C. and Francis, J. (1989) Letting the chat out of the bag: deconstruction, privilege, and accounting research. *Accounting, Organizations and Society*, **14**, 1–28.

Arrington, C. and Puxty, A. (1991) Accounting, interests, and rationality: a communicative relation. *Critical Perspectives on Accounting*, **2** (1), 31–58.

Arrow, K. (1964) Control in large organizations. *Management Science*, **10**, 1–36.

Baiman, S. (1982) Agency research in managerial accounting. *Journal of Accounting Literature*, Spring, 154–213.

Baiman, S. (1990) Agency research in managerial accounting: a second look. *Accounting, Organizations and Society*, **15**, 341–71.

Baiman, S. and Evans, J. III. (1983) Pre-decision information and participative management control systems. *Journal of Accounting Research*, **21**, 371–95.

Barley, S. and Kunda, G. (1992) Design and devotion: surges in rational and normative ideologies of control in managerial discourse. *Administrative Science Quarterly*, **37,** 363–99.

Barnard, C. (1938) *The Functions of the Executive*, Harvard University Press, Cambridge, MA.

Barthes, R. (1976) *Sade, Fourier, Loyola*, University of California Press, Berkeley, CA.

Baudrillard, J. (1988) *Selected Writings*, Polity Press, Oxford.

Baxter, J. and Chua, W. (2003) Alternative management accounting research—whence and whither. *Accounting, Organizations and Society*, **28** (2–3), 97–126.

Beaver, W. and Demski, J. (1974) The nature of financial accounting objectives: a survey and synthesis. Supplement to the *Journal of Accounting Research*, **15**.

Becker, S. and Green, D. (1962) Budgeting and employee behavior. *The Journal of Business*, **35**, 392–402.

Bedford, N. (1974) Discussion of opportunities and implications of the report on objectives of financial statements. *Studies on Financial Statement Objectives, 1974*, Supplement to the *Journal of Accounting Research*, **15**.

Bennis, W. (1966) *Changing Organizations*, McGraw-Hill, New York.

Berger, P. and Luckmann, T. (1966) *The Social Construction of Reality*, Doubleday & Co., New York.

Best, S. and Kellner, D. (1991) *Postmodern Theory: Critical Investigations*, Guilford Press, New York.

Bhimani, A. (ed.) (2006) *Contemporary Issues in Management Accounting*, Oxford University Press, Oxford.

Bhimani, A., Horngren, C., Datar, S. *et al.* (2008) *Management and Cost Accounting*, Financial Times Press, London.

Bingham, N. (1996) Object-ions: From technological determinism towards geographies of relations. *Environment and Planning D: Society and Space*, **14**, 635–57.

Birnberg, J. (1992) Managerial accounting: yet another perspective. *Advances in Management Accounting*, **1**, 1–19.

Birnberg, J. and Shields, J. (1989) Three decades of behavioral accounting research in the United States. *Behavioral Research in Accounting*, **1**, 75–108.

Birnberg, J., Shields, M. and McGhee, W. (1980) The effects of personality on subjects' information processing: a reply. *The Accounting Review*, **55**, 507–10.

Birnberg, J., Turopolec, I. and Young, S. (1983) The organizational context of accounting. *Accounting, Organizations and Society*, **8**, 111–29.

Bloomfield, B., and Combs, T. (1992) Information technology, control and power: the centralization and decentralization debate revisited. *Journal of Management Studies*, **29**, 459–82.

Bloomfield, B. and Vurdubakis, T. (1997) Vision of organization and organization of vision: the representational practices of information systems development. *Accounting, Organizations and Society*, **22** (7), 639–68.

Boland, R., Jr (1989) Beyond the objectivist and the subjectivist: learning to read accounting as a text. *Accounting, Organizations and Society*, **14** (5/6), 455–68.

Boland, R., Jr and Pondy, L. (1983) Accounting in organization: a union of natural and rational perspectives. *Accounting, Organizations and Society*, **8** (2/3), 223–34.

Boland, R., Jr. and Pondy, L. (1986) The micro dynamics of a budget-cutting process: modes, models, and structure. *Accounting, Organizations, and Society*, **11**, 403–22.

Bottomore, T. (1984) *The Frankfurt School*, Tavistock, London.

Bourdieu, P. (1977) *Outline of a Theory of Practice*, Cambridge University Press, Cambridge, UK.

Bourdieu, P. (1990) *The Logic of Practice*, Stanford University Press, Stanford, CA.

Bourdieu, P. (1995) *Sociology in Question*, Sage, London.

Bourdieu, P. (1998) *Practical Reason*, Stanford University Press, Stanford, CA.

Bower, J. (1970) *Managing the Resource Allocation Process*, Division of Research, Graduate School of Business Administration, Harvard University, Boston, MA.

Braverman, H. (1974) *Labor and Monopoly Capital: The Degradation of Work in the Twentieth Century*, Monthly Review Press, New York.

Briers M. and Chua, W. F. (2001) The role of actor-networks and boundary objects in management accounting change: a field study of the implementation of activity-based costing. *Accounting, Organizations and Society*, **26**, 237–69.

Broadbent, J., Laughlin, R. and Read, S. (1991) Recent financial and administrative changes in the NHS: a critical theory analysis. *Critical Perspectives on Accounting*, **2**, 1–30.

Brownell, P. (1981) Participation in budgeting, locus of control and organizational effectiveness. *The Accounting Review*, **56**, 844–60.

Brownell, P. (1983) The role of accounting data in performance evaluation, budgetary participation and organizational effectiveness. *Journal of Accounting Research*, 456–72.

Brownell, P. and Dunk, A. (1991) Task uncertainty and its interaction with budgetary participation and budget emphasis: some methodological issues and empirical investigations. *Accounting, Organizations and Society*, **16**, 693–704.

Brownell, P. and Hirst, M. (1986) Reliance on accounting information, budgetary participation and task uncertainty, tests of a three-way interaction. *Journal of Accounting Research*, 241–9.

Brownell, P. and McInnes, M. (1986) Budgetary participation, motivation, and managerial performance. *The Accounting Review*, **61**, 587–600.

Bruns, W., and McKinnon, S. (1993) Information and managers: a field study. *Journal of Management Accounting Research*, Fall, 84–108.

Bruns, W. and Waterhouse, J. (1975) Budgetary control and organization structure. *Journal of Accounting Research*, 177–203.

Brunsonn, N. (1985) *The Irrational Organization. Irrationality as a Basis for Organizational Action and Change*, Fagbokforlaget, Copenhagen.

Brunsonn, N. (1990) Deciding for responsibility and legitimation: alternative interpretations of organizational decision-making. *Accounting, Organization and Society*, **15** (1/2), 47–59.

Bryce, R. (2002) *Pipe Dreams: Greed, Ego and the Death of Enron*, Public Affairs, New York.

Bryman, A. (1984) Organization studies and the concept of rationality, *Journal of Management Studies*, **21**, 4.

Burchell, S., Clubb, C., Hopwood, A. *et al.* (1980) The roles of accounting in organizations and society. *Accounting, Organizations and Society*, **5**, 5–27.

Burgstahler, D. and Sundem, G. (1989) The evolution of behavioral accounting research in the United States. *Behavioral Research in Accounting*, **1**, 75–108.

Burns, J. (2000) The Dynamics of Accounting Change. Inter-play between new practices, routines, institutions, power and politics, *Accounting, Auditing and Accountability Journal*, **13** (5), 566–96.

Burns, J. and Baldvinsdottir, G. (1999) *Hybrids: The Changing Role of Accountants in Stam Plc.* Working paper.

Burns, J. and Raivio, J. (eds) (2001) Management accounting change, Special issue, *Management Accounting Research*, **12** (4)

Burns, J. and Scapens, R. (2000) Conceptualizing management accounting change: an institutional framework. *Management Accounting Research*, **11**, 3–25.

Burns, T. and Stalker, G. (1961) *The Management of Innovation*, Tavistock, London.

Burrell, G. and Morgan, G. (1979) *Sociological Paradigms and Organizational Analysis*, Heinemann, London.

Busco, C. and Quattrone, P. (2009) How management practices diffuse: the Balanced Scorecard as a rhetorical machine (with Cristiano Busco), working paper presented at the seminars of the accounting department of Harvard Business School, Manchester Business School, Babson College and the EAA Annual Congress, Tampere.

Busco, C., Quattrone, P. and Riccaboni, A. (eds) (2007) Management accounting change. Special issue, *Management Accounting Research*, **18** (2).

Cadbury, A. (1992) *The Financial Aspects of Corporate Governance*, Gee & Co., London.

Caglio, A. (2003) Enterprise Resource Planning systems and accountants: towards hybridization? *European Accounting Review* **12** (1), 123–53.

Capolino, G., Massaro, F. and Panerai, P. (2004) *La grande truffa*, Classe editori, Milano.

Carruthers, B. (1995) Accounting, ambiguity and the new institutionalism. *Accounting, Organizations and Society*, **20** (4), 313–28.

Carruthers, B. and Espenland, W. (1991) Accounting for rationality: double-entry bookkeeping and the rhetoric of economic rationality. *American Journal of Sociology*, **97**, 1.

Carruthers, M. (1990) *The Book of Memory: A Study of Memory in Medieval Culture*, Cambridge University Press, New York.

Carruthers, M. (1998) *The Craft of Thought: Meditation, Rhetoric and the Making of Images. 400–1200*, Cambridge University Press, Cambridge.

Chandler, A., Jr. (1962) *Strategy and Structure*, MIT Press, Cambridge, MA.

Chandler, A., Jr. (1977) *The Visible Hand: The Managerial Revolution in American Business*, Harvard University Press, Cambridge, MA.

Chapman, C. (1998) Accountants in organizational networks. *Accounting, Organizations and Society*, **23** (8), 737–66.

Chapman, C. (ed.) (2005) *Controlling Strategy: Management, Accounting, and Performance Measurements*, Oxford University Press, Oxford.

Chapman, C., Hopwood, A. and Shields, M. (2007) *Handbook of Management Accounting Research* (2 vols), Elsevier, Oxford.

Chapman, C. and Kihn, L.-A. (2009) Information system integration, enabling control and performance. *Accounting, Organizations and Society*, **34** (2), 151–69.

Chenhall, R. (1986) Authoritarianism and participative budgeting: a dyadic analysis. *The Accounting Review*, **61**, 263–72.

Chenhall, R. (2007) Theorising contingencies in management control systems research, in *Handbook of Management Accounting Research* (eds C. Chapman, G. Hopwood and M. Schields), Elsevier, Oxford, vol. I, pp 163–206.

Chenhall, R. and Morris, D. (1986) The impact of structure, environment, and interdependence on the perceived usefulness of management accounting systems. *The Accounting Review*, **61**, 58–75.

Chenhall, R. and Morris, D. (1991) The effect of cognitive style and sponsorship bias on the treatment of opportunity costs in resource allocation decisions. *Accounting, Organizations and Society*, **16**, 27–46.

Cherrington, D. and Cherrington, J. (1973) Appropriate reinforcement contingencies in the budgeting process. *Journal of Accounting Research: Empirical Research in Accounting: Selected Studies*, 225–53.

Chow, C., Cooper, J. and Waller, W. (1988) Participative budgeting: effects of a truth-inducing pay scheme and information asymmetry on slack and performance. *The Accounting Review*, **63**, 111–22.

Christensen, J. (1982) The determination of performance standards and participation. *Journal of Accounting Research*, 589–603.

Chua, W. (1986) Radical developments in accounting thought. *The Accounting Review*, **61** (4): 601–32.

Chua, W. (1988) Interpretive sociology and management accounting research: a critical review. *Accounting, Auditing and Accountability Journal*, **1** (2), 59–79.

Chua, W. (2007) Accounting, measuring, reporting and strategizing—re-using verbs: a review essay. *Accounting, Organizations and Society*, **32** (4–5), 487–94.

Ciborra, C. (and associates) (2001) *From Control to Drift. The Dynamics of Corporate Information Infrastructures*, Oxford University Press, Oxford.

Clark, I. (1985) *The Spatial Organisation of Multinational Corporation*, Croom Helm, London.

Clark, J. (1923) *Studies in the Economics of Overhead Costs*, University of Chicago Press, Chicago.

Clarke, T. (2007) *International Corporate Governance: A Comparative Approach*, Routledge, London.

Clegg, S. and Dunkerley, D. (1980) *Organization, Class, and Control*, Routledge & Kegan Paul, London.

Cobb, J., Mitchell, F. and Innes, J. (1992) *Activity Based Costing: Problems in Practice*, The Chartered Institute of Management Accountants, London.

Cohen, M., March, G. and Olsen, J. (1972) A garbage can model of organization choice. *Administrative Science Quarterly*, **17** (1), 1–25.

Collins, F. (1978) The interaction of budget characteristics and personality variables with budgetary response attitudes. *The Accounting Review*, **53**, 324–35.

Collins, F., Munter, P. and Finn, D. (1987) The budgeting games people play. *The Accounting Review*, **62**, 29–49.

Cooper, C., Taylor, P., Smith, N. and Catchpowle, L. (2005) A discussion of the political potential of social accounting. *Critical Perspectives on Accounting*, **16** (7), 951–74.

Cooper, D. (1980) Discussion of "Towards a political economy of accounting." *Accounting, Organizations, and Society*, **5**, 161–6.

Cooper, D., Everett, J. and Nue, D. (2005) Financial scandals, accounting change and the role of accounting academics: a perspective from North America. *European Accounting Review*, **14** (2), 373–82.

Cooper, D., Hayes, D. and Wolf, F. (1981) Accounting in organized anarchies: understanding and designing accounting systems in ambigous situations. *Accounting, Organizations and Society*, **6** (3), 175–91.

Cooper, D. and Morgan, W. (2006) Case study research in accounting. *Accounting Horizons*, **22** (2), 159–78.

Cooper, R. and Kaplan, R. (1988) Measure costs right: make the right decisions. *Harvard Business Review*, 96–103.

Cooper, R., Kaplan, R., Maisel, L. *et al.* (1992) *Implementing Activity-Based Cost Management: Moving From Analysis to Action*, Institute of Management Accountants, Montvale, NJ.

Covaleski, M. and Dirsmith, M. (1986) The budgeting process of power and politics. *Accounting, Organizations and Society*, **11**, 193–214.

Covaleski, M. and Dirsmith, M. (1988) The use of budgetary symbols in the political arena: an historically informed field study. *Accounting, Organizations and Society*, **13**, 1–24.

Covaleski, M. and Dirsmith, M. (1990) Dialectic tension, double reflexivity and the everyday accounting researcher: on using qualitative methods. *Accounting, Organizations and Society*, **15**, 543–73.

Covaleski, M., Dirsmith, M. and Jablonsky, S. (1984) Traditional and emergent theories of budgeting: an empirical analysis. *Journal of Accounting and Public Policy*, **4**, 277–300.

Covaleski, M., Dirsmith, M. and Michelman, J. (1993) An institutional theory perspective on the DR6 framework, case-mix accounting systems and health-care organizations. *Accounting, Organizations and Society*, **18**, 65–80.

Cruver, B. (2003) *Anatomy of Greed: The Unshredded Truth from an Enron Insider*, Arrow, London.

Culbert, S. and McDonough, J. (1980) *The Invisible War: Pursuing Self Interests at Work*, John Wiley & Sons, Inc., New York.

Culbert, S. and McDonough, J. (1985) *Radical Management: Power Politics and the Pursuit of Trust*, The Free Press, New York.

Cyert, R. and Ijiri, Y. (1974) Problems of implementing the Trueblood objectives report. Supplement to the *Journal of Accounting Research*, **12**, 29–42.

Cyert, R. and March, J. (1963) *The Behavioral Theory of the Firm*, Prentice Hall, Englewood Cliffs, NJ.

Czarniawska, B. (1997) *Narrating the Organization*, University of Chicago Press, Chicago, IL.

Czarniawska, B. (2008) *A Theory of Organizing*, Edward Elgar Publishing, Cheltenham, UK.

Daft, R. (1992) *Organizational Theory and Design*, West Publishing, St. Paul, MN.

Daft, R.. and Macintosh, N. (1978) A new approach to design and use of management information. *California Management Review*, **26**, 82–92.

Daft, R. and Macintosh, N. (1981) A tentative exploration into the amount and equivocality of information processing in organizational work units. *Administrative Science Quarterly*, **26**, 207–24.

Daft, R. and Macintosh, N. (1984) The nature and use of formal systems for management control and strategy implementation. *Journal of Management*, **10**, 43–66.

Dalton, G. and Lawrence, P. (1971) *Motivation and Control in Organizations*, Irwin, Homewood, IL.

Dean, J. (1957) Profit performance measurement of division managers. *The Controller*, 423–8.

Dearden, J. (1960) Interdivisional pricing. *Harvard Business Review*, **38**, 117–26.

Dearden, J. (1961) Problems in decentralized financial control. *Harvard Business Review*, **39**, 72–80.

Dearden, J. (1987) Measuring profit center managers. *Harvard Business Review*, **65**, 84–88.

Dechow, N. and Mouritsen, J. (2005) Enterprise resource planning systems, management control and the quest for integration. *Accounting, Organizations and Society*, **30** (7–8), 691–733.

DeCoster, D. and Fertakis, J. (1968) Budget induced pressure and its relationship to supervisory behavior. *The Journal of Accounting Research*, 237–46.

Dent, J. (1990) Strategy, organization and control. *Accounting, Organizations and Society*, **15**, 3–26.

Dermer, J. (1973) Cognitive characteristics and the perceived importance of information. *The Accounting Review*, **48**, 511–19.

Dermer, J. (1990) The strategic agenda: accounting for issues and support. *Accounting, Organizations and Society*, **15**, 67–76.

Dermer, J. and Lucas, R. (1986) The illusion of managerial control. *Accounting, Organizations and Society*, **11**, 6.

Derrida, J. (1976) *Of Grammatology*, John S. Hopkins University Press, Baltimore, MD.

Derrida, J. (1978) *Writing and Difference*, Routledge & Kegan Paul, London.

Dirsmith, M. and Jablonsky, S. (1979) MBO, political rationality and information inductance. *Accounting, Organizations and Society*, **4**, 39–52.

Donzelli, F. (1986) *Il concetto di equilibrio nella teoria neoclassica*, La Nuova Italia Scientifica, Florence.

Dopuch, N. (1993) A perspective on cost drivers. *The Accounting Review*, **68**, 615–20.

Dopuch, N. and Sunden, S. (1980) FASB's statements on objectives and elements of financial accounting: a review. *The Accounting Review*, 1–21.

Drever, M., Stanton, P. and McGowan, S. (2007) *Contemporary Issues in Accounting*, John Wiley & Sons, Inc., New York.

Dreyfus, H. and Rabinow, P. (1983) *Michel Foucault: Beyond Structuralism and Hermeneutics*, University of Chicago Press, Chicago.

Driver, M. and Mock, T. (1975) Human information processing decision style theory and accounting information systems. *The Accounting Review*, **52**, 490–508.

Duncan, K. and Moores, K. (1989) Residual analysis: a better methodology for contingency studies in management accounting. *Journal of Management Accounting Research*, **1**, 89–103.

Dunk, S. (1989) Budget emphasis, budgetary participation and managerial performance: a note. *Accounting, Organizations and Society*, **14**, 321–4.

Dunk, S. (1990) Budgetary participation, agreement on evaluation criteria and managerial performance. *Accounting, Organizations and Society*, **15**, 171–8.

Dunk, S. (1992) Reliance on budgetary control, manufacturing process automation and production subunit performance: a research note. *Accounting Behavior and Organizations*, **17**, 195–204.

Dunk, S. (1993) The effect of budget emphasis and information asymmetry on the relation between budgetary participation and slack. *The Accounting Review*, **68**, 400–10.

Earl, M. and Hopwood, A. (1980) From management information to information management, in *The Information Systems Environment* (eds H. Lucas, Jr. *et al.*), North Holland, Amsterdam.

Eckel, L. G. (1976) Arbitrary and incorrigible allocation. *The Accounting Review*, **53**, 764–77.

Emmanuel, C. and Otley, D. (1985) *Accounting for Management Control*, Van Nostrand Reinhold, Wokingham, UK.

Emmanuel, C., Otley, D. and Merchant, K. (1992) *Readings in Accounting for Management Control*, Chapman & Hall, London.

Engels, F. (1987) *The Condition of the Working Class in England*, Penguin, New York.

Espenland, W. and Stevens, M. (2008) A sociology of quantification. *European Journal of Sociology*, **49**, 401–36.

Ezzamel, M. (1992) *Business Unit and Divisional Performance*, Chapman & Hall, London.

Ezzamel, M. (1994) Organizational change and accounting: understanding the budgeting system in its organizational context. *Organization Studies*, **15** (2), 213–40.

Ezzamel, M. and Hart, H. (1987) *Advanced Management Accounting: An Organizational Emphasis*, Cassell, London.

Ezzamel, M. and Hoskin, K. (2002) Retheorizing accounting, writing and money with evidence from Mesopotamia and ancient Egypt. *Critical Perspectives on Accounting*, **13** (3), 333–67.

Feldman, M. and March, J. (1981) Information in organizations as signal and symbol. *Administrative Science Quarterly*, **26**, 171–86.

Ferrara, W. (1960) Idle capacity as a loss—fact or fiction. *The Accounting Review*, **35**, 490–6.

Ferrara, W. (1961) Overhead costs and income measurement. *The Accounting Review*, **36**, 63–70.

Ferrara, W. (1963) Relevant costing—two points of view. *The Accounting Review*, **38**, 719–72.

Ferrara, W. (1990) The new cost management accounting: more questions than answers. *Management Accounting*, 48–52.

Fess, P. (1963) The relevant costing concept for income measurement: can it be defended? *The Accounting Review*, **38**, 723–32.

Fess, P. and Ferrara, W. (1961) The period cost concept for income measurement: can it be defended? *The Accounting Review*, **36**, 598–602.

Flori, L. (1636), *Trattato del modo di tenere il libro doppio domestico con suo essemplare composto dal P. Lodovico Flori della Compagnia di Gesù per uso delle case e dei collegi della medesima Compagnia nel Regno di Sicilia*, in Palermo, per Decio Cirillo.

Foucault, M. (1977) *Discipline and Punish*, Allen Lane, London.

Foucault, M. (1980) *The History of Sexuality Volume 1: An Introduction*, Vintage Books, New York.

Fox, L. (2003) *Enron: The Rise and Fall*, John Wiley & Sons, Inc., Hoboken, NJ.

Frank, W. (1990) Back to the future: a retrospective view of J. Maurice Clark's studies in the economics of overhead costs. *Journal of Accounting Research*, 153–60.

Fremgen, J. (1962) Variable costing for external reporting. *The Accounting Review*, **37**, 76–81.

Friedman, A. (1994) *Spider's Web: The Secret History of How the White House Illegally Armed Iraq*, Bantam, New York.

Friedman, M. (1935) *Essay in Positive Economics*, University of Chicago Press, Chicago.

Froud, J., Williams, K., Haslam, C. *et al.* (1998) Caterpillar: two stories and an argument. *Accounting, Organizations and Society*, **23** (7), 685–708.

Fusaro, P. and Miller, R. (2003) What went wrong at Enron: everyone's guide to the largest bankruptcy, in *Liar's Poker* (ed. M. Lewis), Penguin Books, New York.

Galbraith, J. (1973) *Designing Complex Organizations*, Addison-Wesley, Reading, MA.

Galbraith, J. (1977) *Organization Design*. Addison-Wesley, Reading, MA.

Geneen, H. (1984a) The case for managing by the numbers. *Fortune*, October 1, 78–81.

Geneen, H. (1984b) *Managing*, Avon, New York.

Geymonat, L. (1970) *Storia del pensiero filosofico e scientifico*, vol. II, Milan.

Giddens, A. (1976) *New Rules of Sociological Analysis*, Hutchinson, London.

Giddens, A. (1979) *Central Problems in Social Theory*, Macmillan, London.

Giddens, A. (1984) *The Constitution of Society*, Polity Press, Cambridge.

Ginzberg, M. (1980) An organizational contingencies view of accounting and information systems implementation. *Accounting, Organizations and Society*, **5**, 369–82.

Goldratt, E. (1992) From cost world to throughput world, in *Advances in Management Accounting* (ed. M. Epstein), JAI Press, Greenwich, CT.

Gordon, L. and Miller, D. (1976) A contingency framework for the design of accounting information systems. *Accounting, Organizations and Society*, **1**, 59–69.

Gordon, L. and Smith, K. (1992) Postauditing capital expenditures and firm performance: the role of asymmetric information. *Accounting, Organizations and Society*, **17**, 741–58.

Govindarajan, V. (1984) Appropriateness of accounting data in performance evaluation: an empirical examination of environment uncertainty as an intervening variable. *Accounting, Organizations and Society*, **9**, 125–35.

Govindarajan, V. (1986) Decentralization, strategy, and effectiveness of strategic business units in multibusiness organizations. *Academy of Management Review*, **11**, 844–56.

Govindarajan, V. (1988) A contingency approach to strategy implementation at the business-unit level: integrating administrative mechanisms with strategy. *Academy of Management Journal*, **31**, 828–53.

Govindarajan, V. and Fisher, J. (1990) Strategy, control systems, and resource planning: effects on business unit performance. *Academy of Management Journal*, **33**, 259–85.

Govindarajan, V. and Gupta, A. (1985) Linking control systems to business unit strategy: impact on performance. *Accounting, Organizations and Society*, **10**, 51–66.

Granlund, M. (2001) Towards explaining stability in and around management accounting systems. *Management Accounting Research*, **12**, 141–66.

Greiner, L. (1972) Evolution and revolution as organizations grow. *Harvard Business Review*, **50**, 37–46.

Groot, T. and Lukka, K. (eds) (2000) *Cases in Management Accounting: Current Practices in European Companies*, Pearson Education, Harlow.

Guess, R. (1981) *The Idea of a Critical Theory: Habermas and the Frankfurt School*, Cambridge University Press, Cambridge.

Gul, F. (1984) The joint and moderating effects of personality and cognitive style on decision making. *The Accounting Review*, **59**, 264–77.

Gupta, A. and Govindarajan, V. (1984a) Build, hold, harvest: converting strategic intentions into reality. *Journal of Business Strategy*, **4**, 34–47.

Gupta, A. and Govindarajan, V. (1984b) Business unit strategy, managerial characteristics, and business unit effectiveness at strategy implementation. *Academy of Management Journal*, **27**, 24–41.

Gupta, A. and Govindarajan, V. (1986) Resource sharing among SBUs: strategic antecedents and administrative implications. *Academy of Management Journal*, **29**, 695–714.

Gupta, M. (1993) Heterogeneity issues in aggregated costing systems. *Journal of Management Accounting Research*, Fall, 180–212.

Guyer, J. (2004) *Marginal Gains: Monetary Transactions in Atlantic Africa*, University of Chicago Press, Chicago.

Habermas, J. (1979) *Communication and the Evolution of Society*, Beacon Press, Boston, MA.

Hall, R. (1962) The concept of bureaucracy: an empirical assessment. *American Journal of Sociology*, **69**, 32–40.

Handy, C. (1992) Balancing corporate power: a new federalist paper. *Harvard Business Review*, **70**, 59–72.

Hansen, A. and Mouritsen, J. (1999) Managerial technology and netted networks. "Competitiveness" in action: the work of translating performance in a high-tech firm. *Organization*, **6** (3), 451–71.

Harvey, D. (1989) *The Conditions of Postmodernity*, Basil Blackwell, Oxford.

Harvey, D. (1990) *The Condition of Postmodernity: An Inquiry into the Origins of Cultural Change*, Basil Blackwell, Oxford.

Hayes, D. (1977) The contingency theory of management accounting. *The Accounting Review*, **52**, 22–39.

Hebdige, D. (1988) *Hiding in the Light*, Routledge, London.

Hedberg, B. and Jönsson, S. (1978) Designing semi-confusing information systems for organizations in changing environments. *Accounting, Organizations and Society*, **3**, 47–64.

Heilbroner, R. (1980) *Marxism: For and Against*, W.W. Norton, New York.

Henre, J.-F. (2006) Management control systems and strategy: a resource-based perspective. *Accounting, Organizations and Society*, **31** (6), 529–58.

Herman, E. and Chomsky, N. (1988) *Manufacturing Consent: The Political Economy of the Mass Media*. New York: Pantheon.

Hiromoto, A. (1988) Another hidden edge—Japanese management accounting. *Harvard Business Review*, **66**, 22–6.

Hirst, M. (1981) Accounting information and the evaluation of subordinate performance: a situational approach. *The Accounting Review*, **56**, 771–84.

Hirst, M. (1983) Reliance on accounting performance measures, task uncertainty, and dysfunctional behavior: some extensions. *Journal of Accounting Research*, 596–605.

Hirst, M. and Baxter, J. (1993) A capital budgeting case study: an analysis of a choice process and the roles of information. *Behavioral Research in Accounting*, **4**, 187–210.

Hodgson, G. (1988) *Economics and Institutions: A Manifesto for Modern Institutional Economics*, Polity, Cambridge.

Hofstadter, D. (1979) *Gödel, Escher, Bach: An Eternal Golden Braid*, Basic Books, New York.

Hofstede, G. (1967) *The Game of Budget Control*, Koninklijke Van Grocum, Assen, Netherlands.

Hogart, R. (1991) A perspective on cognitive research in accounting. *The Accounting Review*, **66**, 2.

Hogart, R. (1993) Accounting for decision and decision for accounting. *Accounting, Organizations and Society*, **18**, 5.

Hogart, R. and Reder, M. (eds) (1987) *Rational Choice: The Contrast Between Economics and Psychology*, University of Chicago Press, Chicago.

Höpfl, H. (2000) Ordered passions: commitment and hierarchy in the organizational ideas of the Jesuit founders. *Management Learning*, **31** (3), 313–50.

Hopper, T. (1990) Social transformation and management accounting: finding the relevance in history, in *Accounting and Organizational Action* (eds C. Gustafsson and L. Hassel), Abo Academy Press, Abo, Finland.

Hopper, T. and Armstrong, P. (1991) Cost accounting, controlling labour and the rise of the conglomerates. *Accounting, Organizations and Society*, **15** (5/6), 405–38.

Hopper, T., Laughlin R. and Miller, P. (1991) The New Accounting History: an introduction. *Accounting Organizations and Society*, **15**, 395–403.

Hopper, T. and Macintosh, N. (1993) Management accounting as disciplinary practice. *Management Accounting Research*, **4**, 181–216.

Hopper, T. and Powell, A. (1985) Making sense of research into the organizational and social aspects of management accounting: a review of its underlying assumptions. *Journal of Management Studies*, **22** (5), 429–65.

Hopper, T., Scapens, R. and Northcott, D. (2007) *Issues in Management Accounting*, 3rd edn, Prentice Hall, Financial Times, London.

Hopper, T., Storey, J. and Willmott, H. (1987) Accounting for accounting: towards the development of a dialectical view. *Accounting, Organizations and Society*, **12**, 437–56.

Hopwood, A. (1973) *An Accounting System and Managerial Behavior*, Saxon House, Farnborough, Hampshire, UK.

Hopwood, A. (1987) The archeology of accounting systems. *Accounting, Organizations and Society*, **12** (3), 207–34.

Horngren, C. and Sorter, G. (1961) Direct costing for external reporting. *The Accounting Review*, **36** (1), 84–93.

Horngren, C. and Sundem, G. (1990) *Introduction to Management Accounting*, Prentice Hall, Englewood Cliffs, NJ.

Horngren, C., Sundem, G., Teall, H. and Selto, F. (1993) *Management Accounting*, Prentice Hall, Toronto.

Hoskin, K. W. (1994) "Boxing clever": for, against and beyond Foucault in the battle for accounting theory. *Critical Perspectives on Accounting*, **5** (1), 25–56.

Hoskin K. and Macve R. (1986) Accounting and the examination: a genealogy of disciplinary power. *Accounting, Organizations and Society*, **11** (2), 105–36.

Hoskin, K. and Macve, R. (1988) The genesis of accountability: the West Point connections. *Accounting, Organizations and Society*, **13** (1), 37–73.

Hoskin, K. and Macve, R. (2000) Knowing more as knowing less? Alternative histories of cost and management accounting in the US and the UK. *The Accounting Historians Journals*, **27** (1), 91–149.

Humphrey, C. and Lee, B. (eds) (2004) *The Real Life Guide to Accounting Research. A Behind-the-Scenes View of Using Qualitative Research Methods*, Elsevier, Oxford.

Hutcheon, L. (1989) *The Politics of Postmodernism*, Routledge, London.

Innes, J. and Mitchell, F. (1990) The process of change in management accounting: some field study evidence. *Management Accounting Research*, **1** (1), 3–19.

Inoguchi, R., Nakajima, T. and Pineau, R. (1958) *The Devine Wind*, Naval Institute Press, Washington.

Jameson, F. (1984) Postmodernism of the cultural logic of late capitalism. *New Left Review*, 52–92.

Jazayeri, M. and Scapens, R. (1999) *Implementing ERP Systems: Accounting Implications of the SAP Implementation at Building Materials Inc*, working paper, University of Manchester.

Jensen, M. and Meckling, W. (1976) Theory of the firm: managerial behavior, agency costs and ownership structure. *Journal of Financial Economics*, **76**, 305–60.

Johnson, H. (1992) *Relevance Regained: From Top-Down Control to Bottom-Up Improvement*, The Free Press, New York.

Johnson, H. and Kaplan, R. (1987) *Relevance Lost. The Rise and Fall of Management Accounting*, Harvard Business School Press, Boston, MA.

Jones, T. C. (1992) Understanding management accountants: the rationality of social action. *Critical Perspectives on Accounting*, **2** (3).

Jones, C. and Dugdale, D. (2002) The ABC bandwagon and the juggernaut of modernity. *Accounting, Organizations and Society*, **27** (1–2), 121–64.

Jönsson, S. and Grönlund, A. (1988) Life with a sub-contractor: new technology and management accounting. *Accounting, Organizations and Society*, **13**, 513–34.

Kanter, R. (1992) *The Challenge of Organizational Change: How Companies Experience It and Leaders Guide It*, Maxwell Macmillan, New York.

Kaplan, R. (1983) Measuring manufacturing performance: a new challenge for managerial accounting research. *The Accounting Review*, **58**, 686–705.

Kaplan, R. (1993a) Research opportunities in management accounting. *Journal of Management Accounting Research*, Fall, 1–14.

Kaplan, R. (1993b) *The Romance of the Arabists*, Macmillan, New York.

Kaplan, R. and Atkinson, A. (1989) *Advanced Management Accounting*, Prentice Hall, Englewood Cliffs, NJ.

Kaplan, R. and Norton, D. (1996) *The Balanced Scorecard: Translating Strategy into Action*, Harvard Business School Press, Boston, MA.

Kenis, I. (1979) Effects of budgetary goal characteristics on managerial attitudes and performance. *The Accounting Review*, **54**, 707–21.

Khandwalla, P. N. (1972) The effect of different types of competition on the use of management controls. *Journal of Accounting Research*, **72**, 275–85.

Kilduff, M. (1993) Deconstructing organizations. *Academy of Management Review*, **18**, 13–31.

Kilmann, R. (1983) The costs of organization structure: dispelling the myths of independent divisions and organization-wide decision making. *Accounting, Organizations and Society*, 341–57.

Kim, K. (1988) Organization coordination and performance in hospital accounting information systems: an empirical investigation. *The Accounting Review*, **63**, 472–89.

Kirsh, S. (1995) The incredibly shrinking world? Technology and the production of space. *Environment and Planning D: Society and Space*, **13**, 529–55.

Kuhn, T. (1970) *The Structure of Scientific Revolutions*, University of Chicago Press, Chicago.

Kurunmaki, L. (1999) Professional vs financial capital in the field of health care—struggles for the redistribution of power and control. *Accounting, Organizations and Society*, **24** (2), 95–124.

Lamalle, E. (1981–82) L'archivio di un grande ordine religioso. L'Archivio Generale della Compagnia di Gesù. *Archiva Ecclesiae*, **24/25** (1), 89–120.

Lambert, R. (2007) Agency theory and management accounting, in *Handbook of Management Accounting Research* (eds C. Chapman, A. Hopwood and M. Shields), Elsevier, Oxford, pp. 247–68.

Langton, J. (1984) The ecological theory of bureaucracy: the case of Josiah Wedgwood and the British pottery industry. *Administrative Science Quarterly*, **29**, 330–54.

Latour, B. (1986) Visualization and cognition: thinking with eyes and hands, in *Knowledge and Society: Studies in the Sociology of Culture, Past and Present* (eds H. Kuklick and E. Long), JAI Press, London, pp. 1–40.

Latour, B. (1987) *Science in Action. How to Follow Scientists and Engineers through Society*, Harvard University Press, Cambridge, MA.

Latour, B. (1988) The politics of explanations: an alternative, in *Knowledge and Reflexivity. New Frontiers in the Sociology of Knowledge* (ed. S. Woolgar), Sage, London.

Latour, B. (1991) *We Have Never Been Modern*, Sage, London.

Latour, B. (1999) *Pandora's Hope. Essays on the Reality of Science Studies*, Harvard University Press, Cambridge, MA.

Latour, B. (2005) *Reassembling the Social. An Introduction to Actor-Network Theory*, Oxford University Press, Oxford.

Laudan, L. (1977) *Progress and its Problems*, University of California Press, Berkeley, CA.

Laughlin, R. (1987) Accounting systems in organizational contexts: a case for critical theory. *Accounting, Organizations and Society*, **12**, 479–502.

Law, J. (1997) Heterogeneities. Paper presented at the meeting on "Uncertainty, Knowledge and Skill," 6–8 November, 1997 at Limburg University, Diepenbeek, Belgium (co-organized by Organisation Research Group, Limburg University, and the Centre for Social Theory and Technology, Keele University).

Lee, T. (1995) Shaping the US academic accounting research profession: the American Accounting Association and the social construction of an elite. *Critical Perspectives on Accounting*, **6** (2), 241–61.

Lee, T. and Williams, J. (1999) Accounting from the inside: legitimating the accounting academic elite. *Critical Perspectives on Accounting*, **10** (6), 867–95.

Lee, Z. and Lee, J. (2000) An ERP implementation case study from a knowledge transfer perspective. *Journal of Information Technology*, **15**, 281–8.

Lipari, C. (1984) Sulla funzione generale di controllo aziendale. *Annali della Facoltà di Economia e Commercio dell'Università di Palermo*, anno XXXVIII, No. 1–2.

Loft, A. (1986) Towards a critical understanding of accounting: the case of cost accounting in the UK, 1914–1925. *Accounting, Organizations, and Society*, **11**, 137–9.

Lowe, E. and Shaw, R. (1968) An analysis of managerial biasing: evidence from a company's budgeting process. *The Journal of Management Studies*, **5**, 304–15.

Lowe, J. (1992) *The Secret Empire: How 25 Multinationals Rule the World*, Business One Irwin, Homewood, IL.

Lukka, K. (1988) Budgetary biasing in organizations: theoretical framework and empirical evidence. *Accounting, Organizations and Society*, **13**, 281–301.

Lukka, K. (1990) Ontology and accounting: the concept of profit. *Critical Perspectives on Accounting*, 239–61.

Lukka, K. (1994) *Cost Accounting Practice in Finland*, Working Paper, Turku School of Economics and Business Administration.

Lyotard, J. (1984) *The Postmodern Condition: A Report on Knowledge*, Manchester University Press, Manchester.

Macdonell, D. (1986) *Theories of Discourse: An Introduction*, Basil Blackwell, Oxford.

Macintosh, N. (1981) A contextual model of information systems. *Accounting, Organizations and Society*, **6**, 39–53.

Macintosh, N. (1985) *The Social Software of Accounting and Information Systems*, John Wiley & Sons, Ltd., Chichester, UK.

Macintosh, N. (1990) Annual reports in ideological role: a critical theory analysis, in *Critical Accounts* (eds D. Cooper and T. Hopper), Macmillan, London, pp. 153–72.

Macintosh, N. (1994) The profit manipulation phenomenon: the ethics of profit manipulation: a dialectic of control analysis. *Critical Perspectives in Accounting*, **6** (2), 289–315.

Macintosh, N. (1995) The profit manipulation phenomenon: a dialectic of control perspective. *Critical Perspectives on Accounting*, **6** (4), 289–315.

Macintosh, N. and Daft, R. (1987) Management control systems and departmental interdependencies: an empirical study. *Accounting, Organizations and Society*, **12,** 40–61.

Macintosh, N. and Free, C. (2008) *Bourdieu's Logic of Practice Theory: Possibilities for Research on Management Accounting and Control.* Queen's University, Canada: working paper series.

Macintosh, N. and Hopper, T. (eds) (2005) *Accounting: the Social and the Political*, Elsevier, Oxford.

Macintosh, N. and Scapens, R. (1990) Structuration theory in management accounting. *Accounting, Organizations and Society*, **15** (5), 455–77.

Macintosh, N. and Scapens, R. (1991) Management accounting and control systems: a structuration theory analysis. *Journal of Management Accounting Research*, **16**, 131–58.

Macintosh, N. and Williams, J. (1992) Managerial roles and budgeting. *Behavioral Research in Accounting*, **4**, 23–48.

Macve, R. and Hoskin, K. (1994) Writing, examining, disciplining: the genesis of accounting's modern power, in *Accounting as Social and Institutional Practice* (eds A. Hopwood and P. Miller), Cambridge University Press, Cambridge.

Malmi, T. (1997) Towards explaining activity-based costing failure: accounting and control in a decentralized organization. *Management Accounting Research*, **8**, 459–80.

March, J. (1988) (ed.) *Decisions and Organizations*, Basil Blackwell Ltd., Oxford. (Italian translation, *Decisioni e organizzazioni*, Il Mulino, Bologna, 1993.)

March, J. and Simon, H. (1958) *Organizations*, John Wiley & Sons, Ltd., London.

Marx, K. (1944) *Economic and Political Manuscripts contained in Marx and Engels' Selected Works*, Lawrence & Wishart, London.

Mayo, E. (1933) *The Human Problems of an Industrial Civilization*, Macmillan, New York.

Mayo, E. (1945) *The Social Problems of an Industrial Civilization.* Harvard University Press, Cambridge, MA.

McGhee, W., Shields, M. and Birnberg, J. (1978) The effects of personality on a subject's information processing. *The Accounting Review*, **53,** 681–7.

McKendrick, N. (1961) Josiah Wedgwood and factory discipline. *The Historical Journal*, **4,** 30–55.

McKendrick, N. (1970) Josiah Wedgwood and cost accounting in the industial revolution. *The Economic History Review*, **24**, 45–67.

Mckenzie, D. (2006) *An Engine Not a Camera. How Financial Models Shape Markets*, MIT Press, Boston, MA.

McNair, C. and Mosconi, W. (1989) *Beyond the Bottom Line: Measuring World Class Performance*, Dow Jones-Irwin, New York.

Menzies, H. (1980) The ten toughest bosses. *Fortune*, April, 62–9.

Merchant, K. (1985) Budgeting and propensity to create budgetary slack. *Accounting, Organizations and Society*, **11**, 201–10.

Merchant, K. (1987) *Fraudulent and Questionable Financial Reporting: A Corporate Perspective*, Financial Executives Research Foundation, Morristown, NJ.

Merchant, K. (1990) The effects of financial controls on data manipulation and management myopia. *Accounting, Organizations and Society*, **16**, 297–313.

Merchant, K. and Manzoni, J.-F. (1989) The achievability of budget targets in profit centers: a field study. *The Accounting Review*, **64**, 539–58.

Merchant, K. and Rockness, J. (1994) The ethics of managing earnings: an empirical investigation. *Journal of Accounting and Public Policy*, **13**, 79–94.

Merchant, K. and Shields, M. (1993) Commentary on when and why to measure costs *less* accurately to improve decision making. *Accounting Horizons*, **7**, 76–81.

Meyer, J. (1986) Social environments and organizational accounting. *Accounting, Organizations and Society*, **11** (4/5), 345–56.

Meyer, J. and Rowan, B. (1977) Istitutionalized organization: formal structure as myth and ceremony. *American Journal of Sociology*, **83** (2), 340–63, reprinted in Powell, W. and Di Maggio, P. (eds) (1991) *The New Institutionalism in Organizational Analysis*, University of Chicago Press, Chicago.

Mia, L. (1988) Managerial attitude, motivation and the effectiveness of budget participation. *Accounting, Organizations and Society*, **13**, 465–76.

Mia, L. (1989) The impact of participation in budgeting and job difficulty on managerial performance and work motivation: a research note. *Accounting, Organizations and Society*, **14**, 347–58.

Milani, K. (1975) The relationship of participation in budget-setting, to industrial supervisor performance and attitudes: a field study. *The Accounting Review*, **50**, 274–84.

Miles, R. and Snow, C. (1978) *Organizational Strategy, Structure and Process*, McGraw-Hill, New York.

Miller, P. and Napier, C. (1993) Genealogies of calculations. *Accounting, Organizations and Society*, **18** (7/8), 631–47.

Miller, P. and O'Leary T. (1987) Accounting and the construction of a governable person. *Accounting, Organizations and Society*, **12** (3), 235–65.

Miller, P. and O'Leary, T. (1990) Making accounting practical. *Accounting, Organizations and Society*, **15**, 479–98.

Miller, P. and O'Leary, T. (1994a) Accounting, "economic citizenship" and the spatial reordering of manufacture, *Accounting, Organization and Society*, **19** (1), 35–54

Miller, P. and O'Leary T. (1994b) Governing the calculable person, in *Accounting as Social and Institutional Practice* (eds A. Hopwood and P. Miller), Cambridge University Press, Cambridge, pp. 98–115.

Miller, P. and O'Leary, T. (1998) Finding things out. *Accounting, Organizations and Society*, **23** (7), 709–14.

Mintzberg, H. (1972) The myths of MIS. *California Management Review*, **15** (1), 92–7.

Mintzberg, H. (1975) The manager's job: folklore and fact. *The Harvard Business Review*, **15**, 49–61.

Mintzberg, H. (1979) *The Structuring of Organizations*, Prentice Hall, Englewood Cliffs, NJ.

Mouritsen, J. (1994) Rationality, institutions and decision making: reflections on March and Olsen's rediscovering institution. *Accounting, Organizations and Society*, **19** (2), 193–211.

Munro, R. (1999) Power and discretion: membership work in the time of technology. *Organization*, **6** (3), 429–50.

Nagel, E. (1963) Whole, sums, and organic unities. *Philosophical Studies*, **3** (2), 17–32, reprinted in Lerner D. (ed.), *Parts and Wholes*, Macmillan, London.

Nagel, E. (1968) *The Structure of Science*, Harcourt, Brace & World Inc., New York.

Neimark, M. (1990) The king is dead. Long live the king! *Critical Perspectives on Accounting*, **1** (1), 103–14.

Neimark, M. and Tinker, T. (1986) The social construction of management control systems. *Accounting, Organizations and Society*, **11** (4/5), 369–96.

Newell, S., Huang, J., Galliers, R. and Pan, S. (2003) Implementing enterprise resource planning and knowledge management systems in tandem: fostering efficiency and innovation complementarity. *Information and Organization*, **13** (1), 25–52.

Noreen, E. (1987) Commentary on Johnson and Kaplan's "Relevance Lost." *Accounting Horizons*, **1**, 110–16.

Noreen, E. (1991) Conditions under which activity-based cost systems provide relevant costs. *Journal of Management Accounting Research*, **3**,159–68.

Nørreklit, H. (2003) The Balanced Scorecard: what is the score? A rhetorical analysis of the Balanced Scorecard. *Accounting, Organizations and Society*, **28** (6), 591–619.

Norris, C. (1992) *Uncritical Theory*, University of Massachusetts Press, Amherst, MA.

Oakes, I., Townley, B. and Cooper D. (1998) Business planning as pedagogy: language and control in a changing institutional field. *Administrative Science Quarterly*, **43**, 257–92.

Oldroyd, D. (1986) *The Arch of Knowledge. An Introductory Study of the History of the Philosophy of Science*, New South Wales University Press, Kensington.

O'Malley, J. (1994) The Society of Jesus, in *Religious Orders of the Catholic Reformation* (ed. R. deMolen) Fordham University Press, New York, pp. 132–64.

Onsi, M. (1973) Factor analysis of behavioral variables affecting budgetary slack. *The Accounting Review*, **73**, 535–48.

Otley, D. (1978) Budget use and managerial performance. *Journal of Accounting Research*, **16**, 122–49.

Otley, D. (1980) The contingency theory of management accounting: achievement and prognosis. *Accounting, Organizations and Society*, 413–28.

Otley, D. (1983) Concepts of control: the contribution of cybernetics and system theory to management control, in *New Perspectives in Management Control* (eds T. Lowe and J. Machin), Macmillan, London.

Otley, D. and Berry, A. (1980) Control, organization and accounting. *Accounting, Organizations and Society*, **5**, 231–44.

Otley, D. and Dias, F. (1982) Accounting aggregation and decision performance: an experimental investigation. *Journal of Accounting Research*, **20**, 171–88.

Ouchi, W. (1977) The relationship between organizational structure and organizational control. *Administrative Science Quarterly*, **22**, 25–113.

Ouchi, W. (1979) A conceptual framework for the design of organizational control mechanisms. *Management Science*, **25**, 833–48.

Parker, L., Ferris, K. and Otley, D. (1989) *Accounting for the Human Factor*, Prentice Hall, Sydney.

Parsons, T. (1937) *The Structure of Social Action*, McGraw-Hill, New York.

Penno, M. (1984) Asymmetry of pre-decision information and managerial accounting. *Journal of Accounting Research*, **22**, 177–91.

Perrow, C. (1967) A framework for the comparative analysis of organizations. *American Sociological Review*, 194–208.

Perrow, C. (1970) *Organizational Analysis: A Sociological Review*, Wadsworth, Belmont, CA.

Perrow, C. (1972) *Complex Organizations: A Critical Analysis*. Scott, Foresman & Co, Glenview, IL.

Perrow, C. (1986) *Complex Organizations*, 3rd edn., Random House, New York.

Posner, B. and Schmidt, W. (1986) Values and the American manager: an update. *California Management Review*, **32**, 202–16.

Poster, M. (1990) *The Mode of Information: Poststructuration and Social Context*, Polity Press, Cambridge.

Power, M. (1997) *The Audit Society: Rituals of Verification*, Oxford University Press, Oxford.

Preston, A., Cooper, D. and Coombs, R. (1992) Fabricating budgets: a study of the production of management budgeting in the National Health Service. *Accounting, Organizations and Society*, **17** (6), 561–93.

Puxty, A. (1993) *The Social and Organizational Context of Management Accounting*, Academic Press, London.

Quattrone, P. (2000) Constructivism and accounting research: towards a trans-disciplinary perspective. *Accounting, Auditing and Accountability Journal*, **3** (2), 130–55.

Quattrone, P. (2004) Accounting for God: accounting and accountability practices in the Society of Jesus (Italy, XVI–XVII centuries). *Accounting, Organizations and Society*, **29** (7), 647–83.

Quattrone, P. (2006) The possibility of the testimony. A case for case study research. *Organization*, **13** (1), 143–57.

Quattrone, P. (2009) Books to be practiced. Memory, the power of the visual and the success of accounting. *Accounting, Organizations and Society*, **34**, 85–118.

Quattrone, P. and Hopper, T. (2001) What does organisational change mean? Speculations on a taken for granted category. *Management Accounting Research*, **12** (4), 403–35.

Quattrone, P. and Hopper, T. (2005) A "time-space odyssey": management control systems in multi-national organisations. *Accounting, Organizations and Society*, **30** (7–8), 735–64.

Quattrone, P. and Hopper, T. (2006) What is *IT*? SAP, accounting, and visibility in a multinational organization. *Information and Organization*, **16** (3), 212–50.

Ramirez, C. (2001) Understanding social closure in its cultural context: accounting practitioners in France (1920–1939) *Accounting Organizations and Society*, **26** (4–5), 391–418.

Reider, B. and Saunders, G. (1988) Management accounting education: a defense of criticisms. *Accounting Horizons*, **2**, 58–62.

Richardson, A. (1987) Accounting as a legitimating institution. *Accounting, Organizations and Society*, **12**, 341–56.

Robbins, L. (1932) *An Essay on the Nature and Significance of the Economic Science*, Macmillan, London. (Italian translation: *Saggio sulla natura e sull'importanza della scienza economica*, UTET, Torino, 1947.)

Roberts, J. (1990) Strategy and accounting in a U.K. conglomerate. *Accounting, Organizations and Society*, **15**, 107–26.

Roberts, J. (1991) The possibilities of accountability. *Accounting, Organizations and Society*, **16** (4), 355–68.

Roberts, J. (1996) From discipline to dialogue: individualising and socialising forms of accountability, in *Power, Ethos and the Technologies of Managing* (eds R. Munro and J. Mouritsen), International Thompson Business Press, London, pp. 265–81.

Roberts, J. (2009) No one is perfect: the limits of transparency and an ethics for "intelligent" accountability. *Accounting Organizations and Society*, **34** (8), 957–70.

Roberts, J. and Scapens, R. (1985) Accounting systems and systems of accountability—understanding accounting practices in their organizational contexts. *Accounting, Organizations and Society*, **15**, 443–56.

Roberts, J. and Thomas, E. (2002) Enron's dirty laundry: how a vicious 10-year rivalry between two top executives helped create the sex-drenched, out-of-control corporate culture that ultimately wrecked the company. *Newsweek*, 11 March.

Robson, K. (1991) On the arenas of accounting change: the process of translation. *Accounting, Organizations and Society*, **16**, 547–70.

Robson, K. (1992) Accounting numbers as "inscription": action at a distance and the development of accounting. *Accounting Organizations and Society*, **17** (7), 685–708.

Roethlisberger, F. and Dickson, W. (1939) *Management and the Worker*, Harvard University Press, Cambridge, MA.

Ronen, J. and Livingston, J. (1975) An expectancy theory approach to the motivational impacts of budgets. *The Accounting Review*, **50**, 671–85.

Rose, M. (1991) *The Post-Modern and the Post-Industrial*, Cambridge University Press, Cambridge.

Roslender, R. (1992) *Sociological Perspectives on Modern Accounting*, Routledge, London.

Ryan, B., Scapens, R. and Theobold, M. (2002) *Research Method and Methodology in Finance and Accounting* (2nd edition), Thomson, London.

Ryan, M. (1982) *Marxism and Deconstruction: A Critical Articulation*, John S. Hopkins University Press, Baltimore, MD.

Salmon, W. (1989) *Four Decades of Scientific Explanation*, University of Minnesota, Minneapolis, MN.

Sampson, A. (1974) *The Sovereign State of ITT*, Fawcett, Greenwich, CT.

San Miguel, J. (1976) Human information processing and its relevance to accounting: a laboratory study. *Accounting, Organizations and Society*, **1**, 357–73.

Sarup, M. (1993) *An Introductory Guide to Post-Structuralism and Postmodernism*, University of Georgia Press, Athens, GA.

Scapens, R. (1985) *Management Accounting: A Review of Recent Developments*, Macmillan, London.

Scapens, R. and Roberts, J. (1993) Accounting and control: a case study of resistance to accounting change. *Management Accounting Research*, **4**, 1–32.

Schatzki, T., Cetina, K. and von Savigny (eds) (2001) *The Practice Turn in Contemporary Theory*, Routledge, London.

Schick, A., Gordon, L. and Haka, S. (1990) Information overload: a temporal approach. *Accounting, Organizations and Society*, **15**, 199–220.

Schields, R. (1991) *Places on the Margin. Alternative Geographies of Modernity*, Routledge, London.

Schiff, M. and Lewin, A. (1968) Where traditional budgeting fails. *Financial Executive*, 57–63.

Schiff, M. and Lewin, A. (1970) The impact of people on budgets. *The Accounting Review*, **45**, 259–68.

Scott, S. and Wagner, E. (2003) Networks, negotiations, and new times: the implementation of enterprise resource planning into an academic administration. *Information and Organization*, **13**, 285–313.

Shank, J. (1981) *Contemporary Managerial Accounting: A Casebook*, Prentice Hall, Englewood Cliffs, NJ.

Shank, J. (1989) Strategic cost management: new wine or just new bottles. *Journal of Management Accounting Research*, **1**, 47–65.

Shank, J. and Govindarajan, V. (1989) *Strategic Cost Analysis: The Evolution from Managerial to Strategic Accounting*, Irwin, Homewood, IL.

Shank, J. and Govindarajan, V. (1992) Strategic cost management: the value chain perspective. *The Journal of Management Accounting Research*, **4**, 179–97.

Shields, M. (1995) An empirical analysis of firms' implementation experiences with activity-based costing. *Journal of Management Accounting Research*, Fall, 148–66.

Shore, C and Selwyn, T. (1998) The marketization of higher education: management discourse and the politics of performance, in *The New Higher Education: Issues and Directions for the Post-Dearing Universities* (eds D. Jary and M. Parker), Staffordshire University Press, Stoke-on-Trent.

Simon, H. (1960) *The New Science of Management Decision*. Harper & Row, New York.

Simon, H. (1976) From substantive to procedural rationality, in *Method and Appraisal in Economics* (ed. S. Latsis), Cambridge University Press, New York.

Simon, H. (1983) *Reason in Human Affairs*, Stanford University Press, Stanford, CA.

Simons, R. (1987) Accounting control systems and business strategy. *Accounting, Organizations and Society*, **2**, 357–74.

Simons, R. (1990) The role of management control systems in creating competitive advantage: new perspectives. *Accounting, Organizations and Society*, **15**, 127–43.

Simons, R. (1991) Strategic orientation and top management attention to control systems. *Strategic Management Journal*, **12**, 49–62.

Simons, R. (1992) The strategy of control. *CA Magazine*, March, 44–50.

Simons, R. (1995) Control in an age of empowerment. *Harvard Business Review*, March–April, 80–8.

Sloan, A., Jr. (1963) *My Years with General Motors*, McFadden-Bartell, New York.

Smart, B. (1985) *Michel Foucault*, Tavistock, London.

Smith, C., Whipp, R. and Willmott, H. (1988) Case study research in accounting: methodological breakthrough or ideological weapon. *Advances in Public Interest Accounting*, **2**, 25–40.

Solomons, D. (1965) *Divisional Performance: Measurement and Control*, Financial Executives Research Foundation, New York.

Soya, E. (1989) *Postmodern Geographies. The Reassertation of Space in Critical Social Theory*, Verso, London.

Sparti, D. (1995) *Epistemologia delle scienze sociali*, NIS, Rome.

Stedry, A. (1960) *Budget Control and Cost Behavior*, Prentice Hall, Englewood Cliffs, NJ.

Strathern, M. (2000) The tyranny of transparency. *British Educational Research Journal*, **26** (3), 309–21.

Swartz, M. and Watkins, S. (2003) *Power Failure: The Inside Story of the Collapse of Enron*, Doubleday, New York.

Taylor, F. (1911) *The Principles of Scientific Management*, Harper, New York.

Taylor, M. and Thrift, N. (eds) (1982) *The Geography of Multinationals. Studies in the Spatial Development and Economic Consequences of Multinational Corporations*, Croom Helm, London.

Thomas, A. (1969) The allocation problem in financial accounting theory. *Studies in Accounting Research No. 3*. American Accounting Association, Sarasota, FL.

Thomas, A. (1974) The allocation problem: part two. *Studies in Accounting Research No. 9*. American Accounting Association, Sarasota, FL.

Thomas, A. (1975a) Accounting and the allocation fallacy. *Financial Analysts Journal*, **68**, 37–41.

Thomas, A. (1975b) The FASB and the allocation fallacy. *The Journal of Accountancy*, 65–8.

Thomas, A. (1978) Arbitrary and incorrigible allocations: a comment. *The Accounting Review*, **53**, 263–9.

Thompson, J. (1967) *Organizations in Action*, McGraw-Hill, New York.

Thompson, J. and Tuden, A. (1959) Strategies, structures and processes of organizational decision, in *Comparative Administration Studies* (eds J. D. Thompson and A. Tuden), University of Pittsburg Press, Pittsburg, PA.

Thomson, G. (1991) Is accounting rhetorical? Luca Pacioli and Printing. *Accounting, Organizations and Society*, **16** (5/6), 572–99.

Thomson, G. (1998) Encountering economics and accounting: some skirmishes and engagements. *Accounting, Organizations and Society*, **23** (5/6), 283–323.

Thornton, D. (1988) Theory and metaphor in accounting. *Accounting Horizons*, **2**, 1–9.

Tichey, N. and Sherman, S. (1993) *Control Your Destiny or Someone Else Will*, Doubleday, New York.

Tinker, A. (1980) Towards a political economy of accounting: an empirical illustration of the Cambridge controversies. *Accounting, Organizations and Society*, **5**, 147–60.

Tinker, A., Merino, B. and Neimark, M. (1982) The normative origins of positive theories: ideology and accounting thought. *Accounting, Organizations and Society*, **7** (2), 167–200.

Tinker, T. and Neimark, M. (1987) The role of annual reports in gender and class contradiction at General Motors: 1917–1976. *Accounting, Organizations and Society*, 71–88.

Tomkins, C. and Groves, R. (1983) Everyday accountant and researching his reality. *Accounting, Organizations and Society*, **8** (4), 361–74.

Tversky, A. and Kahneman, D. (1981) The framing of decision and the psychology of choice. *Science*, **211** (4481), 453–8. (Italian translation, in L. Filippini and A. Salanti (eds) *Razionalità, impresa e informazione. Letture di Microeconomia*, G. Giappichelli Editore, Turin, 1993.)

Vaivio, J. (1999) Exploring a "non-financial" management accounting change. *Management Accounting Research*, **10**, 409–37.

Vamosi, T. (2000) Continuity and change; management accounting during processes of transition. *Management Accounting Research*, **11**, 27–63.

Varela F., Thompson E. and Rosch E. (1991) *The Embodied Mind, Cognitive Science and Human Experience*, Massachusetts Institute of Technology Press, Boston, MA.

Vattimo, G. (1983) "Dialettica, differenza, pensiero debole," in *Il pensiero debole* (eds G. Vattimo and P. Rovatti), Feltrinelli, Milan.

Wakefield, N. (1990) *Postmodernism: The Twilight of the Real*, Pluto Press, London.

Waller, W. (1988) Slack in participative budgeting: the joint effect of a truth-inducing pay scheme and risk preferences. *Accounting, Organizations and Society*, **13**, 87–100.

Walsh, E. and Stewart, R. (1993) Accounting and the construction of institutions: the case of the factory. *Accounting, Organizations and Society*, **18**, 783–800.

Waterhouse, J. and Tiessen, P. (1978) A contingency framework for management accounting systems research. *Accounting, Organizations and Society*, 413–28.

Watson, D. and Baumler, J. (1975) Transfer pricing: a behavioral context. *The Accounting Review*, **50**, 466–74.

Weber, M. (1947) *The Theory of Social and Economic Organization* (eds A. Henderson and T. Parsons), The Free Press, Glencoe, IL.

Weedon, C. (1987) *Feminist Practice and Poststructural Theory*, Basil Blackwell, Oxford.

Weick, K. (1979) *The Social Psychology of Organizing*, Addison-Wesley, Reading, MA.

Weinwurm, E. (1961) The importance of idle capacity costs. *The Accounting Review*, **36**, 418–21.

Wickramasinghe, D. and Chandana, A. (2007) *Management Accounting Change. Approaches and Perspectives*, Routledge, London.

Williams, J., Macintosh, N. and Moore, J. (1990) Budget-related behavior in public sector organizations: some empirical evidence. *Accounting, Organization and Society*, **15**, 221–48.

Williamson, O. (1973) Markets and hierarchies: some elementary considerations. *American Economic Review*, **63** (2), 316–25.

Williamson, O. (1991) Comparative economic organization: the analysis of discrete structural alternatives. *Administrative Science Quarterly*, **36** (2), 269–96.

Willmott, H. (1986) Unconscious sources of motivation in the theory of the subject: an exploration and critique of Giddens' dualistic models of action and personality. *Journal for the Theory of Social Behavior*, **16**, 105–21.

Willmott, H. (1996) Thinking accountability: accounting for the disciplined production of the self, in *Power, Ethos and the Technologies of Managing* (eds R. Munro and J. Mouritsen), International Thompson Business Press, London.

Woodward, J. (1965) *Industrial Organization: Theory and Practice*, Oxford University Press, London.

Woolgar, S. (1988) *Science: The Very Idea*, Routledge, London.

Wright, J., Winter, W., Jr., Zeigler, S. and O'Dea, P. (1984) *Advertising*, McGraw-Hill Ryerson, Toronto.

Zimmerman, J. (1979) The costs and benefits of cost allocations. *The Accounting Review*, **54**, 504–21.

Index